What the Rabbis Said

What the Rabbis Said

*The Public Discourse of
Nineteenth-Century
American Rabbis*

Naomi W. Cohen

NEW YORK UNIVERSITY PRESS
New York and London

NEW YORK UNIVERSITY PRESS
New York and London
www.nyupress.org

Library of Congress Cataloging-in-Publication Data
Cohen, Naomi Wiener, 1927–
What the rabbis said : the public discourse of nineteenth-century
American rabbis / Naomi W. Cohen.
p.   cm.
Includes bibliographical references and index.
ISBN-13: 978-0-8147-1688-5 (cl : alk. paper)
ISBN-10: 0-8147-1688-1 (cl : alk. paper)
1. Rabbis—United States—Office—History—19th century. 2. Jewish
sermons, American—History and criticism. 3. Judaism—United
States—History—19th century. 4. Jews—United States—Social
conditions—19th century. 5. Jews—United States—Identity.   I. Title.
BM652.C64 2008
296.6'10973—dc22   2007050442

For my children and their children

Contents

Acknowledgments		ix
Introduction		1
1	The Muzzled Rabbi	13
2	From the Words of Sabato Morais	33
3	Heroes and Villains	53
4	Meant for Children	74
5	Rabbi versus Rabbi	94
6	Restoration to Palestine	113
7	Rabbis under Attack	131
8	The New Antisemitism	150
9	The World's Parliament of Religions	177
10	Building a Profession	198
	Notes	217
	Index	247
	About the Author	261

Acknowledgments

I have studied and written about the history of American Jews in the nineteenth and first years of the twentieth centuries ever since my days as a graduate student. In much of my early research I was struck by the lack of published material on the English-speaking American rabbi, and my interest in the topic took root. This book is meant to address, if only partially, the need for a full history of the rabbinate. To be sure, numerous articles and books that were published over the years have dealt with aspects of the subject and offer new data or revised interpretations of facts commonly known, but to my knowledge none has approached the material on the English discourse thematically in the way that I have. My analysis does not purport to be an all-inclusive study of the nineteenth-century rabbi or his office, nor does it fill in all the lacunae emerging from so broad a topic. But by tracing the activities and statements of rabbis—some prominent and distinguished in their time and many less so—on various themes, it adds to our knowledge of religious leaders and their stands on major issues that engaged the Jewish community. In that form it is a commentary on the social history of Jews in the United States before 1900. At least as important, it points to areas of scholarly research yet to be treated in depth. As a recognized Jewish historian told me many years ago, it is best to always leave something for others to do; in this case, much is left.

My book rests for the most part on primary sources in which the sermons and other public statements of the rabbis are examined. I have also drawn from secondary works in American and American Jewish social history that discuss individual rabbis and/or themes that the book develops. Their data have enriched my findings. The material from both the published and unpublished sources bears out the major thesis of this study: that the rabbis labored primarily to create an identity for American Jews that fused Judaism with Americanism.

It is a pleasure to acknowledge those whose advice, help in amassing data, and warm encouragement contributed in no small measure to my work: Jeremy Cohen, Judith Rosen, Nancy Ordway, Avital Cohen, Esther Goshen, Mira Levine, Lottie Davis, Yoel Darom, Adina Feldstern, and the late Geoffry Wigoder. But I do not minimize their aid when I single out a few for special mention. My friend and library consultant, Esther Green, responded cheerfully and indefatigably to my numerous requests for materials from various libraries. Special thanks also go to a close friend, Francine Klagsbrun, for reading portions of my manuscript and offering wise counsel throughout the lengthy process of writing this book. I am grateful as well to Robert Seltzer, a loyal colleague for many years, for his unstinting interest and invaluable help. Last but certainly not least, I am fortunate to have worked with Jennifer Hammer and Despina Papazoglou Gimbel, my editors at New York University Press, who combined professional skills with friendliness and understanding. Any errors that remain are solely my responsibility.

My family as always has been a constant source of encouragement. I lovingly dedicate this book to my children and grandchildren.

Introduction

American Jews of the nineteenth century forged a community that ultimately became the largest and most powerful in Jewish history. Their influence on the shaping of American Jewry transcended that of the small group that had settled in the country before the founding of the Republic and in many ways even that of the immigrant masses who arrived after 1880. Besides contributing to the economic and political development of the nation, those post-Revolutionary Jews, largely of Central European extraction, left a rich legacy of social institutions—philanthropies, schools, fraternal orders, and defense agencies—to succeeding generations. They experimented with different forms of synagogue practices, and they began the institutionalization of the Reform and Traditionalist movements.[1] In all those areas the rabbi was a pivotal figure, playing the multifaceted role of preacher, spiritual guide, educator, and communal leader.

Particularly rewarding for this study of the rabbi as preacher are the rabbis' discourses to their congregations. Indeed, rabbinic sermons, a distinct genre of Jewish literature, offer a rich menu for studying Jewish development in the United States. As yet, however, the corpus of sermons delivered before 1900 has rarely been analyzed.[2] This book helps to fill that void with an examination of sermons, lectures, and other rabbinic statements in English relating to episodes in American Jewish religious history that have frequently been neglected. The chapters focus on each rabbi's actions and reactions to various events and currents of thought that he faced during his career. His words not only addressed matters of concern to the community but also shed light on the rabbi himself. Relying principally on primary sources, I have in most cases organized the material subject by subject instead of rabbi by rabbi. The chapters are not linked by a single story line, nor are they in strict chronological order. Most of my data deal with the last third of the century, but I put those chapters which treat earlier material in the first half of the book. Thus, while each chapter is quite distinct from the others, together they comprise what may be called a "rabbinical commentary" on events and persons.

Although the practice of preaching among Jews can be traced back to ancient times, scholars have found no evidence of weekly rabbinic discourses in the American colonial period. Clearly, the small numbers of Jews who were concentrated in colonies that accepted religious differences were unreceptive to practices in New England like enforced attendance at weekly Sunday sermons or religious homilies for special occasions. In general, a sermon during Shabbat prayers wasn't commonplace among European Jews who immigrated before mid-century. Most had not been exposed to sermons as a standard feature of religious services. Some may have known of the early Reform attempts in Germany to incorporate sermons, but more were accustomed to the tradition of rabbinic preaching but twice a year, once on the Sabbath before Yom Kippur and once on the Sabbath before Passover.[3] After the Civil War, when a congregation of East European Jews in Rochester, New York, questioned the very need of a rabbi, how much less interested in sermons it doubtless was.[4]

The one who instituted sermons in the vernacular on a regular basis was Isaac Leeser, the *hazzan* (reader or minister) of the Sephardic congregation, Mikveh Israel, in Philadelphia. Leeser began preaching in 1830 —his inexperience doubtless explained his description of his first sermon as a "painful experience"—and, despite objections from the laymen, he persisted. He was not the first to call for sermons. Six years earlier the would-be Reformers of Charleston's Beth Elohim had asked among other things for a weekly English discourse on the Torah reading. While the Reformers saw their short-lived efforts for changes in the service as means to harmonize their ritual with the usages of Protestant America, Leeser the Traditionalist fixed on the sermon principally as an instrument to counter religious apathy and to strengthen traditional Judaism.[5]

The waves of German Jewish immigrants to the United States after the mass trek of the 1830s and 1840s reinforced those pioneer efforts. Unlike their brethren in Germany, the new immigrants did not have to win political emancipation, but for the purpose of social integration they too cared about services that would win Christian respect. Whether the motive was modernization, integration, or shoring up the strength of the synagogue, and whether the sermon was to be delivered in English or German, many old and new congregations soon looked for rabbis who would function also as preachers. Early but unsuccessful schemes for a rabbinical seminary, Zion College of 1855 and Maimonides College of 1868, included "practical elocution" or homiletics in their curricula. By the end of the 1870s the first permanent seminary, Reform's Hebrew Union College, required its graduating seniors to study two hours of homiletics weekly and to deliver their student sermons at the school's religious services.[6]

Despite Leeser's early efforts, more time passed before preaching became an accepted part of Traditionalist as well as Reform services. A Christian writer who studied traditional Jewish life in New York City commented in 1870: "The sermon is not regarded by orthodox Jews as a very important part of the Sabbath service. In some synagogues no sermon is preached; in others a short one is delivered in the German language; but it is rare indeed that a sermon in English is heard, for to the present hour, no Rabbi lives in the United States who was not born and educated on the Continent of Europe."[7]

The writer failed to indicate that the use of English corresponded not only to the training of the rabbi but also to the pace of assimilation. In cities or towns where the Jewish population was less dense than in New York, assimilation and hence the use of English for sermons made more rapid strides; where the Jewish population was considerable, assimilation was slower and the German Jews held on longer to their native tongue. By the 1880s and 1890s, however, as one study observes, the sermon had become a standard feature of traditional services and English was rapidly supplanting German as its language.[8] When vast numbers of East Europeans arrived after 1881, a completely different genre of rabbis and sermons, now in Yiddish, gave rise to a totally new style of American Traditionalism. Indeed, the differences between the two kinds of Orthodoxy, largely determined by whether they originated in Central or Eastern Europe, outweighed those between the earlier Traditionalists and the Reformers.[9]

The sermons of Reform rabbis predominate in the discussion in this volume. Not only were they more readily available than those of the Traditionalists, but also the Reformers overall enjoyed a higher status within American society. They were better established and in wealthier congregations, and the more rapid use of the vernacular in the governance and sermons of their synagogues won them greater notice from their Christian counterparts as well as from the secular press. Readers of this book will quickly become acquainted with the outstanding rabbis of the time. None is presented as *the* hero, but certain names are repeated more frequently than others—Isaac Leeser, Isaac Mayer Wise, Max Lilienthal, Kaufmann Kohler, Sabato Morais, Samuel Isaacs, and Emil G. Hirsch. These men were heard on virtually every subject, and they stamped their particular styles on what they preached. Traditionalist or Reformer, conservative or progressive, each differed from his colleagues. So marked were the variations that distinguished one from the other that readers of this volume will often be able to predict how each would react to certain matters. Where the first rabbi might be primarily an instructor of universal morality, the second was an expounder of rabbinic sources and *halachah* (Jewish law), the third a polemicist decrying social institutions, and the fourth a speaker identifiable by an ironic and sarcastic style.

The style of preaching, influenced to some degree by European models, varied from rabbi to rabbi and synagogue to synagogue.[10] Most sermons purported to be enlightening or edifying, but the rabbi's appearance and delivery determined how the message was transmitted. Style was also influenced by the audience that heard a particular sermon or lecture. Rabbis spoke one way to their congregations and differently to fellow rabbis, another way to children, and yet another way to mixed or Christian audiences. Moreover, synagogue members, even when they became accustomed to preaching, did not agree on what they wanted in a sermon. A few looked for evidence of the rabbi's erudition, some enjoyed emotional or sentimental orations that "inspired" them, and still others preferred ethical but inoffensive generalities. A greater consensus obtained on what the rabbi should not discuss; this included political issues and subjects likely to alienate his Gentile neighbors.

More than a survey of rabbinical sermons and other public statements, then, this book probes the rabbis' answers to one underlying question: What is the proper American Jew? The subject bears on two major themes analyzed in some depth—Americanism and Jewish identity. How the rabbis interpreted each theme, and how they labored to prove the compatibility of each with the other, reflected their beliefs and the ways in which they sought to shape the behavior of American Jews.

The first public experiences of the early American rabbi were exercises in acclimatization. Usually born and trained in Europe, he needed to define his own role as minister and decide how best to function as a model for the members of the community. At the same time he worked at carving out new relationships vis-à-vis his congregants, his colleagues in the rabbinate, the Protestant and Catholic religious leaders in his city, and the demands and expectations of his new country. It was incumbent upon him to remember that in all those areas he was a representative of Jewish

Americans. Most noteworthy about his initial experiences was the rabbi's rapid Americanization. Rabbis quickly developed a keen appreciation of American ideals and traditions, and they never tired of instructing their flocks, usually immigrants and the children of immigrants, in America's fundamental values of liberty and equality.

Some went further and equated the essence of Americanism and the spirit of the Constitution with the tenets of Judaism. On that premise they stood for the synthesis of their faith and culture with the American creed.[11] All agreed, rabbis and congregants alike, that because the Jews, a very small minority, reaped the benefits of freedom and security unknown to them in the Old World, they were obligated to reciprocate by Americanizing rapidly and by demonstrating genuine gratitude and unalloyed loyalty to "this blessed land." Positing a virtual contract with the country, they felt obliged to prove that their concerns were no less American than those of their fellow countrymen. Since their primary aim was to ensure acceptance of Jews within the larger society, they could not afford to criticize or appear too different from non-Jews. It followed that what the rabbi said or didn't say—particularly on subjects like Jew-hatred in the United States, Zionism, and American politics—stemmed from a strict interpretation of appropriate public behavior on the part of the Jewish minority.

In the process of acculturation, the rabbi himself became Americanized. Aside from his use of English he differed markedly from the pre-Emancipation rabbis. Whereas they were the scholars, the interpreters of *halachah,* and the judges in Jewish courts, the religious leaders of American synagogues assumed entirely new functions as early as the colonial era. In response to the needs of the largely Jewishly uneducated first settlers who neither wanted nor needed Talmudic sages, the rabbi became pastor and spiritual guide, as well as spokesman to the Christian world. As mediator between the Jews in his congregation or his city and the non-Jewish world, he explained the meaning of synagogue practices and Jewish beliefs and customs to Protestant and Catholic clerics. He attended inter-denominational affairs, served on school boards and library committees, and secured the support of his congregation to city-wide enterprises.

In a study of the first two hundred years of Jewish life in New York that has become a classic, Hyman Grinstein relates how the rabbi extended his role still further by participating actively in the social and philanthropic activities of the larger community. Focusing on Gershom Mendes Seixas, the famous unordained preacher of the Revolutionary period who led New York's first synagogue, Shearith Israel, Grinstein tells how the Christian ministers accepted Seixas as a bona fide and equal member of the clerical profession. Like them, he spoke on national fast days and prayer days proclaimed by the government, and he was recognized as the religious representative of the Jews. The importance of the preacher's position was strengthened still further by state laws on the incorporation of synagogues and the performance of marriages.[12] Many of the early practices lived on, and as the rabbi and his sermons came increasingly to resemble his Christian counterparts, a foundation was laid for future generations on which to build.

During the second half of the nineteenth century the rabbis, now almost always ordained, became more fully Americanized. Those who were flung into communities where their only colleagues were Protestant and Catholic clerics felt increasingly pressed to deliver their sermons in the vernacular and to adopt a style more American than European. They needed to learn American history and about American heroes and holidays, material that they incorporated into their sermons. The education in Americanism absorbed by congregants who heeded the rabbi's message was thereby also enhanced.

Although the rabbi's reactions to Christian leaders varied, running the gamut from suspicion and hostility to full cooperation, he worried about Gentile opinions of his sermons. Like the laymen whom they led, the rabbis adopted an accommodationist posture on American affairs and took great care not to offend public, especially Protestant, opinion. Only the very independent ones, acting out of fear for Jewish security, dared to criticize non-Jewish spokesmen. When problems like persecution in Europe or anti-Jewish discrimination in America called for public awareness, most rabbis gladly welcomed Christian sympathy and support. By the end of the century some had even exchanged pulpits with their Christian colleagues. Full-blown interfaith activities were still in the distant future, but signs of active interreligious cooperation were increasing.[13] In light of such factors, a focus on the English rather than German or Yiddish discourses allows for a deeper evaluation of elements involved in the emergence of the Americanized rabbi and sermon. A comparison of American with European sermons, which lies beyond the scope of this study, would very likely find that the differences between the two in style and substance indicate the rapid progress of Americanization.

Like the theme of Americanism, that of Jewish identity in one form or another pervaded most sermons. In nineteenth-century America, both

Christians and Jews defined a Jew as one who professed a religious belief in Judaism. Although the number of Jews who disavowed religious affiliation was increasing, many of them still resorted to the synagogue at least for religious rites of passage. Reform rabbis denied the national dimension of Judaism, and they, like their Traditionalist colleagues, concentrated on the meaning of religious identity. What did Judaism as religious belief mean? To what extent was a Jew bound by biblical and rabbinic law? Since both Reformers and Traditionalists faced the ravages of assimilation on synagogue membership, most rabbinic discourses pleaded against religious apathy and indifference.

The problem had begun before 1800. A young Jewish matron of Virginia, writing to her parents in 1791, said that her children could not be raised as anything but Gentiles because "Jewishness is pushed aside here."[14] In the free environment of the 1800s, Jewishness was increasingly pushed aside, and more and more Jews were intermarrying or otherwise leaving the fold. As early as 1845 Rabbi Samuel Isaacs, a Traditionalist, commented on the laxity in observance of the Sabbath: "In the days of yore violators were . . . publicly stoned to death . . . but now we court their society, give them the first honors in the synagogue, call them up to hear the law recited which anathematizes the Sabbath violator."[15] Indeed, average American Jews had little against the synagogue, but except for the rites of passage they had nothing much for it. Reform Rabbi Maurice Harris of New York formulated the issue in one blunt statement: the Jews have survived persecution, he said, but "can we survive Emancipation?"[16]

Not only was the spirit of Christianity that suffused the institutions and customs of Americans a snare, but the lure of being an unfettered "nothingarian" was doubtless even more attractive. Free of government regulation and the discipline of their pre-Emancipation corporate existence, many Jews turned their backs on the faith that had guided their ancestors for generations. They ignored the dictates of Jewish religious survival and chose the more comfortable path of total assimilation that in most cases stopped short of conversion. The postbellum influences of materialism, secularism, socialism, and scientific advances—which affected churches as well as synagogues—only accelerated the process. Rabbis repeatedly spoke out against succumbing to the new "isms," but they were usually preaching to the converted—that is, those who attended religious services. How to instill meaning and vibrancy into a seemingly lifeless religion, be it Reform or Traditionalist, was a problem that rabbis acknowledged before 1900 but tackled more forcefully only in the next century.[17]

The theme of Jewish identity underlay the growing rift between Traditionalists and Reformers. Since both the modern Reform movement and the twentieth-century Conservative movement were primarily products of the American environment, the subject of denominationalism, one that emerged from the American experience, looms large. To be sure, Western Europe had modern Reformers and moderate Traditionalists, but for several reasons, including government pressure, neither group was able to flourish the way it did in the United States. Nineteenth-century rabbinic sermons in America that illustrate the evolution of the denominational movements of Reform and moderate Traditionalism, as well as the debates between rabbinical proponents of each, are particularly instructive.

Neither movement was a cohesive body much before 1900; each was still groping for a definition of itself and a fixed and unified stand on normative Jewish beliefs and traditions. As Hasia Diner has observed, "reform" did not necessarily mean "Reform," and changes adopted by one synagogue were not necessarily acceptable to another. The Orthodox, or right-wing Traditionalists, furthest removed from modern currents of thought, had no problem with what a Jew needed to observe, but they took longer to adjust to changes in ritual and even to the rabbi/preacher and the English discourse. Indeed, the very idea of a sermon was repugnant to some precisely because it was viewed as a product of Reform.[18] While Orthodox preachers rarely ventured beyond the interpretations of revered scholars of the past, Reform rabbis explained how new interpretations were demanded in light of Reform's principles. Beset by divisiveness within their own ranks, the right-wingers and moderate Traditionalists failed to mount an effective counterattack against the rabbis who spoke for dramatic religious change.

America's acceptance of congregational autonomy also bore on the subject of denominationalism. For one thing, the principle of autonomy encouraged the mushrooming of new synagogues. American Jews were a heterogeneous group, and even within a single congregation differences in place of origin, language, and religious customs abounded. Often the rabbi or his sermons alienated some of his members, thereby accounting for the not unusual phenomenon of secessions from established synagogues. Distinctions dividing one congregation from another grew sharper too. Since the immigrants of that period settled in far-flung communities throughout the United States where they soon identified with the interests of a specific geographical area, it was quite probable that the preachers and sermons of one community had little attraction for the congregants of another. That setting explains why each autonomous synagogue had to mend its internal defenses before it was prepared to consider denominational much less interdenominational unity. Understandably, the plans of a few nineteenth-century rabbis for a Jewish religious union that would promote the purposes of education, philanthropy, and Jewish defense were usually unproductive. The legacy of separate denominations, each with its own institutions, as well as the search for overall unity, was bequeathed to succeeding generations.

A study of sermons logically asks how well the rabbi met the needs of his congregation and community. Much, of course, depended on the rabbi himself—his intellectual abilities, his charisma, and his goals. One can assume that the average rabbi aimed at leaving an imprint on his flock. He looked for an attentive and decorous audience: one that practiced the normal Jewish and civic virtues and would heed his admonitions on the responsibilities of an informed and religiously inspired Jew. To those ends he, the preacher, attempted to reach his audience by making every sermon an educational lesson on some aspect of religion and the Jewish cultural heritage. In that sense he aimed at a dialogue, using words and images that would trigger an intellectual or emotional reaction within individual listeners.

A minority of rabbis advanced original ideas which they believed could contribute to a richer, more meaningful Jewish existence—Sabato Morais worked for a uniform liturgy to unite congregations; Henry Berkowitz appealed for Jewish social action to ameliorate the abuses of a capitalist system; Joseph Krauskopf founded the National Farm School in Doylestown, Pennsylvania, for putting Jews back on the soil; and Emil G. Hirsch called for university chairs in Jewish studies to raise the respectability and popular knowledge of Judaism. Such rabbis explained their vision to their congregations and spoke of its benefits to the community. They gave a variety of meanings to the word "community": they could be referring to the community (*kehillah*) of the synagogue itself, or to the city, the country, world Jewry, or even humanity at large, but in all cases they asked their congregants to benefit others as well as themselves. Calling for lay participation in the realization of his scheme, the rabbi attempted to gain the congregation's endorsement and cooperation. Success with his own congregation could make his project a model for others removed from his *kehillah.* For such rabbis, the men of vision, satisfaction lay in suggesting an enhanced Jewish way of life that furthered the ends of both Jewish survival as well as community service. At the very least, the discussions and ideas that they raised testified to the ongoing vibrancy of the Jewish religious tradition.

While this volume concentrates on the themes of Americanism and Jewish identity, it also points to other issues that emerge from rabbinic sermons. One was the question of communal leadership. Did the rabbis speak for the community at large on nontheological issues like the abridgment of Jewish rights or the condition of Jews abroad? Did rabbis share authority with laymen who assumed the tasks of Jewish defense? Why did the influence of rabbis qua rabbis weaken in the twentieth century? Divisions within the community and the autonomy of each congregation precluded the rise of nationally recognized Jewish leaders, rabbinic or lay, until the generation of Jacob Schiff and Louis Marshall. Except for Anglo-Jewish periodicals published by rabbis themselves, and random gestures by Reform's Central Conference of American Rabbis, most nineteenth-century rabbis, except for Isaac Leeser, contributed little to the unity or national leadership of their fellow Jews.[19]

Another significant point relates to the interplay between European and American rabbis. In the nineteenth century the cross-fertilization of ideas worked at first in one direction only, from the Old World to the New. Most American rabbis had received their secular and/or rabbinic education in Germany or England, and since some had served in European pulpits, they and their early sermons reflected much of what they had absorbed. Personal contacts and correspondence reinforced the transatlantic connection. Moreover, American rabbis were usually well versed in the writings of foreign Jewish scholars and religious leaders. If they hadn't read the actual works, they turned to the Anglo-Jewish press, which often carried excerpts or summaries of significant portions. Either way American sermons frequently alluded to European books on religion. To receive further guidance on problems that they and their congregations faced, early religious leaders also addressed questions on doctrine and ritual to prominent European rabbis and synagogues. At times, as in the case of Rabbi Isaac Schwab's answer to antisemite Goldwin Smith, which was patterned on the sermon of Rabbi Hermann Adler of London, ideas and actual wording of a particular foreign work crept into American sermons.[20] Not surprisingly, however, as the American community matured and found Old World customs ill-suited to their situation, the gap between the American and European rabbis widened.

Since ordained rabbis did not appear in the United States until the 1840s, most material used here is from the second half of the nineteenth century. Some of the topics, like the magazine for children or the World's Parliament of Religions, may be unfamiliar, but even more so are the rabbinic reactions to them. Although a sermon often addressed multiple issues, most chapters present a composite picture of rabbinic positions on a particular subject. A topical arrangement permits greater latitude for exploring the views and styles of various preachers and for judging how well they addressed the issues. Did they relate their sermons and other public statements to contemporary happenings? Were they knowledgeable about Jewish history and traditions? How sensitive were they to the sentiments of their audience? Did they draw from Christian preachers or literature? These are only some of the questions that are raised. Not every preacher was an ordained rabbi—for example, Isaac Leeser, Morris Raphall, and Samuel Isaacs were not—nor was every rabbi a preacher, but because they were all identified as rabbis, and because the Sephardic minister or *hazzan* functioned like the Ashkenazic rabbi, I use the words rabbi, *hazzan*, Jewish minister, and preacher interchangeably.

The writer of a book on Jewish preaching before 1900 faces numerous difficulties. Many sermons were lost or survived in fragmentary form, and, very likely, the edited or published version of the sermon differed substantially from the one actually delivered. Others failed to identify the preacher or his authority, the language in which the original draft was written, or even the date and occasion for the sermon. Nor can the reader always learn from the extant text what stimuli prompted the preacher to choose his topic. Upon the historian remains the task of resolving those difficulties and of ferreting out information about the preacher's style, the character of his audience, and his reputation as a speaker.[21]

Similar problems apply to research in early American Jewish sermons. Perhaps the most important obstacle is that of availability. Most preachers did not save their sermons, and only those with a drive for literary immortality pushed for publication. Publication in turn necessitated recourse to receptive periodicals—Jewish or non-Jewish journals impressed for any reason by a particular rabbi, or, more important, those edited by the rabbis themselves—or to personal or congregational funds earmarked for that purpose. Complicating the task still further is the fact that many of the American sermons, both in manuscript and in print, are undated. Because of the difficulties in analyzing the background of a particular sermon, the reader looks for mention of a specific event in the text, be it an economic panic, the sinking of the *Maine,* or the expulsion of the Jews from Moscow, for chronological guidelines.

Most primary materials, which constitute the core of this book, come from Anglo-Jewish periodicals, books in which sermons were reprinted, and relevant manuscript collections. For greater depth in assessing and comparing rabbinic views, and since rabbis often felt freer about discussing certain subjects from the lecture podium instead of the pulpit, I have included data from rabbinic addresses to general audiences and from secular newspapers or journals. Differences among rabbis and between rabbis and congregations are explored, but although Christian opinions are occasionally included, the book doesn't purport to be an in-depth study of Protestant or Catholic sermonica.

At the end of the century, Isaac Mayer Wise, the builder and leader of the Reform movement in the nineteenth century, concluded: "The sermon in the American synagogue . . . became not only an integral part but the main part of the divine service."[22] The findings of my examination of Traditionalist and Reform sources prove that the sermons and other rabbinic statements had a significance that transcended religious services. Indeed, they go far in illuminating the larger social history of American Jews who labored to adapt to a distinctly new environment and culture.

1

The Muzzled Rabbi

Ordained rabbis first arrived in the United States in the 1840s, and their initial encounters with their fellow Jews were frustrating if not downright painful. They found a group untutored in things Jewish and for the most part uninterested in religious observance. As Jews rapidly succumbed to the forces of assimilation and secularization, their knowledge of Hebrew was fast disappearing and the wherewithal for a Jewish education was virtually nil. Without colleagues, teachers, and libraries, the new rabbi often felt very much alone. Abraham Rice, the first rabbi in Baltimore, who could tolerate his position for only nine years, described his situation to a friend in Germany: "I dwell in complete darkness, without a teacher or companion. . . . The religious life in this land is on the lowest level, most people eat foul food and desecrate the Sabbath in public. . . . Thousands marry non-Jewish women. Under these circumstances my mind is perplexed and I wonder whether it is even permissible for a Jew to live in this land. . . . I often think of leaving."[1]

Compounding their discomfort, rabbis who sought to meet the challenges of religious indifferentism through "edifying" or instructional sermons confronted serious congregational restraints that limited the freedom of the pulpit. To be sure, the preachers could discuss matters within the synagogue—the form of religious services, prayers and usages, educational problems[2]—and they could chide the congregants for their religious transgressions, but otherwise the restraints severely limited both the subjects and the substance of the rabbi's sermons. Overall, what the average sermon discussed and, equally important, what it omitted reveals an unexpected aloofness from most contemporary events. True, early sermons talked about outstanding happenings, notably slavery and the Civil War,[3] but for the most part rabbinic discourses, particularly those delivered before 1880, rarely considered the world of the non-Jewish majority or, for that matter, that of foreign Jews. Any attempt, therefore, to glean from the sermons the responses of the Jewish community and its rabbis

to specific occurrences or to ongoing political and economic developments yields sparse results. Never did American Jews of the early nineteenth century produce a corpus of sermons like that of the first ministers of colonial New England which included religious interpretations and
substantive guidance on secular as well as theological matters.[4]

A major reason explaining the limited scope of the early Jewish sermon
was the contest for power between the members of a congregation and
their spiritual leaders. Lay control of the American synagogue, like that
which obtained in European Jewish communities, had been fixed long before the first rabbis arrived in the United States. In colonial days power
rested with a small number of laymen who governed the *kehillah*. The
earliest extant constitution of Shearith Israel, the first synagogue in New
York, broadly defined the authority of the *parnas* (lay leader of the synagogue) and his two associates who comprised the ruling board: "That
with the fear of God they may act as their Conscience shall dictate."[5]
Even with the arrival after mid-century of university-trained intellectuals—men like David Einhorn, Samuel Hirsch, and Kaufmann Kohler—
rabbis remained little more than hired help. Isaac Leeser of Philadelphia's
Mikveh Israel told the story of one religious leader (very likely Leeser
himself) who complained to a congregant about an infringement of his,
the rabbi's, rights. The layman's curt answer was to the point: "You, sir,
have no rights, you have only duties to perform."[6] Some forty years later,
a prominent member of the Union of American Hebrew Congregations
(UAHC), a lay-led organization of Reform congregations, reaffirmed one
aspect of lay control when he stated that "in no case should a [rabbi] have
a voice in the counsels or practical administration of the Union."[7] The fact
that Protestant churches similarly controlled the minister made the rabbi's
lot no easier.[8]

Circumstances favored the ongoing subjugation of rabbis to lay leadership. Economically mobile congregants, many uncouth and unlettered,
could still boast that they, former peddlers or sons of peddlers, were the
successful ones and that they and not their rabbis scored far higher in the
American moneymaking race. Those laymen preferred that their spiritual leaders stick to safe subjects like love of God and country. A rabbi
who discussed current sociopolitical events or expressed opinions at odds
with those of his congregants threatened to disrupt the comfortable status quo or, even worse, arouse negative criticism from non-Jewish fellow

Americans. Indeed, the rabbi may have even censored himself precisely to avoid such consequences. Gradually, as sermons gained wider acceptance, lay demands changed. By the end of the century laymen looked increasingly for rabbis who possessed oratorical skills and who cut a good figure in non-Jewish circles.

Lay-imposed restraints on the rabbis laid bare a deeper question: How absolute was the authority of a single rabbi or a group of rabbis? The matter came up at the 1892 meeting of Reform's Central Conference of American Rabbis (CCAR) at which the rabbis considered the requirement of circumcision for proselytes. Rabbi Henry Berkowitz, who canvassed the opinions of his colleagues, assumed that authority belonged to "the rabbis of this land in whom is vested the authority to decide all such matters." The president of the CCAR, Isaac Mayer Wise, agreed with Berkowitz, but others took an opposite stand. Chicago's Bernhard Felsenthal maintained that although the rabbi occupied an exalted post, his opinions, or those of a group of rabbis, were not sacred; in no way did they transcend those of laymen qualified by education to interpret Jewish law: "If it should be the case that a man qualified and competent to be a teacher in Israel should not occupy a rabbinical chair . . . this man can have, and ought to have, nevertheless, the same authority as anyone who is a rabbi in office." He argued that democracy guaranteed individual rights and freedom of conscience, matters that could not be decided by majority vote. Since American Jews revered Jeffersonian democratic principles, they could not recognize the power of any clerical body to legislate on religious doctrine. That would be both anti-Jewish and anti-American. Emil G. Hirsch agreed— "There is no distinction in Judaism between layman and clergyman"—but when the vote was taken the following year, only a partial compromise was reached.[9]

Preaching added to the duties of the nineteenth-century rabbi but failed to raise his status or increase his independence. As Rabbi Isaac Mayer Wise, the architect of Reform Judaism in America, later recalled, the early rabbi was a jack-of-all-trades, from teacher to gravedigger. His salary was low, his tenure uncertain, and the respect he commanded negligible. Wise campaigned early on for better conditions for the rabbi, whose lot apparently approximated that of many Christian ministers. In 1855 his weekly newspaper, the *Israelite*, reprinted an article from the *Western Christian Advocate*, which advised that if congregants attended services regularly and paid decent salaries, they would perhaps get better sermons.[10] But poor sermons were not uncommon. A small item that also appeared in the *American Israelite* (the name had been changed in 1873) gave the following recipe for a bad sermon:

> Take a small quantity of ideas, which everybody knows, paste them on a Bible text, put in two or three funny anecdotes, pour on them three or four quarts of filtered words, stir well with the quill of a spread eagle, spice well with patriotism, liberty and great nation pepper, throw the whole liquid upon paper, dry it in the moonshine of sentimentalities, then cut it in slices of equal size, and you have a sermon which will hurt nobody.[11]

Whatever their quality, sermons too were controlled by laymen, who judged whether the contents of the rabbi's discourses were appropriate. Tempers ran high on the issue of a free pulpit, even resulting once in a physical brawl between Wise and some congregants during his early ministry in Albany.[12] Indeed, some synagogues opposed the very inclusion of any sermon in religious services. Isaac Leeser had his own problems. Although he preached his first sermon in 1830, followed by a series of discourses published six years later, the early sermons first received the congregation's approval in 1843. Some congregants, however, still opposed preaching, and the issue contributed to a serious rift some years later between the laity and the preacher. Effectively restraining the rabbi in the pulpit, laity also frowned on independent rabbinic voices outside the synagogue. The same Leeser reported that as a rule rabbis were not admitted to public meetings: "If they are, prudence teaches them not to touch upon any subject which might perchance be unpleasant to their flocks; for sad experience has proved to them how little they gain who have an independent opinion of their own."[13]

Nor were the rabbis free to discuss political matters in their sermons. More than any other immigrant group, American Jews shied away from injecting their interests into the contemporary political arena. They thought that such behavior contradicted proper Americanism. Only when Jewish equality was at the heart of a problem, as in the case of Sunday laws or Thanksgiving Day proclamations in Christological form, did they speak out. Rather, they followed what may be called an informal code of political abstinence.[14] The code was based on arguments voiced since Emancipation that Jews were part of the larger body politic—merely Frenchmen, Germans, or Englishmen who happened to be Jewish—and not a separate collectivity with its own concerns. In essence it was a code of political neutrality or even political invisibility. It proscribed Jewish political clubs and political rallies; it banned support for specific candidates who happened to be Jewish; it preferred that Jews stay aloof from public office; and, denying the existence of a Jewish vote, it warned religious and lay communal leaders against attempts to influence Jewish voters. Bifurcating Jewish behavior into two spheres, one private and Jewish and one public and political, it led to countless ambiguities and inconsistencies on the place of Jews, individually as well as collectively, in American politics. Nor did it impress Christian politicians who repeatedly appealed for Jewish political support. The fact that leading Anglo-Jewish periodicals reiterated the rules time and again indicates that Jews themselves often honored the code in the breach.[15]

The truth of the matter was that insistence on a politically invisible group was more un-American than minority politics. A political system that James Madison interpreted in *The Federalist* as a reflection of the special interests of contending factions expected voters to express their concerns through the ballot. An insistence that Jewish needs were less legitimate than those of merchants or farmers or workers was artificial and indeed self-defeating, especially for a group that was a minority both religiously and ethnically. Had Jews been less afraid of calling attention to themselves or less intent on currying favor with the native Protestants, they might have seen that hiding their political interests only sheared them of any strength that was rightfully theirs within the American system. Their posture operated neither to serve the interests of the Jewish group nor to convince the Christian majority that the Jews differed from them only in matters of faith. Nevertheless, Jewish leaders kept their silence and trusted that the Constitution and "enlightened public opinion" would protect their special interests. Meantime, political abstinence closed numerous sermons to issues of major public concern.

The riddle of Jewish identity first assumed major proportions in the Age of Emancipation. What was a Jew? Did Judaism preach Jewish distinctiveness or survival as Jews, or did it preach universalism? Nineteenth-century American Jews searched for a workable compromise that accommodated their identities both as Americans and as Jews. Their first priority was for unqualified acceptance as Americans, no matter how sincerely they may have resolved to abide by their religious heritage. If the United States in all good faith recognized them as equal citizens, it was incumbent upon them to respond by sharing and living up to American values. As a small minority, and one saddled with the baggage of age-old Christian suspicions and bigotry, Jews had to convince their compatriots that Jewish behavior was above reproach. More self-conscious now than in pre-Emancipation days, they sought to prove that they could comfortably balance their Judaism with Americanism. America had accepted religious differences from the beginning of the Republic, and thus in some ways the task was facilitated. The compromise they arrived at amounted to a quasi-"Marranoism." Within the synagogue and their homes Jews could retain distinctive practices and beliefs, but publicly any opinions or actions on the part of the Jewish community regarding American political and social issues implied that Jews constituted an identifiable entity in areas other than religion.

If such restraints applied to all Jews, how much more so did they inhibit rabbis? Since American Jews gloried in the country's fealty to the separation of church and state, they considered it un-American to tolerate "priestcraft" in politics. Jews deplored especially the influence of Christian ministers in the political arena, and consistency demanded that they fix the shackles of political invisibility on their own clergy. True, popular Protestant ministers like Wendell Phillips and Henry Ward Beecher held forth on political themes to admiring audiences,[16] but because of such discourses they were discounted as proper models by their Jewish counterparts. Rabbis usually agreed with the divorce of religious from secular concerns, but even if they hadn't, considerations of salary and job security would have kept them from injecting material into their sermons that could be interpreted as partisan Jewish interests. On the premise, therefore, that the synagogue and pulpit must steer clear of most contemporary matters, the code often resulted in muzzled rabbis and dull sermons.

In the 1850s Rabbi Isaac Wise, who piously preached that it was wrong to degrade the sanctity of religion by mixing it with low and corrupt politics, was scolded for going back on his own words. Since he took sides in the North/South conflict over the territory of Kansas, and since he publicly endorsed the Democratic Party, some critics aired their grievance in the municipal press. "We had supposed when we subscribed for his paper," they said, "that it was his purpose to make it a religious paper, totally eschewing all political subjects; and . . . we have been deceived in this." A few years later when Wise received the Democratic nomination for state senator, the board of his synagogue ordered him to turn it down. It also resolved to tell the rabbi that "the Board disapproves of all political allusions in his sermons and to discontinue same." On the eve of the Civil

War when a few rabbis entered the debate on slavery, they were similarly scolded by the lay boards of their synagogues.[17]

Criticism of rabbis who crossed the boundary between proper and improper remarks subsided only gradually. American Jews never indulged in heresy trials the way some Protestant churches did, but echoes of the shackled rabbi resonated even at the turn of the century. In the 1890s a prominent member of Temple Emanu-El publicly denounced a New York rabbi for "disgraceful and indecent" behavior because he had spoken at an anti-Tammany meeting against police harassment of Jewish food vendors in the urban ghettos. Since "Jews take no part in politics as Jews," the layman said, the rabbi's behavior was "disgraceful and indecent." And, in the first decade of the twentieth century Stephen Wise's insistence on freedom of the pulpit at Temple Emanu-El figured prominently in the board's rejection of his candidacy for rabbi.[18]

By the end of the century more rabbis were disregarding the conventional lay-imposed restraints on their public statements and defending their right to free speech. Rapid acculturation made the first-generation immigrants increasingly secure in the American setting and less afraid of the image they projected. The rabbi too became more Americanized and bolder with respect to his congregants. Not every rabbi was blessed with the ego or charisma of outstanding independents like Stephen Wise or Emil G. Hirsch, but doubtless some by sheer dint of personality removed the gags and preached freely to their congregations. Others retained some measure of their independence by venting their opinions through books and articles, popular lectures to non-Jewish as well as Jewish audiences, and various philanthropic or educational institutions.[19]

Still others, admittedly only a small number, insisted publicly that rabbis could not avoid political issues. Since they regularly preached on morality, and since politics also involved morality, why was that subject taboo? Commenting on the increasingly liberated rabbi, Rabbi I. L. Leucht of New Orleans counseled his colleagues at the 1897 convention of Reform's Central Conference of American Rabbis to take heart: "The position of 'rabbi' in most cases is now honorably independent and independently honorable. Even the threatening frown of the well-fed Parnass has lost a great deal of its terror, and the stiffly starched collar in which he has forced his proud neck is no longer woundingly bored into the quivering flesh of the trembling teacher of Israel."[20]

In 1892 two prominent rabbis discussed the legitimacy of preaching on social morality from the politically neutral pulpit. One, a respected

Traditionalist of Philadelphia, Marcus Jastrow, equivocated. He maintained, "The only legitimate province of the pulpit is *religious instruction and religious inspiration.*" But since men sought spiritual truths from their religious leaders, the rabbi could not ignore issues that bore on moral values. Jastrow thereby opened the door to free pulpits, for what issues could not be related to morality? However, he continued, the rabbi had to remain in the background; he must neither lead movements for social reform nor preach about them. If he did, he would arouse fear of "clerical rule" and actually delay the course of moral progress. Jastrow's colleague, Reform Rabbi Joseph Silverman of New York's Temple Emanu-El, reasoned differently. If the rabbi ignored the moral aspects of public issues, not only would he be left with a "dead" pulpit (Silverman's word for sermons without substance), but it was his duty as guardian of morality to discuss political matters that impinged on everyday life. Perhaps, as has been suggested, the difference between the two positions stemmed from Reform's reliance on morality, above theology, for sermonic material.[21]

Other examples show how some rabbis broadly construed morality to cover involvement in politics. David Philipson of Cincinnati defended his talk in 1889 on civil service reform by stating that the clergy's concern for religious welfare legitimately included every level of moral behavior. Rabbi Henry Berkowitz took a similar stand. In the 1880s when labor and agrarian unrest was sweeping the country, Berkowitz injected the theme of "social justice," the Jewish equivalent of the Christian Social Gospel movement, in his discourses. One of the first to preach on causes like the freedom and dignity of labor, he was by no means a radical social reformer whose words would alienate his middle-class congregants. Nevertheless, he too felt impelled to explain why he broke the code of political neutrality:

> It has been said . . . that the question I have undertaken to present to you . . . was out of place in the Jewish pulpit, or, for that matter, in any pulpit. . . . But so firmly convinced was I of the opposite opinion that when I was told that no Jewish minister had ever yet spoken out authoritatively on this subject, it became to me an overwhelming duty and necessity to do so.[22]

As the century wore on, the sermon, whether censored by the laity or by the rabbi himself, slowly changed, and it included matters not broached earlier. Evidence from two collections of nineteenth-century rabbinical discourses that are analyzed below considers the progress made for freedom of the pulpit after 1880.

In 1881 the firm of Bloch and Company in Cincinnati published a book called *The American Jewish Pulpit: A Collection of Sermons by the Most Eminent American Rabbis*. It included twenty-six sermons in English on the Sabbath, holidays, and other occasions delivered by twenty rabbis, most of whom were Reform Jews. A notable exception was the Traditionalist, Sabato Morais.[23] All selections were undated except for one which bore the notation, in Hebrew, "Eve of the New Year, 5641 (1880)"; hints in the texts indicated, however, that they were probably delivered a short time before publication. The book lacked an introduction explaining how or why the selection was made, but the place of publication and the fact that six sermons were written by Reform leader Isaac Wise of Cincinnati suggests that he directed the entire project. Contributors to the book were unevenly identified—some by name only; some by name and city; and some by name, city, and congregation. The themes they discussed were addressed to urban and rapidly assimilating Jewish congregations whose socioeconomic level was comfortably middle class. The size of the city made little difference in the levels of erudition and sophistication displayed in the sermons. The rabbi of Evansville, Indiana, a city with only 375 Jews, sounded very much like his colleague from Baltimore where Jews numbered some ten to fifteen thousand.[24]

The published sermons totally ignored contemporary American affairs and Jewish opinions on specific issues. Major political developments like the end of Reconstruction and state and national elections, and economic questions like the long depression of the 1870s or agitation over bimetallism were bypassed. Rabbis from the states of the Old Northwest made no mention of the rising protest movements by farmers in their section, and Rabbi Henry Vidaver of San Francisco did not reflect on the burning issue of Chinese exclusion that was gripping California. Isaac Wise indicted political leaders guilty of corruption, but he didn't mention specific names or scandals. Indeed, the only concrete allusion to an American happening appeared in a sermon, "The Offering of Isaac," by Rabbi Max Landsberg of Rochester, New York. Landsberg referred to the religious sacrifice of a child at the hands of her fanatical parents in Pocassett, Massachusetts, in 1879, a story highlighted by the nation's press.[25] Together the omissions testified to a scrupulous commitment to the principle of Jewish political invisibility.

Rabbis did respond, however, to new intellectual currents. Some who bemoaned the desertion of the synagogue, particularly by the youth, blamed socialism ("a stepping back . . . into barbarism"), "pestiferous" atheism, "ruinous" nihilism, and the immoral practices those ideologies unleashed.[26] A far more dangerous challenge came from science, Darwinian theories in particular. On that topic, one that involved neither American politics nor the position of the Jews in American society but that did threaten loyalty to the synagogue and to religion generally, the rabbis felt freer about expressing themselves. Explaining why he was injecting the profane into the holy and going beyond the conventional bounds of sermons, one rabbi said: "I will depart from my usual course to notice . . . one of the most recent creations of modern thought, known as the doctrine of Evolution or development. I do this . . . because I happen to know that the confidence with which it has been urged by some, has caused perplexity and pain to many pious persons around us."[27]

After the Civil War, Americans increasingly debated the ideas of evolution and, most startling of all, the transformation of species put forth in Darwin's works, *The Origin of Species* (1859) and *The Descent of Man* (1871). Accepted first by scientists, the ideas of evolution and transformation of species proceeded to conquer scientific circles and the universities before working their way into popular journals. Although the linkage of man with lower species horrified the clergy, they were by the 1880s fast succumbing to the new teachings and attempting a reconciliation between science and religion. Jewish clergymen were also caught up in the controversy over the truth of evolution, and specimens of their answers appeared in the *American Jewish Pulpit*. Like Christian clerics they entertained a wide range of views, from the outright denial of the validity of Darwinism to the formulation of compromises that would bridge their faith and the new biology.

Since almost all contributors to the 1881 volume were Reformers, men who predicated their movement on the need to rid Judaism of outmoded laws and customs and harmonize its religious forms to the temper of the age, they endowed Judaism with an evolutionary nature, one that adapted to the spirit of successive eras. It might be assumed, therefore, that Reformers in general were least threatened by scientific evolution. Not so. Were they to permit unlimited range to science, they would be putting at risk what they too cherished as *immutable* tenets of Judaism: the existence of God, creation by design, the creation of man in God's image, the divine mission of Israel, and eternal moral verities. Such rabbis would not abandon Judaism and a Jewish identity for science. They said that Reform could accept scientific advances but man needed religious faith for interpreting the mysteries of life. Benjamin Szold of Baltimore added: "The higher law for man's guidance is not the product of science. . . . It is . . . an ingredient of his higher nature." Even Max Lilienthal of Cincinnati, a defender of religious change, warned against total reliance on "the scalpel" or the "chemist's crucible." He said that if scientific theories transcended their legitimate sphere, they would destroy all moral responsibility.[28]

Positing man's innate need for religion, and that both science and religion were two separate spheres equally legitimate for advancing civilization, the Reform rabbis who preached about evolution resembled those Protestant ministers whom Sidney Mead has called the "romantic liberals," or the moderates on issues of theological and social change. Some rabbinic sermons and lectures also echoed the older doctrines of American transcendentalism—the existence of an Oversoul, or the sum total of what is good; the spark in man that permitted him to grasp the Oversoul or the Infinite; the bridge between the individual and the Infinite. Others added that since Judaism put no limits on free scientific inquiry, and since Reform Judaism was adaptable to change, it had little to fear from the new biology. Wasn't Reform's openness to scientific change an additional proof of its superiority over Orthodoxy? The two Traditionalist contributors to the *American Jewish Pulpit,* Abraham De Sola and Sabato Morais, found their own reasons for disputing science's challenge to religious faith. De Sola argued that the theory of evolution was speculative rather than scientific; Morais claimed that science confirmed "what Moses taught," because creation, even if the result of evolutionary changes, could not deny the unity of design and the role of a Creator or Prime Mover. Unlike the Christian scene, where liberal in theology usually meant a readiness to accept Darwinism, Jewish Reformers and Traditionalists were not necessarily of opposite minds with respect to evolution.[29]

Two Reform rabbis of Chicago, Bernhard Felsenthal and Emil G. Hirsch, found no reason to consider whether Judaism conflicted with science. While Felsenthal insisted that Judaism allowed the scientist unlimited freedom, Hirsch elaborated on the theme of Judaism as conduct rather than confession. Nondogmatic and itself subject to evolution, Judaism did not dichotomize as did other religions between scientific and religious truths. Therefore, he said, it alone had no call to search frantically or futilely for reconciliation between old beliefs and new knowledge. Both he and Felsenthal, proudly touting the superiority of Judaism and its adaptability to change, defined "superior" as Reform Judaism. Thus, if measured solely by the new science, a Reform identity scored higher than an outworn Traditionalism.[30]

None of the sermons in the 1881 volume, Traditionalist or Reform, defended the theory of the transformation of species. Traditionalist De Sola maintained that there was no evidence of "separate species of animals being produced from other species," and Radical Reformer David Einhorn sneered at theories popularized in the press and embraced by immature youth that man was "nothing but an animal." Einhorn's son-in-law, the renowned theologian Kaufmann Kohler, expatiated more fully: "Never will man be robbed of his crown of divine nobility; never will he allow himself to be ranked among baboons and chimpanzees. Darwinism, so far as it renders the world an interaction of mere mechanic forces, tends, like socialism, its twin brother, to glorify the struggle not for right, which is celestial, but for *might* which is brutal."[31]

Emil G. Hirsch recalled years later in his usual sarcastic way how he was introduced to Darwinism during his days in high school: "We high school boys took great pleasure in writing compositions and delivering addresses on the hypothesis of evolution. We were very proud to say that we were descended from the ape and monkey, and some of the high school boys really verified that theory. When you heard them proclaim it, every doubt was banished from your mind—they furnished the illustrations."[32]

Since intellectual currents like Darwinism found their way into Jewish sermons, one can conclude that the avoidance of sociopolitical themes that accounted for the muzzled rabbi was deliberate and not because congregations were too ignorant to comprehend them. The very fact that two rabbis could cite the names of Tyndall and Huxley (among others)[33] proves that they were addressing listeners who were at least superficially aware of the debates of the era. To be sure, German Jewish laymen, like their brethren in Germany, may have admired *Bildung* for its own sake, whether or not they fully understood the preacher's erudition. Nevertheless, the choice of themes points to a maturing middle-class Jewish community. No longer raw immigrants, they increasingly resembled the members of well-established urban Christian churches. It also meant that their children, who could more readily climb the American educational ladder, were fast becoming sensitive to the antireligious implications of modern science.

While the rabbis appraised the new biology and how it enticed Jews away from the synagogue, they simultaneously denounced the spirit of materialism so rampant in the post–Civil War era among Jews and society at large. Actually, preachers had lamented Jewish worship of Mammon long before 1881. Sharp-tongued David Einhorn for one had charged American Jews with having bred a generation of "spiritual midgets." Synagogues had become more beautiful on the outside, he said, but devotion within them grew weaker. In a statement worthy of any respectable Jew-hater, he stated that Jews "not only worship the golden calf—*but pick up the pieces of the broken tablets and try to sell them!*" (emphasis added).[34] Several of the contributors to the 1881 collection continued the attack. Linking materialism to sensualism and libertinism, they called it destructive of religion and of conscience and moral responsibility. The materialist, they predicted, was slated for an ignominious death, and only religion could save him from the pitfalls of "an aimless, God-forsaken world." Not only did the materialist sell his own soul to Mammon, but he betrayed the next generation as well. As Isaac Wise asked rhetorically: "Who will deny the necessity of saving our own sons and daughters from . . . the destruction of this age of gross materialism, which seeks pleasure, gratification, pomp, ostentation, tinsel and toys more than truth, light, happiness and true manhood?" The sensual, scandal-loving and excitement-seeking generation had "no aim beyond crude selfishness."[35]

Both the sermons on the shortcomings of scientific inquiry and those on the dangers of materialism had the same purpose: to stem the drift away from the synagogue. How well they succeeded was an entirely different matter. Similar scoldings had been heard before, if not specifically about science and materialism, then on other snares that led to religious apathy. Moreover, the targeted audience, the young adults and their parents, were doubtless those who no longer attended religious services regularly. As more and more Jews received a formal secular education, the more likely they were to have been won over by the new science or by the pragmatic desire to expand the economic successes of their fathers. Whatever the cause, they had for all intents and purposes already strayed from the fold. Perhaps the most important result was the growing realization on the part of some religious leaders that they needed somehow to revivify the package they were marketing.

The collection of 1881 omitted any discussion of Christianity or Jewish/Christian relations. Usually circumspect on that subject, except for denunciations of missionaries who targeted the Jews, a few rabbis did find fault with elements of the Christian faith. Some said that the "fictions"

of the Eucharist and divine resurrection, and the belief in eternal dam-
nation for nonbelievers, made for the superiority of Judaism. Bernhard
Felsenthal asserted that "whatever is good and true in them [Christianity
and Islam] they have directly appropriated from the treasures of Judah."
But Christianity went "astray," and by incorporating non-Jewish heathen
doctrines became "idolatrous." Falk Vidaver referred to the "cruel and
atrocious acts" perpetrated in history by the "religion of love." He added
that only when Christians emulated the virtues of Abraham the Patriarch
could they "boast of being good Christians."[36] None, however, spoke on
how Jews did or should relate to their Christian neighbors.

Conspicuously absent as well, but not unusual for sermons delivered
before 1880, was mention of the rising tide of antisemitism worldwide. At
a time when American Jews were reeling under the pressure of increased
social discrimination in the wake of the Seligman-Hilton affair of 1877,
and when measures were intensifying to pass a Christian amendment to
the Constitution or to strengthen Sunday laws and religion in the classroom, the sermons kept quiet. So too with respect to the steadily dete-
riorating condition of the Jews in the newly unified German Empire and
in Eastern Europe.[37] The Jewish community carefully watched developments, but most of their spiritual leaders were as yet not ready to share
such concerns with their congregations. Kaufmann Kohler did admit that
"darkness still prevails round about us," but he insisted nonetheless that
the Jewish situation was improving.[38] Kohler's seeming blindness can be
explained by a variety of reasons. First, Reform's mission to spread the
universalist prophetic message was rooted in the Enlightenment's ideas
of optimism. Moreover, like American rabbis in general, Kohler would
not question Jewish confidence in a free America. He may have been attempting to shore up Jewish morale, or to prove that Jewish patriotism
remained steadfast in Western nations despite bigotry, or to avoid the
possible exacerbation of popular antisemitism by admitting its existence.
Whatever the explanation, his message sounded a false note.

A second collection of sermons appeared in 1896. The CCAR, the organization of Reform rabbis, had resolved a year earlier to publish an annual
collection of sermons, but that of 1896 was the first and last of a projected
series. A volume of thirty-seven sermons delivered by twenty-seven rabbis, five of whom had contributed to the earlier collection, its stated purpose was to provide a better understanding of modern Judaism and Jewish
religious thought. The rabbis said that "it is anticipated that this book will

be of interest to preachers and laymen of all denominations, who may desire to learn what Judaism has to say in regard to the vital questions of the day." It aimed in addition at aiding "the smaller communities which have no rabbis and wish to conduct divine services on the chief holy days."[39] Besides sermons the book included lectures and addresses delivered outside the synagogue. Unlike its predecessor of 1881, it was limited to Reformers. Jewish identity meant adherence to Reform; if non-Jews read the book, they might have overlooked the fact that the writers of the sermons did not speak for the entire Jewish community.

Classifying the sermons according to the same fields that we used for *American Jewish Pulpit*—American politics, intellectual currents, Jewish/Christian relations, antisemitism worldwide—we can more easily search for significant changes in the post-1880 discourses. True, the substance and style of the discourses did not differ dramatically from the earlier volume. Devoted mainly to holidays, the sermons for the most part bore the same characteristics: they were edifying and moralistic, and they indulged in optimistic presentations of Reform's future and its interpretation of the mission of Judaism. Although the CCAR had promised a look at Judaism's stand on contemporary "vital questions," the rabbis still ignored the crucial issues of American domestic affairs—workers' strikes, the Populist Party, rampant political corruption in city and state governments, and the rise of the Progressive movement. The code of political abstinence held firm for the most part, and barring several exceptions, Jewish affairs at home and abroad, like the intensified persecution in Russia, the Dreyfus affair, and the numerous problems attendant on the heavy immigration of East European Jews, were neglected too.

Nevertheless, and despite those many qualifications, seeds of change were germinating. The muzzled rabbi and his limited sermon were giving way to a freer style more involved with contemporary institutions and currents of thought. The fact that lectures were included in the 1896 book suggests that the lines between morally edifying sermons and informative talks were becoming more fluid and that Jews like other Americans responded enthusiastically to the introduction of the popular educational lecture. At the same time, the preachers appeared to grow bolder with respect to the laity. With the establishment of the Hebrew Union College (1875) and the efforts of the CCAR to boost the professionalism of the rabbinate, the status of the rabbi slowly improved. As a result, it was doubtless likely that some rabbis dared more readily than before to criticize their own congregants.

Most reminiscent of the 1881 collection was the theme of science versus religion. Although the Reform rabbis had stated in their Pittsburgh Platform of 1885 that "the modern discoveries of scientific researches in the domains of nature and history" did not conflict with Judaism, many contributions to the 1896 volume again emphasized the limitations and inadequacies of scientific inquiry. Among other things, they said that just as earthly things lacked constancy, so did science and scientific knowledge. "Spurious rationalism" overlooked the soul of man, and science failed to unravel the mysteries of God and human faith.[40] Similarly, a good number of contributors continued the earlier attack on materialists and materialism, and a few went on to scoff publicly at atheists and agnostics.[41] More forcefully than in 1881 they also indicted their own congregations, whose impressive holdings were recorded in the U.S. census of 1890, and warned them against the worship of gold. Rabbi Leon Harrison of St. Louis said bluntly: "You have all more than you actually need to live and make life worth living. . . . The limit of purchased happiness is fixed. You cannot buy more than a certain amount of pleasure, food, shelter, clothing, physical enjoyment. And they are no permanent investment." To counteract such insidious influences, rabbis called for a renewed religious faith and the need of strong Jewish homes and schools.[42]

In a sermon delivered on Sukkoth, Rabbi Emil G. Hirsch developed a new theme related to materialism, that of social justice. The subject had engaged him, like Rabbi Henry Berkowitz, since the 1880s, and in one of the most original sermons included in the volume he elaborated his ideas. An early exponent of social justice, which, like the attempt by liberal Protestant churches and clergy in the Social Gospel movement to apply the moral teachings of scripture to contemporary social problems, Hirsch exhorted his congregants to substitute the values of humanity and brotherhood for rampant capitalism. Unlike most of his colleagues, he preached for the rights of labor and the economically downtrodden and, more specifically, against Jewish slums and sweatshops: "Property is our own only to do therewith what shall prosper the common life. The right to possess is limited by the duty to utilize one's own for the social good." Although his sentiments doubtless ruffled his wealthy parishioners, Hirsch persisted. Insisting that it was his duty as a rabbi to raise the subject, he boldly dismissed the usual restraints on sermons: "If the minister to-day cannot plead for the poor, if he cannot speak for the weak and the down-trodden, then, indeed, there is no use for him." If he, Hirsch, were to be fired for his uncensored talk, he would leave the pulpit and seek another type of employment. Acknowledging the "generous provisions" that his congregation had made for him, he conceded that he was freer than the average rabbi, underpaid and without tenure, to raise controversial subjects.[43]

The onslaught of scientific advances and materialism led a few rabbis, admittedly a very small minority, to dismiss the usual optimism of their colleagues and consider the spiritual crisis that faced the Reform movement. By the last decade of the century serious Reformers were acknowledging that an overrationalized and diluted Judaism had failed to sustain a vibrant faith and command the loyalty of the young people.[44] Since the average layman perceived Reform as a negative creed chipping away at old customs and rituals, he came to doubt both its relevance for himself and its very lastingness. Sociologist Nathan Glazer wrote some fifty years ago: "Around the turn of the century, it would not have been far-fetched for an historian of ideas to predict a merger between Reform Judaism and liberal Christianity." Indeed, there were Jews, and not just Ethical Culturist Felix Adler, who, matter of factly or happily, envisioned a gradual absorption of American Judaism into a vague form of moralistic, universalistic Unitarianism. One contributor to the 1896 volume of sermons candidly challenged his flock to face that possibility: "The un-Judaized Jew, the mongrel type of half-breed that is so common today, has no reason to stand apart and preserve his separateness. . . . It devolves upon those chosen out for a high mission among the nations of the earth, to either live up to their calling . . . or lose their useless identity and merge themselves into the population of the world." Nevertheless, as historian Benny Kraut has shown, Reform rabbis held on to basic theological beliefs and were at best ambivalent about a merger of Judaism with Unitarianism.[45]

New topics for sermons emerged in the collection of 1896. One atypical sermon was the contribution by Gustav Gottheil, rabbi of Temple Emanu-El, on "Judaism and Temperance." Gottheil's remarks, at a time when the crusade of the "drys" was heating up, not only broke with the conventional apolitical sermon but also indicated that the larger community expected the Jews to take a stand on controversial issues. Perhaps, as has been suggested, Christians asked for explanations of Jewish traditions in order to add legitimacy to their own opinions. Rabbi Gottheil said that the Jews, a sober people, had no cause to practice total abstinence or to sympathize with asceticism. He thought that prohibition was a utopian fantasy; it wrongly threatened an industry that provided many jobs, and it could only drive moderate drinkers "into the camp of the rum-sellers." He suggested that a wiser alternative, and one which both Jews and social reformers could support, was legal regulation of the liquor traffic.[46]

Rabbis also delved more deeply into the subject of Jewish/Christian relations. Those berating Jews who succumbed to the attractions of the churches insisted that a comparison of theologies showed Judaism's superiority over Christianity. Judaism neither posited original sin and the depravity of man nor required a mediator between man and God. Without fixed dogma or creed, it assured the individual's freedom of thought. Referring to the widely publicized heresy trial of the Presbyterian minister, Charles Briggs, Emil G. Hirsch said:

> Was ever [a] Jew tried for subscribing to a new doctrine on the Bible? Was I ever summoned before a council because I stated in the hearing of a company of forty-five rabbis . . . that I believe that not a single word of the Pentateuch was written by Moses? . . . We Jews know that freedom of thought and freedom of expression is the very vital element in Judaism.[47]

Louis Grossman similarly pointed out the shortcomings of Christianity, but he injected a new note into the debate by taking issue with contemporary Christian thinkers who scoffed at Jewish "legalism." He disputed the charge heard in circles of biblical critics, a charge that was a common euphemism for Judaism's alleged indifference to higher moral issues and hence an explanation for its inferiority to Christianity. Concerned by the inroads of higher criticism into popular books and journals, Grossman prepared several answers:

1. Legalism was no sin, and Christianity too had its full share of law.
2. Judaism with its contributions to the arts and humanities could not be dismissed as legalism.
3. Jewish law, an evolving way of life rather than mere theological dicta, sustained the Jewish community.[48]

Three contributions to the 1896 volume, first prepared in connection with the World's Parliament of Religions of 1893, also commented on Jewish/Christian relations. At the Jewish Denominational Congress that immediately preceded the parliament and at the parliament itself, rabbis attempted to elucidate the beliefs and ceremonials of Judaism to an international assembly of representatives of numerous faiths from around the world. All gave lip service to one purpose—to promote interfaith peace and harmony—but unlike some non-Jews, both at the parliament and in its immediate aftermath, they did not embrace ideas of a single universal religion. Despite similarities that seemingly united Judaism and some Christian creeds, particularly Unitarianism, and despite a readiness to unite with non-Jews against religious intolerance, rabbis refused to renounce their identity or the independence and legitimacy of their faith. Rabbi Moses Gries of Erie, Pennsylvania, advised his audience of Jews and Christians not to slur over the "fundamental differences" dividing religions. He and colleagues Maurice Harris of New York and Joseph Stolz of Chicago mentioned two differences in particular: different interpretations of individual salvation and a belief in a man-god or at least a more than human mortal. When Jewish teachings were compared with Christian, the former were usually judged superior. Since the relevance of Judaism was ongoing, the three were in agreement: Unity on social issues, yes; Merger, no.[49]

Perhaps even more significant, a discussion of antisemitism in the 1896 volume, a relatively new subject for the preachers, manifested a freer approach by rabbis to contemporary realities. True, some still resorted to oblique allusions like "dark clouds" and "the Hamans are still with us." Only one preacher paid serious attention to the rampant social ostracism in the United States, and a few stubbornly insisted that the brightness of the Jewish condition, especially in America, was in no way dimmed.[50] Nonetheless, several preachers did mention Russian barbarism, and others rebutted the bigots' favorite charges of Jewish economic parasitism, arrogance and exclusivity, and disloyalty. In a decade of heightened nationalism, when even "respectable" antisemites charged that Jews were forever aliens—a peculiar race and a state within a state—Jewish defenders countered by pointing up the parallels between Judaism and Americanism and the direct impact of Jewish ideals on the Founding Fathers.[51] Stating that the "curse and shame of anti-Semitism is uppermost in the minds of the noblest Israelites," one rabbi explained further that Jew-hatred was a barometer of a nation's political democracy. His point, which was picked up and expanded by Jewish defense agencies in the next century, went as follows: "The Israelites of every country are the infallible thermometers of that country's civilization. Let a people begin to degenerate morally, and the first symptoms of that degeneracy will show themselves in prejudice and ill-will against the Jews."[52]

A Hanukkah sermon by Emil G. Hirsch entitled "The Ancient Anti-Semite and His Modern Successors" merits special attention.[53] Flowery rhetoric aside, the discourse revealed Hirsch's wide grasp of secular subjects, while it developed the theme of antisemitism without any anchor in biblical or rabbinic verses (to be discussed below). Notable for its modernity, the rabbi boldly put forth novel interpretations and remedies for Jew-hatred that made the sermon, like that on social justice, one of the most impressive in the 1896 volume.

All products of the last quarter of the nineteenth century, the sermons discussed in this chapter reveal how the restraints imposed and self-imposed on freedom of the pulpit explained the silence of most rabbis on contemporary events. Not all agreed on the challenges of science to religion, but all deplored the ravages of a materialistic age. Grappling with a central problem that all faced—the inability of congregations to ensure and retain the loyalty of American-born members and their children—rabbis faulted congregants made captive by the inroads of secularization. Only a very few suggested ways of revitalizing the religious life of the synagogue. Those who preached the message of Jewish social justice may have pleased a portion of their membership as well as liberal Christians, but in essence they were fashioning social justice into a surrogate for religion.

On two points, however, the rabbis preached alike. First, irrespective of denomination, be they Reform or Traditionalist, Radical Reformers or moderates, their sermons conveyed a boundless love of the United States. Second, despite the challenges of the nineteenth century to religion and religious observance, they repeatedly validated the retention of a Jewish identity. They reminded their audiences that Judaism had contributed much to world civilization throughout history and that its mission for humanity was still both timely and legitimate.

2

From the Words of Sabato Morais

In a study such as this, in which Reform rabbis predominate, a more equitable balance of the opinions of Reformers and Traditionalists is obtained by examining the discourses of Sabato Morais. A moderate Traditionalist, Morais exemplifies the religious and political beliefs of one kind of non-Reformer. He succeeded Isaac Leeser, also a Traditionalist but one whose work is better known, at the Philadelphia synagogue, Mikveh Israel.[1] There, in a long career of more than forty-five years, Morais labored to reconcile his interpretation of Judaism to the realities of American life. This chapter emphasizes his differences with his Reform and other Traditionalist colleagues and testifies to the wide spectrum of religious beliefs that separated rabbi from rabbi.

In 1851 the prestigious Sephardic congregation in Philadelphia, Mikveh Israel, appointed Sabato Morais to the post of *hazzan*. Italian-born Morais, who was only twenty-eight at the time, succeeded Isaac Leeser, and he remained with the congregation until his death in 1897. Reared in a Traditionalist family that supported Italian liberalism and unification, he had studied with Italian rabbis. He spent five years as a Hebrew teacher in London where he became acquainted with a leading communal figure, Moses Montefiore. Morais learned of a position at Mikveh Israel after an English woman he had met visited her daughter in Philadelphia. Upon her return she asked him if he would be interested in serving as minister in the post recently vacated by Leeser. Although his experience in England was his sole preparation for an American pulpit, Morais accepted the synagogue's offer.[2]

Historian Arthur Kiron's study of Morais concentrates on the rabbi as an exemplar of enlightened Orthodoxy. Kiron explains that during his years in Italy and England Morais absorbed the teachings of a secular enlightenment that he melded with rabbinic Judaism. Steeped in the Sephardic heritage, he was a firm republican who championed religious liberty, humanism, and universalism. Morais carried those ideals with him across the ocean, and in the New World he added the belief in American exceptionalism to his creed. His Judaism so interpreted allowed him to preach the need for rapid acculturation—with no diminution of loyalty to his ethnic roots—along with religious observance. Irrespective of its origin, his philosophical/theological position placed him in the ranks of the moderate Traditionalists.[3]

Scholar, writer, educator, and active participant in Jewish affairs, Morais modified his European-bred Traditionalism under the influence of his American experiences. Quite aware that Jews in the New World, without proper schooling in their history and tradition, were fast succumbing to the lures of secularization and the ease of religious indifference, he worked to instruct the Jewish community in the riches of traditional Judaism even as he reminded them of their obligations as Americans. A predominant figure of his time, he published more sermons during the Civil War period than any of his rabbinical colleagues.[4] According to a ledger of newspaper clippings that Morais kept, both early and later sermons as well as many of his numerous statements were picked up and printed by Philadelphia newspapers and by his friend, Rabbi Samuel Isaacs, the founder and publisher of the *Jewish Messenger* in New York.[5]

Morais became well known among Reformers too. For a while he cooperated with Reform and supported changes in ritual and custom primarily for the sake of religious unity among the contending factions, but as the Reform movement became more assertive, he distanced himself and hardened his defense of Traditionalism. Because of his scholarly writings, his good press, and his prestigious synagogue, he was by the 1880s the acknowledged leader of the moderate Traditionalists. His labors made him the exemplar of religious centrism, endeavoring to adapt Judaism, still in a state of flux, to a free environment, and he led the moderates in what only later would be known as Conservative Judaism. Morais was a founder of the Jewish Theological Seminary (1887), always the center of gravity of the twentieth-century Conservative movement, and its first president.

Although difficulties with the English language and his timid and modest nature made the young Morais apprehensive about preaching, he refused to discontinue the practice that had been instituted by his predecessor. To dispense with sermons would be a step backward, he said, and he insisted that the sermon was a necessary device for reaching the young people. His early efforts as preacher came at a time when lay control of the synagogue was firmly entrenched. His preaching was less than brilliant, and he himself was well aware that his audience did not always respond positively. In an undated sermon, he admitted that although he preached only nine months each year, some congregants would have preferred to eliminate the sermon entirely. He enumerated the grounds on which he may have evoked disapproval: "When I thought to teach, I became wearisome; when I conceived to have offered good counsel, I was considered tedious; when I imagined to have chosen a pleasing style, I created a disgruntled impression; when I sought to give spiritual gratification, I have been deemed out of time and out of place."[6] It wasn't long, however, before Morais won the right to preach throughout the year and to speak from a free pulpit.

An examination of Morais's sermons reveals that his public discourses, other than those dealing exclusively with the religious duties of an observant Jew, fell into distinct categories. Among the most interesting were his opinions on the right of rabbis to discuss contemporary political issues, his defense of American Jewish equality, and his views on traditional Judaism. Each category in turn came with a set of guidelines, or what we may call "codes" of proper rabbinic discourses. The codes themselves were hardly Morais's personal invention. The principle of political neutrality or invisibility, which underlay the first and second categories, had been set by the community at its very inception, and the code of traditional Judaism had been fixed by the Talmud and by generations of rabbinic commentaries. How well Morais conformed to or deviated from the codes, and how his statements resembled or differed from those of his rabbinical colleagues, reveals major issues of concern to nineteenth-century Jewish religious leaders. Morais was at times inconsistent, but because he modified his guidelines in answer to specific social changes, and because he often acted independently, his career merits added interest.

Unlike the typical rabbi of mid-century America, Morais fought for and won the right to a free pulpit. An early tiff with the officers of the synagogue arose during the Mortara affair, the case in 1858 of a little Jewish boy of Bologna, Italy, who had been secretly baptized by a servant and forcibly removed from his home several years later by papal guards. The rabbi desperately wanted the American government to condemn the Vatican's action, but President James Buchanan turned down such pleas. Morais participated in a delegation to Buchanan, but the committee's request for the president's intervention "on the side of human rights" was summarily rejected. When Morais sought to continue the pressure by omitting the Sabbath prayer for the government, the board of Mikveh Israel vetoed the idea. For Jews to brazenly snub the American president on a Jewish issue not only contradicted the political code—that is, Jews were to refrain from injecting Jewish issues into the political arena—but appeared fraught with danger. As the rabbi recalled in a sermon some twenty-three years after the event: "My feelings were worked up to a pitch, which led to a collision between myself and the temporal officers of our congregation, and in which I was of course defeated."[7]

An interesting footnote to the Mortara affair came in a sermon preached by Morais many years later on the new antisemitism in Germany. Recalling his prior experience, he thought an appeal to Washington on the subject would be futile. Unlike many of his colleagues, however, he also frowned on public statements on behalf of German Jews voiced by American Christian clerics. Those statements, usually embellished with praise of Jews and Judaism, drew his bitter reaction: "In my ears," he said, "the praises bestowed by ministers of the Nazarene creed sound like patronage, which I heartily loathe. I don't wish my people to be patted and talked about pitifully because they are dealt foully with by a wicked world. I would rather we be spoken of as an unyielding, uncompromising race than lauded for having given the Church which claims supremacy, its man-god." On that issue he dismissed a long-established practice of Jewish defense that called for enlisting prominent Christians to speak for the Jewish cause in the public square. For example, Rabbi Marcus Jastrow, his colleague in Philadelphia, was one rabbi who disagreed with Morais. In favor of statements by German Christians in support of Jews, Jastrow said that the Christians also acted out of self-interest, because they opposed the race hatred that the German antisemites preached. Morais was unmoved. Here too he was the independent rabbi who didn't hesitate to challenge the community's accepted opinion.[8]

Not long after the Mortara case the issue of muzzling Morais resurfaced. The story told by historian Bertram Korn relates that the rabbi, an outspoken opponent of slavery and a staunch supporter of Lincoln and the Union, was criticized by a group of congregants for his political partisanship during the Civil War. When the board thought to resolve the matter by voting to dispense with all English sermons unless requested by the synagogue's president, Morais successfully organized a group of laymen who petitioned for a reversal of the decision. The board yielded partially, announcing that all sermons were to be "religious discourses" delivered at the president's discretion. Morais was not entirely satisfied, and at his urging in April 1865 a large majority of the congregation voted him permission to preach on "moral and religious" issues whenever he chose and on "the subjects of the day." The rabbi yielded somewhat, too, and in one undated sermon he asked his congregants to make their opinions on his sermons, both negative and positive, known to the board.

The parameters so defined proved eminently flexible for Morais. Ironically, despite his victory, his sermons until the 1880s usually heeded the strictures on political invisibility, and Mikveh Israel had little to criticize about their unmuzzled rabbi. Indeed, Morais's published and unpublished papers reveal that he handled most topics, touching even slightly on domestic politics in newspaper articles and lectures and not in religious discourses. He himself said in one sermon that "the Synagogue is not the arena of politics."[9] Only in the later years of his ministry did he broaden the scope of his sermons and inject political matters, like the exclusion of Chinese immigrants, corruption in government, rights of workers, and American foreign policy. He said then that temporal subjects did belong in the pulpit; rabbis were obligated to preach against evil.[10] If individual members of the congregation ever contested his choice of topics, they refrained from public censure of their rabbi.

The Philadelphia rabbi made his opinions known on a wide variety of subjects, but his independence appeared less pronounced when he discussed aspects of the condition of American Jewry. His talks in defense of American Jewish equality and against Jew-haters, especially those before 1880, show that he usually abided by the restraints imposed by the political code. To be sure, in his case the restraints were mainly self-imposed, but as examples discussed below show—particularly with regard to advice on proper Jewish responses to discrimination—he heeded what was tantamount to a "halfway" code: that is, visibility only where constitutional rights were concerned. At the same time, however, his sermons and other statements provided valuable instruction for the congregation on the basic principles of the American ethos.

From a family that had championed the cause of Italian liberalism, Morais rejoiced in the freedom that he and his fellow Jews enjoyed in the United States. His praise of the country, its founders and the Constitution, and its mission as haven of the oppressed was unstinting. Equating the essence of Israel with that of America, he taught that each had a role for the benefit of humanity: "Israel would dispel the clouds of heathen barbarism, America widen the horizon of human civilization." Morais also emphasized—and here the congregation gave its full approval—the blessings of America specifically for the Jews: "Under the broad aegis of [America's] matchless Constitution, we have dwelt . . . in perfect security." In light of such sentiments the rabbi's encouragement of rapid accultura-tion easily followed. Love of Lincoln and the Union during the Civil War resonated in the sermons he delivered on special fast days and days of thanksgiving proclaimed by the president. Not only did the rabbi identify wholly with America and American history—"our Republic," "our military achievements," "the genius of our immortal predecessors of revolutionary memory"—but also he found support in Jewish history for the cause of the Union and against secession. On one occasion he asked rhetorically: "When was Judea tranquil within and respected without? Was it not when the twelve tribes formed a glorious unit under the scepter of one sover-eign? [And] from what period do the declining of our ancient power and our unheard-of disasters date? Is it not from the unpropitious time that Judah and Israel became two separate kingdoms?" On another occasion Lincoln wrote a letter of gratitude to Morais for his pro-Union stand.[11]

Morais's ardent patriotism did not blind him to issues that he per-ceived as impinging on Jewish constitutional rights. On such matters he was not alone, since other rabbis also believed that fundamental issues of Jewish equality exempted them from the customary political restraints. Especially sensitive to executive or legislative attempts on both the fed-eral and state levels that recognized the favored status of Christians and Christianity, they publicly opposed the stigma of second-class citizenship foisted on Jews and Judaism by such actions. In 1868, for example, Morais joined six other Philadelphia rabbis who protested the Thanksgiving Day message of Governor John Geary calling on the citizens of Pennsylvania to pray that "their paths through life may be directed by the example and instructions of the Redeemer [Jesus], who died that they might enjoy all the blessings." The issue was an old one. Jews had participated in Thanks-giving celebrations with Christians since the eighteenth century, but gov-ernors of various states had repeatedly addressed their messages to Chris-tian citizens alone. Jews understandably took offense; not only did such pronouncements set them apart from their compatriots as less than equal, but also the Christological allusions testified to the more encompassing and frightening specter of America as a Christian state. Seeking vari-ous ways to demonstrate their opposition, some Jews boycotted the holi-day and kept their businesses open. At the same time, Jewish communal leaders protested publicly against Christian phraseology; they argued that such proclamations were unconstitutional, depriving them of the freedom of conscience that was rightfully theirs. (Technically, their argument was inaccurate; it was *equality* of religion and not *freedom* of religion that was abridged.) Morais recalled in his Thanksgiving Day sermon of 1868 that the gubernatorial proclamation a year earlier had been similarly objectionable, but now again, despite protests from many Jews, the governor repeated the insult.[12]

The rabbis' response to Geary stated first that the "freedom-loving authors of the American Constitution" had produced a document that "opened indiscriminately to all the avenues of greatness, so that the position now filled by a follower of the theories of Calvin or Wesley may tomorrow be occupied by the descendant of Abraham, or perchance by a free-thinker." It followed, they added, that Geary's proclamation violated Jewish rights: "We object to its encroachment on 'the immunities' we are entitled to share with all the inhabitants of Pennsylvania, and we appeal to . . . our fellow-citizens that [the governor's deed] may be universally stigmatized as an offense against liberty of conscience . . . and derogatory to the honor of the noble state he represents." In Morais's words: "Allow no man, however loftily stationed, to dictate, or even intimate to the denizens of this land, by the rites of what church they ought to worship their Creator." Morais received letters of protest from Christian ministers bluntly reminding him that Pennsylvania was a Christian state. The rabbi apologized sarcastically to such complaints; he had learned, he replied, that Jews could not complain about infringements of their rights but were expected to show gratitude for crumbs that Christians threw at them. Morais put up a good fight, but he noted regretfully that only one newspaper had picked up the story of the rabbinic protest.[13]

Twelve years later the same question arose. Henry Hoyt, then governor of Pennsylvania, issued a Thanksgiving Day proclamation in which he referred to the state as a "Christian Commonwealth." In an open letter to the press, Morais chided Hoyt for dividing the citizenry into Christians and Jews. We are all part of one humanity, he said. Individual Jews also protested, and this time the protesters succeeded. Disavowing any religious prejudice, Hoyt removed the offensive phrase by substituting for it the "Commonwealth of Freemen."[14]

In both Thanksgiving episodes Morais may have strayed from the strict interpretation of the political code by addressing what was a gubernatorial order or a political matter, but he never went too far afield. He held the governors alone culpable, and he neither counseled Jews to protest to Geary and Hoyt (or to punish their political parties at the polls) nor advised political rallies, pressure on legislators, or the enlistment of Christian allies. Appealing only to constitutional and humanitarian principles, and to the legacy of the Founding Fathers, he limited his weapons. His message to his congregants, fitting his low-key response, advised them only to keep faith in the Almighty.[15]

As in the Thanksgiving Day episodes, some rabbis, and Morais among them, also protested the injustice and unconstitutionality of Sunday laws that recognized the "Lord's Day" or the Christian day of rest. On one occasion the rabbi of Mikveh Israel devoted a sermon to the subject even as he admonished his flock to observe the Jewish Sabbath. His purpose, he announced, was to refute proponents of Sunday laws who argued that since the holiness of Sunday was rooted in the Jewish Sabbath, Sunday ordinances were in the Jewish interest too. An irate Morais called that argument a "pious fraud." "Is it logical to suppose that we, who are made by the Church weekly to pay the penalty for our attachment to the five books of Moses, will aid the Church in fastening upon the world severe restrictions, pretended to have been derived from those very volumes?" The rabbi assured his audience that he hadn't forgotten about political neutrality: "We choose not to let our voices be heard abroad with remonstrances of a denominational character." He felt impelled to answer, however, because, he said, Jewish law had been dragged into the discussion.[16] Yet again, despite the free pulpit that he had won some twelve years before, Morais still refrained from urging an active Jewish response. Doubtless he feared protests from the laity and from non-Jews that, at the very least, might cause him or his congregation discomfort. The rabbi went no further than to call the objectionable practices a violation of the principles of the Founding Fathers and of church/state separation as well as an injustice to the Jews.

According to Morais, the themes of Americanism and Jewish identity, as in the cases pertaining to the equality owed to professing Jews, more than complemented each other. Indeed, at times they appeared to be fused. Positing a contract between the nation and the Jews, he spoke of the obligations of both parties. It behooved Jews to bond with the American culture and to demonstrate their loyalty to the nation and its ideals. America in turn was duty bound to protect the freedom and equal rights of Jews as Jews that were spelled out in the Constitution. Morais went on to develop the idea of contract beyond assertions of mutual rights and duties. Since Jews were required to defend their rights against any encroachment by the government, their defense of constitutional principles, the rabbi implied, served to guard the greater good—that is, the basic rights of *all* Americans. Indeed, the guardianship of America's basic rights was virtually a God-given role for, as he hinted on several occasions, Jewish faith in God operated in tandem with a faith in the Constitution.

Morais used Jewish law as his excuse for preaching sermons on several other questions then being discussed in the political arena. When Pennsylvania's legislature was considering the abolition of the death penalty, the rabbi said that he was reluctant to use the pulpit for commenting on the matter but for the fact that a popular argument in the debate blamed "barbaric" Jewish law for the retention of capital punishment. He intimated that his own opinion was secondary at best, but he managed to show how the Bible and the ancient sages had formulated escape clauses regarding the use of the death penalty. Another political issue discussed by Morais was prohibition. The rabbi explained that Jewish law did not forbid imbibing liquor and wine, but he was more concerned about denouncing the very few Jewish drunkards within the community. In a third sermon, this one on labor unrest, Morais didn't even seek a Jewish link as an excuse. After the notorious Haymarket strike in 1886, when several radical workers were executed for their violence, he, although sympathetic with labor, criticized socialism and anarchism as well as capitalist abuses. Explaining why he addressed an issue growing more and more politicized, he said: "To let events that stir up communities go unnoticed by the pulpit is impossible."[17] Aside from its substance, the comment testified to his growing impatience with political neutrality.

Far more dangerous than Thanksgiving Day proclamations or Sunday laws in the eyes of nineteenth-century Jewish leaders were movements to Christianize the Constitution—that is, to ground the fundamental law and its derivatives in Christianity. Criticism of the Constitution for ignoring Christianity as the basis of civic morality had been heard ever since the eighteenth-century debates over ratification. During the Civil War popular agitation increased. A group that called itself the National Reform Association (NRA) pushed for amending the Constitution along Christian lines, principally by acknowledging God and Jesus in the preamble. Gaining widespread support, it peaked in the 1870s and again in the 1890s, and it persisted into the twentieth century. Since it presaged legal hardships on non-Christians by the imposition of stricter Sunday laws, Christian teachings in the public schools, and restrictions on holding public office,

Jews feared that their struggle for full religious equality would come to a halt if not regress. Morais argued that while a Christian amendment could not change the way people thought, it could cause fanaticism. Indeed, one Episcopalian minister said openly that those who deviated from the faith of the majority had to expect persecution.[18]

In 1871 at a convention of the NRA the Christianizers made short shrift of their fellow Jews; they either maligned them, ignored them, or equated them with aliens. Morais like other rabbis rose in defense of his coreligionists. Since the gravity of the threat transcended by far any considerations of political neutrality, the Philadelphia rabbi aired his views in a public letter to the secular press. Not only was civilization in general indebted to Jews, he said, but their contributions to the United States were ongoing ever since the Revolution: "[The Jew] bled at Bunker Hill to gain . . . independence, and poured out his treasures to enlarge its boundaries. He fell side by side with his fellow-man professing Christianity in the mighty struggle that saved the Union." Equally important, aside from victimizing the Jews, a Christian amendment offered no benefits to society at large. It could neither eliminate corruption and moral vice nor guarantee the strength of the country. America was a blessing to mankind, he concluded, but it faced a grave threat: "With the Constitution altered as the convention [of the NRA] . . . proposed, America will be a scourge in the hands of the crafty to tear the lives of the powerless, whether they be Jews or Christians." Morais repeated the same arguments when an attempt was made in 1876 to Christianize the constitution of Pennsylvania, but other than alerting the press—a hint at stirring up public sympathy—he offered no plan of resistance.[19]

Some twenty years later, when the voice of the Christianizers cried out against a "godless country," their agenda (which included Sunday laws, religion in the classroom, Christian oaths for holding office, and popular support of a Christian amendment) increased. Congress considered a joint resolution calling for an amendment, and with other rabbis Morais denounced the scheme from the pulpit. Devoting the bulk of his remarks to the dangers of a state-supported church, he lashed out against the Christianizers and their following. Now again, when Jewish equality was on the line, he needed no explanation for deviating from the path of political neutrality. No one could foretell, he warned, what "the persistence of the pietists" or those so anxious to amend the work of the founders of the Republic might bring about: "They are determined to show their own followers, that unless America proclaims her Christianity before the world, she is doomed to perdition." To students of Jewish history, he insisted, the handwriting was on the wall: "They remember what sacrileges were perpetrated in the name of God. They have not forgotten the madness of a fanaticism which kindled the torch of devastation; the bigotry that leveled houses of worship to the ground. They can recall how to avenge a dominant religion the clergy blessed the word that cut to pieces the disaffected. A Christian nation, forsooth!"

Morais was more familiar with the excesses of Catholicism, the dominant faith of his native Italy, but he inveighed as well against the record of Protestantism: "Luther bequeathed a legacy of ill-will against such as refused to accept his reformation. He did not scruple to recommend violence, for his motto was: 'Thunders and lightnings are necessary to clear the atmosphere.'" Protestant Germany and Protestant England were as guilty as pre-modern Spain and France for discriminating against dissenters. He himself, Morais added, while he had lived in England had witnessed the humiliation of the Salomons and Rothschilds forbidden to take their seats in Parliament as a penalty for refusing to swear "on the true faith of a Christian." The obvious lesson for the United States was to adhere faithfully to the separation of church and state.[20]

The word "antisemitism" came into popular usage only in the late 1870s, but Morais avoided the term even in his later sermons. To be sure, he denounced persecution of the Jews in Europe, Asia, and North Africa, but despite the alarming receptivity to racist antisemitism in the United States as well as on the Continent during the fourth quarter of the century, he addressed antisemitism directly in but one sermon, that on the anti-Jewish eruptions in Bismarck's Germany. Never did he refer to Jew-hatred in his remarks on Thanksgiving proclamations, Sunday laws, or a Christian amendment as manifestations of American antisemitism. He may have been reluctant to believe that serious antisemitism, far different from European-like oppression and pogroms, existed in his beloved America—"pietists" and unthinking officials were to blame for any threats to Jewish equality—or he may have feared that concerted Jewish attacks on American prejudice could alienate both non-Jews and concerned Jews.

Much of what Morais said was aimed at public relations. While he reminded the Jews of their obligations to the nation, he explained Jewish customs and traditions to the larger society and rebutted the arguments of Christian missionaries. Taking note of mounting social discrimination in America, he responded to antisemitic slurs.[21] On two separate occasions he, unlike most Jews and sympathetic Gentiles, blamed the discrimination on the victims as well as on the perpetrators. Since both incidents concerned members of the powerful and well-connected Seligman banking family, they aroused public interest nationwide. The first involved Joseph Seligman, a friend of President Grant, who in 1877 was denied entry into the Grand Union Hotel in Saratoga just because he was a Jew, and the second concerned Seligman's nephew Theodore, who applied for membership in the prestigious Union League club in 1893 and was blackballed for the same reason. Much was said in criticism of those responsible for the discrimination, but Morais wasted no sympathy on the Seligmans. Why must Jews seek out places that didn't want them? Furthermore, since neither Seligman displayed any self-respect as a Jew or respect for his faith, he didn't merit any better treatment. Neither money nor social contacts with members of the government or other prominent non-Jews, of which both men could boast, mattered: "We must . . . be impeachably moral, steadfastly pious, well-informed, refined, polished, gentlemanly in the best and truest sense of the word." By their own doing Jews had put a stigma on the word "Jew." Morais's words were not calculated to win him popularity, particularly since they contradicted Jewish efforts against social discrimination, and indeed they did not escape popular censure.[22]

A singular example of Morais's response to Jew-baiting in America was his denunciation of the popular revivalist and agitator, Dwight Moody. Missionaries to the Jews in the nineteenth century used both the carrot and the stick to ply their trade among non-Christians, but Moody, who chose the stick, was different. Unlike the stereotypical backwoods revivalist, he was the preacher who brought traditional religion to native Americans on the urban frontier seeking to bridge their former way of life with the realities of the industrial age. Middle class in aspirations and values, they were as yet uncomfortable with the scientific and secularist challenges to religion. Moody shared their attitudes; he identified with businessmen, and he applied business principles to his own revivalist campaign. Although he claimed that he honored the Jews because they were the people destined to convert the world to Christianity, he incited his audiences against them.

The winter of 1875–1876 marked a high point in Moody's revivalist crusade. Before tens of thousands in major American cities, he lashed out at the Jews. At one meeting in Philadelphia he made full use of the age-old myth that the Jews were guilty of deicide. Not only did he recount the story of the crucifixion in lurid detail, but he also claimed that a thousand

Jews who had met in Paris in 1873 boasted of having killed the Christians' God. Morais responded to Moody in a sermon titled "The Israelites and Their Detractors." No Jew would have believed, he said, that on the eve of America's centennial celebrations a man "ostensibly [on a] holy mission" would have tried to "inflame the passions of multitudes against law-abiding Hebrews." But fortunately, because the setting was America and not a land without the tradition of liberty and constitutional rights, "bloodshed and plunder" by Christian mobs did not follow. The rabbi denied Moody's charge of deicide, but, unlike the feisty Isaac Wise who repeatedly challenged Moody to a debate on the story of the passion of Jesus, he ignored the particulars of the evangelical's anti-Jewish brief. Here too Morais acted in accordance with the common restraints on a rabbi, and he refused to indulge in invectives or to counsel a popular response: "We will not, my brethren, desecrate this spot devoted to prayer and spiritual instruction. . . . Never will we pervert our sanctuary from its holy purpose." In justification, however, of considering Moody from the pulpit at all, he insisted that Jews earned respect only if they remained faithful to Judaism. It behooved American Jews, therefore, to keep the faith, the most effective shield against bigots like Moody, and to dedicate themselves to the protection of "that matchless inheritance of the sages of the Revolution." Faith in the Constitution and in God's mercy to Israel was the reassurance that Morais gave his congregation. He went no further in probing the causes and manifestations of Jew-hatred, nor did he suggest other possible ways of amelioration.[23]

Morais ministered to Mikveh Israel at a time when Reform Judaism was winning over large numbers of Jews and congregations. Unlike the movement in Europe, which on occasion met opposition from the government, Reform in the United States appeared to be enjoying limitless success. It attracted those Jews who sought a modern religion free of antiquated Traditionalist rules, taboos, and rituals as well as notions of a separate peoplehood. Appealing primarily to the more acculturated and affluent members of the community, Reformers offered a form of worship Americanized in language and style that would be understandable and acceptable to non-Jews. They would show Americans thereby that Jews differed from them only in matters of faith. Reform's progress encountered little effective resistance from Traditionalists, principally because they lacked a unified and creative leadership that could challenge the dissenters in a meaningful fashion. Clinging to a seemingly stagnant creed that bred a mood of religious apathy among the congregants, the Traditionalists found it difficult if not impossible to retain the loyalty of the faithful.

Morais was a moderate Traditionalist; on a religious scale he stood to the left of the right-wing Orthodox, particularly the extremists. Always aware of the demands of acculturation, he accepted Jewish conformity to popular mores as long as such practices neither conflicted with the essentials of Judaism nor constituted steps to the Christianization of Jews or their faith. He also expected Jews to exhibit a pride in their heritage and to hold fast to ties that bound them to a living Jewish group. As Kiron concludes: "This effort to formulate an acculturated Jewish version of religion [and] politics . . . without shedding Jewish particularism sets him apart from the familiar identification of Jewish life in America during that same time as leading to reform and assimilation." True, like other Traditionalists, he regarded the Shabbat, the dietary laws, and prayers in the Hebrew language as inviolate, but he aimed for a "rational" or "intelligent conservatism" or an "enlightened Orthodoxy."[24] The terms "Conservative" and "Conservatism" were not yet used for a specific movement or ideology.[25] When Morais spoke or wrote those words, he meant Traditionalism or the opposite of Reform. His loyalty to what he knew as "Historical Judaism" notwithstanding, Morais did not oppose all change in age-old Jewish practices. In one sermon, sounding much like Reformers, he called for "lopping off excrescences" and rejecting "whatever is the offspring of prejudice and superstition, engendered by clannishness resulting from ages of social debasement."[26] But unlike Reformers, and despite shifts in his own position over the years, he defended the need to observe traditional rituals.

As a foremost exponent of moderate Traditionalism who wanted his congregation to be *the* model of moderate Traditionalism, the Philadelphia rabbi, in the footsteps of his likeminded predecessor, Isaac Leeser, contested Reform and Reformers throughout his ministry.[27] Time and again he reiterated his basic objections to the movement that "deformed" Judaism. Neither Leeser nor he would countenance changes by unauthorized rabbis or changes that conflicted with the Orthodox tenets of creation ex nihilo, Sinaitic revelation, or the coming of the messiah. Usually Morais linked his critique to three larger themes that constantly engaged him: the need for communal unity, the education of Jewish youth, and the dangers of imitating the Gentiles. He spoke both as a defender of normative Jewish teachings and a force for a stronger American Jewry.

Questioning Reform's logic and legitimacy, Morais charged that Reformers, who had begun as revilers of rabbinism and the oral law, also tampered with the Torah and ended up in total disbelief. Claiming to rest on higher principles, Reform ignored the ceremonials needed to implant those principles. As for Reform's deification of reason, Morais added: "Let reason be the hand-maid of religion but never our sole director." Since Reformers were bent on aping Gentile services, as in the removal of Hebrew from the liturgy and the use of the organ and mixed choir, they were trapped by the mania for innovation. Instead of rebuilding, they overthrew. Individual rabbis, often poorly educated for the rabbinate and answering to no authority but their congregation, introduced changes that destroyed the belief in a Jewish national identity and led logically to Christianity. In short, Reform was thoroughly destructive. Wreaking "synagogal devastation," it was the "anti-religion" unable to prevent youth from leaving the fold, or the "Moloch" that made for the Christianization of Judaism.[28]

The rabbi had several friends among Reform rabbis, like Bernhard Felsenthal of Chicago, but when Mikveh Israel fell on hard times, he refused as a matter of principle to appeal for funds from Jews opposed to his conservatism. Rather, he turned for support to Sir Moses Montefiore, an Orthodox Jew and the renowned leader of British Jewry. Although Montefiore may have understood something different by conservatism and moderate Traditionalism, he responded warmly: "Your . . . ardent desire to preserve in your Synagogue the principles of conservatism has afforded me much pleasure." That Morais felt constrained to turn for help from abroad is testimony to the lack of unity among American counter-Reformers.

Yet despite his rebuttals and barbs, a note of ambivalence with respect to Reform crept into Morais's activities. For one thing, he cooperated with his Reform colleagues on matters like Thanksgiving Day proclamations, Sunday laws, and a Christian amendment to the Constitution. More important, he was willing to compromise with Reform for the sake of higher goals—Jewish unity and Jewish education. Unity, he said, would strengthen Judaism in America and show the world that the religion of American Jews was neither pointless nor apathetic. When Reformers established the Union of American Hebrew Congregations (UAHC) in 1873, which at first was not exclusively Reform, he urged every congregation, Traditionalist as well as Reform, to join. Another of his higher goals, that of educating young people, led him to amend his own insistence on a traditional education and to serve for a few years on the board of examiners of Reform's rabbinical seminary, Hebrew Union College (HUC) in Cincinnati. In a contest between education and denominational loyalties, he ranked the former above the latter. As he said, even if a professor at HUC repudiated the oral law, the courses he taught were better than nothing! At the same time, however, Morais contradicted his acceptance of HUC by agitating for the establishment of a Traditionalist seminary. He said later that the Reform school educated its pupils for destructive purposes and that it therefore ran counter to basic Jewish needs.[29]

Concern about the lack of unity and a readiness to compromise with Reform prompted Morais to put forth a bold plan for a uniform synagogue ritual. Not only was he willing to sacrifice the Sephardic *minhag* (mode), the one in which he was reared and the one that governed Mikveh Israel, but his plan ran counter to the common practice in America of organizing congregations according to the immigrants' geographical origin and forms of worship. As early as 1867 Morais outlined his suggestions in articles for the *Jewish Messenger*. His purposes, he wrote, were to achieve unity and peace and to bring back to the fold those who had strayed from the synagogue. Arguing against the preservation of rituals imported from other countries, he advocated an American liturgy adapted or altered to serve the desires of the present generation. Although he condoned the right to make changes in religious services if they were sanctioned by recognized rabbinical authorities—a gesture that might appeal to moderate Reformers—he hoped that the unity achieved by a uniform ritual would disarm the enemies of traditional Judaism. Morais later told his congregation that the community had not responded to his plan; individual rabbis were making their own changes in ritual and Reform was "more rampant" than ever.[30]

Deploring the strides of the Reform movement, Morais watched apprehensively when, in 1869, thirteen rabbis met in Philadelphia and adopted a creed for Reform that was diametrically opposed to rabbinic Judaism. Building on earlier Reform conferences in Germany, the assembled rabbis specifically negated much of the traditional code regarding marriage, divorce, and circumcision. The general principles they formulated were even more radical: rejection of a personal messiah and the restoration of the Jews to Palestine, rejection of the sacrificial system and the priesthood, denial of bodily resurrection, the need to give up Hebrew in the liturgy, and an affirmation of a mission that required the dispersion of the Jews outside Palestine.

Since the resolutions were publicized in the American press, Morais felt impelled to answer. Appealing to his like-minded colleagues, he said that Jews would not be swayed by the Reformers, because Traditionalism shuddered at the anomaly of rabbis who were supposed to be "the appointed guardians of Biblical and traditional laws" but who substituted their own principles. Only Christians, out of a lack of understanding, praised the resolutions adopted in Philadelphia and hailed them "as a stride towards the Christianization of our race." The rabbi charged that the Reformers were bent on removing "every trace of the ancient covenant," and their resolutions were the product of "rashness unbecoming all intelligent beings." How could they affirm "the selection of Israel as a religious people" at the same time that their decisions contradicted that very principle? Summing up his remarks, he said: "To a conscientious Israelite," the Philadelphia conference was "but a mad effort to erase with a stroke of the pen, what the finger of God wrote in letters of fire."[31]

Despite his bitter denunciation of the Philadelphia conference, Morais continued to urge adoption of a uniform ritual, a subject that best illustrated his inconsistency with respect to a strict Traditionalist code. Between 1869 and 1885 his pressure reached a new peak, and in 1875 he expatiated at length and more forcefully on the principles regarding ritual that he had outlined previously. This time he elaborated on changes he was willing to accept in a uniform prayer book for the sake of unity and for reaching the youth. Keep the impregnable core, he advised, but much of the rest—that is, "what relates to the ordinances followed by the ancients in the performances of sacrificial rites . . . what relates to Mishnaic and Talmudic lore"—could be deleted. In effect, the move would have strengthened the Reformers, since a uniform "American" liturgy that renounced the Sephardic rite and Talmudic injunctions catered to the tastes of Reform's congregants. Morais believed that a uniform ritual might have checked Reform's progress: "Unhappily the golden opportunity for preventing the inroad of Radicalism was lost, but it is the duty of all who love the law to come to the breach. If to defend points that must be kept impregnable, we are forced to yield others not so important, let us not hold back and fold our arms, looking on while the whole edifice is being razed to the ground." The plan drew criticism, however, from both Traditionalists and Reformers, and no further action was taken.[32]

The flames of controversy between the opponents and defenders of Reform were fanned still further in 1883, when, at a banquet to honor the first graduating class of HUC, non-kosher food was served. While

Traditionalists protested angrily, Isaac Wise's *American Israelite* showered insults on the critics. In one issue it said: "Stop that noise over the culinary department of Judaism. Nobody has appointed those very orthodox critics overseers of that Kitchen and taskmasters of the stomach!"[33]

The final break came two years later. In 1885 Reform rabbis assembled in Pittsburgh and drew up a platform for their movement that resembled the principles formulated in 1869. Called Reform's Declaration of Independence, it affirmed the God-idea, a dedication to spiritual elevation, and the universal mission of Judaism. Although it accepted the Mosaic code with significant qualifications, it rejected the *halachic* laws concerning dietary restrictions as well as restoration to Palestine and a revived temple service. More afraid now of Reform's ultimate success, Morais delivered an impassioned sermon attacking "the Ministers who . . . virtually declared that what fails to please the modern Jew ought to be abolished." He explained that during the years between the Philadelphia and the Pittsburgh conferences, Reform "has been seething," finally reaching "the highest degree of effervescence." Morais expressed his bitterness in a long tirade against the Radical Reformers and the implications of the 1885 platform:

> They [the Radical Reformers] became the leading spirit of the [Pittsburgh] convention. Hence, circumcision was denounced as "a relic of African barbarism"; Sunday services were recommended for such "places where their necessity is felt"; laws regulating diet were set down "as foreign to our mental or spiritual state." . . . By not insisting on the Abrahamic rite, we will inevitably lead to entangling domestic alliances; by holding a worship similar to the Sabbath on the first day of the week, we will suicidally lead the rising generation to the Church; by permitting all sorts of viands we will . . . encourage a dangerous approximation to gentiles. But the recent platform discloses features more abhorrent to honest Jewish hearts than even those which I have just pointed out. It presents a threatening look against the Pentateuch. It makes us feel that if the Convention at Pittsburgh in 1885 proves more successful than that of 1869 at Philadelphia, the five books of Moses will be sacrilegiously cut down to the size of scarcely one! Its platform declares that the Sinaic [*sic*] legislation was meant to train a people for their residence in Palestine, that consequently only its moral code and such of the ceremonies as are adapted to modern civilization can be accepted. It states furthermore that the conception of Divine Providence and of Justice in the sacred volumes is imperfect, that

it simply reflects the primitive ideas of olden ages. . . . Stripped of verbiage, condensed in a few lines, the gist of the high-sounding platform is an attack on Mosaism, as a thing unfit for our time.

Perverting the teachings of Judaism, he concluded, such beginnings could only lead to dire consequences. In his words, "Reform has been fruitful of harm, but barren of the good which Mosaico-Talmudical Judaism produced."[34]

Morais's criticisms of the Reform movement continued, but now he was less ambivalent than before and less likely to compromise even for the sake of unity. In one sermon he recalled that there had been times when he had advocated changes in the services, but now he saw that changes had not improved synagogue attendance. Breaking his ties with the UAHC and HUC, he lashed out against two of the most prominent Reform leaders, Isaac Wise and Kaufmann Kohler. In a Yom Kippur sermon of 1889 he went so far as to anathematize a Philadelphia colleague and Reformer, Joseph Krauskopf, and his synagogue, Keneseth Israel—in Morais's words a "temple of heresy"—for profaning the Jewish creed. Vowing to strengthen the "true" worship, Morais now said that the best way to counter Reform and to save the true Judaism from total destruction was through the proper education of rabbis and teachers. His support of a Traditionalist rabbinical seminary directed by a faculty of Traditionalists, a plan that had engaged him for many years, increased markedly immediately after the Pittsburgh conference. Calling for well-trained qualified spiritual leaders, he warned his fellow Jews that Reform's Hebrew Union College "will unavoidably continue to give us teachers and preachers of a mind antagonistic to the faith which our fathers preserved at the cost of their lives. We need not possess extraordinary acumen to foresee the consequences—vulgar compromises which will lower Sinai and exalt Cavalry, or to say it plainly, the Christianization of the religion of Moses." Although Arthur Kiron maintains that Morais envisioned the school as the embodiment of his long-held belief in "rabbinic humanism," unpublished statements by Morais emphasize the anti-Reform purpose of the seminary.[35] He appealed to the oldest synagogue in America, Shearith Israel of New York, wealthy, prestigious, and Traditionalist, to take the lead in establishing a college that would produce "faithful expounders of Rabbinism" and "able defenders of conservatism." The break of the anti-Reformers like Morais from Hebrew Union College had reached a climax.[36]

*

The preparatory work of Morais and other Traditionalists culminated shortly thereafter in the establishment of the Jewish Theological Seminary. Its founders like Morais called it a "counteracting force" to the evils of Reform and referred to its supporters as "Jews of America faithful to Mosaic law and ancestral tradition." The new institution signified the formal split of American Judaism into two wings, the Reformers and the anti- or non-Reformers. The school began classes in 1887 in rooms donated by Shearith Israel, and President Morais, who called the seminary his Benjamin or the child of his old age, devoted the last ten years of his life to its development. Whether or not the founding of the seminary marked the inception of the Conservative movement in America remained a subject of debate for later historians.[37]

Work for the Jewish Theological Seminary was the final chapter in an active career of communal service, and it earned Morais well-deserved acclaim. The writer George Alexander Kohut called the rabbi "fearless and undaunted . . . in things pertaining to the sacred cause of Israel" and "unique and unequaled in the history of American Judaism." He resembled, Kohut said, the Ezra of biblical times.[38] Another glowing tribute came from Joseph H. Hertz, the first graduate of the seminary who became chief rabbi of Britain. Morais was outstanding, Hertz said, for the "saintliness" of his character, for his rigorous scholastic and moral demands of rabbinical students, and for his "heroic" fight on behalf of "Divine Law."[39]

3

Heroes and Villains

The American sermon of the nineteenth century was more often than not a lesson in morality. "Good" and "evil" were absolutes that
brooked no compromise, and virtue always triumphed. Drawing for the
most part from the Bible, the average rabbi usually based his sermon on
the weekly portions from the Pentateuch, the Prophets, and the Hagi-
ographa that were read in the synagogue on the Sabbath or on holidays.
From the vast array of heroes and anti-heroes that he had before him, he
easily found the appropriate figures for his messages. The most commonly
cited heroes were the Patriarchs, Moses, the prophets, and Kings David
and Solomon. While the heroes, or the admirable Jews, manifested the
essential virtues of courage, wisdom, public service, and defense of the
nation, their opponents were the anti-heroes. Familiar characters in the
Bible frequently became generic terms; a Moses, a Daniel, a Joshua represented the heroes, and their opposites, a Pharaoh and a Haman, were
the quintessential villains. The preacher of those edifying sermons sent a
clear message to those who heard or read his discourses: Behave like the
righteous and resist the evil-doers. Three of the most popular figures that
emerged from sermons, lectures, and newspaper articles of the century
were Mordecai, the symbol of good, and Haman and Amalek, the symbols of evil. The symbols in turn reflected the favorite themes of rabbinical sermons. The good taught the lessons of patriotism and public service
that the Jew owed to America, and the evil, the would-be destroyers of
Judaism and Jews, were best challenged by a strong Jewish identity and
loyalty to the larger Jewish group.

The *Jewish Messenger* of New York frequently called in its early years for
"representative men" to strive for the good of Judaism and Jews within the
United States. The *Messenger,* one of the first major Anglo-Jewish periodicals of long duration, was founded in 1857 by Rabbi Samuel M. Isaacs.
Isaacs had been educated in England, but in 1839 and without receiving

official ordination he moved to New York where he served at B'nai Jeshurun and then at Shaaray Tefila. At B'nai Jeshurun he was the first rabbi to preach regularly in English to an Ashkenazic congregation. He capped his active involvement in Jewish communal work with the founding of the *Messenger*, which he edited and published with the help of his sons until his death in 1878. His Traditionalist religious posture and his conservative stand on political and economic issues which, for the most part, were preserved by his sons until the paper ceased publication in 1902, attracted a wide readership of established middle-class Jews.[1]

Isaacs's call for representative men was primarily a plea for defenders of Jewish group interests. As such, it was a serious critique of Jewish leadership, or lack thereof, in mid-century America. His definition of group interests was broad; it ranged from the state of educational facilities in small Jewish communities to the needs of persecuted foreign Jews. Anti-Jewish discrimination by American governments, whether federal, state, or local, begged for attention, and so did discrimination by social institutions like clubs, resorts, and schools. Isaacs's search for defenders never meant that he questioned the greatness of America. Rather, he fingered the few who, he said, tarnished American ideals and kept the country from living up to its promise.

Since the overriding American Jewish goal was always for legal equality and acceptance as equals within the larger American society, and since Jews also fought discrimination that made Judaism a less than equal faith in the American marketplace of religions, nineteenth-century Jews desperately needed able defenders. The ongoing tasks of defense became the essential ingredients of American Jewish leadership. Although on every Jew rested the responsibility to project a positive Jewish image, particularly since the misdeeds of one reflected on the entire community, Isaacs searched for Mordecais, or men whose public behavior made them exemplars for the Jewish group nationwide. Public-spirited leadership that aroused and guided Jewry might even be able to achieve some form of communal unity.

In antebellum America, circumstances doomed Jewish attempts at unity just as they militated against the rise of national leaders or defenders. American Jews were a far-flung heterogeneous group divided by language, customs, and religious rites that they had brought with them from Europe. Immigrants to ever-changing communities in the New World, they were too unsettled and too inexperienced to make Jewish defense or union one of their top priorities. Defense, a few also argued, implied that Jews doubted the ability even of America, the model of freedom, to fully protect a non-Christian minority. Temple Emanu-El of New York, for example, protested the need of an early attempt at Jewish union, the Board of Delegates of American Israelites. It argued: "It would be a mistake for Jews to act together for social and political purposes for thus they would become an *imperium in imperio* in America, and others would believe that the Jews felt they were in exile."[2]

Attempts at union and defense were also stymied by the American principle of congregationalism. Like most American Protestant churches, the places of worship that Jews established were autonomous and answered only to themselves. Since the United States never mandated any form of communal organization, like the consistorial system in France or the office of chief rabbi in England, only crises or extraordinary events at home or abroad motivated Jews to search for national spokesmen. To be sure, ever since colonial days congregations had chosen officers and committees to deal with the governance of the synagogue as well as with schools and charities, but their functions were generally limited to individual institutions or geographically small localities. Ad hoc committees treated specific issues and usually disbanded after completing their task. On occasion, as in the case of the powerful missionary groups, Jews attempted to co-opt Christians to defend them against the proselytizers.[3]

The first significant extension of the boundaries of Jewish defense beyond the individual synagogue came with the long-lived Anglo-Jewish periodicals that were established between 1840 and 1860. Most important were the *Occident,* the *Messenger,* and the *Israelite* (later the *American Israelite*). The journals reported and commented on events affecting Jews locally and nationwide, they defended American and foreign Jews against the charges of Jew-haters, and they prescribed a proper code of behavior for the American Jew within his own as well as within the non-Jewish community.[4] All three were founded and edited by rabbis—Isaac Leeser of the *Occident,* Isaacs of the *Messenger,* and Isaac Mayer Wise of the *Israelite* —a fact that explained a penchant for moralizing and a special interest in sermons and other rabbinical activities. Since all the periodicals could boast of readers scattered throughout the country and even abroad, each rabbi/editor enjoyed a reputation that extended far beyond his local congregation. They represented different religious and political viewpoints, which frequently led them to criticize their competitors, but all decried the lack of American Jewish unity and the dearth of proper leaders. Only the *Messenger,* however, called appropriate leaders the representative men, or the Mordecais.

Isaacs, who more than anyone else fixed on Mordecai above all the biblical luminaries, never explained his choice of a hero. It may have been because the biblical Mordecai lived outside his own land, and Isaacs was preaching to Jews in exile. But although modern scholarship has denied the veracity of the book of Esther —one prominent scholar called the Book of Esther "a mock-learned disquisition," perhaps with kernels of truth, "to be read as the opening of a carnival-like celebration"[5]—Isaacs apparently followed the text literally. A Traditionalist Jew, he would hardly have shrugged off the importance of any biblical book, even one that could be construed as a license for heavy drinking and general merriment, particularly if it contained material so suitable for rabbinic discourses.

Mordecai's heroic rescue of the Jews from annihilation, was, of course, the rabbi's primary focus, but he may have been prompted as well by several other reasons. The Mordecai in the scroll (*megillah*) of Esther was not commissioned by God; a man of flesh and blood who neither received nor relayed divine communications, his exploits were within the reach or at least the comprehension of ordinary mortals. Besides, the *megillah* which never mentions God was not a religious text. Its message was the same for believer and nonbeliever; for Orthodox, Traditionalists, and Reformers. The deeds of the ideal Mordecai were incapable, therefore, of stoking the fires of denominational disputes and divisiveness. Furthermore, the man who refused to bow down to Haman, Mordecai was portrayed by Isaacs as the symbol of resistance to tyranny. Loyal American and loyal to his English heritage, Isaacs chose a theme that drew on England's Glorious Revolution of 1689 and the words of America's Tom Paine and Thomas Jefferson. In the eyes of the *Jewish Messenger,* Mordecai was *the* representative man, the American-like Jewish leader par excellence. To be sure, the first Mordecai operated in a hostile environment, light years away from conditions in America, but American Jews too and their persecuted brethren abroad needed able defenders.[6]

Time and again, usually during the Purim season, the *Messenger* defined a Jewish leader as one who emulated the conduct of Mordecai, a man aiming not at "personal aggrandizement or vain glory, but a desire to elevate Israel religiously, morally, and socially." Viceroy to King Ahasuerus, Mordecai was, the paper wrote, "great for the Jews, seeking the good of his people, and speaking peace to all his seed." The *Messenger* admitted, however, that not every Jew could be a leader or representative man. Specifically the paper called for one "who, for his wealth or for his rank, stands high in the estimation of his fellow-citizens." But wealth and standing were not enough. A Mordecai "must study the welfare of his people, spiritually and worldly. He ought to advocate all works of good among them, and by his own greatness, his own purse, his own fortunate situation, and his widespread influence, advance the moral and intellectual position of his . . . nation." The paper ignored the representative man's need of political power or the fact that the authority of the biblical Mordecai derived from the king and not from his own abilities.

Such wealthy and influential individuals, the *Messenger* continued, were those "whose benevolence is continuous and liberal, and who take the honor of Israel in their keeping when any ignorant or bigoted assailant dares to cast an affront upon '*their* people.'" They were men of "intellectual greatness"—a term that was not explained—and patriotic Americans, ready to render meritorious public service. Although the paper demanded neither a grounding in Jewish culture nor religious observance, it insisted on a consistent "attachment" to Judaism. Attachment had a public dimension; it meant a sensitivity to and awareness of non-Jewish actions that debased Judaism or Jewry. Since Jews too could be guilty of such deeds, a leader's responsibilities included the need to hasten the assimilation of their less knowledgeable, even "less-civilized," brethren. Americanization, the *Messenger* was saying, was the first step to appropriate conduct. To find all those qualities in one person was indeed a tall order, but singly or together the desirable behavioral traits fit the man whose prime motive, like Mordecai's, was to improve the Jewish condition.

At the same time that the *Messenger* described the character and actions of the representative man, it injected its own criticism of affluent American Jews: "We have among us gentlemen of acknowledged social position, of 'old families' . . . but no true pride of race." They led lives of studied indifference to the welfare of their fellow Jews and showed no sympathy with movements for their advancement. Mordecais were extremely rare. Jews might produce clever politicians, able professional men, talented artists, or men of letters, but they were so busy and so engrossed in their own affairs that they had neither time nor interest to spare for their fellow Jews. Those indifferent men were "too prone to bow to Haman because he is Prime Minister and not bold enough to assert their manhood and dignity as *Jews*." And because such men were not inspired to guide and elevate their brethren, the Jews were tolerated and patronized, but not treated as brothers.

Who chose a Mordecai? Isaacs never considered the input of the rank and file in the selection of a representative man. Was he to be appointed by a given constituency or did he merely assume leadership? The biblical Mordecai became the king's vizier by royal fiat, but in a democracy, where the government was officially religion-blind and without regulations on how Jews were to organize themselves, a Mordecai could not be chosen by American officialdom. From the examples discussed below of European heroes, it appears as if Isaacs's Mordecai simply arose out of his own vague idealism and selflessness. Nor was a Mordecai empowered in any way by his fellow Jews. They might be impressed by his acts of benevolence, but they had no influence on his conduct.

Before the Civil War the *Messenger* said that there might not be an immediate need in America for a Mordecai, but less than ten years later it insisted that mounting social discrimination against Jews proved that the "Hamanic spirit" was on the ascendant. "We are waiting with unwonted patience and no little apprehension the advent of an American Mordecai."[7] It offered weighty proofs for its claim that complete equality and fraternity still eluded the Jew: serious and respectable Americans agitated for a constitutional amendment that would make Christianity the law of the land, insurance companies and mercantile agencies blackballed Jews just because they were Jews, and even members of Congress were guilty of publicly defaming the Jew. In sum, Americans held fast to the images of the Jew as a pariah and a petty trader "who would sell himself body and soul to make money."[8] Only representative men or Mordecais, the paper insisted, could turn public contempt into respect.

Deploring the absence of representative men in America, Rabbi Isaacs claimed that the status of Jews in the nations of Western Europe, just because of their representative men, was higher than that in the United States.[9] The examples he cited were men who had devoted much effort for the attainment of Jewish legal rights in their own countries and in distant lands of Eastern Europe, the Near East, and North Africa: Adolphe Crémieux of France; Gabriel Riesser of Germany; and Sir Moses Montefiore, Sir Francis Goldsmid, and Sir David Salomons of England. Isaacs, who maintained close contact with the land of his youth, was particularly fond of the English heroes. An editorial in the *Messenger*, which praised

Goldsmid for his work on behalf of Serbian Jews and deplored the absence of American Mordecais read in part:

> Boldly he takes upon himself the mission of *speaking* and *acting* for his unhappy co-religionists, and nobly he represents to his government the wrongs done those of his race who are living in the midst of anarchy under the dominion of Christians [in the Balkans] who are worse than the Turks. Is he ashamed to acknowledge that he is a Jew? Does he adopt any euphemism to conceal that "hated epithet," and proclaim himself simply interested in the fate of unfortunate victims of tyranny? . . . But, no— there is no false pride, no paltry shame, no squeamish morbidity about him. He is a Jew [who] represents Jewish sentiment and asks sympathy and aid for his brethren in faith. . . . We are mortified and pained to find among the American Israelites, who have enjoyed opportunities for contributing to the creation of a better and more kindly sentiment towards their brethren, so few who have taken the slightest interest in the elevation of the Jew in the eyes of his fellow men. . . . We have lamented the absence of a Mordecai from American Jewish annals. . . . We contend that the Hamanic spirit is in the ascendant, in spite of the progress of civilization. We contend that for a successful overthrow of the Haman, who not being able to exterminate the Jews would ostracize them and brand them as outcasts,—Mordecai must yet arise in America.[10]

Just as Mordecai had become a generic term for the proper Jewish protector, so were the words Haman and Hamanic synonymous with Jew-hatred.

Isaacs excluded rabbis, foreign or American, from his consideration of appropriate leaders. He may have thought that rabbis lacked the financial resources or public status that contributed to popular recognition, or he may have sought to avoid any charges that he was seeking power for himself. Looking back to past years, he found no American exemplars of representative men. He gave a half-hearted nod of praise to Mordecai Manuel Noah for combating antisemitism after his return from the post of consul to Tunis,[11] but he totally ignored a veteran rabbi, Isaac Leeser. Indeed, none could fill Isaacs's requirements as well as Leeser. The Traditionalist rabbi of Philadelphia had ardently defended Jews and Judaism in the United States, and his attachment to his faith was unquestionable. Not only did he labor to improve the communal infrastructure with devices like the Sunday school, a Jewish translation of the Bible, and a Jewish publication society, but also he constantly pressed for intercongregational unity. At the same time that he defended Jewish rights in the political arena and against the missionaries, he preached a code of proper civic and social behavior for American Jews. And, in the spirit of Isaacs's representative men, he also agitated against disabilities of Jews in foreign lands.[12]

Although Esther, the heroine of the Purim story, received passing praise for her deeds on behalf of her people, she rarely appeared center stage. The entire scheme for destroying Haman was usually depicted as Mordecai's, and she, albeit dutifully, followed his instructions. A different portrayal of Esther came in a sermon in the 1890s by Rabbi Max Heller of New Orleans, an early graduate of Reform's Hebrew Union College. Heller also lauded the beautiful Esther for her shyness and obedience, and he thought her courage was noteworthy. Indeed, as Heller explained, she staged the precise setting for an appeal to the king. Esther could have kept silent, the rabbi said, but despite her "shrinking modesty" she chose to speak up when Jews faced the threat of extermination. Her behavior, Heller continued, set an example for contemporary Jews, for they were obliged to protest openly when domestic and foreign conditions caused injustices. Nevertheless, his praise of Esther "as a fair vision of womanly dependence and obedience" that "few heroines of history or fiction" could rival doubtless offended the early champions of women's rights. In his words:

> Submission, service, the shy constraints which sit so well upon a noble countenance are her principal charms; Jewess, orphan, exile, it is but natural that loveliness and self-effacement should surround her as with a halo of unconscious purity. It is in such as she that aggressive women with their bold claims of masculine privileges might recognize wherein, by nature's immutable law, is found woman's highest beauty and grandest dignity.[13]

Just as Mordecai was the exemplar of good, Haman, his adversary in the Purim story and theological counterpoise, represented evil. Haman, the man who desired to destroy Mordecai's people, became the symbol of those who mercilessly persecuted Jews throughout their long history. Tradition explained that Haman carried the seed of evil; he was a descendant of Esau and of the Amalekites, the nation that had attacked the Israelites from behind on their trip through the desert. For their cowardly behavior, striking first at the weak and the stragglers in the Israelite camp, God had decreed an everlasting holy war against those progenitors of Haman.

The biblical narrative recounts how the children of Israel battled with the nation of Amalek on their trek through the desert. Exodus 17:11, 14–16 reads: "Then, whenever Moses held up his hand, Israel prevailed; but whenever he let down his hand, Amalek prevailed. . . . Then the Lord said to Moses, 'Inscribe this in a document, as a reminder, and read it aloud to Joshua: I will utterly blot out the memory of Amalek from under heaven.' And Moses . . . said . . . 'The Lord will be at war with Amalek throughout the ages.'" A passage in Deuteronomy 25:17–19 repeats the admonition: "Remember what Amalek did to you on your journey after you left Egypt—how, undeterred by fear of God, he surprised you on the march, when you were famished and weary, and cut down all the stragglers in your rear. Therefore, when the Lord your God grants you safety from all your enemies around you . . . you shall blot out the memory of Amalek from under heaven. Do not forget!" The biblical account is unclear as to whether God or the Israelites would wage the war, but either way it was God who commanded the extermination of Amalek in a war that would last throughout time.

Who the Amalekites were and why God ordered an ongoing holy war against them is a vast subject lying beyond this study, but it is correct to conclude that from the beginning Amalek became the quintessential symbol of evil and, like Haman, Israel's most bitter enemy. "Never will the throne of God—the Lord of Truth, Justice, and Love—be fully established until the seed of Amalek—the principle of hatred and wrongdoing—be destroyed forever." In rabbinic literature, reasons are sought for God's unusual decree. Some rabbis pointed out that since Amalek was the first nation to contest the invasion of Palestine by the Israelites, its action could encourage others; others explained that the command to "Remember" actually referred to the sins of Israel.[14] Whatever the accepted reason, post-biblical generations read the verses from Deuteronomy on the Sabbath before the Purim holiday, which fittingly became known as *Shabbat Zakhor* (the Sabbath of Remembrance).

While references to Haman's name and reputation were straightforward and commonplace among Jews of every era, the image of Amalek caused modern rabbis in nineteenth-century America some discomfort. Doubtless the biblically ordered ongoing holy war embarrassed them.[15] To be sure, other biblical stories, like those about the not-too-righteous patriarchs and their dysfunctional families, posed difficulties, but the Amalek episode taken literally was far more disturbing. How could a universal God who was a just and merciful God command eternal vengeance on an entire nation? Were the Christians correct in calling the Hebrew God cruel and vengeful and contrasting Him with their god, the so-called god of love? Why had the Bible singled out Amalek when similar imprecations could be leveled against Egypt or Babylonia? Modern rabbis never tried to excuse Amalek by arguing, for example, that its resistance to conquest and "occupation" by the Israelites, invaders who had not poured their blood into the soil of Palestine, was justified. Nor did they minimize Amalek's wrongdoing by equating it with other wars against the Israelites. In their interpretations Amalek was different. The embarrassed rabbi was left therefore with two options: he could either ignore the subject entirely or reinterpret the meaning of Amalek in ways more palatable to a modern audience. Those who chose the latter course usually fixed on social conditions or institutions that were inherently evil as surrogates for the biblical Amalek.

The following analysis of a few sermons from various decades of the nineteenth century reveals how some American rabbis dealt with the problem. Retaining Amalek, sometimes used interchangeably with Haman, as evil incarnate, they discussed the personification of Amalek in contemporary happenings that threatened American or American Jewish well-being. All delivered by Reform rabbis, they showed how denominational teachings were woven into rabbinic discourses irrespective of the sermon's exact topic. Like the *Jewish Messenger*'s description of the duties of representative men, they also emphasized the interests of the group, or the group dimension of Jewish identity, over and above the interests of the individual Jew. Among other things, they indicated thereby the seeming inconsistency between Reform's definition of Judaism as merely a religion and its affirmations of Jewish peoplehood and Jewish ethnic concerns.

Two forceful sermons on Amalek were delivered by Rabbi David Einhorn. The rabbi had come to the United States from Germany in 1855 to serve at Har Sinai Temple in Baltimore. He had participated in the German conferences of Reformers in the 1840s, and in America he spread their teachings through sermons and his own periodical. Becoming known almost immediately as a Radical Reformer—that is, an extremist with respect to the repudiation of traditional law—he was reputed to be a rabbi who spoke with the "fire of a prophet" and the first rabbi to inject polemics into the sermon.[16]

An outspoken abolitionist, Einhorn had attacked the institution of slavery for several years before the Civil War, and he continued the practice after the war broke out. Since he was embroiled in the clashes between the Unionists and Confederates in the border state of Maryland, supporters urged him to leave Baltimore for his personal safety. He fled to Philadelphia, and although he thought to return, the board of Har Sinai decided on muzzling their rabbi. They told him that for his sake and that of the congregation it would be safer "if in the future there would be no comment from the pulpit on the excitable issues of the time." That condition was unacceptable to Einhorn, and he remained in Philadelphia until he was called to New York.[17]

From his pulpit in Philadelphia's Keneseth Israel, Einhorn held forth on current issues. On *Shabbat Zakhor* of 1864 he preached a lengthy sermon on Amalek and its modern equivalent, slavery. The war against Amalek, he posited, was a war for God and His people, a war of right versus wrong, and hence a war of self-defense rather than vengeance. In contemporary America the "enslavement of race," which degraded human beings created in God's image, was the work of Amalek. Replying to arguments advanced by the South and its defenders, Einhorn disputed the claims that history and the Bible sanctioned slavery. Slavery may have existed among the ancients, but "can ancient custom indeed, convert an atrocious wrong into right?" Morality and progress had since decided, and would continue to decide, otherwise. Moreover, slavery did not fit the *spirit* of the Bible: "It is true, the institution of slavery was introduced . . . into the Mosaic code, but only . . . because the deeply rooted evil could not be at once eradicated, and only with the intent to surround the detestable institution with ordinances mitigating the evil." Einhorn the Reformer did not hesitate to denounce the defenders of slavery for their literal or fundamentalist reading of the Bible. Attacking thereby the fundamentalists among the Orthodox, the rabbi maintained that they too were enslaved: "It is only the slaves of the letter that deny [the] capability of development —it is only they that convert the letter of the Bible into a slave-whip." To those like Morris Raphall, the distinguished Traditionalist rabbi of New York whose widely read sermon in 1861 had argued that slavery was condoned by the Bible,[18] Einhorn's discourse was a forceful reply that targeted two enemies: slavery and the unenlightened among the Jews as well as non-Jews.[19]

The preacher's tirade included a warning to his fellow Jews too. Since Amalek oppressed *all* weak minorities, it was responsible for a second kind of slavery in America, "enslavement of conscience." In this part of his address Einhorn singled out the group pressing for a Christian amendment to the Constitution. Organized during the Civil War, the movement begun by Presbyterian ministers argued that America's suffering in the war was a sign of God's punishment of a nation that was not sufficiently Christian. Calling for an acknowledgment of Jesus as the source of legal authority and for Christianity as the law of the land, the plans of the Christianizers according to Einhorn were the work of Amalek. Since spokesmen for the movement pointed specifically to Jews among their opponents, the rabbi predicted that if the movement were to succeed, the opposition would be deprived of the rights of citizenship. Instead of "a palladium of liberty of conscience," the Constitution would be "a prison-fortress of religious tyranny"; "America would become not merely a Christian State, but a real Church State, and Washington a second Rome."[20]

He also foresaw conflicts among the Christian denominations that would inevitably turn into another bloody civil war. Einhorn addressed the problem with his customary vigor and denounced what he called an attempt to substitute the "sons of Shem" for the "sons of Ham." He added that aside from the Christianizers, other "Hamans" were reviving old stereotypes of the Jews by calling them a "peculiar nation" made up solely of "traders." He resented both charges; "traders" showed an ignorance of Jewish contributors to learning and civilization, and "nation," which held Jews to be more than a religious group, was utterly groundless. American Jews, he warned, must not be lulled into a false sense of security. "Let us make war upon this Amalek; let us meet this newly-budding religious animosity with all honorable weapons at our command!" He didn't say what such weapons were, but in light of his activity in Baltimore he doubtless meant unrelenting verbal and written attacks.

To triumph over Amalek meant that Jews had to war against a third type of slavery, one within their own midst, or in Einhorn's words, "enslavement of the spirit." In this segment of his sermon the rabbi addressed his remarks to Jews who sacrificed the spirit of Judaism for materialistic, this-worldly goals. His indictment of such Jews was a lengthy one. Because of an overpowering lust for gain they had abandoned their God-given mission, neglected their synagogues and schools, desecrated the Sabbath, and no longer lived a virtuous family life. Since they profaned the name of God by yielding to base temptations, it was no wonder that non-Jews asked, "Where is your God?" Yes, the rabbi concluded: "The staff of God has fallen from our hands, and, despite all pomp and glitter, we creep weary and exhausted [like the feeble Israelite stragglers who were Amalek's first victims], sighing and panting, through a vast desert affording no oasis . . . to become a prey for Amalek." Einhorn's solution was obvious—only a free and revived religious spirit as preached by Reform would enable Jews to withstand all the faces of Amalek.

The rabbi drew his material from contemporary events—the Civil War, the Christian amendment movement, and the increasing impact of materialism and secularism on the Jewish community. The evils of Amalek were instigated by Jews as well as by Christians. As the preacher of Reform, Einhorn included certain themes that were among the cardinal teachings of classical Reform: the repudiation of fundamentalists who refused to recognize the evolution of Judaism, the denial of Jewish nationhood, and the mission of a Jewry, no longer a nation, dispersed throughout the world to preach the word of God. Interpreting each "enslavement" as a moral sin, Einhorn was at one and the same time the impassioned crusader against immorality and the defender and chastiser of the Jews. His sermon may have been confrontational; even his congregants may have shuddered lest he antagonize their Christian neighbors or alienate their fellow Jews. But ever independent, the Reform rabbi refused to retreat.

In 1870, when Einhorn, then in New York, preached on *Shabbat Zakhor,* slavery had ended but, the rabbi said, the evils of Amalek, ever the symbol of "falsehood and wickedness," persisted. Turning specifically to the Amaleks within the Jewish community, he reproached the right-wing Orthodox for religious hypocrisy that masked true faith and for their religious indifference. The honest Orthodox, he said, were but a small number: "The great mass deems it all right to throw off all that is practically inconvenient and to clamor theoretically for every traditional iota." These hypocrites, the same so-called Orthodox who secretly violated the Law, were the Amalekites, or in contemporary terms those who evoked Gentile contempt for Jews and Judaism. Perhaps even worse were the indifferent Jews, Amalekites who were totally removed from Judaism and approached the synagogue only if they needed a place for their dead in a Jewish cemetery. Orthodoxy or Traditionalism was to blame, for it had failed to rid the community of the spirit of Amalek. Clearly, only Reform could defeat that enemy.[21]

Einhorn focused a major portion of his 1870 address on two external Amaleks. He called them the two faces of Christianity, "Popery and

Puritanism." Different from most of his rabbinical colleagues, the rabbi was unafraid of challenging the faith of American Christians at that relatively early date. Prompted by the Vatican Council then in session, he lambasted some features of "Popery"—the doctrine of papal infallibility as well as the Syllabus of Errors. The latter document set the seal of papal disapproval on nineteenth-century ideologies like Naturalism, Socialism, and Freemasonry; it proclaimed the Roman Catholic Church's control over culture and science as well as education; and it rejected freedom of conscience and worship for non-Catholics. Condemning the list of "errors" and its influence even in America, Einhorn summed up the document as follows: "He [the pope] desires that everything be literally anathematized that bears the glimmer of the culture of our century . . . that there be anathema [on] every pure human emotion, every scientific research, every rational thought, every republican, yea even constitutional system of government!" Civilization may have progressed, but "the aim of annihilating Amalek by the sword of intellect has not been reached yet by far." He contrasted the Syllabus of Errors with the series of curses, mostly on immoral acts, proclaimed by Moses to the children of Israel before they crossed the Jordan. Whereas the papal list served as the "executioner of liberty," the Jewish list advanced ethical progress. It proved, therefore, that Judaism was superior to Catholicism and that the light of Mosaism was necessary to continue the battle against the darkness of Amalek.

Puritanism or Protestantism was also guilty of immorality. Heeding the call of Amalek, the Christianizers still worked for a constitutional amendment that would recognize Christianity as fundamental American law. Amalek's jealousy toward Israel, the same jealousy it bore in ancient times, had made Judaism the spurned religion. By perpetuating such evils both Catholicism and Protestantism lagged behind the Jewish faith. Their abuses proved yet again that it was incumbent upon Jews to combat the internal and external Amaleks. Indeed, American Jews could ill afford to be trapped by a misplaced sense of security. Repeating some of what he had said in 1864, he claimed that the strongest weapon for the defeat of Amalek in all its forms was a religious one. If Jews revived the spirit of their faith and followed the path of Reform, they would spread the message of the Unity of God and brotherhood of man throughout the world and thereby speed the redemption of humankind.

Of all the rabbis discussed here in connection with Amalek, Einhorn was the most prominent and his sermons the most confrontational. He sought the modern Amalek in the changing needs of the Jews at a specific

time, and he found it in persons, like the pope, the Christianizing ministers, Orthodox Jews, as well as in impersonal forces of evil.

Far different from Einhorn's two sermons both in content and tone was
one in 1876 by Rabbi Isaac Schwab of Evansville, Indiana. Schwab admonished his congregants to remember Amalek's evil, but he suggested that
Israel had not been totally guilt-free. Citing old rabbinic interpretations
that blamed the people's transgressions for Amalek's merciless attack, he
called the Amalekites the divine rod for punishing the Israelites. Medieval writers, he continued, similarly interpreted the calamities suffered by
Jews at the hands of the Catholic Church, but they also noted the various
transgressions by the Jews. Some married Gentiles, some were "greedy of
money and gain," and some had "a haughty mind bent on rule or ruin." The
rabbi didn't explicitly expatiate on the wrongdoings of American Jewry,
but he made it clear that he included all modern Jews in his indictment.
By blaming Jews for succumbing to the snares of Amalek, Schwab's message spread the guilt for the unrelieved suffering of Israel in pre-modern
times. But post-biblical Israel had a "spiritual" defense against Amalek's
evil: "As long as the people looked up to God, putting themselves to His
will and guidance, they were victorious; when not, they were beaten." Israel's culpability gave Schwab a way of bridging the past with the present,
for it contained a timeless lesson for his audience.[22]

Schwab also enlarged the interplay among Amalek, God, and Israel
by introducing a fourth element: an external force from the non-Jewish
world. In the modern era, he said, Amalek represented the dark forces
that combated intellectual progress. Victory over Amalek first came in
the wake of the Enlightenment, when liberal writers, the "champions
of culture," began to uproot those forces: "They crushed the time-worn
prejudices . . . of sect and caste, and broke the chains of bondage flung
around the weak mankind by the domineering princes of darkness." True,
Schwab called the Enlightenment a tool of God, but nonetheless his reliance on the march of civilization depersonalized the Amalek story still
further. More than a contest limited to Israel and Amalek, the struggle
against wickedness and sin had become universalized. The rabbi ended
on an optimistic note. We have seen the progress made by the march of
civilization to relieve mankind's suffering, he said: "Amalek, the evil one,
plaguing others for opinion's sake, is now extinct almost everywhere.
And what is yet left of him here and there will and must ere long vanish
before the rays of civilization." Although Schwab said that God was and

will be "our strength, our fortress and refuge," even He appeared tangential at best.

Unlike Einhorn, Schwab didn't preach any form of denominational Judaism, Orthodoxy or Reform, nor did he mention specific events of the day. Since he indulged largely in generalities, one wonders how impressed his congregation was.

In 1881 a *Shabbat Zakhor* sermon by Rabbi Henry Vidaver of San Francisco appeared in a collection of American Jewish sermons. Titled "Israel a Missionary People," its purpose was to interpret the cruel and vengeful God of the Amalek story for modern Reform Jews.[23] Remembrance of Amalek was indispensable, Vidaver posited, for preserving an idea that pervaded the long history of Israel from its beginning until the present day: "It was and is the idea of Israel's struggles; implying the struggles against Amalek, that is against 'Idolatry' in all shapes and manners, against inhumanity in all ways and forms. It was and is the idea of Israel's triumphs, implying the triumph of truth, the triumph of a pure faith in the 'Unity' of God and the moral elevation of the human race." Wherever pure faith in God's unity and mankind's elevation were victorious, it was a victory for Israel.

Having identified Israel's ongoing struggle against Amalek with a broader universalism, the rabbi launched into an explanation and defense of Reform's interpretation of Israel's mission. God made Israel a kingdom of priests, a missionary people to propagate "His divine light of pure faith" to a common humanity. The aim was not to convert the nations to Judaism—Israel did not need to augment its numbers—but to propagate the *idea* of Judaism. It was always Israel's duty, Vidaver said, "to help in the uplifting of the human mind to . . . the purest conception of the Deity as *One* absolute Godhead, and the uplifting of the human heart to the blessed conception of humanity as the broadest, most comprehensive principle of love." Vidaver's repeated use of the word "uplift" paralleled the biblical verse that Israel prevailed against Amalek when Moses "lifted up" his hands, while repetition of his words "One God" or the "Unity of God" may have been purposely directed against the Christian trinity. Vidaver's emphasis on the need to carry the word of God to humanity worldwide validated another Reform principle: the necessary dispersion of the Jews throughout the nations.

As missionaries, the rabbi said, Israel acted silently throughout its history. Unlike the American proselytizers familiar to the Jews who relied on "pious cant" and sanctimonious words, they used neither salaried preachers nor tract societies to spread their message. Nor had they ever indulged in forced conversion by acts of torture to which they themselves had been subjected at the hands of fanatical Christians or Muslims. In its ongoing war against Amalek, Israel silently fought the tyranny and oppression of dogmatic creeds that, "Amalek-like, pounce upon helpless innocence and seek its destruction." But when Amalek attacked, whether in the ancient period or the Middle Ages, Israel "lifted up" its heart, and Judaism triumphed. Armed with the Jewish virtues of chastity, industry, and scholarship, Israelites survived their ordeals with patience, perseverance, and pure faith. The rabbi concluded with a charge to the present generation to emulate the labors and endurance of their forefathers.

Vidaver's forceful sermon was tightly organized, and it was an able defense of Reform. But like Schwab's, it made no mention of contemporary events. The rabbi never mentioned issues that troubled American Jews, like social discrimination, Sunday laws, or the Christian amendment group. Nor did he allude to the growing rift between the Reformers and the Traditionalists or to problems within the synagogue. In essence his address, like Schwab's, was one of generalizations rather than specifics. It too had a timeless quality about it; with only slight emendations it was appropriate for all periods and places. A sermon of that sort was unlikely to arouse a negative reaction from the laymen who preferred to control the pulpit, but the reader remains clueless as to what in particular prompted him to see the danger of Amalek at that time.

Children too heard sermons about Amalek. Hermann Baar, a German-born rabbi and educator who wrote a weekly column for the *American Hebrew* called "Sermons for the Young," served as superintendent of a Jewish orphan asylum in New York. There he instructed the children in Bible by talks on the Torah portion of the week. One short Purim address entitled "Ancient and Modern Amalek" appeared in his two-volume work, *Addresses on Homely and Religious Subjects Delivered before the Children of the Hebrew Orphan Asylum* that was published in 1885. Internal evidence suggests that the Purim sermon was delivered in the early 1880s.[24]

Using language that appears far too difficult for an audience of children, Baar may have been catering to the adults who frequented the orphan asylum for religious services. When he explained the lesson of *Shabbat Zakhor,* he told how Amalek emerged as the enemy of Israel in the days of King Saul (1 Samuel 15) and again in the character of Haman. "My children," he said, "old Amalek is dead, but in dying he has transmitted . . . the famous Amalek spirit." He pointed to the different forms of anti-Jewish discrimination and persecution then current in the world that were products of the Amalek legacy:

> This Amalek spirit . . . has written against us in books and in pamphlets, it has preached against us in pulpits and on platforms, it has assailed us in hotels and places of amusement, it has even crept into the hot, burning brains of skillful and eccentric musicians; in barbarous countries, like Russia, it has plundered our brethren, desecrated their homes, slaughtered their families, and taken possession of their hard-earned wages and properties.

Of all the sermons discussed here, Baar's was the only one to offer examples of the new racist antisemitism of the last quarter of the century. The first half of his list of Amalek's legacies fit conditions in Western Europe and the United States; the second half was doubtless prompted by the wave of Russian pogroms in 1881–1882. That very few children, if any, knew about discrimination in America and Europe, or about bigots like American preacher Dwight Moody and German composer Richard Wagner, or about the Russian pogroms was clearly not a deterrent.

Baar raised two issues. First, why did Amalek hate the Jews? To be sure, Jews were not perfect, and Baar enumerated the virtues that Israelites, his name for contemporary Jews, still had to cultivate: modesty, simple and unostentatious behavior, intellectual rather then material aspirations. But Jews could boast of virtues that surpassed those of many nations: a loving family life, compassion, and philanthropy. Although talk of a family life may have been inappropriate for an audience of orphans, Baar tried to instill pride as well as self-criticism in the youngsters. For the few who understood the sermon, the idea that Jews were at least partially to blame for the modern Amalek may have taken root.

Second, what could the Jews do to defeat their enemy? Since the biblical text says that "the Lord" will be at war with Amalek, the struggle is literally left up to God. But Jews could help, the speaker said. Just as Moses had told Joshua to choose someone to fight the nation that stood in the path of Israel's conquest of Palestine, so must contemporary Jews choose vigorous defenders. Sounding much like Samuel Isaacs on the need of a Mordecai, he said: "We have to select men who, by pen or word, by influence or practical deeds, have to defend Judaism and our brethren. . . . No lukewarmness will do." With proper leadership and proper religious devotion, virtuous Jews, wanting only to live in friendship with all others, would fight prejudice and thus contribute to the inevitable disappearance of the Amalek spirit. Different from the sermons of Einhorn and Schwab, Baar's remarks did not trumpet the principles of Reform. Although he was known as a Reformer—he had served for a very short time in a Reform synagogue in Washington—his discourse well suited a nondenominational audience.[25]

Frederick de Sola Mendes, a Traditionalist who over the years shifted himself and his congregation to the ranks of Reform, officiated as rabbi of the West End Synagogue in New York. In 1895 he delivered a short sermon of limited scope on *Shabbat Zakhor*,[26] and like his colleagues he substituted the Amalek spirit for the Amalek of the Bible. An annual Sabbath of Remembrance was necessary, he said, because the Amalek spirit was still alive and well. More than a fleeting memory of that nation's cowardly attack on the Israelites, the Sabbath before Purim alerted Jews to an everlasting danger: "Remember that the spirit of Amalek is limited to no country, no race, no period, that in every clime, among every race where we dwell, and in every period of culture or of non-culture, the spirit of the Ishmaelite is ready to strike, the spirit of cowardice is lying in wait for the hindmost, the weak and the weary."

Jews needed annual reminders that the "War of the Lord" was an eternal and ongoing struggle, Mendes said, and American Jews were no exception. Directing his message to Jewish parents, he graphically described the Amalek-like lures and snares that beset their children:

> Here we are doing our best to bring up our children in the way they should go, striving to impress our adult youth by means of religion with a love for all that is pure and just . . . and there come the Amalekites of the day to fall upon them and cut them off. . . . Amalekites of the newspaper, who pour daily into our homes columns of suggestion and example culled by preference from the lowest dregs of society; Amaleks of the press and library, who supplement those vile attacks by more elaborate and persistent ones in the shape of the suggestive novel and sensational story; Amalekites of the stage, who, instead of describing upon the boards lofty ideals of classic minds, gloat over the ones of salacious scribblers [and] seek their materials in the unsavory records of the courts of law.

It was up to the parents, therefore, to uproot the evils of Amalek by closing their homes to inappropriate reading material, by boycotting offensive plays, by warring against the evils of drink, and by praying for divine help. One wonders, however, why Mendes assumed that parents themselves had escaped the harmful influences of Amalek.

Mendes's discourse, which sounded very much like the diatribes of any moralistic group of the time, like the Women's Christian Temperance Union, testified to the acculturation and secularization of postbellum American Jews. Indeed, Jews too read contemporary fiction and attended the opera and theater. But whatever the validity of Mendes's charges, the sermon ignored the vital issues troubling all Americans during that turbulent decade: Populist agitation, the struggles of workers and consumers against the giant industrial combinations, and the impact of the mass immigration from Eastern Europe on the existing Jewish order. It would have been quite natural had he equated Amalek with czarist Russia or if, like middle-class American Jews, he had preached against the Silverites or the Pullman strikers of the 1890s. As it stood, the sermon could have suited any decade after the Civil War.

In broader terms, Mendes's sermon was a call for Jewish identity. The rabbi added a different twist by pleading with Jews to live up to their reputation. Didn't they as well as Christians often praise Jews for virtues like sobriety and virtuous family life? To recapture what he called "all that is pure and just" was the duty of the modern Jew. According to Mendes, Jews also needed to pray for divine help, and he doubtless meant prayer in the manner of Reform.

The sermons discussed here made Amalek into an impersonal and timeless force, an eternal evil at war with God or God's chosen people. All preachers stressed the duty of Jews to keep the faith, and they generally called for self-improvement. Their sermons built on the group dimension of Jewish identity. Jews may not have constituted a nation in the political sense, but individual Jews suffered at the hands of Amalek because they belonged to a particular and separate *collectivity*. Except for Baar, the rabbis ignored contemporary antisemitism, and one wonders whether the stress on self-improvement indicates that the rabbis too, like some Jewish commentators in the Gilded Age, blamed Jewish manners or behavior, rather than the lack of able defenders, for the discrimination.[27] On the question of whether Jews had other ways of fighting the external Amaleks, the sermons kept silent. None dared to advise Jewish political action.

Even if they understood that important issues were solved by the ballot, they would hardly have deviated so radically from communal bans on Jewish participation in politics. Nor, in spite of the various forms of the Amalek spirit, did they contest the optimistic belief of the nineteenth century in the march of progress.

The symbols of Mordecai, Haman, and Amalek provided nineteenth-century rabbis with oft-used ideas for Purim sermons. In twentieth-century sermons, however, the figure of Mordecai the hero lost much of its importance. To be sure, one rabbi, claiming that the persecutors of the Jews generation after generation were ultimately defeated, maintained that while the Hamans had died, Esther and Mordecai lived on. But in his interpretation they were depersonalized. They had become the symbols of the entire Jewish people and, "typical of the Jew, always remain. As such they are deathless."[28] Except for children's stories, the image of the individual Mordecai, the public-spirited man devoted to the service of his people, largely faded.[29] Like corporate America after World War I, the Jewish community went through a managerial revolution. As a result, the representative men so eagerly sought by the *Jewish Messenger* decades earlier, or the Mordecais, were replaced by paid professionals who charted policy for defense organizations like the American Jewish Committee, the American Jewish Congress, and the Anti-Defamation League.

The image of Amalek, however, lived on in the twentieth century. It was magnified in the ongoing tragedies endured by the Jews. In the 1920s Amalek accounted for the devastating pogroms in the Ukraine; in the 1930s and 1940s it reached unimaginable heights in the deeds of Hitler and the Nazis; and after World War II it took the form of obstacles imposed by England on the survival of the Displaced Persons and the creation of a Jewish state. No matter which cloak it donned, Amalek or evil kept alive the call for remembrance and the duty of Jews to wage an unremitting war against their would-be annihilators. As one twentieth-century rabbi reminded his congregation: "While Amalek and Haman are dead, their reincarnations are not. In every generation there arise new Amaleks and Hamans to fill the vacancies left by their predecessors and they do their work as effectively as those who came before them."[30]

4

Meant for Children

American rabbis knew that sermons and synagogue services in general failed to hold the interest of the youth or to teach them about Judaism. In the pre–Civil War era men like Isaac Leeser, Isaac Mayer Wise, Sabato Morais, and Max Lilienthal supported synagogue schools or classes that would shape the child into model Americans and model Jews. While Americanization proceeded almost naturally from the very air that the children breathed, molding a Jewish identity required sustained effort, particularly in light of formidable competition from an indifferent home upbringing and a secular or Protestant-flavored public school. After the war Rabbis Lilienthal and Hermann Baar found other extra-synagogue ways to engage the youth. The former taught through a periodical for children and the latter through sermons and religious instruction at an orphanage. The themes they discussed, like those in sermons heard by adults, stressed both Americanism and a positive Jewish identity. Here the rabbi appears primarily as the communal activist whose Jewish concerns extended beyond his synagogue pulpit. The work of Lilienthal and Baar broke new ground in precedents left for succeeding generations. Lilienthal's periodical set an example for twentieth-century juvenile magazines, and Baar's sermons anticipated later concern on how to instill Jewish content into extra-synagogue agencies funded by the community, like hospitals, homes for the chronically ill, settlement houses, and reformatories.

In 1874 Reform Rabbi Max Lilienthal of Cincinnati launched one of the first American periodicals for Jewish children, the *Hebrew Sabbath School Visitor,* shortly renamed the *Sabbath Visitor* and hereinafter called the *Visitor.* To teach the youth, the rabbi said, was his "sacred task." Planned for youngsters aged seven to fourteen, the four-page illustrated magazine resembled Christian and secular journals of the time—like *St. Nicholas* and *Youth's Companion*—in its efforts to impart good character and a meaningful religious faith to its readers. Like them the *Visitor* stressed the proper conduct expected of American "ladies" and "gentlemen." Lilien-thal, who was editor of the *Visitor* until his death, also wrote the bulk of the material. In the manner of the contemporary edifying sermon, he, a master "edifier," tailored the teachings of the average nineteenth-century sermon to juvenile tastes in order to elevate the youngsters morally and spiritually. The biblical verse that he fixed to the journal's masthead in both Hebrew and English summed up his message: "Listen to advice and accept discipline/ In order that you may be wise in the end" (Proverbs 19:20). Aside from its moralistic character, the *Visitor* under Lilienthal's direction provided later readers with a view of the social life of American Jews during the years 1874–1882.

The new journal served several of the rabbi's purposes. Concerned about the growing indifference of American Jews to a Jewish education, he aimed primarily at bringing the doctrines and values of Judaism—faith, virtue, and proper deportment—directly into the home and the existing Sabbath (or Sunday) schools. Targeting the generation most vulnerable to assimilation, he hoped too that the material in the journal would raise the standards of those schools in terms of substance and pedagogical techniques. The greater his audience, the better the chances of equipping the younger generation with pride in their Jewish heritage and an ability to defend themselves against both prejudice and the blandishments of Christian missionaries. After Lilienthal's death in 1882 the journal limped along under a succession of editors, Reform rabbis in the main, who duplicated neither his passion for the magazine nor his engaging style. In 1893 it passed out of Reform sponsorship.[1]

Lilienthal came well prepared for the tasks of teaching children via a journal.[2] Before he immigrated to the United States, he had written popular articles for European periodicals, and he continued the practice when he arrived in America. He also held fast to what proved to be a lifetime commitment to a broad secular education. The roots of that commitment were planted at an early age. Munich, the city of his birth, had imbibed currents unleashed by the French Enlightenment and the Jewish *haskalah* (enlightenment), and there he studied the sciences and humanities according to modern methods of a secular *Gymnasium* and university. He prepared simultaneously for the rabbinate, and during those years were sown the seeds of his later identification with Reform Judaism. Unable to receive a rabbinic post in Germany, he accepted an offer to serve the Jewish community of Riga. Once in Russia, he was commissioned by the czarist government to modernize the Jewish schools nationwide and thereby modernize Russian Jewry. Despite strenuous efforts to revamp traditional Jewish education along the lines of the secular and "scientific" German model which he had tried first in Riga, his Russian mission collapsed. His European options few at best, Lilienthal set sail for America in 1845.

His failure in Russia notwithstanding, the rabbi continued to press for a modern education for the young. In his installation address to the three congregations in New York to which he first ministered, he declared that their God-given mission was to educate their children "as Jews, as good men, as useful citizens." He established a day school under the aegis of the three congregations, and he experimented with new curricula and modern pedagogical methods.[3] His name as an educator spread when he founded a private boarding school in the city after temporarily leaving the pulpit. The timing was auspicious. Given the Protestant character of the American public school, new immigrants from Central Europe preferred the private Jewish boarding schools that flourished in the 1840s and 1850s. Lilienthal's school boasted a modern course of study that included a heavy concentration in English along with foreign languages, Jewish studies, mathematics, and physical training. Working for both rapid assimilation and at keeping Jewish youngsters within the fold, the rabbi was known for the personal attention he gave individual students. One graduate recalled in a letter to his former headmaster: "I felt as if I was in my own father's house. . . . Every scholar will look upon you as a second father, and as our warmest friend." In 1855 Lilienthal was persuaded to accept a rabbinical post in Cincinnati, where he became a close associate of Isaac Mayer Wise. He frequently contributed to Wise's periodical, the *American Israelite,* and despite his Orthodox background, he became, like Wise, a moderate Reformer.

Armed with praise from New York on his skill as an educator, Lilienthal served on Cincinnati's Board of Education, and he worked for the establishment of the University of Cincinnati. He also set out to raise the standards of his synagogue's Sabbath school. His aim had not changed since 1845—he planned to make the students "enlightened" Jews and model American citizens. Toward that end he began the *Hebrew Sabbath School Visitor,* a pedagogical device for use in the Sabbath school. In the very first issue of the magazine, the rabbi "spoke" to the children:

Welcome, thrice welcome, my dear good children! How pleased I am to find you all regularly attending your Sabbath school! How glad I am to see you all so orderly, so attentive, so anxious to learn. . . . Good children ought to be rewarded. And therefore I have resolved to visit you every Sabbath morning, and bring you a nice paper full of instruction and amusement. We shall talk together about our sacred Jewish religion.

Promising stories from the Bible, the Talmud, general history and other subjects, as well as anecdotes and riddles, Lilienthal foresaw "a splendid time together." But he conditioned his promise: "provided you be good at home, attend regularly to your Sabbath school and the divine service, and be, in every respect, young ladies and gentlemen." On those terms the readers would find the *Visitor* one of their "best friends" and "instructive companions." Touting the magazine as a joint venture with the young readers, he asked the help of the superintendents and teachers in the Sabbath schools, as well as parents, to distribute the *Visitor* and to solicit subscriptions. He never doubted that they shared the same aim —"the inculcation of the beauty and morality of our holy religion."[4] Setting his sights beyond Cincinnati, he sought to reach children in outlying areas without synagogues or schools and to raise the standards of Sabbath schools overall. His ambitious agenda reflected the desperate need of the schools at the time to upgrade curricula, teaching staffs, and materials.[5]

The rabbi lost no opportunity to preach the message of how to "be good." In the stories he wrote, whether ancient or modern tales, he not only molded the characters and their behavior along lines of good and bad, but he often interrupted the narrative to draw a moral lesson from a particular incident in the story. In other instances pieces were set in the form of conversations with children. Stories from the Bible, Talmud, and Jewish history were retold in modern parlance, even as the rabbi peppered the accounts with comments to his "dear children." Simultaneously, he taught the need of religious faith based on knowledge. A long series about weekly meetings of a personal "Visitor," clearly Lilienthal himself, with several Jewish boys, at which he, the master teacher, answered his disciples' questions about religion, history, and proper behavior, provided him with a particularly appropriate podium. As he said, "It is so nice to know something and explain it to others." In a different series, this one about the young virtuous Nellie, a devotee of religion and learning who taught biblical stories to her younger siblings and had them memorize verses from the Bible, Nellie was the dedicated teacher par excellence. In one chapter her mother promises her a reward for her efforts. No, says the little girl, I don't teach the younger ones for the sake of a reward; I only want them to know about God and the Bible.[6]

To "prove" that children easily comprehended and appreciated the messages, Lilienthal included the reactions of the *Visitor*'s small group of boys within the actual text. For example, one boy who was impressed by the teacher's wide range of learning promised enthusiastically at the end of one session: "I shall spend every leisure hour I have in acquiring some useful knowledge." Lilienthal's heroes and heroines were all paragons of virtue—they were modest and hardworking, honest and responsible, loyal to their faith—and of course well behaved. The rabbi's list of good manners included a host of subjects ranging from cleanliness, grammatical speech, the proper way to leave a room filled with guests, and consideration for parents and the elderly to the use of a handkerchief! Never examine what you cough up in a handkerchief, he admonished. "Nothing is more vulgar except spitting on the floor."[7]

Despite the magazine's overly sweet and sunny outlook, parents heartily approved of the *Visitor,* and judging from the volume of letters received, the magazine grew increasingly popular with the youngsters. Correspondence with readers, usually expressing joy at receiving the journal, was eventually handled as a separate department by a "Cousin Sadie." By choosing a handful of letters for publication, the editor provided children eager to see their name in print with another reason to read and subscribe to the *Visitor.*

A typical issue of the early *Visitor* contained a story based on the Bible, one from the Talmudic or later medieval period, and one on an aspect of modern Jewish history or on a prominent modern personage—statesman, artist, religious figure or musical composer. Among the journal's nineteenth-century Jewish heroes, whom Lilienthal called "Our Modern Mordecais," were England's Sir Moses Montefiore, France's Adolphe Crémieux, and Germany's Eduard Lasker. The editor even included a story about the famous American Unitarian minister, William Ellery Channing.[8] History and biography also appeared in the magazine's marking of American and Jewish holidays. Those days received full coverage, and Lilienthal carefully explained their meaning and significance for American Jewish children. In all the stories, biographical sketches, and holiday tales, fact and fiction mingled. Like the bulk of the periodical's contents, they too bore the message of faith and morals. The rabbi's style and personal touch along with an ability to translate complex or dull issues into familiar terms captured and sustained the children's interest. Most impressive to the modern reader was Lilienthal's obvious respect for his readers, even those totally ignorant of the subject under discussion. He was their wise friend who understood their questions and seriously weighed their opinions.

Aside from the abundance of morality tales, the journal discussed other subjects. For one thing it emphasized the importance of charity. Here too the *Visitor* included non-Jewish as well as Jewish causes. It called annually for contributions to the Alliance Israélite Universelle for its work on behalf of foreign Jews, and, as in the case of the yellow fever epidemic that hit the United States in 1878, it appealed for the relief of all victims. With Jewish orphans in mind but in no way meant for middle-class Jewish business families, it supported Hebrew Free Schools as well as agricultural colonies planned by the Union of American Hebrew Congregations (UAHC). On the lighter side, shorter pieces or fillers abounded. They told of natural phenomena, of exotic foreign lands, and of famous sites like Mount Vernon, Monticello, and Bunker Hill. One piece discussed the "true" facts of Shylock; another, the Transcendentalist poet Margaret Fuller; a third, the relations of William Penn with the Indians; and still another, George Washington's false teeth.[9] Lighter still were the items of amusement that Lilienthal had promised—jokes, anecdotes, and puzzles. Before 1880 there were but few items on foreign affairs and current events.

The *Visitor* drew its audience from the rising middle class of Jews from Central Europe. A commentary on the rapid mobility of the country's Jews, the stories talked about Jewish families like those of its readers, families in midwestern cities who lived comfortably without financial worries and who could afford to employ at least one servant. The father was the typical merchant or small businessman, and the sons often went to college and trained for the professions. Nellie's father, for example, was a shopkeeper who traveled east periodically to buy supplies, and her older brother studied medicine. The family belonged to a Reform synagogue, and the children attended the Sabbath school in addition to the municipal public school. Testifying to the growing strength of the Reform movement, the customs in their synagogues or temples were no longer Traditionalist. Now the places of worship provided organs and choirs and confirmation ceremonies for both girls and boys, and they also condoned greater laxity in Sabbath and holiday observances. Ironically, although the *Visitor* supported the equality of sexes in the synagogue, some items in the periodical were specifically directed to boys and others to girls.

The journal taught the tenets of Reform Judaism, and when it reported on Jewish religious affairs in various parts of the country, it limited its coverage exclusively to holiday celebrations under Reform's auspices and to Reform institutions like the UAHC and Reform's rabbinical seminary, Hebrew Union College. The worlds of the *Visitor* and that of its readers, where middle-class status, a drive for mobility, Americanization, and loyalty to a modernized Judaism were the norms, made the two worlds mutually reinforcing. Not until the presence of large numbers of East Europeans was felt after 1875 did the static but familiar setting depicted in the *Visitor* undergo any changes.

"I love my religion," Lilienthal entitled one editorial. He attributed the statement to one of the boys in the Visitor's group of students who went on to explain his pride in his faith and his readiness to defend it. The editor said that the boys had fully absorbed his, the Visitor's, lessons about Reform as well as his pointed rebuttals of anti-Jewish stereotypes. From that same editorial one can also infer Lilienthal's sharp criticism of Orthodoxy. Defense of Reform Judaism went along with the rabbi's message of good relations with Christians. To be sure, missionaries who maligned the faith of the poor and defenseless Jewish immigrants upon whom they preyed, and Christian rowdies who indulged in name-calling and foul language in street scuffles, required forceful responses. But otherwise Jewish and Christian children made friends with each other; they played together and visited each other's homes; and the rabbi and Christian minister informally shared opinions. The journal left it unclear, however, whether there was a limit to fraternization and where, as in the celebration of Christmas, the line should be drawn.[10]

Lilienthal tried hard, moreover, to teach a Judaism tailored to Christian tastes. For example, in telling the story of Abraham's sacrifice of Isaac, he deviated from the original text. The Bible relates that when Abraham picked up the knife to slay his son, he was stopped by an angel of God. According to Lilienthal, however, Abraham restrained himself, reasoning, in words not used in the biblical account, that God did not desire the sacrifice because "[God] is love and mercy and goodness."[11] The rabbi scored twice thereby: he denied the popular charge of Christians that the Hebrew God was a cruel and vengeful God, and he portrayed the Jewish God in terms akin to those used by Christians about the New Testament's "God of love."

The *Visitor*'s favorite theme aside from faith and morals was the glory of America. Each Jew was "a patriot to the very core of his heart," the editor said, and he supplied countless lessons in civics and on famous people and places. Lilienthal would have preferred an America with complete separation of church and state, and he voiced his support of the secular public school through the pages of the *Visitor*,[12] but that grievance did not detract from America's greatness. The exemplar of liberty and peace to other lands, the United States extended its full blessings to the Jews. The latter, owing the nation their undying gratitude, had contributed and continued to contribute meaningfully to its development. Aren't you proud of your country?, the rabbi asked rhetorically. He took special pride in a Jewish boy he had recommended to West Point who served courageously in the American army.[13] Doubtless such sentiments as well as the Puritan-like virtues that the paper taught commended it to non-Jews. Indeed, the *Visitor* boasted of Christian readers just as it included material from non-Jewish sources.

Lilienthal's personal penchant for German culture notwithstanding, he insisted that American Jews could never be charged with dual loyalties. They were members of a religion only and not a nationality that aspired to a homeland of its own. Ethnicity in general as well as other ethnic groups were also ignored by the *Visitor*. The journal asserted that Jews were patriots in whatever land they lived, loyal even to states like Germany and Russia in which they suffered cruel persecution. Denying any contemporary Jewish interest in a Jewish Palestine, Lilienthal printed only a few scattered pieces on sites and customs of that land. In his synagogue he refused on principle to follow the Traditionalist practice of commemorating the destruction of the two ancient Hebrew temples on the fast day of Tisha b'Av (the ninth day of the Hebrew month of Av) and his periodical followed suit. Dispersion and exile were "providential," he said, and a cause for rejoicing. God is with us, and we have found our home in America. The German-born rabbi turned American went even further by making Americanism part of his religion. In a story set on the eve of the fourth of July, the Visitor's boys heard their teacher ecstatically extol the greatness of the country. One of the young lads, a choirboy in the temple, was thereupon moved to sing a well-known verse from the book of Psalms: "Give thanks unto the Lord for He is good, for His righteousness endures forever." Yes, answered the Visitor, Jews should add the Hallel prayers (psalms on God's greatness and goodness which include that verse and which are recited on holidays and the New Moon) to their prayers on July 4th. Like many other Reform rabbis, Lilienthal linked the American ideals with those of Judaism and he called Passover Judaism's Fourth of July.[14]

Almost pollyanna-ish in outlook, the *Visitor* preferred to report on the achievements of Jews and how they advanced in the world rather than on the troubles that assailed them. Indeed, it announced in 1878, and at a time when discrimination in Russia was very much alive, that persecutions were over.[15] Extremely little coverage went to current events at home and abroad and even less to antisemitism. Popular use of negative stereotypes of Jews was noted and condemned, but for the most part discrimination in America was ignored. A short account of the Seligman-Hilton affair appeared, but the rising tide of exclusion of Jews from schools, clubs, resorts, and employment was not discussed. One interesting anonymous piece related the experiences of a bright young man at a New England university who was ostracized by his fellow students as soon as he revealed that he was a Jew. The point of the story, however, was not social discrimination on campuses but how to overcome it: "Our aim," the hero says, "must be to teach the Gentile that the Jew differs from him, if at all, in his religious opinions only; that we are Americans as they are; that we have the same code of morals and the same notions of right and wrong, the same love of the good and the same impatience with the bad." Behaving always as the virtuous gentleman and a man of honesty and self-respect, the student was soon received in the most exclusive and aristocratic homes of Boston.[16]

While optimism about the Jewish future in the United States never flagged, the placid world of the *Visitor* was somewhat disrupted around 1880 by the new racist antisemitism in Europe. The waves of persecution in Germany and Russia could not be totally ignored, and reports of the Jewish situation in those countries increased markedly. But glaring omissions obtained here too. The response of Jews and non-Jews worldwide to the pogroms and to the European antisemites was inadequately reported, while any serious consideration of the responsibility of American Jews for the victims was ignored. The *Visitor* conceded that progress for the European Jews was temporarily halted, and it did approve of relief for impoverished Russian Jews when they arrived in the country, but its more important lesson was: Be grateful you live in America.[17]

The *Visitor* went through various changes in the course of its existence. It expanded the number of its pages, and it appeared at times as a biweekly or monthly. After Lilienthal's death in 1882, his successors, beginning with a string of Reform rabbis, changed the character and style of the magazine. To be sure, an emphasis on faith and morals persisted, but in line with the tastes of a particular editor, certain features were added or expanded and others omitted. Contributions from readers and laymen generally increased, sermons by Reform rabbis were introduced as a standard feature, and for some stretches of time virtually no mention at all was made of current events or American political and foreign affairs. Despite a rapidly changing society in the last two decades of the nineteenth century, the new forces shaping American and American Jewish life were largely ignored.

In its later years the journal paid more attention than ever before to individual Sabbath schools. Lesson plans for the schools were introduced, and efforts to create a union of Sabbath schools were encouraged. In 1891 the *Visitor* spelled out an additional aim—to counter the passion of the young for "trashy" literature and to develop in them a taste for "ennobling" material.[18] Aware that its first readers were in most cases no longer children, it also sought to reach post-confirmation youth and, indeed, the entire family. No change, however, was more telling than the end of Lilienthal's service as editor. Each succeeding editor, and none stayed for very long, put his own imprint on the journal, and sterner and more austere styles largely erased the founder's sprightly and friendly tone. Some thought the *Visitor* was rapidly going downhill, and two years before it ceased publication one critic called it "a mess of trash." The same critic added in horror that at one point the journal had been edited by a non-Jew![19]

There were flaws in the magazine even during Lilienthal's tenure, particularly in the eyes of a modern reader. Aside from its "goody-goody" tone which could become cloying, it left little to the imagination. The style of its main pieces was didactic, the characters were two-dimensional, and by purposely avoiding controversial subjects the magazine did not encourage an exchange of views. Only scant attention was paid to the condition of foreign Jews, and not until the violent anti-Jewish persecution in Europe in the 1880s did the *Visitor* discuss manifestations of Jew-hatred. An explanation of its omissions, albeit only a partial one, came a few years after Lilienthal's death. Then the journal stated that its consistent policy had been to avoid subjects that could breed controversy and dissension. But despite its shortcomings, the *Visitor* under Lilienthal's guidance was put on a firm foundation. His contemporaries admired the rabbi's skills as an educator and his passionate interest in Jewish youth. His work with the magazine was, they said, a true "labor of love."[20] His pioneering efforts at managing the *Visitor* reaped long-term benefits too, for the rabbi blazed a trail for Jewish children's magazines of the next century.

*

A frequent contributor to the *Visitor* during its post-Lilienthal period was Hermann Baar, a rabbi and educator from Germany. In the United States he earned a reputation as the director of the Hebrew Orphan Asylum (HOA) of New York. At that post he wrote numerous sermons and lectures for the *Visitor* in which he, like Lilienthal, replicated the substance of the average adult sermons. Delivered for the most part to the children in the asylum, they perpetuated the journal's themes of faith and morals.

The origins of the HOA went back to 1822. One story tells that when a Jewish veteran of the Revolution fell critically ill, he applied for aid to leaders of his community. Funds were raised on his behalf, and after his death the residue became the seed money of the Hebrew Benevolent Society. Whatever its genesis, the largely Sephardic-controlled society rapidly developed into a dominant communal institution separate from a synagogue, and in time it merged with similar charitable societies of German and other Jewish groups. The newly named Hebrew Benevolent and Orphan Asylum Society opened a temporary orphanage in 1860 with room for thirty children, and, with municipal assistance it moved to a larger building in 1862 that was planned for two hundred inmates. The ever-increasing numbers of immigrants and of fatherless families in the wake of the Civil War demanded a further expansion of facilities. Not only had it become more difficult to discharge children at the stipulated age of thirteen, but more and more single parents were for a fee placing their children, known as "half orphans," in the home. Some twenty years later the society erected a four-story building described by observers at its dedication as "new and palatial." The spacious structure with room for one thousand inmates included dormitories, a modern kitchen, and what were called "swimming baths." Its announced purpose was both practical and idealistic: to prepare the youngsters for future careers and to inculcate in them the principles of virtuous living. Like other Jewish orphanages it adopted the norms of its middle-class founders and supporters on educating its wards to become moral individuals and loyal Americans. Reform Rabbi Kaufmann Kohler, who directed religious training at the institution, also thought that orphans so trained would have a salutary influence on poor children who were not privileged to live in such plush surroundings![21]

The administration of the asylum and supervision of its day-to-day operations was the responsibility of Hermann Baar. Baar had been schooled in secular and Jewish studies in his native Germany. Attracting wide public attention in various European and American cities for his work as a rabbi, educator, and journalist, he reached the pinnacle of his career in his post at the HOA which he filled from 1876 to 1899.[22] His expertise in the theory and methodology of modern pedagogy—he himself was an admirer of the Pestalozzi schools—earned him the respect of American Jewish communal leaders; Rabbi Kohler called him a "wise and loving school-man."[23] During the last quarter of the nineteenth century, when new ideas on the introduction of scientific principles in philanthropy and philanthropic institutions were germinating, Baar's work appeared particularly significant.

In addition to his administrative duties, Superintendent Baar preached regularly to the orphans on Sabbaths and religious holidays. Attracting outside visitors to the home, many of his popular addresses were published, some in his book *Addresses on Homely and Religious Subjects* and more in American Jewish periodicals. The sermons used here come from the *Sabbath Visitor,* where a piece by Baar appeared in almost every issue from mid-1884 through 1892. Although we can date their appearance, his talks were applicable to any decade. True, references to rampant materialism or agitation for an eight-hour working day or the name of Adolf Stoecker, the notorious German antisemite, showed that they were written in the last quarter of the nineteenth century. But for the most part the sermons, which emphasized what nineteenth-century Americans would have called the "eternal verities," were not time bound.

A review of Baar's numerous talks reveals that the preacher concentrated on different facets of one theme alone: the importance of character building. As he repeatedly told the youngsters in the HOA, a good character lay at the heart of one's self-fulfillment and happiness. Admittedly, no one person was totally good or totally bad, but only with a good character could a person be of benefit to himself, the community, and humankind at large. Cultivation of the proper virtues along with faith in God and one's fellowmen were the means to those ends. The superintendent's list of virtues resembled Lilienthal's but was considerably longer. Baar added attributes like self-reliance and self-restraint, truth and honesty, courage, gratitude to teachers, a wise choice of friends, consideration of others, diligence and perseverance at work, cleanliness, a readiness to make sacrifices, and even good penmanship.[24] Other virtues rounded out the picture. A person with an exemplary character understood that education was essential but that wisdom was less important than a good heart, that resilience and a measure of toughness were necessary to adjust to life's hard knocks, and that good deeds were called for without any thoughts of reward. Moral worth and merit, not riches, Baar often said, made for happiness. He admitted that virtuous behavior was not always easy; indeed, the highest treasures of life—freedom, independence, courage—came from "self-denial" and privation, and individuals had to be grateful for their portions in life.[25] One wonders, however, if those children who were placed in the asylum because their parent or parents could not afford to support them would rank good deeds above material privation.

Baar usually elucidated his theme on behavioral traits with lessons from the Bible or the lives of great men—living and dead, Jewish and non-Jewish. The orphans were taught Jewish history, Bible, and prayers, but unlike the *Visitor* under Lilienthal, Baar paid little attention to the wisdom of the Talmudic sages. In one sermon he added that he was never at a loss for a topic because he picked up on what he heard from the youngsters. Using anti-heroes as well as heroes—for example, in the story of Absalom's revolt against David—he illustrated the struggle of evil against good. Although there was a God, and although upright people prayed to him, God rarely figured in the equation. Baar did say that repentance erased wrongdoing, but for the most part the way to proper behavior was the individual's independent choice. In Baar's words, a person was the architect of his own fortune and destiny.[26]

In his choice of biblical models, Baar showed a marked preference for certain characters, and he often referred to his favorites. He revered Moses, the leader par excellence, and his favorite prophet was Jeremiah, "Israel's greatest patriot."[27] He taught the children that the suffering endured by those two men on behalf of their people made them especially worthy of emulation. Although he never repeated a sermon word for word, he often alluded to the lessons that made certain biblical tales richer for him than others. The story of Moses' father-in-law Jethro, for example, had more than one message; it showed the sagacity and measured judgment of a man, even one from a different nation, and it also underscored the modesty of a wise statesman, Moses, who was not too proud to heed constructive criticism. At times, the superintendent explained that the same individual embodied both faults as well as virtues: King Solomon may have been a man of reason and wisdom, but he was spoiled by too much luxury; Miriam was Moses' caring sister and the musical heroine of the exodus from Egypt, but she deserved to be punished for criticizing her brother's marriage to a Cushite woman; the modest and generous Rebecca was a perfect wife for Isaac, but she was deceitful in trying to win the birthright for her younger son. Baar's discourses were full of examples of how he differed with the literal word of the Bible. The promise to the patriarchs that their progeny would be as numerous as the stars did not mean actual numbers but rather, like the stars, Jews would be scattered all over the world. And, the same Miriam who was guilty of gossip and slander may not have been totally wrong, since she doubtless wanted to preserve the dignity of her family.[28]

The superintendent taught the rudiments of a nondenominational Judaism in his weekly talks, but in fact he was a moderate Reformer. His prior experience included service in Reform temples, and the *Visitor,* on whose editorial board he served for a while, was a Reform journal. Some visitors to the HOA also observed that the religious services followed the ritual of New York's Temple Emanu-El.[29] The contents of the sermons confirmed his loyalty toward Reform rather than Traditionalism. Like all good Reformers Baar often emphasized the universal mission of Jews to teach the unity of God and brotherhood of man above the demands of Jewish law and ritual. And, like most rabbis, the superintendent demanded a religious-like patriotism from American Jews. For example, he once said that the strongest sentiment after love of home and love of God was love of country. In another sermon he spoke of the incomparable blessings of America—liberty, no caste system, welcome to the oppressed from foreign lands. The country perhaps was not the greatest in fine arts or culture, but it was unsurpassed in charity and benevolence. Any intolerance, he concluded, came from Europe. It was only fitting, therefore, that the HOA labor in paternalistic fashion to Americanize the children of immigrants by impressing on them the values and mores of the nation. American holidays were celebrated, and portraits of Americans adorned the walls. As Reena Friedman relates in her comprehensive study of Jewish orphanages, even the purpose of the HOA's marching band, organized during Baar's administration, was to inspire patriotism.[30]

Compared with the average sermon of the day, Baar's message was a model of brevity, for he usually spoke no longer than ten to fifteen minutes. In other respects his talks resembled the "edifying" and moralistic Protestant sermons of nineteenth-century Germany whose style was popular in America. Avoiding the subject of theology, he chose a topic which he elucidated and illustrated, and he closed with a prayer for the well-being of his audience. Like a rabbi speaking from a synagogue pulpit, Baar chastised as well as taught. For the Jewish community at large he preached against ostentatious behavior, be it manifested in funerals or weddings; the money could be better spent on charity, he said. He found fault as well with nonbelieving lay congregational leaders who set an example for religious indifference. Both laity and rabbis, he added, should never regard the ministry as a money-making proposition.[31] To be sure, since Baar spoke to a captive audience of four hundred to six hundred wards at HOA, there was no need for him to curry favor with "parishioners." Otherwise, the format of his addresses replicated that of the congregational rabbi. Whether or not the reader of today considers Baar's sermons appropriate for young children, they were well received by the Reform sponsors of the *Visitor.*[32]

Overall the sermons contained interesting and even dramatic material, but the superintendent frequently sacrificed the comprehension of his audience for the sake of rhetoric. No doubt many children, no matter how attentive, were unable to understand all his words or allusions. The following are examples of how unintelligible at times his sermons must have been for youngsters:

> On a rule of pedagogy: "A science of pedagogical knowledge and instructions has been marked out and promulgated which has had the greatest influence upon the development of our public school life."[33]
>
> On the biblical Aaron: "He must have been mortified to see how severely and fiercely his priestly dignity and position was undermined and assailed through the vulgar hostility of his own relative, Korach, and his mutinous gang."[34]
>
> To the monitors at the HOA: "Your and our own influence upon the children must be like that of Pericles in ancient times. Pericles was noted . . . as one of the ablest and most illustrious statesmen of his age. In eloquence he was superior even to a Gladstone."[35]

Nor were the orphans likely to recognize names like von Treitschke, Kosciuszko, Diogenes, Cardinal Mezzaponti, and Benjamin Disraeli.

One also questions the superintendent's lack of sensitivity when he spoke on a second favorite topic, the joys and riches of family life. Although the youngsters were doubtless unaware that Baar had been fully orphaned by the age of ten, and although he spoke only once about his mother, his sermons seemed quite inappropriate when he talked glowingly about the warmth, loyalty, unity, and mutual respect within an exemplary family. "After all," he stated in one sermon on Naomi and Ruth, "all mothers-in-law are not so bad!"[36] He expressed his sympathy for orphans in general and reminded them that God had found a place for many great men in history who had been orphans.[37] Indeed, the orphans ought to be grateful to their new home, especially since the training they received at the HOA was superior to that of many children from families with both parents. On one occasion he even said that at least as orphans they wouldn't be spoiled the way Jacob had spoiled Joseph.[38] Again, it is doubtful whether such words effectively comforted the bereaved children. Had Baar conducted discussions of the ideas he raised, they might have had a different impact.

Embedded in Baar's litany of virtues were the evils of bad conduct —that is, the consequences of idleness, dishonesty, greed, laziness, misplaced concern for creature comforts, and lack of self-discipline. Confronted with that vast array of human frailties, the children of the HOA would be hard put to follow his strictures on the need for optimism.

Baar wove his experiences at the asylum into his addresses, frequently preaching on the behavior expected of the orphans. The laziness and indifference of the children, he said, made the work of the HOA an uphill task. A stern taskmaster, Baar often reminded the orphans how grateful they should be for their more than decent living conditions, their simple but adequate food, their good training at the hands of helpful teachers, and their numerous benefactors within the community. There were those, he added, who flagrantly disobeyed the rules of the asylum: "Many of you would rather live on bread the whole day and enjoy the liberty of running about, than to live here among us in comfort and ease, and be restricted by order and discipline." The asylum had its share of what he called "street boys," those who hit, lied, bullied, and vandalized property, and who gave the HOA a bad name. On some occasions Baar's patience wore thin; how could a child who received so much from us write us an "insolent" letter of complaint, he once asked.[39]

The worst offenders according to the superintendent's sermons were those who lied. Time and again his talks to the children emphasized truthfulness: a man's moral character rested on truthfulness, and lying betrayed cowardice and the want of honor. He assured the guilty ones that they weren't too old to change, but as matters stood, he claimed that only a few in the HOA told the truth. In one sermon Baar minced few words:

> For many years have I tried to make you truthful and have constantly entreated and requested you to be open and frank in all your words, acts and doings. And yet, with all my attempts, I do not think that I have been very successful; for I do not hesitate to tell you that most of you have

no idea of truthfulness. Whether you do not understand the great moral significance of this virtue, or whether you are too feeble in comprehension to see what an honor it is for man to adorn himself with this, God's greatest attribute, I do not know.

Discipline was clearly a major problem in the orphanage, for in the same sermon Baar also lashed out at those who struck their fellow inmates:

> Again, no day passes that I do not exhort you not to touch or to strike your fellow-orphans. If I could collect those words which I have spoken in this matter, I am sure I could fill with them a whole volume; I even did not fail to punish you often severely for the committal of such acts. And yet, every time that I step among you I hear complaints that you strike your fellow-orphans.

You have hard hearts, he concluded; like Pharaoh who oppressed the Israelites, you do what you please and have no inclination to do what is right.[40]

Infractions of the numerous rules of the asylum were punished, but publicly Baar explained that he judged the offenders fairly and that he made his rebukes gently and privately. Never did he reveal how he whipped children who didn't pass morning inspection. At the funeral of one inmate, the superintendent praised the child for having been a "model inmate," or, in his words, for submitting patiently and unquestioningly to the will of Providence.[41] Whether the will of Providence also meant the will of Baar was unclear, but problems of obedience persisted.

Baar also discussed the matter of monitors in his sermons on behavior. From his words one learns that there were approximately two dozen monitors, boys and girls, or as he called them "monitors and monitoresses," for over five hundred children. He explained that their duties were to help the staff in the management of the asylum by keeping the inmates orderly, truthful, and diligent. Requirements for the posts of monitors included the willingness to undertake duties and the ability to take criticism well. However, and therein lay the problem, "How seldom is it that we find among the children of our home here the right and proper material for services and offices of this kind." Some children, Baar added, showed thereby a lack of ambition or a spirit of "unselfish devotion." Admitting their difficult tasks, he claimed that the monitors would ultimately benefit, for the posts would help them in later life to discharge their duties properly.[42]

A recent history of the HOA by Hyman Bogen devotes an entire chapter to the regimented living and rigorous discipline imposed on the orphans during the Baar administration.[43] The more horrific details, reading like pages out of *Jane Eyre,* came from information gleaned by the author from alumni of the institution. They told how the boys were organized into military-like companies headed by monitors and were inspected daily for cleanliness and appearance. The monitors commanded the dormitories and dining room where the same precision and obedience were expected. The orphans wore uniforms, they were forbidden to speak to each other during meals, they were forced to finish everything on their plates, they were permitted to play but a few hours weekly, and visits by parents were allowed only once every three months. Perhaps worst of all, they were at the mercy of the monitors who devised all sorts of physical punishments for infractions of the rules. Whether Baar himself was aware of what transpired is an open question, but to all who recalled his tenure the authoritarian superintendent was hardly the "wise and loving school-man" described by Rabbi Kohler. The author of the asylum's history concluded: "Never again would life for the residents be as remorselessly controlled and restrictive." The conditions explain why the orphans did not consider the post of monitor an honor or a goal toward which to strive. In an institution run so harshly it was more than likely that those who became monitors were regarded by their peers as having joined the enemy in an ongoing battle of "us versus them." Surprisingly, however, alumni of the HOA remembered the Baar era "with a good deal of pride and affection."[44]

In the course of his numerous messages Superintendent Baar frequently mentioned the orphans' need to prepare themselves for a future occupation. The young girls claimed little attention, for they were usually placed as domestics. As for the boys, Baar's standard advice was to avoid the mercantile and commercial fields and look rather to mechanical and technical trades. Both the Bible and the ancient sages, he claimed in one sermon, praised craftsmen; wasn't the famous Bezalel, who was appointed by Moses to construct the tabernacle in the desert, a master architect and builder? Eager to see the boys go on for training at the Hebrew Technical Institutes, he also said that knowledge of a trade provided greater economic security than occupations dependent on the fluctuations of business cycles.[45] On one occasion he told how disappointed he was when the HOA lost the opportunity to place two boys in the American navy because of their families' objections.[46] To be sure, successful businessmen figured prominently in the Jewish circles that supported the asylum, but they agreed with Baar. The charge that Jews avoided the productive occupations of agriculture and crafts in favor of business had become more popular in the brief of the new antisemitism, and American Jewish leaders sought to refute the negative stereotype of the unproductive small businessman.

There was little indeed that supporters of the HOA, rabbis and laymen, could fault in Baar's sermons. None denied that Jewish children required training in religion and moral behavior. The patrons of the HOA were also "for" God and virtue and "against" sin and wrongdoing. Since many of them were conservative self-made men, they liked Baar's emphasis on self-reliance and the work ethic, and they agreed with his condemnation of American labor unrest.[47] They too expected obedience from children, and they questioned neither the superintendent's strict regimen nor his harsh discipline. Under his administration the HOA scored higher than non-Jewish orphan asylums in various matters of health and performance,[48] and accordingly they took pride in the HOA. Since the asylum was no different in kind from most philanthropic institutions, Christian as well as Jewish, it was eminently American. Supporters could also reap satisfaction from the knowledge that the HOA refuted any claim that Jews were responsible for turning loose a generation of untrained and uneducated paupers upon the city. They proved yet again the popular image that Jews took care of their own.

As for Baar's intended audience, the orphans themselves, there is little information on how they reacted to the sermons. Bogen's book contains a single item: "One Baar alumnus recalled that he often fell asleep during the sermons and is sure he wasn't the only one. However, he added, the sermons were good 'when he listened.'"[49]

Were Baar and Lilienthal representatives of the genteel tradition so dominant in the second half of the nineteenth century? R. Gordon Kelly, a historian of early American journals for children, has explained that juvenile periodicals were sponsored by the "gentry," a class committed to propagating the appropriate roles and behavior of "ladies" and "gentlemen" in tandem with religious values.[50] Although Lilienthal's *Visitor* sounded much like a product of that genteel tradition, there is no evidence indicating that he or Baar considered themselves its spokesmen. The analysis presented in this chapter reveals that since the children they addressed were largely from immigrant families of Eastern Europe, and since their mentors and sponsors were the established Jews of Central European origin, neither stratum had been in the country long enough to have produced a gentry of its own or to have been accepted by old established American families. More important, the rules of behavior taught by Lilienthal and Baar were grounded in Jewish and not Protestant sources. Much as the Puritan ethic derived from the Bible, accounting thereby for many similarities with Jewish teachings, Christianity and not Judaism shaped the values of nineteenth-century America.

At the same time, however, neither Lilienthal nor Baar can be separated from his American environment. Their messages that aimed to inculcate an appreciation of Jewish values and conduct were embedded in words and descriptions drawn from the American experiences of their readership—the homes they lived in, the schools they attended, the holidays they celebrated, and the non-Jews with whom they associated. By emphasizing biblical virtues, the rabbis could and did equate proper Jewish deportment with virtuous American behavior. Since the children heard similar messages from their public school teachers, they could easily comprehend the demands of an American way of life. Lilienthal and Baar took them even further by teaching how easily rapid acculturation could be combined with a modernized Jewish religion.

5

Rabbi versus Rabbi

In medieval society and until their legal emancipation in the Western world, Jews constituted a distinct collective body. A corporate group within the feudal structure, they, the non-Christians, lived for many centuries under special regulations imposed by local rulers. While intercourse between Jews and Gentiles was severely limited, internal governance of the Jewish ghetto, where permitted by the authorities, followed Talmudic and rabbinic teachings. The era of the French Revolution and Napoleon changed conditions in Western Europe. Ghettos were destroyed, and Jews who were now absorbed as individuals into the nation-state received rights that whittled down much of the inequality heretofore endured. In the United States where a feudal structure and official ghettos never existed, the small numbers of Jews in the colonies were generally tolerated. The new state constitutions of the Revolutionary period granted some political liberties, and still others were provided in the federal Constitution and Bill of Rights.[1]

Although absolute political equality was yet a distant goal, few if any nineteenth-century American Jews would have forgone the blessings of Emancipation enshrined in the state and federal constitutions. The new freedom, however, posed a sharply different problem: Was the price exacted of Jews too high? Indeed, Reform Rabbi Maurice Harris of New York asked in all seriousness whether Jews could survive Emancipation. He explained that freedom had two sides—freedom to observe and freedom to neglect. True, Emancipation permitted the individual Jew to enjoy rights of which he had never dreamed. Free to practice as well as to neglect his religious customs and heritage, he rapidly found his way into the political and economic mainstream of the new nation. But, at the same time, freedom from a separate corporate existence and from rabbinic authority weakened chances for the survival of the Jewish group and the preservation of Judaism.[2]

American Jews could neither go back to the medieval ghetto nor resurrect the Talmudic legal system that had regulated dealings between Jews and Christians. The options that remained for reconciling Judaism with the modern world were few in number. Jews could renounce all forms of religious identification and become merely "nothingarians"; they could convert to Christianity; they could affirm their loyalty to Orthodox Judaism by totally ignoring the demands of a secular lifestyle and a modern climate of opinion; or they could purposely break with Traditionalist axioms and plot the course of a totally Reformed Judaism.

The first and second options were, of course, unacceptable to rabbis. Their unqualified loyalty to the individual freedoms of the American creed notwithstanding, they were the Jewish survivalists, or those opposed to the extinction of the Jewish people. They also knew that despite the pervasiveness of popular anti-Jewish imagery, nineteenth-century Americans preferred believers irrespective of persuasion to those who repudiated religion in any form. Notwithstanding their insistence on the need of Jews to accommodate to the United States—always a popular message in rabbinic discourses—they never hinted in any fashion at compromises with Christianity. We are a separate people, Isaac Leeser insisted: "We should be a light to [non-Jews], but are on no account to suffer our light to be darkened by the shadow of their unbelief." Rabbis showed little love for Judaism's daughter religion. Not only was Christianity responsible for the centuries of persecution suffered by Jews, but also the religion of a Christian in no way surpassed that of a Jew. Therefore, conversion to Christianity and rejection of Jewish Law was "moral cowardice" or treason.[3] In sum, Jewish religious leaders were left with the options of adhering to Orthodoxy or following the Reformers, who renounced the teachings of the Talmud and rabbinic authorities and shaped their faith in the spirit of modernity.

Two major debates in the middle of the nineteenth century show how rabbis argued the merits of their positions on Judaism in modern America. They also show how the lines separating American Jewish denominations grew sharper. Unlike religious disputations of ancient and medieval times that pitted defenders of different faiths against each other, the two debates under consideration here were totally within the Jewish camp; each featured a Traditionalist rabbi who crossed swords with a Reformer. Since the ultra-Orthodox and the extreme Reformers were rarely involved, the debaters were drawn from the moderates of each group. Each debater, however, did not distinguish among the variations in the side he attacked.

The Traditionalists spoke out against all Reformers, and the Reformers lumped together all the Traditionalists, the moderate compromisers along with the right-wing Orthodox. At stake was the course of American Judaism, one that provided the optimum balance between the demands of Americanism and Jewish identity.

Ironically, more united the disputants than divided them. Both sides admitted that the familiar but static character of European Orthodoxy could not be replicated in the United States. Like all aspects of civilization, religion could hardly dismiss the scientific advances of the age. How to adjust Judaism to the "spirit of the age"—what to retain as inviolate and what irrelevancies to excise—became the central point at issue. Both sides remembered that in light of their identification with American ideals and values, modifications of their faith that were too outlandish for American tastes were unacceptable. As for congregational life, Traditionalists and Reformers experienced the same problems—the ignorance and apathy of congregants; the inability of the synagogue to retain the loyalty of its membership, most particularly that of the youth; inadequate religious schools and materials; and the need to train a native American ministry. Since religious leaders of all stripes favored some sort of institution to unite American Jews and their congregations, efforts from within the religious factions for intercongregational unity also ranked high on the agenda of the moderates. But unless a meeting of minds was first reached on the essentials of Judaism, unity would remain as elusive as ever, and the needs of Jewish defense or Jewish education that transcended the individual synagogue would remain unaddressed.

The advantages in the debates discussed here lay with Reform. More affluent and better organized than Traditionalism, its growth had been rapid. In large measure its progress was unchecked because its Traditionalist opponents lacked the unity, the leaders, and the wealth to mount effective resistance. Moreover, Reform in practice and beliefs appeared better suited to the dynamics of change in modern American surroundings. Aside from any appeal it wielded on ideological grounds, it attracted Jews ready to shrug off the values of what they perceived to be a stagnant religious tradition.

A major disputation between Traditionalists and Reformers, represented respectively by Isaac Leeser and Max Lilienthal, took place in 1856–1857. Leeser and like-minded friends and colleagues had felt the winds of change within the Jewish camp even earlier. Their apprehension grew in the first decades of the nineteenth century, when echoes of the clashes between Reformers and Traditionalists in Western Europe—their opinions as well as the innovations they instituted in prayers and schools—resonated in synagogues and rabbinical statements across the Atlantic. Immigrants to the United States from 1840 to 1860, better acquainted with the changes in Germany, brought the new ideas with them. Leeser explained in 1844: "With an increase of immigration from Europe, persons tinctured with all the modern heresies have mingled among us."[4] He blamed the "heresies" on Jewish ignorance and on a keen desire to ape the Gentiles. Americans too, he pointed out, took careful note of measures by Reformers that included both modest changes, like the use of the vernacular in the service, and more extreme acts like the disregard of Shabbat and dietary laws, circumcision, and intermarriage with non-Jews.[5]

Through the pages of the *Occident,* the journal that he founded in 1843, Leeser traced the development of Reform and its "fallacies."[6] Growing out of the Age of Reason and the French Revolution that deified reason and scientific inquiry, Reformers shared with the secular ultraliberals "a rage for destroying" the institutions and laws of the ancients. Instead of fixing the old, Reform preferred to discard it: "Let it then not surprise you that so many systematic attacks are made upon the remains of our ancient learning by persons whose greatest pleasure it is to decry what they do not understand and to despise every thing ancient, as though every day must bring forth a new system of wisdom." A deceptive and insincere movement, Reform indulged in "jesuitical priestly cunning" to mislead the people.[7]

The rabbi applauded free inquiry, and he repeatedly stated that religion could go along with reason, but he denied that scientific advances negated faith. His brief against Reform rested on principles that he had developed and repeatedly explained from the very beginning of the *Occident's* appearance. He criticized the haste of the Reformers who neither detailed their program nor indicated their end goals; working without proper authorization from recognized religious leaders, Reformers made changes that displayed widespread ignorance of the opinions of pre-modern rabbinic sages. Most important, Reformers questioned the basic tenets of Judaism. According to Leeser, they failed to acknowledge that Jews, a separate people, had to guard their separatism in order to preserve the sanctity of Jewish law as well as the traditional concepts of the unity of God and the mission of Israel. To be sure, some of the rabbinic rituals and prayers that were accumulated throughout the ages had outlived their usefulness for the modern Jew—Leeser himself strayed from Orthodoxy with his sermons in the vernacular and his translations of the Bible and prayers into English—but the teachers of Reform indiscriminately hacked away at Tradition and thereby weakened the very foundations of the faith. To live according to the "spirit of the age," which became the mantra of Reformers, did not justify challenges to the absolutes of faith and morals. "Are we to practice immorality because a Louis XIV or Charles II or a George IV happens to set an unblushing example of royal impudence?"[8] Old was not necessarily wrong, Leeser insisted. The precepts of the Lord were unchangeable: "Right is right . . . even if not one man remains faithful."[9]

The barrage of criticism against Reform notwithstanding, Leeser and his friends rarely indulged in ad hominem attacks. The *Occident* opened its pages to articles and letters by Reformers as well as Traditionalists. Leeser at first was generous in his praise of the moderate Reform leader Isaac Mayer Wise, and he reprinted sermons by another moderate, Max Lilienthal, the man who would be his adversary in 1856.[10] When Wise suggested that he and Leeser could work together on behalf of national Jewish unity, the latter was prepared to overlook Wise's Reform sentiments. Unlike other Traditionalists who refused to sit down with the enemy, Leeser was ready to compromise. He tried to explain:

> I am a reformer, as much so as our age requires; because I am convinced that none can stop the stream of time, none can check the swift wheels of the age; but I have always the *Halachah* [normative Jewish Law] for my basis; I never sanction a reform against the *Din* [a basic Law]. I am a reformer, if the people long for it, but then I seek to direct the public mind on the path of the *Din*.

With two objectives in mind, bringing Reform back to tradition and achieving national unity for dealing with problems like Jewish education, Leeser agreed to a meeting of congregational leaders in 1849. But given the divisions within the community the entire project was aborted.[11]

Leeser had compromised for the sake of cooperating with Wise, the man soon to emerge as the influential leader of the rapidly burgeoning German Jewish population of the Midwest. He saw no justification, however, in sparing two rabbis of Charleston's Reform synagogue, Beth Elohim. In 1843 he laced into Gustav Poznanski for introducing the organ into religious services and for abolishing observance of the second day of holidays—changes, Leeser said, that caused disunity within the congregation. He now regretted that he had recommended Poznanski for the post of rabbi before the candidate abandoned his Orthodox beliefs.[12] A dozen years later he tore into a lengthy sermon by Maurice Mayer that bitterly attacked the Talmud and the hypocrisy of Orthodoxy. Saying that God gave the Truth and commanded the rituals, Leeser called for Traditionalists to fight back.[13]

Leeser's reaction to Mayer's abusive comments was one indication of the widening breach between the Traditionalists and the Reformers in the decade after the attempted conference of 1849. Although Reform had begun in individual synagogues with relatively minor emendations to the religious services, it presaged a potential for far-reaching changes. Increased immigration of German Jews after the revolutions of 1830 and 1848 mounted steadily, and the new arrivals, in part because of their liberal political orientation, showed little enthusiasm for enriching the yet scanty resources for preserving the traditional faith. True, the emotional and psychological needs engendered by adjustment to the new environment tended to keep new arrivals within the fold, but alienation from what they equated with the servility of the ghetto militated against the reestablishment of congregations with widespread communal control. Since the American government showed no interest in whether or not Jews opted for religious affiliation, freedom from the synagogue was facilitated. Many immigrants settled in outlying areas of the Midwest, and lacking rabbis, schools, and teachers, Traditionalist institutions had little with which to attract and keep them.

Some Jews were concerned about mass desertions from Judaism and the possibility of communal anarchy resulting from the variety of customs engendered by Reform, but their numbers were largely offset by the majority that preferred to discard religious laws that widened the gap between them and non-Jewish Americans. Dietary laws, for example, limited the free association of Jews with their Gentile neighbors and so did the traditional minutiae of Sabbath observance. For the sake of the Jewish image as well as their own social goals, Jews were also embarrassed by the impressions that Orthodox, or rigid Traditional, religious services left on Christian visitors. Decorum was virtually nil, religious honors were sold, men wearing hats and prayer shawls swayed as they chanted unintelligible Hebrew prayers aloud and independently of each other, and the interminably long service was unrelieved by dignified organ music or modern sermons. While the face of Jewish denominationalism was being shaped—the Orthodox on one side, the Reformers on the other, and the compromisers somewhere in the middle—the signs at least on the surface pointed to an ultimate Reform victory.

The first and last attempt to unify the opposing camps was the Cleveland Conference of 1855. Following the model of the three major conferences of German Reformers a few years earlier, Wise and Lilienthal convened a meeting of religious leaders to hammer out a common ground on matters of Jewish law, liturgy, and education. According to one biographer, Lilienthal, who was now a prominent associate of Wise, wrote newspaper articles explaining the moderate Reform position that he hoped would rule the gathering. For the welfare of future generations, he said, he and Wise proposed a program "to prevent the endless desertions and splits . . . to banish indifference, which has taken hold of a large portion of the Jewish community, and . . . to inspire the Jews with a new love for their religion." Eager not to offend the opposition, he promised that the Reformers would base their recommendations on biblical and Talmudic authority. Indeed, Wise's original platform maintained that the Bible was divinely inspired and so was the Talmud. Since "the Talmud contains the logical and legal development of the Holy Scriptures," the platform affirmed that "its decisions must guide us in all matters of practice and duty." Invitations to the conference had gone out to Traditionalists, but Leeser was the only rabbi who attended for that faction. He said that if the Reformers crafted a system that rested on the Bible and oral tradition, it would be carefully entertained. Delighted with the early passage of Wise's proposals, he believed that his side had scored a crucial victory. Nevertheless, when the Reform-controlled assembly continued deliberations and amended the resolutions on divine inspiration and on the authority of the Talmud, serious opposition from Traditionalist rabbis and synagogues to the conference and to Leeser personally grew in intensity. At first the Philadelphia rabbi did not relinquish the goal of unity for the purpose of restoring the moderate Reformers to Judaism, but the attacks propelled him further to the right. As a result, his influence as a potential mediator among the groups waned considerably, and the lines defining the denominations grew sharper. Meantime, the prestige and reputation of his antagonist in the oncoming debate, Max Lilienthal, were on the rise.[14]

Like Leeser, German-born Lilienthal had witnessed the divisions in his native land between Reformers and Traditionalists, and he too had sided with the latter. At the same time, despite the failure of his mission to

Russia, he remained committed to the need of modernizing Jewish education. He arrived in New York in 1845, where he first ministered to three
congregations. His inaugural sermon expressed opposition to Reform innovations, and in the pulpit he asked only for decorum at services and the
institution of the confirmation ceremony. After a few years as headmaster
of a boarding school for Jewish boys, he was invited in 1855 to fill a pulpit
in Cincinnati.[15] There, in the Queen City, his career took a decided turn
toward Reform. As a friend and close associate of Isaac Wise and a frequent contributor to Wise's newspaper, the *Israelite,* he followed Wise in
the path of moderate Reform.

His new allegiance could hardly have been a total surprise. His experi-
mentation with modern progressive methods in education was sooner the
work of a Reformer than that of a Traditionalist, and so were the changes
on decorum and confirmation that he introduced in his first congregations. While in New York he had also hinted at the rectitude of Reform
within the Talmudic framework. The seeds of change blossomed when he
teamed up with Wise. The latter may have entertained the larger objectives with respect to the development of an American Reform *movement,*
but it was often Lilienthal who worked out the particular points in a logical and scholarly fashion. By the time of the Cleveland conference he was
fully prepared to challenge the Traditionalists.

Points of issue that had absorbed the conference of 1855 were debated
publicly after the meetings closed, but the acrimony generated by the proceedings foreclosed the possibility of resuming the sessions. Moderate Reform and moderate Traditionalism were still fluid categories that could
be changed or even harmonized, but the spirit of cooperation had largely
dissipated. Leeser felt betrayed by Wise's faction, and the friendly association he had enjoyed with the Cincinnati men in the pages of the *Occident*
gave way to new tensions. The Cleveland assembly also laid bare distinctions between Leeser and Lilienthal that would work in a debate to the
latter's advantage. The preparation that he had done for the conference
showed a richer knowledge and deeper appreciation of both Jewish and
secular sources. His skills as a popular writer transcended Leeser's. Blessed
with an engaging style, his writing was far less prolix and better organized
than his rival's. Moreover, since Leeser had begun his public criticism of
Reform as soon as he founded the *Occident,* he did not feel impelled at
times to answer Lilienthal point by point. Unlike a more skilled debater,
he merely directed his audience to articles and sermons he had written

from 1843 to 1856. Lilienthal, however, spent more time studying Leeser's exact words for contradictions and inconsistencies, and his well-taken attacks on the Philadelphian's position came easily.

Leeser did not give up completely on his goal of unity after the Cleveland conference. Although he continued to scorn the arbitrary approach to innovations on the part of individual leaders and congregations, he would have accepted an international assembly of important rabbis to decide the legitimacy of specific reforms. Toward that end he raised a question shortly after the conference: "Are all the measures of the reformers wrong?" Again admitting that he himself favored certain changes, he promised that if "authoritative alteration" restored communal peace, he would not oppose it. The very question, however, was a tactical blunder. Lilienthal cleverly seized on it and welcomed the Philadelphian to the Reform camp. When the latter charged that he had been misrepresented, Lilienthal accused him of self-contradiction and of refusing to confront the pressures of the times within the community. In response Leeser said he would welcome a religious debate provided it was free of Wise's customary "vulgar invective": "We wish to improve, not to please the spirit of the age but the spirit of religion." And so the sparring began. Never a formal debate wherein the two disputants met and presented their positions and rebuttals, it was carried on in the press, with Leeser speaking through the *Occident* and Lilienthal through the *Israelite*.[16] Doubtless the debate harbored personal motives in addition to the issue at stake. Each side was jockeying for communal power and was loath to yield to its rival in any fashion.

Lilienthal fittingly called his first three letters to Leeser, printed in the *Israelite* of December 1856, "The Spirit of the Age." He defined the spirit of the age as the sum of those ideas that governed all aspects of social life and their inescapable effect on religion. His survey began with the Middle Ages. He maintained that Judaism at that time, conforming to the temper nurtured by the Catholic Church outlawing free investigation, reason, and science, also hardened dogma and made study subservient to religious authority and blind faith. According to the spirit of the following age that began with the Protestant Reformation, reason and free inquiry gradually penetrated the thinking of Christians about Jews and of Jews themselves. Moses Mendelssohn and his group, like the later nineteenth-century Reformers, drew fire from the fanatical antirationalist Orthodox, but nevertheless they persisted. What they absorbed from their setting and applied to Judaism contributed to the upward spirit of progress that governed the course of general human history as well as that of their religion. The ideas set into motion by the Protestant Reformation that flowered into political liberalism defined the spirit of the modern age. Judaism could not lag behind the other modern movements. And just as the effect of those ideas embodied in Emancipation was welcomed joyfully, so should their religious form—Reform Judaism—be similarly received. Was it logical for Leeser, Lilienthal asked, to welcome Jewish political rights while simultaneously denying changes in religion? Both stood or fell together.

Lilienthal presented a deterministic scheme of historical development. Positing the ongoing course of progress, his essays on the spirit of the age reduced themselves in essence to the proposition that the rise and progress of Reform Judaism was unstoppable. It followed that the individual Jew, buffeted by the advances in civilization, had little choice in the matter.

In three succeeding letters Lilienthal considered his rival's accusations that Reform had destroyed Jewish unity and had violated rabbinical codes. Reform was not, he retorted, the product of irreligious or capricious minds as Leeser had said but was founded on the "natural development of history" effected by "Divine Providence." He argued that in light of Reform's basic principles it was no longer possible to abide by all the traditional strictures:

> Your [Leeser's] party rests on the medieval principle of authority, the reform party on the acknowledgment of reason, as declared by the spirit of the age. Your party is founded on the unlimited belief in tradition, the reform party on the results of critical and historical investigation. Your party claims equal right and title for all our biblical, traditional, and rabbinical codices; the reform party denies this. Your party asserts that Judaism must remain confined within the limits of its national particularity; the reform party maintains that, according to its messianic ideas, Judaism has to lead the van, in order to accomplish the acknowledgment of the only "One" by the whole human race. Your party expects the fulfillment of this prophetic promise from some supernatural occurrence; the reform party asserts that, in the development of the human race and the dutiful cooperation of men, the ways and means are given for attaining this sublime aim and end.

Instead of living in the past, Reform fired the imagination of the rising generation and signaled "the bright anticipation of the future." Thus, as matters stood, since Reform was a legitimate product of the temper of the times, it could not be undone and disunion was inevitable.[17]

Leeser responded to "The Spirit of the Age" but did not backtrack on previous statements: "The courageous man . . . will be taught lessons of prudence by passing events; yet he will not discard the teaching of bygone experience as the mother of true wisdom." His proof came from the Patriarchs and the Prophets who all acted against the prevailing customs of the age, and he advised Lilienthal to read their stories in the Bible.[18] Lilienthal in turn addressed his fourth letter to an early charge by Leeser on how the Reform movement destroyed rabbinical codes that interpreted the Bible and tradition. He countered with the argument that since premodern rabbinical authorities had sanctioned changes in customs over the centuries, change had long been an acceptable tool. Turning to specific and seemingly outdated practices that still obtained in some Orthodox circles, he asked if Leeser would abide by the prohibition that mandated head coverings for married women. Similarly, would he keep to the bans of carrying on Shabbat or refraining from the use of wine touched by Gentiles. Since the modern age did away with those outdated customs, Leeser would have to admit that retrogression was a "moral impossibility." The Reformer thus impaled his foe on the horns of a dilemma: you can maintain that legislative power on religious matters ceased with the Bible or Talmud, he said, or you can admit that it was bequeathed to later generations. Either way the nineteenth-century Jew had the right to deviate from the decisions of the post-Talmudic sages.[19]

Lilienthal's articles were thoughtful, knowledgeable, and carefully constructed. Leeser, not as well organized, had little new to add to his previous discussions. He repeated his major criticisms, and he continued to challenge Reform's method and its particular beliefs. At the end of January 1857 he posed a series of questions to his rival that ranged from theological tenets to specific practices. Did Lilienthal accept traditional teachings on the coming of the messiah or the restoration of Palestine and the temple service? Did he believe that that all mankind would recognize God's kingdom and law at the end of time? How did he stand on the procedure for admitting proselytes? Was it proper for a Jew on a journey to eat meat slaughtered by a non-Jew or to frequent a public coffee house on the Sabbath? How many times daily should a Jew pray? Was it necessary for him to put on phylacteries and to affix a *mezuzah* on his door? The very questions indicated how far Traditionalism within the entire community had eroded and how ready American Jews were was to discard the Traditionalist responses that Leeser eagerly sought. The Philadelphia rabbi also said that if Lilienthal answered the queries, he, Leeser, would come up with others. He wanted to elucidate, he said, the aims of each side. As matters stood, Reform had matured rapidly by 1857: "It has outgrown its childish age, and presents itself as a rebel against the *Bible,* not to mention the Talmud."[20]

Lilienthal advised his opponent to keep to the central issue, the legality of overhauling both customs and codes. But since Leeser gave no satisfactory reply, he resolved that the "chit-chat" had gone far enough. He planned to publish his articles in Germany where, he said, he was assured of more learned opponents and a more enriching interchange.[21] He thereby signaled the end of the debate, one that lessened the power of the moderates in both camps. Meantime, Lilienthal's position scored higher on the scale of Americanism. It reflected the optimism and belief in progress that the country had symbolized from its beginning, and it echoed the popular belief that men make law and that they could not be eternally fettered by the legal dictates of previous generations. While the Traditionalists, on the defensive, were the standpatters, the antiauthoritarian Reformers exuded an image of vitality so attractive to the newly emancipated American Jew.

In 1894, Kaufmann Kohler, the foremost Reform theologian, delivered a eulogy on the death of Alexander Kohut. Kohler called him an ardent American and eloquent preacher, but he dwelt at greater length on Kohut's scholarship. Out of genuine awe for the man whose Talmudic knowledge was recognized worldwide, Kohler praised the "distinguished master," an "ornament" of Jewry, a "diadem" in the crown of Jewish erudition, who added new luster to American Judaism. Like the rabbis of old, Kohler said, Kohut had a thirst for Jewish learning, and his ideal was to live and, if necessary, to die for the Law. Although he was not fully appreciated in a utilitarian America, he gave an impetus to rabbinic study and research that Gentiles too respected.[22]

It certainly was not unusual for a rabbi to eulogize a colleague, but some might have found Kohler's tribute somewhat puzzling. Without any reference in the eulogy, he had sparred with Kohut less than ten years earlier in another major disputation between a Reformer and a Traditionalist.[23] At that time, the goal of uniting both camps was still elusive, and during the three decades after the Leeser-Lilienthal exchange Reform had become more solidly entrenched. By 1885 it boasted its own rabbinical seminary, Hebrew Union College, and union of congregations, Union of American Hebrew Congregations (UAHC). It had also been reinforced by the immigration of prominent Radical Reform rabbis, intellectuals like Samuel Adler, Samuel Hirsch, and Kohler. While the mass exodus from Eastern Europe was beginning to swell the ranks of the right-wing Orthodox, the condition of the moderate Traditionalists, without new leaders or creative ideas, appeared static. Admittedly, Reform had its problems too. The Darwinian challenge to religion played havoc with the synagogues as it did with the churches, and movements like Ethical Culture, Christian Science, and different forms of spiritualism attracted some affiliated Jews. Religious indifference and ignorance continued to grow, and even Reformers admitted their failure to stay the trend among Jews. Within the Reform movement individual congregations and rabbis often struck out on their own, veering further away from traditional practices and from the moderate course staked out earlier by Lilienthal and Wise. Both Reform and Traditionalism were sorely in need of reinforcements—the former to produce positive content and direction for a movement that was fast threatening American Judaism with anarchy and a spiritual vacuum, the latter to come up with a positive alternative to Reform.

For their needs, the anti-Reformers eagerly hailed the arrival to the United States of Alexander Kohut. Born in Hungary, Kohut came from a learned Orthodox family. He was formally educated in Budapest and at the Breslau Theological Seminary, and he earned his doctoral degree at the University of Leipzig. While still a student he embarked on his lifework, a multivolume dictionary of the Talmud through which he revealed his proficiency in languages and philology. By the time he was invited to the pulpit of New York's Congregation Ahavath Chesed in 1884, the forty-two-year-old rabbi had established a name as an able orator and erudite scholar. In addition to his rabbinical duties he had lectured, published, and served as a district school superintendent. As a result of his public activities he was elected to the Hungarian parliament as a representative of the Jews, a post that he never filled because of his decision to emigrate.

Doubtless it was his fame and not his Traditionalism that accounted for his invitation to Ahavath Chesed. Otherwise the congregation would hardly have had any reason to select him. It was a Reform synagogue: members did not observe the Sabbath, minor holidays, or dietary laws;

during the services the men and women sat together; the services followed a nontraditional prayer book, and music was included. Probably
unfamiliar with American conditions in more than a general way, Kohut
tried to win the congregation back to traditional practices. A sympathetic
friend and biographer who called Kohut a "conservative Reformer" admitted that the rabbi was guilty of occasional inconsistencies but that he
chose the "middle way." A segment of Kohut's inaugural sermon illustrated the point: "Truth, in Religion, is doing God's will. I consider that to
be the truth which is taught by the rabbinical Jewish doctrine, but usages
which cannot be based on the teaching of the Talmud, I reject. . . . I offer
you the old and the new in happy and blended union."[24]

Kohut expatiated on that theme when, three weeks after his inaugural
sermon, he began a series of weekly discourses on the well-known Mishnaic text, *Ethics of the Fathers*. Boldly and in learned fashion he challenged
the religious beliefs and practices of American Jews. He began with the
proposition that the continued existence of the Jewish community rested
on the authority of the Torah and the rabbis, or in other words on commitment to tradition. "The chain of tradition," he said, "continued unbro-
ken from Moses through Joshua, the elders, the Prophets and the Men
of the Great Synagogue, to the latest times. On this tradition rests our
faith, which Moses first received from God on Sinai. On this foundation
rests Mosaic-rabbinical Judaism today; and on this foundation we stand.
Whoever denies this on principle . . . disclaims his connection with the
bond of community of the house of Israel." Clearly, since Reform broke
the chain, it was not the proper course.

Kaufmann Kohler, then rabbi of Temple Beth-El in New York, immediately rose to defend Reform, but despite a series of sermons by Kohler,
Kohut did not give way: "A Reform which seeks to progress without the
Mosaic-rabbinical tradition is a deformity—a skeleton without flesh and
sinew, without spirit and heart. It is suicide." Reform which distilled religious truths into mere principles made Judaism bodiless and caused
its evaporation. Were Jews to burn the bridges to their past and yield to
every whim of irresponsible religious leaders, the result would be chaos
and death. But was all change unacceptable, was Judaism closed forever
or did it need continuous development? Kohut's answer was both yes and
no: "I answer Yes, *because Religion has been given to man;* and as it is the
duty of man to grow in perfection as long as he lives, he must modify
the forms which yield him religious satisfaction, in accordance with the

spirit of the times. I answer No, in so far as it concerns the Word of God
. . . and His unchangeable Law." Only recognized religious authorities, he
concluded, could decide what changes were permissible.[25]

Although a recent arrival to the country, Kohut deplored the perva-
sive religious indifference that he observed. In his opinion the key to the
problem was the dearth of proper American rabbis. The typical rabbi, he
said, preached too much and studied too little. Congregations needed
to respect the authority of their rabbis, but on the congregation lay the
responsibility of appointing men able to deliberate questions of change:
"Only when the rabbis of this country shall be moved by a common endeavor for wise moderation . . . only when conservative progress rather
than ungovernable speed shall characterize our religious movement, can
the outlook for Judaism be hopeful."[26] Kohut wasn't the only rabbi to find
fault with the quality of the rabbinate, but his criticism rested on the basic
issue that divided Reformers and Traditionalists.

Despite Kohut's willingness to entertain proper religious changes, the
anti-Reformers enthusiastically greeted his sermons. Morale rose in Traditionalist circles; they had found a worthy defender. The sermons, which
appeared weekly in the columns of the Anglo-Jewish press, were widely
discussed and attendance at Ahavath Chesed soared. Not that Kohut refrained from criticizing the type of Orthodoxy which he called narrow, fa-
natic, or "blind letter-worship." If Judaism were a "closed book," the result
would be petrifaction. Jews had the right to make changes in religious usages and interpretations of the "non-essentials" in accordance with changing opinions and mores. He gave two examples of justifiable, middle-of-
the-road alterations that might raise the level of piety—the right to excise
certain passages from the traditional prayer book, and the right to permit
mixed seating at synagogue services. Critical of both religious extremes,
Kohut advocated a Judaism of the "golden mean."

Kohut found a scholarly rabbi of equal intellectual acumen in Kaufmann Kohler. Born in Bavaria in 1843, Kohler, like Kohut was raised and
educated in a strictly Orthodox environment. Introduced to secular subjects at the universities of Munich and Berlin, he underwent a spiritual
crisis that led to his break with Traditionalism. His thesis, in which he
suggested the evolution of the "God-idea" among the ancient Hebrews,
also argued for freeing religion from a stagnant past. He chose a rabbinical instead of scholarly career, but since the Orthodox had banned his
book, he had no chance of a post in Germany. In contact with Reform
leaders in the United States, he accepted a pulpit in Detroit in 1869. There

and in his next congregations—he was at the prestigious Temple Beth-El in New York when he debated Kohut—he preached Reform and its relevance for modern man. At first he was associated with the radical wing of American Reform championed by David Einhorn. The latter became his father-in-law as well as his new spiritual father.[27]

Both Kohler and Kohut were battling over the future of American Judaism. They had discussed their theological differences privately, but now they sought a wider audience. Kohler delivered a series of five sermons titled "Backward or Forward," which like Kohut's were given wide coverage in the press.[28] After expressing his respect and "highest regard" for Kohut—it was indeed a very civilized and gentlemanly-like interchange—he began with a flat refutation of his adversary's statement that those who denied the Mosaic-rabbinic tradition were no longer Jews:

> Must we, after having dropped the obsolete observances of by-gone days, after having worked for thirty-five years in this country for emancipation from the yoke of Mosaico-Talmudical Judaism, again bend our neck to wear it in order to be complete Jews in the sense of orthodoxy, or may we persist in claiming, as we did thus far, to stand on a far higher ground, while discarding a great many of the ceremonial laws of the Bible and tradition, and placing ourselves on the standpoint of prophetical Judaism, with the Messianic aim as its world-embracing goal?

While Kohut's Judaism was "retrospective" and looked back to the lifestyle of our forefathers, Reform, Kohler said, looked forward to a brighter future. It was obvious which brand of Judaism was preferable—the one that wailed over the ruins of the past and the downfall of blind worship of authority, or the one that stood for building up a universal religion proclaimed by the Prophets.

Affirming that modern man could not deny the right of free inquiry into religion, Kohler proceeded to deride the minutiae of traditional laws and customs. For example, how relevant was the biblical prohibition on wearing garments made of wool mixed with linen? Should we observe such meaningless practices and explain each as the word of God? The sermon climaxed with a paean of praise to the freedoms inherent in Reform: freedom from the bondage of the letter; freedom for those neglected or excluded, like women, from traditional privileges; "freedom from all fences and hedges which prevent the unfolding of the full truth; freedom from all rust and mould of the past, which disfigure and obscure our bright heritage before the world and check its wholesome growth." The Mosaic-Talmudic tradition that Kohut talked about had outlived its purpose. We look forward and not backward: "Mount Zion" towers high above Mount Sinai.[29]

In his four succeeding sermons Kohler elaborated the same points. Orthodoxy meant fanaticism, intolerance, and observance of petrified forms that collided with modernity. Reform, "a vitalizing power of Jewish history," stood for prophetic ethics that superseded dogmatism, and for superior forms of religious devotion that brought man closer to God and to his fellow men. Kohler declared that the degradation of rabbinism was not his aim, but his words conveyed a different message. He once declared that he preferred "no Judaism at all than that we should bow under the authority of Rabbinism and surrender reason and freedom . . . Rabbinico-Mosaical Judaism is dead." On the other hand, modern Reform was optimistic and progress-oriented. Its essence was "prophetism" and monotheism; it recognized Israel's mission to spread the truths of monotheism and prophetism, and it looked to the "Messianic era of humanity," the highest stage in Judaism's evolution. His emphasis on prophetism and humanity elicited Kohut's disparaging comment—You are only an ethical Jew!—but Kohler stood by his words. Defining Judaism as a living and constantly unfolding revelation, the Reform rabbi totally ignored the plea for moderation on both sides or, as Kohut put it, the golden mean between Traditionalism and Reform. For Kohler it was an either/or proposition—backward with Orthodoxy or forward with Reform.[30]

To be sure, Reform had committed errors, Kohler admitted, and had failed to live up to many expectations. It had overemphasized reason and in the process had sacrificed religious warmth and emotion; it had failed to train the children in the need for daily communication with God; while it busily threw out the "rubbish of the old," it had not introduced enough to replace the old. In sum, it had not yet made the Jew realize that religion was not a law but a positive faculty and privilege of man, "a covenant of God." But Orthodoxy or Traditionalism erred more grievously, for it blinded Jews by a maze of legalisms to the true meaning of their faith and their purpose as Jews. Kohler drew arguments from Jewish law—explaining, for example, how the ancient rabbis had effected change—but he used loaded terms like "ghetto," "Oriental," "liberty," and "progress" to color his brief against Orthodoxy. Although critics charged Kohler with contradictions and inconsistencies, just as others had faulted Kohut, his words sounded more American than those of his adversary. Since Reform's teachings of freedom and tolerance harmonized with the national creed, Kohler's justification of Reform doubtless appealed to those anxious to conform to American tastes. Indeed, both disputants, although relatively new to the United States, were careful to praise the ethos of America.[31]

In many ways the debate of 1885 resembled that of Leeser and Lilienthal. But the superior intellectual level of the second exchange testified to the greater erudition and sophistication of the two disputants. It also revealed how far the quest for an American Judaism had moved from its raw frontier-like stage of pre–Civil War days. The Jewish community was rapidly maturing, and yet the goal of religious unity appeared more unattainable than ever. But the debate had positive results as well. Traditionalists and middle-grounders found a champion in Kohut, and he was enrolled in the ranks of the founders of the Jewish Theological Seminary in 1887.[32] An attempt to blend progressivism and Americanism with a commitment to rabbinical Judaism, that institution became the mother of the Conservative movement in America. At the same time, Reformers like Kohler felt impelled to clarify their position still further.

Kohler called for a conference of Reformers several months after the disputation for the purpose of discussing the requirements of an American Judaism to fit the needs of the time. Scholarly interpretations of the resultant product, the Pittsburgh Platform, have varied, but it was clear to all that Kohler, who dominated the proceedings, aimed for a broad platform, one that was "comprehensive, enlightened and liberal enough to impress and win all hearts, and also firm and positive enough to dispel suspicion and reproach of agnostic tendencies, or of discontinuing the historical thread of the past." Including much of his brief against Kohut, the Pittsburgh Platform remained unchanged for fifty years.[33]

The practice of religious disputations in which one rabbi publicly challenged another on matters of faith and dogma before the community at large subsided after the Kohut-Kohler interchange. To be sure, rabbis in the next century still squabbled among themselves, but Traditionalism versus Reform was no longer a fundamental issue, and matters of concern in both the Jewish and American arenas—such as intermarriage, abortion, church/state separation, Zionism, and gay rights—were handled by the denominations separately. On subjects like those, individual rabbis within the three major groups—Reform, Conservative, Orthodox—usually spoke through their rabbinical and congregational organizations.[34] Nor was it unusual, especially after World War II, for denominations, now represented by lay defense agencies as well as by clerics, to ally themselves with non-Jewish groups. Jews and their congregations were thereby integrated into the American scene still further. Having outgrown the European customs that had shaped their evolution for most of the previous century, they fashioned new patterns of communal organization.[35]

While the two rabbinic disputations contributed to the development of separate denominations, denominationalism in turn often eclipsed the individual rabbi. As the leader of only one synagogue and thus a limited constituency, he became less influential in the larger Jewish community. Except for a few outstanding orators, the rabbis' sermons grew less noteworthy too. Public recognition of the rabbi would depend thereafter on his role in institutions dealing with matters ancillary to the synagogue, like Jewish philanthropy, Zionism, Jewish defense, and academic posts in Jewish studies. Stephen S. Wise and Abba Hillel Silver, for example, were known for their oratory, but their fame reached new heights as Zionist leaders and not as rabbis. For his congregants, the twentieth-century rabbi remained primarily a teacher of synagogue classes and/or the pastor and counselor.[36]

The two nineteenth-century disputations ended attempts to create an American Judaism that united the moderate Traditionalists and moderate Reformers. Leeser had tried in 1856 and Kohut tried in 1885, but both failed. The debates underscored rather how far apart the two sides were. Individual Jews and synagogues could and did move from one camp to another, but they usually followed the lead of the congregation as a whole. No common liturgy or platform was ever adopted, and Isaac Mayer Wise's dream of a "Minhag America"—an American rite for one American Judaism, and the title of his first prayer book—remained just a dream.

6

Restoration to Palestine

Jewish settlers in America brought with them the age-old hope for restoration to Palestine as spelled out in their prophetic teachings and prayers. The traditional belief promised that in the messianic age Israel, by divine action, would be reconstituted as a nation, a holy nation where the glories of Jerusalem and the temple would be restored. But nineteenth-century Jews could not escape the effect of this-worldly ideas on their religion. Against a background of heightened nationalism in Europe and antisemitism on the Continent and in the United States, particularly rampant after 1860, many fixed on Jewish nationalism and a restoration to Palestine as viable here-and-now answers for contemporary Jewish needs. Indeed, before the Basel Congress of 1897 at which Theodor Herzl founded the Zionist movement, they often spoke of some sort of Jewish settlement or colonization in Eretz Yisrael independent of God's timetable. American rabbis too discussed restoration, albeit from different points of view. Their opinions, predicated on their theological and denominational principles, were expressed in the last third of the century usually in connection with developments in international diplomacy or even popular writings. Not only did those opinions indicate how Jewish religious leaders adjusted their articles of faith to pragmatic issues and to the free environment of America, but they also show how Palestine became an issue of contention, hardening divisions among denominations and presaging American Jewish reactions to Herzlian Zionism.

The themes of Zion and of a Jewish restoration to Palestine were not the exclusive province of Jews. Indeed, they had always commanded attention in American religious and secular thought. In colonial New England the Puritans, who incorporated Mosaic law into their civil code and who called their settlements and their children by biblical names, acknowledged the influence of the ancient Hebrews but adapted the theme of Jewish restoration to their own situation. Terms like "the new Jerusalem" or "the new Zion" or "the city on the hill" were not unusual allusions to the Massachusetts Bay colony. During the first decades of the republic, Christians supported missionary societies that propagated ideas on the ingathering of Jews in Palestine in tandem with their conversion to Christianity. As the century wore on, advances in geography and transportation injected a realistic element into Christian interest, and the number of non-Jewish residents, visitors, and pilgrims to the Holy Land steadily increased. Some Christians also expressed their support of a Jewish return to Palestine, and the press reported sporadically on Jewish efforts to buy Jerusalem—a project often attributed to the House of Rothschild and to the Rothschilds' financial involvement in Eastern Europe. Favorable Christian opinion on settling Jews in Palestine, however, did not necessarily derive from a love of Jews. As Martin Luther had said centuries earlier, restoration was the means of removing the hated Jewish race from decent Christian society: "We shall provide them with all the supplies for the journey, only to get rid of that disgusting vermin. They are for us a heavy burden, the calamity of our being; they are a pest in the midst of our lands."[1]

Even before 1881, when racist antisemitism in Europe, especially the brutal pogroms in Russia, sharpened the focus on a refuge for the persecuted, the American Jewish community showed a pragmatic interest in a Jewish Palestine. It was an issue that cut through the Reform and Traditionalist denominations and elicited sympathy as well as opposition. The two wings united only on matters of relief for the needy Jews in Palestine. The missions of Palestinian messengers to the United States in the eighteenth and nineteenth centuries, for example, mustered widespread support among rabbis as well as laity. Like Diaspora Jewry in general, they believed that the pious remnant of students and scholars in Palestinian yeshivas were contributing to the salvation of the entire people, akin to the Christian concept of shoring up grace, and therefore merited financial aid. To be sure, contributions in no way obligated the donors to support restoration, but each of the well-advertised Palestinian missions sparked a new burst of interest in the subject.[2]

Most Reform rabbis had little difficulty in dealing with the issue of Palestine and American Jews. Building on resolutions adopted at the early conventions of German Reformers in the 1840s, they formulated a theology that totally repudiated the traditional belief in a Jewish return to the Holy Land at the end of time. Jews were a religious group and not a nationality; in the words of one prominent participant at the Frankfurt conference of 1845, enlightened contemporary Jews believed that "the destiny of Judaism is not bound up with a Jewish state, but on the contrary, religion itself requires a close and sincere attachment to the commonwealths in which the Jews abide." The messianic age as the early Reformers explained had only a spiritual significance, and biblical prophecies that dealt with a restored Jewish state and temple were anachronistic. A conference of Reformers in Philadelphia in 1869 reaffirmed those principles:

> The Messianic aim of Israel is not the restoration of the old Jewish state
> . . . involving a second separation from the nations of the earth, but the
> union of all men as children of God. . . . We look upon the destruction
> of the second Jewish commonwealth not as a punishment for the sinfulness of Israel, but as a result of the divine purpose . . . which consists in
> the dispersion of the Jews to all parts of the earth, for the realization of
> their high priestly mission, to lead the nations to the true knowledge and
> worship of God.[3]

Sixteen years later the Pittsburgh Platform, the official creed of Reformers for some fifty years, again denied that Israel constituted a nationality or that the traditional messianic hope still had relevance: "We consider ourselves no longer a nation but a religious community, and therefore expect neither a return to Palestine, nor a sacrificial worship under the administration of the sons of Aaron, nor the restoration of any of the laws concerning the Jewish state."[4]

Although not specifically mentioned in the creedal pronouncements, Reform leaders liked to stress the inherent contradiction between a belief in restoration and the prime allegiance of Jews to their country of residence. That principle had been voiced by Western Jewry ever since Emancipation. In 1841 Reform Rabbi Gustav Poznanski of Charleston summed up the sentiment in an oft-repeated statement: "This synagogue is our temple, this city our Jerusalem, this happy land our Palestine."[5] Reformers in the Old and New Worlds added to their anti-restorationist brief as time went on, but for American Reformers the argument that Jews were attached *nationally* only to the lands in which they lived or, in other words, that loyalty to a Jewish homeland was at odds with loyalty to America, became paramount. True, a minority of Reform rabbis sided with the nationalists and restorationists, but they were unable to keep the principal Reform institutions—an organization of rabbis (Central Conference of American Rabbis [CCAR]), an organization of congregations (Union of

American Hebrew Congregations [UAHC]), and a rabbinical seminary (Hebrew Union College)—from lining up against a Jewish state and a Jewish return to Palestine.[6]

Max Lilienthal, a Reform rabbi in Cincinnati, added an interesting footnote to the debate on the conflict of loyalties. He depicted the relationship between Jews and the United States in the form of a contract. Whereas the country was required to maintain the separation of church and state, which was the prerequisite for liberty, equality, and intergroup harmony, Jews were obligated to replace much of their Jewishness with an American identity. Because the United States was living up to its side of the bargain, the Jews had also complied: "Hence, we have given up our sectarian schools and send our children to the [public] schools," and "hence, we have given up all ideas of ever returning to Palestine." In later sermons Lilienthal enumerated all the "obsolete" prayers, including those on exile and restoration that the Reformers had excised from their prayer books in return for full citizenship. He concluded: "We owe no longer any allegiance to Jerusalem, save the respect all enlightened nations pay to this cradle of all civilizing religions. We cherish no longer any desire for a return to Palestine, but proudly and gratefully exclaim with the Psalmist, 'Here is my resting place; here shall I reside; for I love this place.'" If carried further, Lilienthal's "contract" meant that the optimal future of the Jews lay in the United States where, according to Reform's interpretation, the true messianic age would be realized. Just as dual allegiance became central for anti-restorationists and for later anti-Zionists, so did faith in America, the land of promise, become in large measure a surrogate for the traditional faith in Judaism.[7]

Reform rabbis did not debate the issue of divine versus man-made restoration, but the Traditionalists did. On them lay the burden of defending the normative view, which held that restoration would occur in God's good time and at His direction, and that Jews were to refrain from attempts to hasten the messiah's arrival. Accordingly, the ultra-Orthodox dismissed out of hand all talk of a Jewish return to Palestine or any form of political nationalism. Such schemes, some added, encouraged the rise of false messiahs. Moderates, however, found compromises that linked man to the divine process and in essence made him God's partner in that process. One Warder Cresson, a Philadelphian who converted to Judaism and as an observant Jew attempted to promote agriculture among Palestinian Jews, explained the compromise in simple terms. God will bring about restoration, he once wrote in the 1850s, but "it surely must be right for us to endeavor to promote the happy future by some exertions of our own." Nor were those moderates deterred by fears that they were incurring American displeasure. As long as the activity of the restorationists was limited mainly to prayer, public opinion was not aroused.[8]

Isaac Leeser, rabbi of Mikveh Israel in Philadelphia and a leading Traditionalist, discussed his views of a restored Palestine in his monthly journal, the *Occident*. In one article, he devoted much of the piece to a scathing rebuke of contemporary Jews who, denying a belief in a Jewish nation, scorned the traditional prayers for a divinely engineered return. Those prayers, which hoped for the full development of the Jewish character and of Judaism, assured a role in history for the Jewish nation; without such prayers the martyrs and victims of persecution throughout the ages would have died in vain. Even in democratic countries of today, Leeser continued, Jews were subject to disabilities or at least to popular disdain. Only through restoration could they fulfill their mission: "Whether our views be realized, whether speedily or tardily . . . [we] pray for a national restoration, if we have any love for the triumphant though peaceful rule of our religion over our people, and to free them from the moral and physical yoke which will necessarily rest upon us while we have a permanent home nowhere." Elsewhere Leeser explained in more modern terms why Jews needed a state of their own. A Jewish state was a place "where the Jew would not and need not receive his rights as a favor, where there would be no talk of toleration, where there would be no fear of abridgment of privileges, where, in short, the Israelite would be free, not because the stranger grants it, but because his laws, his religion, his faith constitute him a part and parcel of the state itself."

God's role was absolute in restoration, but, the Philadelphia rabbi said, there were signs that human actions played a part in realizing the divine plan. After the European revolutions of 1848 he replaced a religious view of restoration for one that stressed political and practical developments. The international scene was rapidly changing; scientific and mechanical progress was bringing about shifts in population and changes in the balance of power. Hence, it was not totally unlikely that the great powers would take Palestine away from Turkey and place it under the rule of England, France, or Russia. It mattered not if God directed the world powers or if they were moved by this-worldly reasons. Either way they functioned as aids to the Almighty in effecting a Jewish return to their land. Since the article appeared before the Russo-Turkish war of 1877 and the Congress of Berlin of 1878 where the future of the Balkans was considered, Leeser's predictions were hardly farfetched.[9]

Another prominent Traditionalist and a friend of Leeser's, Rabbi Samuel M. Isaacs of New York, was also a mediator on the issue of a divine-human partnership. Sounding much like Leeser, Isaacs spoke through sermons and through the pages of his influential newspaper, *Jewish Messenger*. In 1869 he enthusiastically greeted the opening of the Suez Canal with an editorial called "Palestine Restored." Asking "Is it irrational to connect this extraordinary event with the future of Palestine," the *Messenger* predicted that Jerusalem would be at the center of the revived commercial activity of the Near East. But the canal was a religious omen too. Linked to prophecies of Isaiah and Ezekiel on restoration, it was a sign, Isaacs said, proving that men could work with God in achieving that end. While he maintained that hundreds of thousands of Jews worldwide would seize the opportunity to return to Zion, he lashed out against Reform's claim that the desire for a return conflicted with good Americanism: "If a few demand the abolition of prayers, reciting the Almighty's promise to reestablish the Jewish people in their own land, and charge that those who believe in such restoration cannot be faithful subjects of the country of their birth or adoption, *we* fail to discern the inconsistency of praying that the Temple may be rebuilt [while] maintaining unquestioned allegiance to America, our 'fatherland.'" The editorial concluded: "There is still an undertone of love for the Holy Land which . . . needs but the impulse to be aroused into action. That impetus may be given much sooner than the skeptics of today would credit. Events are pointing to it. This generation may not participate in the return to Palestine, and yet it is possible."[10] Thanks to Leeser, Isaacs, and like-minded men, a bridge between proto-Zionism and moderate Traditionalism was constructed that enabled the moderates to support the rebirth of a Jewish Palestine both before and after the advent of the political Zionist movement.

A few years later, when the *Messenger* reviewed George Eliot's novel *Daniel Deronda*, it enthusiastically praised the book that defended the ideal of a reconstructed Zion, a "new polity" to be the "organic" center of Jews worldwide. Again the newspaper considered the question of leaving restoration exclusively to God. To be sure, it said, Judaism warns us not to speculate about the ways through which God would reestablish Zion, but some work by mankind needs to be done as well. In the eyes of the *Messenger, Daniel Deronda* was a link in the human endeavor.[11]

After 1870 the opinions of Leeser and Isaacs appeared more credible.

Unrest on the part of ethnic groups in the Balkans and the intervention of the great powers in the Eastern problem added a new dimension to widespread considerations of a Jewish Palestine. Both sympathizers and opponents now admitted that the future of that country depended on international diplomacy. In 1876 the *Daily Gazette* of Cincinnati printed a long article happily heralding the coming of a restored Jewish Palestine endorsed by the world powers: "It is not impossible that the Hebrews may yet, with the fall of the Ottoman Empire, be renationalized in their own land, and stand at the head of the future advancing civilization of the East. . . . It looks as if the restoration of the Jewish nationality in Palestine were now emerging from the realm of prophecy into that of actual history." European diplomacy might delay the event, but "the event itself is certain." Other Christians spoke at same time on the imminence of restoration. A sympathetic writer in the *Atlantic Monthly* told of the difficulties in reviving agriculture among Jews in Palestine, but he confidently believed that with the talk then current about a Jewish restoration the land could bloom again.[12]

Many proto-Zionists, like the writer in the *Atlantic Monthly,* talked specifically of revived agriculture as well as commerce in a restored Palestine. The reasoning reflected the common view of many Christians and Jews on the abnormality of the Jewish people who stayed away from working the land and devoted their energies to a life of business and commerce. But if that was an abnormality, it was fast becoming an American characteristic. Increasingly, the effects of the transportation revolution and the rapid strides of industrialization indicated that America's agricultural economy would soon give way to an urban, capitalistic one. Nevertheless, the "agrarian myth," or the long-ingrained belief that virtue and morality inhered in an attachment to the soil—which influenced Zionist thought too—lived on.

The mid-century debate in the Anglo-Jewish press on a return to Zion continued. Reform leader Isaac Mayer Wise challenged the opinions of those like the *Gazette* and the *Messenger* in the columns of his weekly, *American Israelite.* He once wrote:

> In all these beautiful words there are but two slight mistakes, . . . the Jews do not think of going back to Palestine among Bedouins and sandy deserts, and the nations in power do not want them to go there. No European country today would give permission to the Jews to emigrate with their wealth or even without it; and the European Jews have as little an

idea to go as the Rothschilds want to purchase Palestine or be kings of the Jews. It is all dream and fantasy.

Moving from the practical to the theological, the rabbi charged that the idea of a return contradicted the course of history. As the Reformers confidently preached, man was moving toward the establishment of God's kingdom on earth, an era in which all mankind would unite in the worship of one god and the entire world would become "one promised land." With a swipe at the Traditionalist supporters of restoration, Wise added: "Let those who are narrow-minded enough to tie the world's destiny to the soil of a certain strip of country [do so, but] we do not. We expect and will see it come, the unification of the human family, the triumph of truth, and the dominion of goodness."[13] Wise's universalistic posture, which characterized the tenets of Reform, contrasted sharply with the then-current European mood of hypernationalism, but it remained at the core of Reform's anti-Zionism well into the twentieth century.

Wise repeatedly attacked Christian as well as Jewish optimistic predictions on the prospects of restoration. Doubtless he drew some comfort from the fact that Rabbi Sabato Morais of Philadelphia sided with him. Morais, a recognized leader of the Traditionalists and a foremost critic of Reform's theology, spoke out against an imminent Jewish return to Palestine. He had been a fervent Italian nationalist, but Jewish political nationalism was a different matter. True, he preached on the need to preserve a Jewish nationality and the hope for divine restoration. He admitted too that "the Jew will not enjoy tranquility . . . until he possesses a country and a flag." But when and how restoration would occur rested in God's hands. For several pragmatic reasons he also denounced the scheme of man-made restoration as a "chimera." Emancipated Jews would not leave the countries to which they were so strongly attached, especially since a restored but underdeveloped Palestine promised them no benefits. More important for Morais, ideas of a premature messianic age actually delayed the coming of that age. He insisted that Israel first had to carry out its earthly mission as the educator of mankind:

Not by the mere possession of a patch of ground guaranteed by protocols is the aspiration of the pious; not for that they daily supplicate the throne of grace . . . but for the glory of having caused the Divine Spirit to rest on all flesh, for the supreme joy of feeling that doctrines [once] rejected and despised are universally accepted and revered. . . . Then the supremacy of the priest people will be recognized, and . . . [there will be] a regenerated Jerusalem.[14]

Since both Orthodoxy and Reform preached the mission of the Jews, Morais's words may not have sounded so different from Wise's, but unlike Wise he held fast to traditional beliefs in a Jewish nationality and a divinely engineered restoration.

Discussions continued on the issue of a return to Zion, but after 1881 they were marked by a note of extreme urgency. Renewed persecutions and pogroms in czarist Russia that lasted until World War I unleashed a mass emigration of East Europeans. Jews worldwide pondered how best to relieve their fellow Jews and how best to direct them to the most suitable refuges. Inevitably Palestine was drawn into the calculations, and the issue of divine versus man-made restoration paled in significance. At the same time, some Jews took the matter of restoration into their own hands. A group known as *hovevei Zion* (Lovers of Zion) was organized in Russia for the purpose of encouraging Jewish settlement in Palestine. Closely allied to them was the *bilu* (an acronym in Hebrew of the words "O house of Jacob, come let us go") movement, which consisted of the few pioneers who went to Palestine and actually cleared the land and drained the swamps. In the West, banker Baron Edmond de Rothschild, a supporter of the *hovevei Zion,* inaugurated ambitious plans for establishing settlements and developing the economy in a yet barren country. American branches of the Lovers of Zion were established during the 1880s and 1890s, but most lasted only a few years. Philanthropic rather then nationalistic, they focused on the victims in Russia, and from their American audience they asked nothing that would seem to compromise Jewish loyalty to the United States. Supported in the main by recent immigrants from Eastern Europe and a few Traditionalist rabbis, their activities were largely ignored in English sermons and rabbinical statements.[15]

In response to the Russian atrocities, the poet Emma Lazarus composed a series of popular articles under the title of *Epistle to the Hebrews* (1882–1883). The daughter of an old and prominent Jewish family of New York, and a protégé of Ralph Waldo Emerson, she labored throughout her life and in her major writings to find an identity that blended her Jewishness with her Americanism. Despairing of a future for Jews in Europe, she called in the *Epistle* for a modern Jewish state. She was also involved with the East Europeans who fled to America in dire straits, and in 1883 she organized the very short-lived Society for the Improvement and Emigration of East European Jews whose purpose was to raise funds for sending Jews to colonize in Palestine. Influenced by the writings of George Eliot and Leo Pinsker, the precursor of Zionism in Russia who wrote *Auto-emancipation*, and by Laurence Oliphant, British journalist and author of *The Land of Gilead* on behalf of a Jewish return to Palestine, she, like them, believed that only Jewish resettlement in a land of their own could ameliorate the problem of anti-Jewish persecution. The answer to racial antisemitism was the revivification, *by Jews themselves,* of the Jewish spirit and talents in a Jewish land. She too stressed that American Jews were not called on to commit themselves existentially to a new nationality or settlement. Despite that usual disclaimer by the supporters of colonization in Palestine, their opponents continued to raise the specter of dual loyalties. Nor did they accept Lazarus's definition of Jews as a modern nationality.

Rabbinical leaders who commented on Lazarus's proto-Zionism usually adhered to the positions they had carved out before 1881. For example, Isaac Wise jeered at Lazarus's "romantic" notion of race or nation and advised that her energies would be better spent in working for the eradication of Christian prejudice; Sabato Morais repeated what he had said years before: beware of those who support a premature messianic age, because they actually delayed the coming of the messiah and God's plan of restoration. Disagreeing with Wise and Morais, H. Pereira Mendes, rabbi of the prestigious Sephardic synagogue of New York, Shearith Israel, spoke out in favor of Lazarus's opinions.

In the same vein as Leeser and Isaacs before him, Mendes, a moderate Traditionalist, offered a compromise in 1883 for reconciling traditional beliefs in restoration with human efforts. Congratulating Oliphant and Lazarus for encouraging Jewish settlement in Palestine, he optimistically thought that conditions favoring a Jewish return were improving. The commercial possibilities of Palestine had been disclosed, and it was not unlikely that the world powers which had recently intervened in the Balkans against Turkey would act similarly with respect to Palestine. Proof, Mendes concluded, that the prophecies of restoration were "echoed by the voice of History, endorsed by the Law of Human Progress, strengthened by the Law of Justice." God may have predetermined the course of history and the laws of progress and justice, but men collectively carried out His design.[16] Like other compromisers among the Traditionalists, Mendes never said how much God and man would each contribute.

One significant change in the wake of the *Epistle* was the shift in position by the *Jewish Messenger*. As discussed above, the founder and first editor of the paper, Rabbi Samuel Isaacs, was a Traditionalist who supported restoration. After his death his son and new editor, Rabbi Abram Isaacs, aired opposing views. An editorial under the title "A Problematic Champion" denounced Emma Lazarus for spreading the idea—one heartily endorsed by racist antisemites, Isaacs said—that Jews were aliens and strangers who could only be patriots in Palestine. The schemes of Oliphant and Lazarus were "unwise and impractical," he added, and the talk of a Jewish nationality and of a Jewish restoration was an "Oliphant-asy."[17]

A piece by Lazarus that appeared in February 1883 in *Century Magazine* along with a critique by Isaacs carried the debate to a wider audience. Lazarus included a brief survey of the persecution and suffering endured by the Jews throughout their history, and she recounted with deep feeling the torments inflicted on the Jews by the Christian church ever since the reign of Emperor Constantine. Forced into occupations like money lending, pre-modern Jews, "a race of high moral and intellectual endowments," often faced massacres and expulsions. Emancipation in the wake of the French Revolution gave Jews the rights of citizens in the Western world. Where restrictions were removed they showed exemplary loyalty to the lands in which they had made their homes, and they contributed meaningfully to the progress of civilization. Nevertheless, Lazarus insisted, "all the magnanimity, patience, charity, and humanity, which the Jews have manifested in return for centuries of persecution, have been thus far inadequate to eradicate the profound antipathy engendered by fanaticism and ready to break out in one form or another . . . at any moment." The clouds had lifted for a short while only, she warned, but modern Jews, despite a willingness and ability to assimilate, were, in the last quarter of the nineteenth century, again a favorite target of prejudice. From the atrocities in Russia to social discrimination and exclusion in free America, they were yet a race deemed alien and unacceptable. Her answer: *They must establish an independent nationality.*[18]

Convinced that any other solution for antisemitism was at best temporary, Lazarus insisted that the hope of restoration was widespread among both Jews and Christians. The Jews, a race whose creative powers would be reawakened in their own land, would furnish "a new Ezra for their own people." She concluded with a quotation from Mordecai, the spiritual hero of *Daniel Deronda*: "Revive the organic center. Let the unity of Israel which has marked the growth and force of its religion be an outward reality. . . . When our race shall have an organic center, a heart and brain to watch and guide and execute, the outraged Jew shall have a defense in the court of nations . . . And the world will gain as Israel gains."

Isaacs's response came in a letter to the editor of the *Century Magazine.* Although the rabbi appreciated Lazarus's "admirable" historical summary of antisemitism, he continued to deride her proposed solution. Denying that Jews en masse were interested in restoration, he predicted that "every attempt, under present circumstances, to colonize Palestine on any large scale with a view of organizing a Jewish nation" was simply a utopian fantasy that was doomed, in his words, to go up in smoke. As before, Isaacs reacted most sharply to Lazarus's defense of a separate Jewish nationality, particularly at a time when extremist Jew-haters were questioning Jewish loyalty to their adopted lands. But if emigration to Palestine was not the solution to the problem of Russian Jews, then what was?

Isaacs, who believed in the future of Jews and Judaism in the Diaspora, thought that Russian Jewry must remain in Russia. He had two suggestions—first, that Russian Jewish spokesmen mount a fight for Jewish rights; second, that with the aid of wealthy men the Jews be prepared for citizenship by proper "civilizing" schools to train their children. A third condition, one admittedly not within the power of the Jews, was a Russian church that would "strive to awaken a Christianity more in accord with the gentle teachings of its Founder." Isaacs was unrealistic but optimistic. He predicted that if his conditions obtained, the Jewish problem in Russia would be solved in ten or twenty years. Doubtless the rabbi's position found favor with many American Jews; not only did it reflect their dread of any challenge to their patriotism, but also it freed them of any direct responsibility for their "uncivilized" Russian brethren.

Not unexpectedly Reformers hardened their stand against a return to Palestine in the 1880s. Kaufmann Kohler, the rabbi who had been a dominant presence at the Philadelphia and Pittsburgh conferences, took the lead. In the course of a well-publicized debate in 1885 with Rabbi Alexander Kohut, a moderate Traditionalist newly arrived from Hungary, he defended Reformers and their beliefs against Kohut's serious challenges. In one sermon delivered on the Fourth of July he seized the opportunity to repudiate the traditional hope for Palestine which he juxtaposed with American Jewish love for the United States. He said in part:

> We cannot afford any longer to pray for a return to Jerusalem. It is a blasphemy and a lie upon the lips of every American Jew. . . . We love

Jerusalem as the cradle of our national existence, but we do not long for a return. We behold in Jerusalem's overthrow, not a fall, but a rise to higher glory. For us Zion stands for the fulfillment of humanity's keenest hopes and loftiest ideals . . . and "every city of Brotherly Love" forms a part and link of the same. Consequently, we perceive in the jubilant tocsin peals of American liberty the mighty resonance of Sinai's thunder. We recognize in the Fourth of July the offspring of the Sixth of Sivan [traditional date for God's granting of the Torah]. We behold in the glorious sway of man's sovereignty throughout this blessed land the foundation stone for the temple of humanity we hope and pray for.[19]

The same factors that sparked Jewish discussions of a return to Palestine inspired talk on the subject by non-Jewish Americans too. Not all commentators were concerned primarily with the needs or welfare of the Jews. The hate-mongers among them preached rather that modern states would be the chief beneficiaries if the Jew—the eternal alien and indigestible substance within Christian society who conspired against Christendom—were to leave for Palestine.

Less venomous in tone was the voice of Anna Laurens Dawes, the daughter of a Massachusetts senator and a member of proper Bostonian society. She was a racist but hardly a rabble-rouser. Dawes published a long essay called *The Modern Jew: His Present and Future* in which she claimed that Jewish removal to Palestine was the only logical answer to the Jewish Question. She dwelt at length on the admirable qualities of the Jews in history and their contributions to world civilization, but her sincere appreciation changed abruptly when she considered the contemporary Jew and the reasons for antisemitism. Building on the premise of the Jew's racial distinctiveness, she discussed Jewish "faults," and like the outspoken antisemites she elaborated on what she called the Jewish refusal to relinquish their "race bond." If not total assimilation, which included abandonment of circumcision, the Sabbath, and dietary restrictions, the one remedy short of extermination was "wholesale colonization" in Palestine. The world had awakened to the potential of Palestine and its strategic and diplomatic importance. Despite obstacles posed by a divided Jewry and by the larger society, the outlook for successful colonization, buoyed by an awakening Jewish national consciousness, looked bright.[20] The popularity of Dawes's work, reprinted in 1889, indicated how well it was received by aristocratic circles in New England.

Pre-Herzlian Christian support of a Jewish settlement in Palestine peaked in the Blackstone Memorial of 1891. William Blackstone of Chicago, a successful businessman and devout Christian who was genuinely moved by the victimization of the Russian Jews, composed a memorial to President Benjamin Harrison. He asked that the president and secretary of state convince the European powers and Turkey to participate in an international conference considering how best to solve the problem of the Jews. After having spent a short time in the Near East, he found a simple answer: "Why not give Palestine back to them again? According to God's distribution of nations it is their home." Once important for both agriculture and commerce, the land of the Jews was "the center of civilization and religion." Blackstone thus envisioned a restored Palestine, one that more than justified Jewish claims to the land. He buttressed his answer with pragmatic reasons—Jewish and Christian sentiment in favor of a Jewish restoration, the poverty of Turkey that would enable "rich Jewish bankers" to fund a portion of the transaction, and precedents for such international action—but his primary argument was the divine promise:

> There seem to be many evidences to show that we have reached the period in the great roll of the centuries, when the ever living God of Abraham, Isaac and Jacob is lifting up His hand to the Gentiles (Isa. 49:22) to bring his sons and daughters from far, that he may plant them again in their own land. . . . Not for twenty-four centuries, since the days of Cyrus, King of Persia, has there been offered to any mortal such a privileged opportunity to further the purposes of God concerning His ancient people.

Blackstone amassed over four hundred signatures to the memorial, many from the ranks of prominent government officials and publishers. Eight rabbis signed the petition, but opinion in both the Jewish and Christian communities divided sharply. Two Reform rabbis in Chicago, the venerable Bernhard Felsenthal who was a personal friend of Blackstone's and the radical Reformer Emil G. Hirsch, were pitted against each other—the former in support of the memorial, and the latter opposed to what he called a "fool's errand." Other Reformers again raised the arguments that restoration contradicted the true mission of the Jews and that it cast suspicion on the loyalty of American Jews to the United States. Some among them, like Rabbi Solomon Schindler of Boston, went on to warn that Zionism would increase popular antisemitism. In light of the fact that Reform was the strongest and wealthiest organized Jewish denomination, its arguments on allegiance doubtless swayed non-Jews to its stand. A variation of the loyalty issue appeared in the *Jewish Messenger*. Adhering to the anti-restorationist policy of Rabbi Abram Isaacs, the newspaper cautioned Jews in its usual timid fashion to avoid issues that brought notoriety and suspicions of disloyalty. Invoking the age-old specter of *mah yomru ha-goyyim* (what will the Gentiles say?), it advised Jews to keep a low profile and not invoke restoration to Palestine in the face of antisemitism. Nothing tangible came of Blackstone's scheme, but the widespread attention that it aroused testified to both the growing concern over the Jewish problem in Eastern Europe and its fallout in the United States.[21]

During the 1890s, at a time when the European powers were embarked on imperialist ventures in Africa and Asia, the Jewish Question continued to loom large. The *Readers' Guide to Periodical Literature,* for example, introduced a new category called simply the "Jewish Question" for the volume covering 1890–1899. A wide variety of subjects was subsumed under that title, including the general condition of the Jews in Europe, specific manifestations of antisemitism, and a return to Palestine. During that decade ongoing persecution and expulsions in Russia persisted, and so did antisemitic attacks by European Jew-baiters whose articles and personal appearances in the United States fanned the flames of American racism.[22] Exacerbating the plight of Jews still further, the Western nations, who feared the influx of hordes of poverty-stricken aliens, were tightening restrictions on the immigration of Russian Jewish refugees. Finally, the Dreyfus Affair, a severe jolt to Western Jews, proved that even assimilated Jews in the free countries were hardly immune to Jew-hatred. More than ever, conditions seemed ripe for the appearance of Theodor Herzl.

An assimilated Jew who was influenced by the currents of European hypernationalism and what he described as ineradicable antisemitism, Herzl found his answer to the Jewish Question in a Jewish *state*. He outlined a bold plan for achieving statehood in his book, *The Jewish State* (1896) and at the congress at Basel that he convened a year later. There the Zionist platform or Basel program was formulated and the World Zionist Organization was officially launched.

Herzl's well-publicized activities accounted for the continued debate among American rabbis on aspects of Zionism. Some repeated or elaborated their earlier opinions, and others assumed new postures. A good example of those who changed their minds was Gustav Gottheil. Only five years before he "converted" to Zionism and became president of the

Federation of American Zionists, predecessor of the Zionist Organization of America, Gottheil sounded very much like other loyal Reformers. At the World's Parliament of Religions in 1893 he had stated:

> Palestine is venerable to us as the ancient home of our race, the birthplace of our faith, the land where our seers saw visions and our bards sang their holy hymns; but it is no longer our country in the sense of ownership, ancient or prospective; that title appertains to the land of our birth or adoption; and "our nation" is that nation of which we form a part, and with the destinies of which we are identified, to the exclusion of all others.

A decade later the New York rabbi spoke differently: "There is no such thing as an anti-Zionist. . . . How can anyone in whose veins flows Jewish blood oppose the movement?"[23]

As in the pre-Herzlian period the rabbis continued to discuss the shifting developments on the world and Jewish scenes that bore on Zionism and that influenced public opinion. Now as opposed to the earlier discussions the political and practical obstacles facing the movement received greater emphasis. The views of the rabbis still differed, and only during World War II, when an overwhelming majority came out in support of a Jewish homeland, was a decisive consensus reached.

Some themes broached in the proto-Zionist discussions during the last third of the nineteenth century persisted. One concerned the nature of the movement itself: Was a return to Palestine religious or secular? Herzl himself preached in secular, political terms. A Jewish *state* to be licensed by international fiat and built by the efforts of ordinary Jews would, he said, resolve the problem of worldwide and persistent antisemitism. God and religion were hardly factors in the equation. Early critics had charged that a secular movement would make Zionism alien to Judaism, but Herzl focused strictly on *pragmatic* considerations—an emphasis on international diplomacy, rampant persecution in Eastern Europe, the growth of nationalism among subject minorities, the ability of Jews to create an autonomous homeland, and the economic potential of a newly developed country. To be sure, Traditionalists no longer debated the issue of man-made versus divine restoration; they insisted rather that religion would play a positive role in developing a future Jewish state. Toward that end one faction founded a separate organization, Mizrachi, dedicated to the establishment of a state grounded in Jewish tradition where the voice of Orthodoxy would be heard in civil as well as religious matters. Nevertheless, the political and secular emphases of Herzlian Zionism remained fixed at least until World War I and the Balfour Declaration of 1917.

Longer lasting and more important to American Jews was the issue of the compatibility of Zionism with American loyalty. Opponents of Zionism, Jews and non-Jews, adopted an either/or position. Positing that national loyalty was a monolith, they continued to charge that a Jew who supported the idea of a Jewish state cast suspicion thereby on his professions of loyalty to the United States. True patriotism, they said, demanded that his Jewish attachment yield to the American. Reform rabbis had piously affirmed their exclusive fealty to the United States for many years. "First Americans and then Jews," was the way Max Lilienthal had put it in 1870, and they reaffirmed such sentiments during the formative years of American Zionism. In response to the Basel program of 1897 the organization of Reform rabbis resolved that they "totally disapprove of any attempt for the establishment of a Jewish state. . . . Such attempts . . . infinitely harm our Jewish brethren . . . by confirming the assertion of their enemies that the Jews are foreigners in the countries in which they are at home, and of which they are everywhere the most loyal and patriotic citizens."[24] The number of Reform's Zionist supporters grew during the Hitler era, but the opposition, now a minority position, did not evaporate entirely. In 1942 some Reform rabbis, fixed on the idea of dual loyalties and spearheaded the establishment of the rabidly anti-Zionist American Council for Judaism.

For their part, American Zionists were not oblivious to the issue of incompatible loyalties. Even their nineteenth-century precursors had carefully disclaimed any diminution of allegiance to the country. Their purpose, the Lovers of Zion and rabbis like H. Pereira Mendes and Bernhard Felsenthal said, was only to provide a refuge for foreign victims of persecution. In effect that was a two-sided disclaimer: (1) It exempted the United States from the charge of antisemitism, the basis on which Herzl predicated political Zionism, and (2) it exempted American Jews from any existential commitment to settle in Palestine. On those grounds Zionism in the United States quickly became a form of refugeeism. Since American Jews hardly fit the category of refugees, Zionism was no more than a philanthropy for victims of persecution that demanded only financial, political, and moral support.[25]

In the new century Zionism brought a major change in the role of the

American rabbi. The men discussed above, religious leaders all, reached the laity through the pulpit and the press. But their successors, many of whom became prominent in national Zionist organizations, now gained influence as leaders of a *secular* movement.[26] Such rabbis did not alter the areligious cast of Zionism, but Zionism altered their functions and public image. Immersed principally in Zionist affairs, men like Stephen Wise, Solomon Goldman, Abba Hillel Silver, and even their less famous colleagues in far-flung communities, won recognition in non-Jewish circles because of their work for Zionism. For some rabbis Zionist duties took precedence over their congregational functions, and to the average American Jew those rabbis were Zionist leaders first and rabbis only second. In the long run, while the Zionist movement may have enlarged the scope of the rabbis' secular activities, it simultaneously pared down the influence of *rabbinical* authority. The opinions of most rabbis as religious leaders on the subject of Zionism mattered less in the twentieth century than they had in the nineteenth.

7

Rabbis under Attack

Reform rabbis were put on the defensive in 1894 when a prominent layman, Leo N. Levi of Texas, attacked them for their lack of principles and their inconsistencies. Levi challenged the amorphous nature of the Reform movement, or what he called a state of "anomie," and the changes in theology and observance initiated by Reformers. He aimed his attack at the heart of the movement. Hinting at the desirability of reducing Judaism to a fixed creed, he called for answers to two questions: What is Judaism? Who has the authority to alter traditional beliefs and practices? For the moment the rabbis were irritated, even infuriated, but the episode ended without any satisfactory agreement on the essentials of the Jewish faith. Nor did the Reformers reach any consensus on the qualifications for rabbis who made changes in Jewish law. Surprisingly, the episode was self-contained. Concerned religious leaders paid scant attention to the possibility that Levi's criticism could trigger a mass revolt within Reform congregations or that it augured ill for the survival of Jewish identity in America. As for Levi himself, the incident left no lasting scars on his career of communal service.

During the last two decades of the nineteenth century the Reform movement in the United States came to full bloom.[1] While its emendations of Traditionalism proceeded at a dizzying pace, its tripartite structure—a rabbinical seminary (Hebrew Union College), a lay organization of congregational leaders (Union of American Hebrew Congregations [UAHC]), and a rabbinical organization (Central Conference of American Rabbis [CCAR])—took root, and its lordly temples commanded the notice and respect of Christian America. With little significant opposition from Traditionalist leaders, Reform and the future of American Judaism appeared to be one and the same.

At the same time, however, challenges to Reform hegemony were multiplying. After 1880 the hordes of East European immigrants, who rapidly outnumbered the German-dominated established order, were unlikely candidates for the Reform movement. Indeed, their rabbis more often than not held negative views of Reform and spoke of a bleak future for American Judaism.[2] Those newcomers who held on to religion usually established their own Orthodox congregations that presaged a formidable counterforce to Reform. Competition to Reform's influence was also inherent in a newly created Jewish Theological Seminary and the yet dormant seeds of Conservative Judaism, a twentieth-century movement that would appeal in particular to children of the immigrants. From an antithetical direction came the stirrings of secular Zionism that denied the major premises of Reform: that Jews were no longer a people and that Judaism was no more than a religion.

Like American religions in general, Reform was also hit by new intellectual currents within the larger American society when the teachings of secularism, evolution, and biblical criticism invaded the churches and universities. Under their impact Judaism was targeted by theologians and clerics who taught "scientifically" that Christianity was a higher form of religion and that the faith of the Jews was but a fossilized relic of an earlier age. Simultaneously, the Social Gospel movement and the enthusiasm it generated among Christians posed a problem of a different sort. In response, some Reform rabbis and congregations turned to social justice, the Jewish equivalent of Social Gospel, and substituted humanitarian reforms for religion and Jewish identity. Finally, and not the least of all the challenges, a rising tide of social discrimination on the part of fellow Americans targeted all Jews, the acculturated and the immigrants, the Traditionalists and the Reformers. Again, Jewish faith and religious observance were on the line, and it was left to the Reformers, the most rooted and acculturated American Jews, to find appropriate defenses.[3]

A contemporary description by a Charleston rabbi called attention to various elements that accounted for what he called the "parlous state" of Judaism in America:

> The writings of . . . Charles Darwin, Tyndall and Spencer, which had played havoc with the Church, was playing no less havoc with the synagogue. Indifference to all things Jewish prevailed everywhere. Ethical Culture, Christian Science, Spiritualism and the various occult movements were winning an ever-increasing number of adherents from the ranks of Judaism. In some Reform pulpits, the cherished traditions of Israel were openly flouted and a dangerous Universalism was being preached. The

Abrahamic Covenant was denounced as a relic of barbarism, a Sunday Sabbath advocated, and the dietary laws declared to be only antiquarian superstitions. The latest utterance of the last-printed scientific book was the religious pabulum of many Reform congregations.[4]

Compounding all those pressures, threats from within its ranks to the strength and unity of the movement shook organized Reform still further. The determined efforts of Reform rabbis to rid Judaism of age-old rituals and a sense of peoplehood, all in the name of rationalism and universalism, resulted in a cold and unsatisfying product that failed to stir allegiance, let alone passion, among the American-born children of Reform congregants.[5] Defections from the temples increased. Some Jews went to the Ethical Culture movement, some became freethinkers or atheists, some considered merger with the Unitarians, and many were, as others called them, simply "nothingarians."

For rabbis to differ with rabbis, laymen with laymen, and congregations with congregations over how far Reform should take its changes in doctrine and practice was characteristic of all stages of the movement's development. And it was not unusual for individual Orthodox or Traditionalist Jews to lash out publicly against Reform leaders and what they claimed was the movement's religious bankruptcy.[6] It was quite another matter, however, when a prominent Reform layman joined the open attack. Such was the case in 1894 of Leo N. Levi of Galveston, Texas. A well-known speaker and writer, the thirty-eight-year-old attorney was invited to address the council of the UAHC at its biennial convention. Speaking on "The Ideal Rabbi," he sparked an uproar within the Reform camp. The storm blew over in a short time, but it exposed longer lasting issues that continued to beset the course of American Judaism.

The son of an immigrant from Alsace, Levi was born in Texas in 1856. He studied law at the University of Virginia, where he scored well scholastically and earned a reputation for his debating skills. At the age of twenty he joined a prominent law firm in Galveston and was soon made a partner. In that bustling commercial center, which was home to roughly one thousand Jews, he became known for his legal and civic work and for his role in Jewish communal affairs. He served as president of his synagogue, B'nai Israel, and was an active participant in the local lodge of B'nai B'rith and the councils of the UAHC. Chosen as national president of B'nai B'rith in 1900, he spent the last few years of his life in New York.[7]

Levi had pondered the course of Judaism in the United States for some time before his address to the UAHC. He had lectured in 1884 on various aspects of American Jewish development, and at the urging of some listeners had written a long essay, "The Jews of Today: Their Status and Duties," that was serialized for twenty weeks in the leading Reform newspaper, the *American Israelite*. Replete with a brief historical sketch of medieval and post-Emancipation Jewry, and buttressed by impressive references to the works of philosophers, historians, scientists, and men of letters, the essay addressed the problem of American Jewish indifference to Judaism. Levi, who posited his personal veneration for Jewish tradition, maintained that in order for Jews to fulfill their destiny in service to mankind, they had to maintain their integrity as a people and preserve the legacy of Jewish beliefs and rituals. He agreed that manners and customs changed, but he was wary of Reform practices. He charged that the rabbis initiated changes without proper authority and that they went to extremes in hastily discarding rituals. Instead, he insisted, they should have followed a course of "conservative and gradual alteration." When he said that changes in ritual required the sanction of a recognized authority, he was raising the possibility of calling a synod to fill the need.[8] The essay did not bother Rabbi Isaac Wise, the editor of the *American Israelite* and the leader of the American Reform movement. He too had his differences with the Radical wing of Reform, and Levi had specifically categorized him as a moderate, and hence acceptable, Reformer.

Levi's essay was reworked into a short book appearing in 1887 entitled *The Jews of America*. There, among other issues, the author again criticized "revolutionary" Reform while emphasizing the need to preserve the integrity of Judaism and Jewish peoplehood through conservative change.[9] That same year, now focusing exclusively on the abuses of Reform and without distinguishing clearly between moderates and Radicals, he wrote a serious attack that appeared in *Menorah* magazine. Since the piece in *Menorah* was a direct antecedent of Levi's talk in 1894, it merits further scrutiny.

His worry, Levi said by way of introduction to that "open letter," was the fear that American Jews would abandon their religion. Indeed, the Reform movement harbored that distinct possibility. Maintaining that his anxiety and confusion, particularly in light of Reform's lack of cohesiveness, was shared by many laymen, he faulted the rabbis. "I am far more charitable in my judgment . . . than the vast bulk of my coreligionists," he said. "I hear every day the charge made by Jews that not only do the Rabbis preach a distorted and false Judaism, but that they do not believe even the little which they preach." On occasion Levi attempted to defend the rabbis, but his efforts only elicited further accusations from the laymen. "I am answered that many of you," he told the rabbis, "are 'Rabbis for revenue only,' . . . that many of you teach what your congregations like to hear, rather than what it is proper for them to know," and worst of all "that you employ your position in Jewish pulpits to assail before Jewish congregations the most sacred doctrines of Judaism, not even sparing the Torah itself."

He then called on the rabbis to answer the basic question, "What is Judaism," one that he divided into thirty specific queries. Although some lay respondents endorsed the letter, replies from rabbis were very few and, in Levi's opinion, insufficiently comprehensive. Those who did answer stressed vague concepts like ethical behavior, a belief in God, the mission of Judaism, and a "religion of humanity."[10] The attorney was not satisfied, and his discontent festered. One may indeed wonder why, in light of his well-publicized opinions, Levi was invited to address a Reform body, the UAHC, at all. Perhaps the passage of time had dulled the memory of his charges, or his words had struck a responsive chord among the union's lay leaders.

It is unlikely that Levi's critique of Reform and Reform rabbis was prompted by personal experience with his own rabbi, Henry Cohen. Cohen, who trained in England and the West Indies, came to B'nai Israel in 1888 at the age of twenty-five and served the congregation for over fifty years. Rapidly adjusting to his ultra-Reform synagogue, which had been established twenty years earlier and which numbered some one hundred seventy-five families, he became a respected and well-liked figure in the Jewish and non-Jewish communities of Galveston. Defending the need of Reform for the "conservation" of Judaism, he was by choice a social reformer rather than a student of theology. Levi was president of the synagogue when Cohen arrived, and reportedly became one of the rabbi's supporters. Although the attorney left Galveston for New York in 1899, he and his family remained close to Cohen. Levi's untimely death occurred in 1904, and it was Rabbi Cohen's glowing tribute that was included in the *Leo N. Levi Memorial Volume*.[11]

At the 1894 convention Levi announced at the outset that he would "talk back" to the rabbis who constantly criticized the shortcomings of their congregants. He proceeded to indict the movement and its leaders: "[Reform] has never had a great leader. It has none now." He told his hosts that since the UAHC supervised Hebrew Union College, Reform's rabbinical seminary, it was their responsibility to see that the school trained proper rabbis.[12] Placing Reform within the context of a century of rapid change, Levi lashed out at Jews intoxicated by a thirst for novelty who were prepared to cast off anything that appeared outdated. The result was disastrous:

> The movement in which these Jews are and have been engaged is not factive but altogether destructive. It does not build up but tears down. Moreover, its destructive processes are without any rule or system, apparently having no other object than to destroy. And when the destruction is complete, there does not arise upon the ruins . . . any new structure brought about by any process, either natural or factitious, but on the contrary, the destroyers reveling amidst the ruins they have made, challenge the amazement and demand the admiration of those who have witnessed their performance.

Within the Reform movement at large the rabbis were especially culpable, since they succumbed to the iconoclastic spirit of the age and "yielded themselves to the superficial skepticism of the present era." To be sure, Jewish history was replete with examples of differing interpretations of religion, but those Reform doctrines that assaulted the very integrity of Judaism, as rooted in the Pentateuch, were beyond the pale of legitimacy. He conceded the need for minimal changes, separating "the wheat from the chaff," but the actions of Reform rabbis, both on doctrine and praxis had resulted only in "demoralization, acrimony, and strife." He offered details:

> The first and most striking feature . . . is [Reform's] want of system. It has been spasmodic, erratic, and altogether negative. . . . The entire movement is chaotic, sensational, and illogical. . . . It has no unity . . . except that cohesion which arises from negation. Each so-called reformer has been a leader instead of a follower; each has been a law unto himself; each has denied any standard except that formulated by himself; each has denied the leadership of all others and has assumed it for himself. The so-called reform movement in each congregation differs from that of all others, and even in a particular congregation the movement takes its complexion from the minister, who for the time being occupies the pulpit; and so it has come to pass repeatedly, when a minister has died or resigned his position . . . that his successor has preached a so-called

reform Judaism which did not consist with that which prevailed during the incumbency of his predecessor.

As for those rabbis who substituted oratory and entertainment in place of teaching the essential faith, Levi had only contempt. He did not concede, however, that once the door was open for rejecting the "chaff," the very principle of change was legitimized.

The lawyer said he was speaking not to the Orthodox but to "bewildered" Jews like himself who were willing to drop customs and ceremonies not enjoined by the Torah but were unwilling to discard the essentials. On their behalf he asked Reform leaders for a standard or common ground that defined the essence of Judaism and the limits to change. To talk about ethical or moral behavior as they were wont was not enough; Judaism like any religion meant rituals as well. Those who don't live by that requirement, he said, "place themselves beyond the pale of religion." In sum, he continued to search for an answer to his earlier question of "what is Judaism."

The speaker made no reference to the heated debate in 1885 between two rabbis—the leading Reform theologian, Kaufmann Kohler, and the Traditionalist scholar Alexander Kohut. While Kohler had argued for freedom from Mosaic and rabbinic legislation, Kohut had defended the divinity of the Law: "Such a reform which seeks to progress without the Mosaic-rabbinical tradition . . . is a Deformity . . . a skeleton of Judaism without flesh and sinew, without spirit and heart." Nor did Levi mention the Pittsburgh Platform of 1885 which bore Kohler's stamp and which laid down the theological principles distinguishing the Reform movement. He apparently found both the debate and the platform inadequate. He may also have thought that those pronouncements were at best the views of a small minority, for indeed the rabbis who had met in Pittsburgh numbered only nineteen.[13] That Levi had kept abreast of those events was evident in the fact that many of his statements resembled those of Kohut. It is interesting, however, that the lawyer neither read himself out of the Reform camp nor prepared to join the Kohut faction.

Doubtless the attorney grasped the deeper implication and relevance of his questions on the meaning of Judaism. Since the repudiation of Mosaic-rabbinic law in the Pittsburgh Platform and the Kohler-Kohut debate had left Reform bereft of authoritative guidelines and in a virtual state of lawlessness,[14] Levi argued that the movement had failed to fill the void which it itself had created. Indeed, Reform had come to mean only what individual rabbis and congregations said it was. Although autonomy may have reflected the congregational character of American Protestant denominations, it broke sharply with Jewish patterns of change.

Levi explained why he persisted in challenging the rabbis. Every Jew, he said, had the right to demand explicit answers from his rabbi for himself and his children. In conclusion, he called on his fellow Jews, increasingly distrustful of their rabbis, to follow the example of biblical leaders Ezra and Nehemiah and replace the "false priests" with "ideal" rabbis:

> The ideal Rabbi, for whose coming [the Jews] are longing, will be a man imbued with a perfect faith in God's law as written in Torah; he will study it with a broad and liberal mind, seeking always to comprehend the will of the Creator to the end that he may observe it; he will be imbued with this faith and filled with this understanding, devoting himself to teaching and practicing the ancient religion, not as a mere matter of form, but as a vital and forceful agency to accomplish the true development of man's highest nature. To him eloquence will consist in deeds, not words; to him entertainment will only be an incident to instruction; to him theology only an aid to piety; to him ceremonies will be divinely ordered means to a divinely ordered end. . . . Such a man believing, following, teaching and practicing the doctrine, the rites and the ceremonies of Judaism, will stand forth before the eyes of the Jews as a leader to be followed.

A stormy emotional debate that lasted for two sessions broke out at the conclusion of Levi's address.[15] The *New York Times,* which highlighted the story on its front page, called the discussion "about as turbulent as a ward mass meeting." Rabbis in the audience were quick to denounce the traitor in their midst and to defend Reform and themselves. "Motions were made, discussed and voted on half the time without knowing on one side of the house what was being done at the other side," one participant observed. What should have been a mere formality—to thank the speaker and to recommend printing the address in the *Proceedings* of the council—led to bickering and disorder. Some thought that the talk should be printed along with a statement denying that it represented the council's views. It was finally decided to append a hastily written protest from the CCAR to the text of the address. Denouncing the "strictures" on the rabbis, the protest read in part: "These strictures are not founded on facts. Mr. Levi's conception of the reform movement in Judaism is erroneous, and his conclusions have been hastily arrived at, without a thorough study of the question. His sweeping statements, like all generalizations, are un-just." The president of the board of Hebrew Union College feared that the protest was too strong to win approval, but in the end it was passed.[16]

Recalling another address at a Reform convention that was also critical of Reform rabbis, Levi's opponents suggested that greater care be taken thereafter in the choice of speakers. Although the name of the speaker in the earlier episode was not divulged, the reference was probably to the sermon delivered by Rabbi Max Heller of New Orleans to the CCAR in 1891. There Heller was sharply critical of rabbis who substituted lectures on history or religion, or discourses on contemporary scientific and phil-osophical questions, for proper sermons. Moreover, he could not justify those rabbis whose talks on ethics or *mitzvoth* (commandments) drowned the singular Jewish heritage in a universal sea. Either way, Heller claimed, whether as an uninformed dilettante or a preacher who ignored the fact that Jewish "separateness" and tradition forever linked the Jewish past to the present, the errant rabbi was seriously out of line. Instead of serving as the "mouthpiece" of God whose task was to inspire congregants with the riches of their religious legacy, the rabbis, succumbing to "individual-ism gone mad," were weakening Judaism and Jewish identity.[17]

In his own defense Levi said that if he was to blame for the address, the council was equally at fault for having invited him. Moreover, he had told Rabbi Isaac Wise, now the venerated elder statesman of the Reformers, what he planned to say, and Wise had agreed to his appearance before the council. Wise doubtless forgot, because at the convention he admitted that since Levi's lack of sympathy with Reform was on record in speeches and writings, the invitation was a "blunder." Levi could have added, as he had in the *Menorah,* that he represented the views of many congregants, but on that point he kept silent. Nevertheless, his supporters made themselves heard at the convention. They applauded and cheered his address, and a group was promptly organized to underwrite and circulate ten thousand free copies. One observer said that the vote to print the address would not have carried without the speaker's partisans. To be sure, Levi had no plan to foment an outright revolt, but even if he had, it would have miscarried. Many laymen may have shared his sentiments, but the rebels were quickly stifled by a fiery rejoinder from Wise.[18]

Pandemonium gave way to silence when Wise rose to speak. The rabbi lashed out at Levi, once a featured contributor to the *American Israelite.* Wise, a proud man, may also have been personally offended by the at-torney's charge that the Reform movement never had a great leader. The venerable Wise challenged the council in words that reflected the prevailing bitterness unloosed among the rabbis: "Are you going to allow such strictures to be cast upon the rabbinate without a protest? To do so would be an outrage, and must not be permitted." He continued the attack in a statement that appeared in print a few weeks after the convention. He admitted that the talk might have been appropriate had it been delivered before the CCAR, but in the setting of the council it appealed to the laity's base motive of *Rabbinerhetze* (rabbi-baiting), a phenomenon carried over from Germany that was "radically un-American." The intermittent applause for Levi's remarks, the rabbi explained, came not from an understanding of his speech but from a Southern claque out to cheer a "favorite son." Wise erred, however, when he contradicted some facts in Levi's account of the *Menorah* episode. He felt forced to retract on that matter, but in the end he, Wise, had the final word: "I intended not to say anything hard, harsh or anywise offensive to Mr. Levi personally or of his address, not only because I entertain the highest respect and the kindest feelings for Mr. Leo N. Levi but also because I am old and considerate and *Mr. Levi is neither*" (emphasis added).[19]

Reactions to Levi's address appeared in the Jewish press for several months after the convention. Among the writers some recalled other Reform Jews who had seriously questioned the direction of the movement.[20] European Jews chimed in too. The prestigious *Jewish Chronicle* of London agreed with Levi on the deleterious effects of Reform, the *American Hebrew* quoted a statement from Grand Rabbi Zadoc Kahn of France on "The Ideal Rabbi," and from Germany came word that Levi intended to lead an anti-Reform movement.[21]

With varying degrees of surprise, some commentators pointed out that women were also among the critics of the rabbis. Rabbi Louis Grossman of Detroit could not contain his sexist prejudice. He wrote very seriously: "Women are brilliant talkers; but they cannot keep up a long conversation. They scintillate for a few moments, and the brightest woman relapses into the implicit weakness of her sex."[22] The public role of women had been noticed ever since 1893 when, in connection with the World's Parliament of Religions in Chicago, a Congress of Jewish Women was organized, which in turn led to the establishment of the National Council of Jewish Women. At the same time, critiques of American Judaism by Esther Ruskay and Josephine Lazarus also caught the community's attention. While Ruskay expounded on the values of Jewish Traditionalism as opposed to

Reform, Lazarus went beyond Reform by calling for the unity of Jews and Christians in what she called a Church Universal.[23]

As expected, Traditionalists delighted in the discomfiture of their adversaries. A writer in the *Jewish Messenger* praised Levi's courage, and a letter to the *American Hebrew* faulted Reformers who denounced Levi instead of admitting their own weaknesses: "Had they been wise, they would have recognized that, by keeping quiet, they might have established a reputation as gentlemen, and had they taken to heart the lessons inculcated by the oration they might have imbibed enough fervor to preach more effectively in their own congregations." An editorial in the same newspaper, the mouthpiece of the moderate Traditionalists, mocked the Reform rabbis whose criticism of Levi betrayed their own oft-touted devotion to liberalism: "Have these Rabbis, whose principal stock in trade is Liberalism, so little conception of liberality that they cannot gather and deliberately discuss a proposition without losing all sense of courtesy, that they cannot tolerantly and dispassionately endeavor to refute those who express views not in harmony with their own?"[24]

Levi may have caused the rabbis "anguish" as one of them said at the convention, but Reform leaders did not wallow sadly or quietly. They struck back, blasting the Texan and his address. To be sure, most acknowledged that the attorney was thoughtful, serious, honest, a good speaker, and perhaps even bent on constructive rather than destructive criticism. After all, said Emil G. Hirsch, the influential rabbi of Temple Sinai in Chicago whose very words often dripped with vitriol and sarcasm, "not every layman is entitled to the solemn degree of A.S.S." But the charges he and others leveled against the speaker far outweighed a list of his attributes: (1) He was ignorant of Jewish history and culture, and his questions invaded what was rightly the domain of theologians. (2) Because he was an attorney he erred in thinking that Judaism could be defined or pinned down as a legal deposition. (3) He defended the sanctity of Mosaic law, but he, as well as the vast majority of American Jews, did not observe all its "oriental" and "outlandish" laws and rituals.[25]

Hirsch in his newspaper, *Reform Advocate,* led the sneering section. He wrote that Levi and other critics were not commissioned to be "Lord High Sheriffs for God Almighty." The rabbi also referred to the *Menorah* episode, which he claimed had festered in Levi for seven years. Had Levi been forced to contain his anger any longer, the "earth itself would have opened up to swallow the whole breed of rabbis, and none, save Mr. Levi, would have remained to tell the tale!"[26] Other Reform newspapers joined the attack. According to the *American Hebrew,* which relished details of the crisis, the Reform periodicals "fairly bristle with militant denunciations. The contents of Mr. Levi's oration are overwhelmingly hidden under the dense mass of opprobrium heaped upon him as a lawyer for presuming to deal logically and rationally with Jewish problems."[27]

With regard to the substance of Levi's message, some Reformers immediately planned a counterattack. The first Sabbath after the UAHC convention Rabbis Wise and David Philipson, both officers of the CCAR, were guest preachers at Reform temples in New Orleans. In their sermons they repeated classical Reform's beliefs with an emphasis on reason, ethics, and mission of the Jews. The rabbis asserted that in the natural evolution of religion, old laws out of tune with times or those that failed to "elevate," deserved to be discarded. As Wise said, the spirit of the Torah transcended specific laws.[28]

Subsequent criticisms of Levi's address picked up or developed those and other stock themes—Reform Judaism as a "liberated" faith and a "faith universal," how attempts to reduce Judaism to a fixed creed contradicted the "genius" of the faith, and the success of Reform in holding on to Jewish youth. Sensitive also to non-Jewish opinion, defenders of Reform claimed that the movement had carved a respectable image for Judaism in America. Meeting Levi's attack head on, some admitted that the rabbis' freedom of speech had occasionally resulted in "unbridled individualism" or unrestrained license, but the changes introduced by Reform had been made responsibly and were overwhelmingly constructive. In fact, change and fluidity were essential for a living Judaism; it was a religion characterized by free thought and not fixed creed. The answer to Levi and his kind, Emil G. Hirsch told the 1895 convention of the CCAR, was not less Reform but more Reform. Indeed, Reform was very much alive and well, and the movement had no reason "to be perturbed by the ravings of the ignorant and superstitious disciples of medieval ritualism on the one hand, or by the carping of shallow and pretentious fault finders on the other." Doubtless Hirsch put Levi in the second category.[29]

Although they denounced Levi and his address, Reform rabbis could not honestly deny either the discontent within Reform congregations or the widespread religious indifference and apathy among American Jews. On that score they tacitly agreed with the Galveston attorney, and they too groped for answers. Some also looked, albeit in vain, for a definition of Reform that would unite their followers. As Rabbi Maurice Harris had said some months before the Levi episode: "No ten Hebrews agree as to what are the essentials of Judaism." Assessing the situation, two prominent religious leaders, Kaufmann Kohler and Emil G. Hirsch, were then speaking critically of classical Reform and questioning its almost exclusive reliance on reason.

Kohler, for example, wrote: "Reform theology, when based on sole reason as fundamental principle, is, or was, built on sand and quagmire. Reason, which often ends in doubt and anarchy, is a *corrective*, not a *constructive* force of humanity. All the great men and events of history are impelled, not by intellect, but by the inspiring power of faith." In the summer of 1894, when he delivered a conference sermon at the CCAR convention, Kohler fully discussed Reform's reliance on reason at the expense of spirituality. The solution, he said, was for Reform to revitalize that spirituality, to recognize that truth was a matter of heart rather than head, and not Theism, Deism, or any form of universal humanitarianism. In pre-modern days Judaism had fused intellect and emotion, and now again Reform needed to bring spirituality into the homes, synagogues, and everyday life of the Jew by translating past forms into meaningful present day rituals. When a healthy balance was reached between the intellect and the spirit, Reform would be infused with new vigor for the propagation of its mission.[30] Kohler's emphasis on the destructiveness of early Reform and the need of ritual pointed to a new phase in Reform's development.

Hirsch similarly rejected the shallow and "insipid" liberalism of the French Enlightenment and of Moses Mendelssohn and his circle. Hadn't the knowledge unlocked by modern science proved the limitations of the Age of Reason? Whereas early Reformers had needed rationalism to free Judaism from fossilization and to gain Christian toleration, the task of modern Reform was to teach a human religion, steeped in Jewish consciousness and in keeping with the new sciences.

Both Hirsch and Kohler accepted biblical criticism and were influenced by the work of Moritz Lazarus on the psychology of nations. Using terms like "national consciousness," race, and *Volksseele* (soul of a people), the two rabbis emphasized the importance of a Jewish collectivity, a *Volk* (a people) to carry out the God-given mission of the Jews. They were thereby modifying the reliance of classical Reform on the precepts of the Enlightenment and adapting their faith to the climate of the new scientific and nationalistic age. In a dramatic repudiation of early Reform's cosmopolitanism and its insistence that Judaism was only a faith like any other, they now spoke of a Jewish people or ethnic group and of race, national genius, and ethnic soul. Theirs was another manifestation of the balance

American Jews constantly sought between Jewish singularity and integration within a larger and changing American society.[31]

Levi's address doubtless strengthened Kohler's resolve to propagate his
ideas, and in one paper he used his rebuttal of Levi to air his own convictions on how to rectify Reform's errors. Stressing again the need of "a
system of reconstruction and regeneration of our faith," he denounced
the unchecked individualism in Reform and its cavalier repudiation of
ritual that could result in total anarchy or the total unraveling of the religious tradition. In his sermon of 1894 to the CCAR, he also attacked the
idea that Judaism was based solely on cold reason; Judaism was neither
"ethical monotheism" nor "theistic humanitarianism." The answer to the
movement's weaknesses, he asserted, lay not in Traditionalist or Orthodox observances but in the renewal of the Jewish spiritual force through
Reform ceremonials, those that would "invest the home, the Sabbath and
the festival seasons with the character of sanctity and impress the Jew
with the sacredness of his priestly mission among the nations." To be sure,
even spiritually infused rituals did not solve the problem of uniting congregations and rabbis in common beliefs and practices, but Kohler's focus
was primarily on theology. He was confident that if Reform followed the
dictates of spirituality as well as intellect, it could reach the true meaning
of Judaism which was "not legalism, not ritualism nor exclusive nationalism, but the *Prophetic message of the God of righteousness and truth to the
human race, preserved and protected in its purest and loftiest form by Israel,
the Chosen Priest and Martyr Nation.*"

Kohler, the most profound thinker among those who reacted to Levi
publicly, admitted that Levi was correct on several points that were cause
for alarm. Some changes by individual rabbis were arbitrary and presaged
virtual anarchy; others were introduced by rabbis who were primarily bent on imitating the Christians. But Levi was wrong in presenting a
blanket indictment of all Reformers, particularly since he was ignorant of
theology. Turning to the stickiest issue, that of the retention of the Mosaic code, Kohler asked whether Levi himself, or his supporters, lived up
to that standard. More important, Kohler denied that the Law was immutable; change of the Law was a constant, and changes had been made
since the days of the Prophets. Since Judaism was elastic, it could not be
defined in one book. He concluded optimistically that Reform, recogniz-
ing both the elasticity of Judaism and the justification of change, would
continue to develop in the United States.[32]

An offshoot of the Levi episode came in the remarks of H. Pereira

Mendes, rabbi of the oldest Sephardic congregation, Shearith Israel of New York, and a founder of the Jewish Theological Seminary in 1887. In answer to Kohler, he took up the cudgels of Alexander Kohut who had sparred with the Reformer in 1885 and who had died a few months before the UAHC convention. Mendes wrote as an exponent of the moderate Traditionalist faction, and he defended the right of a layman to raise questions about Jewish principles. He was more interested, however, in pointing out what he called contradictions and inaccuracies in Kohler's views. Among other things, he charged that Kohler was "stealing the thunder" of the moderate Traditionalists by defining Reform as "Progressive Judaism," a term that Mendes claimed was used first by his faction. He also questioned Kohler's acceptance of higher criticism. Mendes respected Kohler, and trying perhaps for some sort of understanding between the Reform and Traditionalist camps, he wrote that he willingly accepted "open fencing" among the denominations.

Kohler's reply was only partially conciliatory. He affirmed his personal beliefs in divine revelation and the concept of the chosen people, which were axiomatic to Mendes's Traditionalism, and he claimed that early rabbinic changes in Mosaic law, before Pharisaism became "petrified," were no different from what modern Reform was doing. Recalling the ideas of Abraham Geiger and Zachariah Frankel, two prominent German Jewish thinkers who had influenced both Reform and later Conservatism, he said that their definition of historical Judaism meant "historical growth which implies change according to the circumstances of the time." If Mendes was prepared to accept that premise, "we both stand on the basis of Historical Judaism." Neither rabbi explained the breadth of "circumstances of the time," and so the divide between them was not bridged.

At this point Mendes recoiled:

> I am not prepared to admit that the new leaders of Reform today, outside of some four or five like Dr. Kohler, can even rank with a Geiger or a [David] Einhorn for learning. And I am not prepared to admit that Reform Judaism can claim equal rank with Mosaic and Talmudic Judaism as an historical phase of our religion unless I know whether it believes in Divine Revelation and origin of the Torah, on which Mosaic and Talmudic Judaism insist.

Since American Reform, as Kohler himself admitted, had failed to achieve its promise of a vibrant American Judaism, Mendes suggested that two or three Reformers meet with two or three from his side and come up with a plan that could lead to a stable yet unifying religious system. Kohler ignored that letter, and the faint possibility of a debate, much less a meeting of minds between the opposing groups, quickly evaporated.[33] As it stood, the exchange was another notch in the widening gap between Reformers and moderate Traditionalists.

Other replies to Levi defended the rabbis as well as the nature of the Reform movement. The *Jewish Spectator* commented that more than rabbis were at stake: "To attack Reform rabbis . . . is a pessimistic innuendo against the powers of the human mind, against the progress and recognition of higher spiritual truth." Some defenders shifted the blame for any faults of individual rabbis to the laity. They said that Reform congregants, who succumbed to the beliefs of a secularist and materialist age, were either indifferent, or they prodded their rabbis to radical practices and sensationalistic sermons. Kohler put it this way: "The horses drove too fast and shied, because the bridle of reverence was cast off by the laymen." Another Reform rabbi added that laymen were often embarrassed by the very subject. It was not fashionable to speak about Judaism, he said; congregants disliked the name "Jew," and they distanced themselves from discussions of religious subjects.[34]

Some laymen addressed the matter directly. Lee K. Frankel, a Reform Jew and prominent communal worker in Philadelphia, thought that Levi represented a goodly portion of thinking American Jewry but that he had neglected to consider the duties of the layman. Furthermore, the speaker hadn't posed the real question asked by laymen: not *what* to believe but *why* believe. After offering his own answer to "why believe"—and Frankel was in the small minority that acknowledged the larger problem of the shrinking synagogue attendance—he briefly discussed the obligations of the congregants, which, in his view, amounted to an active rather than passive role in the synagogue. At bottom the layman's duty was to support the synagogue and its projects, specifically to cooperate in educational and philanthropic ventures by personal participation as well as financial contributions.[35]

Two of the most prominent Reformers attributed criticism like Levi's to the laymen's scorn for the rabbi. Isaac Mayer Wise had raised the theme of rabbi-baiting at the convention, and he developed it shortly thereafter in the *American Israelite*: "The more Mr. Levi denounced the reform Rabbis the louder his friends applauded, so that the *Rabbinerhetze* became evident as the theme of that whole oration." Wise deplored the practice, blaming it, an import from Europe, on "disappointed leaders in some eastern cities." Emil G. Hirsch also attacked the "rabbi hater," often the ignorant parvenu; he likened that parvenu to the president of a congregation who despised the rabbi as "one unfit for any useful calling" and who demanded strict compliance with the laymen's directives. Expatiating on the topic, Hirsch devoted two and one-half columns in one issue of the *Reform Advocate* to the rabbi-haters. He bitterly faulted the shallow, uneducated, and unprincipled laymen who were captivated solely by a glib tongue. Had a radical Reformer with "oratorical pomp and rhetorical pyrotechnics" addressed the UAHC convention in place of Levi, Hirsch claimed, the same audience would have been as enthusiastically responsive.[36]

Proud of his reputation as a Radical Reformer and brilliant speaker, Hirsch also laced into his cowardly colleagues who publicly blamed the Radicals for the abuses of which Levi had spoken. As he told the CCAR at one convention: "The impression has gone abroad that we Radicals, in these last years, have been doing nothing but whittle away at Judaism. . . . Nothing is further from the truth than the threadworn charge that Radicalism is the shame-born hybrid of materialism and sensualism." Hirsch was secure in his prestigious position at Temple Sinai, where every week he drew an audience of some fifteen hundred, including many non-Jews, and he saw no need at least publicly to modify his opinions. But irrespective of whom he blamed, he did not appear overly troubled by the shortcomings of Reform beliefs and practices.[37]

One Reform rabbi who agreed with Levi and who fit Hirsch's description of the moderate Reformers arrayed against the Radicals was C. H. Levy of Baltimore. A sermon printed in the *Jewish Messenger* showed that Levy had done some soul-searching. He said that Levi's indictment of all rabbis was too sweeping, but nonetheless the charges were true. Indeed, there were Reformers who sacrificed truth for novelty, who rejected the past in favor of the present, and who were downright destructive of Judaism, taking away "our Sabbath, our Torah, stripping the spirit so that it would freeze in the cold glare of wintry indifference." "A revolution," he continued, "is that which knows no moderation, rushing blindly from one extreme to the other, and that is what some of our leaders have done." He went on to endorse the major criticisms in the attorney's address of the erratic and negative methods of Reform leaders; the demoralization, distrust, and indifference that those methods caused; and the need for a common standard that included ceremonies as well as principles. Like

Levi he also supported a Judaism based on the binding force of the To-rah. It was the duty of the Reform congregation, he concluded, to demand that its rabbi keep faith with the Torah and to rebel if he did not.[38] How seriously Levy's own congregation acted on their rabbi's words remains a question, but he, a lonely defender of "The Ideal Rabbi," left Baltimore within two years.

Levi's speech and the reactions it generated had no tangible effects. Levi neither recanted nor changed his views publicly. Rather, he contin-ued as president of his congregation in Galveston, and in 1900 he was elected national president of B'nai B'rith. Both positions testified to the fact that lay and clerical leaders had not forced him out of either his own synagogue or the Reform camp. The attorney gained added prominence when, as president of B'nai B'rith, he lobbied with Theodore Roosevelt's administration on behalf of Romanian and Russian Jews. In that role he was credited with having drawn up the famous petition to Russia after the Kishinev pogrom of 1903.[39]

Nor were there any dramatic developments in the American Reform movement that resulted from Levi's speech. In 1895 the CCAR decided to publish a collection of sermons. The rabbis did not mention Levi by name, but the words of the resolution suggest that his speech may have in some measure prompted their action. The purpose of the book, they said, was to provide:

> A medium a for the clearer expression and the better understanding of the fundamental doctrines and characteristic aims of modern Judaism and a historical record of the development of the content and expres-sion of Jewish religious thought. It is anticipated that this book will be of interest to preachers and laymen of all denominations, who may de-sire to learn what Judaism has to say in regard to the vital questions of the day.[40]

It is unlikely, however, that the book, which was devoted primarily to hol-iday sermons, would have satisfied Levi. Since Reform did not establish a synod and since the Pittsburgh Platform of 1885 remained the closest it came to the formulation of a uniform creed, the status quo still obtained.

No branch of American Judaism was free of divisiveness among its rab-bis on the meaning of the "true" Judaism. Nor was any immune to the ancillary problems that were laid bare in the Levi affair. Matters like the role and status of the individual rabbi and rabbinical-lay differences had arisen long before Levi, and they lived on after 1894 in Traditional as well as Reform congregations. Common difficulties, however, brought neither the contending denominations nor the different wings within each camp any closer together. American Jews regardless of formal affiliation cooperated on social, political, and philanthropic matters, but on religious issues —on dogma and ritual—they steered separate courses. In the evolution of American Judaism congregational autonomy had won out above intercongregational unity.

Levi's "rebellion" was no more than the proverbial tempest in a teapot. Results of the controversy might have been different had the attorney not focused almost exclusively on the rabbi, an approach that immediately put Reform leaders on the defensive. Had he posed the question of how to keep laymen loyal to the synagogue, an issue that most except for Kohler and Frankel ignored, he could have aired his criticisms at the same time that he initiated some form of cooperative venture between the clergy and their congregants. As the episode played out, however, there were no winners or losers.

8

The New Antisemitism

Echoes of the virulent antisemitism that engulfed German and Russian Jews in the last quarter of the nineteenth century resonated in sermons and other statements of American rabbis. To be sure, America's Jews, made up largely of immigrants or children of immigrants, needed no reminders of the age-old discrimination and suffering that their European brethren had endured and were still enduring. But something new was added to the attacks on Jews after 1870. Instead of the customary religious prejudice that underlay earlier persecution—rooted largely in the popular Christian myths of deicide, ritual murder, and the Wandering Jew—the factor of race abetted by the currents of conservative nationalism, as well as the pseudo-scientific theories generated by Darwinism, helped determine the place of the Jew in society. The new Jew-hatred even sported a name that first came into use in the 1870s: antisemitism.

Commentators and analysts, both Jewish and non-Jewish, debated whether the characteristics of the unsavory Jew as delineated by the racists were innate or acquired and how they could be modified or erased. The liberal weekly *Nation,* although in sympathy with the victims of the new antisemitism, agreed at least in part with the racist argument: "There is some leaven of truth in the contest of Germanism and Jewism—namely, the difference in the national or race character of Jews and Germans, a difference . . . whose existence is one of the most important factors in history."[1] American rabbis also considered the problem. They knew that aside from the need to supply relief to the victims of a more intense hatred, American Jews were directly affected. First, antisemitism in a racist garb tainted Jews worldwide and could easily spread to the Western Hemisphere; second, their security in the United States, of which they constantly boasted, was at least theoretically jeopardized; third, the hordes of victims from Eastern Europe who sought refuge in the United States raised countless problems for the established

Jews. Inevitably the volume of rabbinic discussions on the so-called Jewish Question swelled.

Historians have long debated the subject of antisemitism in the United States, its meaning and its causes.[2] The following account suggests the importance of assessing contemporary Jewish opinions, principally those of American rabbis, who were witness to the impact of European events on their community. Most rabbis discussed here were loath to accept the racist explanation. Strictly defined, racism meant immutability, and if Jews remained forever a people distinct from all others, the path of full assimilation into American society, which most Jews chose, would forever be blocked.[3] Rabbis realized that racism could also shake the layman's pride in a Jewish identity. Furthermore, since racism conjured up discussions of racial superiority and inferiority, it put Jews in a lose/lose situation. To admit to inferiority was suicidal, but a claim of superiority could only compound the hatred of the antisemites.

Some Jews disagreed with the rabbis. For example, the *American Hebrew* once aired an editorial arguing that to be a Jew meant "to be of the Hebrew race" and indeed of a superior race. The editorial elaborated: "Wherever the Aryan has stood for pillage, the Semitic race has stood for peace. When the Aryans pursued the chase, Semites cultivated letters. The law of fittest surviving, aided by the breeding of hereditary qualities in a pure race, has given the Jews a physiological and mental superiority which can be perpetuated only by the perpetuation of the race purity." It followed that religious conversion to Judaism, or indeed Jewish conversion to Christianity, was meaningless, since faith alone did not make a Jew.[4]

In a sermon of 1881 Rabbi Sabato Morais of Mikveh Israel in Philadelphia preached on the subject of racial antisemitism in Bismarck's Germany. Calling it a throwback to medievalism and an "ethnological fanaticism [which] is now striking all Germany with blindness," he presented the central argument of the racists: "The Jews have descended from Shem, the white Christians from Japheth; the country [Germany] belongs to the Japhaites, the Far East is the cradle and ought to be the confines of the Shemites."[5] Seventeen years later, another rabbi, Maurice Harris of New York, testified to the maturation of the ongoing agitation: "Jewish persecution has been raised to the dignity of a philosophy, with a philosophic name to hide its malice. It is made the platform and creed of political parties; it is a new element to be dealt with in the State; it is prosecuted with the precision and the thoroughness of a science. It has its own literature, its press, its propaganda."[6]

A writer of the time elaborated more fully on both the nature of the new antisemitism and its popularity in Germany. He provided an all-inclusive interpretation of the causes and manifestations of racism: "The prejudice is directed against the Jews as a race and manifests itself in all phases of human activity. It seeks its justification in all that the Jews may say, do, or think; it feeds upon popular superstitions, exploded myths, and uncontrollable rumors; and it expresses itself in a variety of acts of intolerance suggestive of the age of medieval barbarism." Almost immediately after the unification of the German state in 1870, he continued, racists began to exploit the country's mood of hypernationalism. Preaching the desirability of a homogeneous society and defining Jews as unwanted and unassimilable aliens, they found a receptive audience. Major segments of German society appropriated racist teachings for their own purposes. The Catholics used it in the church's struggle against Bismarck, economic competitors of the Jews used it to explain the collapse of the market in 1873, and Bismarck used it to undermine the Liberals in politics and the government. Scientists, students, academics, politicians, and popular speakers from all classes of society added to the antisemitic clamor and fed the hatred still further. While historian Heinrich von Treitschke said, "The Jews are our misfortune," populist agitator Wilhelm Marr, who coined the word antisemitism, wrote that a state should include people of the same race and that foreign elements, like the Jews, should be absorbed or eliminated. At the same time, Jews and their property were subjected to physical abuse and violence.[7]

Disturbed and confounded by the German situation, rabbis in America carefully monitored reports and analyses in the American and European press. They pessimistically predicted that the antisemitism sweeping Germany was rapidly infecting countries both to the east, Russia in particular, and to the west. Rabbi Marcus Jastrow of Philadelphia, speaking at a conference of the Jewish Ministers' Association, added that the hatred had even reached America: "A drop of poison has been instilled into the blood of Western nations causing a distemper contagious to its nature, and, there is no use in denying it, the contagion has reached our beloved country . . . [working] its way into the heart of our community, destroying the social peace which heretofore has been its just pride."[8]

The fact that the "poison" originated in Germany troubled the rabbis at least as much as the persecution itself. Most of the established religious leaders had been born and/or educated in Germany, and they treasured the German familial ties and cultural traditions they had brought with them to the United States. One outspoken Germanophile, Rabbi David Einhorn, had even said that Reform Judaism in America stripped of the German language and spirit would wither away.[9] To such Jews, outbreaks of Jew-hatred in Russia or the Ottoman Empire, lands not completely rid of their medieval past, might not have seemed unusual. But racial persecution was totally misplaced in Germany, the birthplace of modern science and scholarship.[10]

The new strain of antisemitism challenged a popular theme of rabbinical discourses. Since "the Jew" irrespective of country was accused of all sorts of vile characteristics, from physical deformity to moral depravity, American Jews soon learned that they stood in the dock with their European brethren. Despite speakers who still insisted that America was different,[11] it followed that the constant rabbinic refrain that America, the exemplar of freedom, differed qualitatively from the other nations required some modification or at least explanation. Indeed, reverberations from abroad coalesced in time with grave economic and social disturbances in the United States during the last quarter of the century and produced what John Higham has called a "likely context for antisemitism." Within that context American Jews felt the hardening of social discrimination and the ever-widening barriers that blocked their full acceptance in society. Many of their fellow American countrymen agreed that the Jew was the alien. The racist teachings of historians at leading American universities and the swelling tide of Jewish immigration from Eastern Europe reinforced the idea of the superior Aryans and the inferior Semites.[12] When popular books brought the racist message directly to the United States, the Jews felt increasingly vulnerable.

Since Americans of all classes were acquainted with the scurrilous propaganda from abroad, it wasn't long before they produced incendiary products of their own. For example, one book, *Judas Iscariot*, that appeared in 1888 focused on the undesirability of American as well as European Jews. Recounting the "abominable" traits of the country's Jews—they were deceivers, cheaters, hypocrites, and swindlers who conspired to destroy "Edom" (Christian states)—the book charged that Jews were "perfidious traitors" who lived by their own archaic laws and were bound only to each other. It concluded with a plan to uproot the Jews from American society and settle them on a reservation in New Mexico. Jew-hatred in America was also reinforced when two dedicated German agitators, Adolf

Stoecker and Hermann Ahlwardt, visited the United States in the 1890s and delivered their messages directly to American audiences.[13]

Racial antisemitism drew forth a host of questions and explanations from rabbis and laity alike. What caused the new antisemitism? How should Jews respond? Were there any remedies or cures? Individuals offered single or multiple reasons; some reversed themselves and suggested reasons they had previously rejected. Others blurred any distinction between religion and race and between religious and racial hatred. The questions cut through classes and denominations, and the answers ranged from the sarcastic to the serious. Rabbis disagreed with rabbis; lay leaders disagreed with rabbis and with each other. The very word "race" added to the confusion. Since the term "ethnic group" was still not commonplace, race was often used loosely, unscientifically, and interchangeably with "a people," or "a nation," or "a nationality."[14] Irrespective of which interpretation was accepted, it was unrealistic to expect a consensus or any collective action by a hopelessly divided community. The one agency that for some twenty years had claimed to speak for American Jews was the Board of Delegates of American Israelites. Established in the aftermath of the Mortara affair[15] and absorbed by Reform's Union of American Hebrew Congregations in 1878, it had never included a majority of congregations. Moreover, it relinquished any say on the German situation after Jewish leaders there advised that foreign pressure was counterproductive.[16]

The definition of the new antisemitism aroused most differences among the rabbis. As one historian has explained, the Reformers were caught on the horns of a dilemma. For one thing, they defined Judaism as a religious faith free of any national dimension, and they were the exponents of a Jewish mission interpreted in universalist rather than narrow nationalist or racial terms. Furthermore, since they stood for the full integration and equality of the Jews in American society, they had no cause to agree with a racial label that emphasized the unique and separatist characteristics of the Jewish minority. Yet at the same time, they were the defenders of a Jewish *people*, an eternal people whose history spanned two millennia and whose rich and distinctive heritage and religion set them forever apart. Understandably, therefore, they reached no consensus on the matter of a Jewish race.[17] Some argued against the very concept of racism. Words like "Aryan" and "Semitic" applied to linguistic categories, and, they said, the attempt to classify human beings according to race was unscientific and inherently false. Nor was it correct to speak of a particular or pure

"Hebrew" race, since there had been many additions to the original Israelites through intermarriage and conversion. Furthermore, "race" was objectionable because it connoted permanence. As Rabbi Abram Isaacs's *Jewish Messenger* pointed out, trappings could change, but according to racists a Jew remained a Jew.[18]

For the most part, the rabbis preferred two other explanations of discrimination: religious prejudice and economic jealousy. The former, often coupled with additional reasons, was far easier to deal with than race. A derivative of the popular image of the Jew as Christ-killer, that form of prejudice dated back to the adoption of Christianity by the Roman Empire. Since Jews liked to say that every generation had its Haman, some judged nineteenth-century European antisemitism to be merely more of the same. Although persecution irrespective of cause or place brought tragedy in its wake, Jews had repeatedly outlived the Hamans. Moreover, just because the pattern was familiar, the outlook appeared less bleak. Don't be misled by the learned term "antisemitism," one respected communal leader advised. The hatred in Germany was no more than an attack on freedom of religion.[19]

Rabbi Adolph Moses of Louisville probed the religious factor more deeply. In a bitter reply to the question posed by a Detroit newspaper, "Why Is the Jew Hated," he claimed that the principal cause of Jew-hatred was Christian preaching about the Jews. The average Catholic priest, he said, had two stock themes for his sermons: the sin of man whose salvation was possible only through Christianity and love of Jesus, and the vilification of the Jews. "Worship of Jesus Christ and hatred of the Jews came to be interchangeable ideas with the priests of the Church." The latter persuaded rulers to strip the Jew of all his rights, and they inflamed mobs with descriptions of how Jewish fiends had tortured Jesus and how Jews used Christian blood for ritual purposes. Vengeance on the Jews for those crimes was "the one supreme duty of a good Christian." Under the tutelage of the church, Christians believed that only a small number of Jews, necessary to bear witness to the truth of Christianity, had the right to survive, and that the ghetto, the yellow badge, and popular riots were no more than signs of God's anger. In short, the Jew, an enemy of God and mankind, was an anathema from the days of Pontius Pilate until the present. Rabbi Moses illustrated the last point with a personal experience of his own. He was once followed, he said, by a gang of Catholic boys who called after him "Sheeny, sheeny Moses, Christ-killer Moses." When he asked them if Christianity permitted such behavior on their part, they neither answered the question nor discontinued their chant. The rabbi concluded with an appeal to the priests: Jews did not deserve Christian hatred at the hands of those who claimed they followed the teachings of Jesus, the teacher of universal love. Prejudice would vanish only when priests taught their congregations that it was a crime to despise Jews.[20]

Isaac Wise responded to the same question that had prompted Moses. He was particularly incensed by the comment of the Detroit newspaper that all groups encountered some form of prejudice and therefore the subject of antisemitism should be dropped. We would if the world did, Wise retorted, and he gave numerous examples of the then current persecution in Central and Eastern Europe. Jews had entertained the idea of progress, he said, but now we know differently. Like his colleague Moses, Wise too fixed responsibility on the teachings of the churches. Not only were Jews blamed for the crime of deicide, but as the "accursed" people they were destined to remain strangers in different lands without a home of their own. That base, Wise maintained, nourished other anti-Jewish charges. Those were the seeds that Christian teachings planted in the minds of children, seeds that yielded an antisemitic harvest. Neither the remarks by Wise nor those by Moses brought answers from the Detroit paper.[21]

The makeup of the audience addressed by rabbis often determined the tone as well as the substance of their comments on Christian doctrines. Whereas both Moses and Wise spoke principally for Jews, others addressed mixed or largely non-Jewish groups. A lecture in Poughkeepsie by Rabbi Gustav Gottheil of New York's Temple Emanu-El was a case in point. Speaking on "Who Are the Jews," a talk that touched on the new antisemitism, he said that the purpose of his talk was to draw Judaism and Christianity closer together. The rabbi mentioned the charge of deicide, but he made no attempt to deny the charge itself. Without the bitterness or rancor of Moses and Wise, he calmly proceeded to refute two so-called proofs that God had rejected the Jews: antisemitic persecution and the forfeiture of the Promised Land. In response Gottheil said that the spirit of God rested on the victims and not the persecutors. As for the loss of the Promised Land, dispersion was a blessing that enabled Jews to carry out their mission. They would be ready for their land only after they had converted all the Christians. Jews believed that they were the Chosen People, he concluded, but only in the sense that they trusted in God and enjoyed a covenant with Him. In essence the rabbi projected the image of a proud Reform Jew who disagreed with Christian dogma but refused to malign his Christian adversaries. He thereby left room for interreligious dialogue if not cooperation.[22]

Gottheil's associate at Emanu-El, Rabbi Joseph Silverman, was equally circumspect. Addressing a mixed audience, he too refrained from open attacks on the church or its tenets. He blamed persecutors in general for their "errors" in misjudging Jews and not for any naked hatred or blind prejudice. Explaining what he meant by errors, Silverman stated: "One of the keenest and most injurious evils that can befall a man or a people is to be misunderstood; perhaps worse is to be misrepresented." Although he didn't say Jews or Christians specifically, the "errors" clearly drew from Jewish experience at the hands of Christian hate-mongers:

> To worship truth and be accused of falsehood; to be religiously virtuous and be charged with vice; to aspire to heaven and, by the world, to be consigned to purgatory; to be robbed of one's identity and be clad in the garb of . . . an inferior being; to see one's principles distorted, every motive questioned, one's words misquoted, every act misunderstood, one's whole life misrepresented, and made a caricature in the eyes of all men, without the power of redress, is to suffer all the unmitigated pangs of inner mortification.

Despite the virtues of the Jews, the errors had taken root and flourished. Silverman asked but one thing from Christian preachers—to desist from the "error" of charging Jews with deicide.[23]

Some rabbis drew a measure of comfort from the belief that the persecutors were the real enemies of Christianity. Not only was persecution a "monstrous blasphemy," but also it resulted in a weaker Christianity. According to Rabbi Silverman, "Russia has set Christianity one or two centuries backward. Antisemitic agitation in Germany will have a similar result. The church is committing a monumental blunder in conniving at this nineteenth century outrage, and must sooner or later be overtaken by her Nemesis. The church should in her own interest . . . rise up in arms against unholy Russia and unrighteous Germany." Religious leaders voiced a belief similar in kind when they asserted that persecution would boomerang and bring suffering to its host country.[24]

The second reason frequently given to explain Western antisemitism was popular envy of the economic successes scored by emancipated Jews. How Jews succeeded in the burgeoning capitalist markets and proceeded to accumulate great wealth that effectively stymied their competitors accounted for resentment and hostility. Antisemites even charged that the now-powerful Jews aimed at the "judaization" of society under their economic domination.[25] Other rabbis commented on the antisemites' use of the Shylock image, a popular stereotype that lent credence to the image of the Jew as cruel and immoral usurer. Not surprisingly a few serious articles in the Jewish press during the years of German persecution dealt with Shakespeare's perversion of the historical fact that the real Shylock was a Christian.[26] The economic reason for antisemitism was developed more fully by Rabbi Wise's *American Israelite*. In perhaps the most sophisticated analysis of the situation it interpreted racist antisemitism as a weapon of conservatives to hold on to the old order despite the inroads of materialism and secularization. What Christians found distasteful in an urbanized, modernized economy seemed to be summed up in the person of the Jew. The newspaper understood that in the contest between modernity and reaction, Western Jews could identify only with the new order.[27]

Reform Rabbi Emil G. Hirsch elaborated on the economic explanation and on other causes of Jew-hatred. In one Hanukkah sermon he said that Russian antisemitism resulted from a hypernationalism that labored to extirpate all languages, religions, and customs that deviated from accepted national norms. Since Jews were the *Versuchsvolk*, the guinea pigs on whom new principles were tested, they were the immediate victims. (Here Hirsch digressed to laud the Russian Jews who preferred to suffer rather than abandon their faith. We Germans hold ourselves superior to the East Europeans, he told his audience, but it is they whose loyalty and idealism make them the true aristocrats.) In Germany, he continued, the cause of antisemitism was economic. Just as Antiochus Epiphanes of the Hanukkah story desired to expropriate Jewish wealth, so in modern Germany, where Jews had become the "dynamo of the industrial activities of the fatherland," Jewish wealth and power evoked an anticapitalist countercrusade. The outrages were permitted, since officials sought thereby to deflect popular protests meant for Bismarck's government. Hirsch's advice on the best way to combat that type of antisemitism, albeit unrealistic, was for Jews to repudiate the individualistic economic creed of laissez-faire and to live the prophetic message of social and communal justice.[28]

The rabbi also examined the American scene. Looking at social discrimination, which was the type of antisemitism that prevailed, Hirsch found the cause in the social climbing nature of the post–Civil War nouveaux riches. Anticipating John Higham's classic interpretation,[29] he argued that the nouveaux riches, specifically the Gentile women, faulted the Jew for his vulgarity, boorishness, and ostentatious behavior. "I do not deny that there are Jews that are vulgar," Hirsch answered, and he pointed to the vulgar display of jewelry and the loud talk and rudeness on their part. "But," he added, "there are as many non-Jews that do the same thing." Although he said that personally he didn't resent exclusionary practices because he had no wish to associate with those who would exclude him, he urged Jews to mind their manners and see that their behavior was above reproach. At least as important was his suggestion that Jews endow programs of Jewish studies at the major universities. He himself had been appointed in 1892 by the University of Chicago where he was one of the first Jews in the United States to hold a chair in rabbinic literature and philosophy. In the rabbi's words, "One Jewish professor, whatever his branch may be, and especially if he teaches Jewish science [a reference to Wissenschaft des Judenthums, the science of Jewish scholarship] and teaches the history of Judaism and the philosophy of Judaism, does more for the generations to be than all other movements to combat prejudice combined."[30]

Members of the same family could and did differ on the causes of the new antisemitism. Rabbi Marcus Jastrow of Baltimore, attempting to explain the meaning of the Jewish Question in an early sermon had this to say: "This is not a religious question or a Jewish question or, as the name of disguise now adopted runs, a Semitic or Aryan question, but one of human civilization, when the feeling pervades all the fair-minded that the ground beneath us is shaking whereupon stands the ladder of progress [that] humanity has repeatedly attempted to climb up and repeatedly failed." It was a universal tragedy, he maintained, because "the economy of the human mind cannot well spare Israel's labor." A few years later the rabbi changed course. Agreeing that more than one cause explained the phenomenon, he refused to single out the religious charge of deicide. No "enlightened" people of the nineteenth century could be guided solely by so ancient a calumny. Irrespective of whether Christianity remained a component of modern antisemitism, Jew-hatred lay dormant in Germany until revived by the "science" of racism. Antisemites could then mobilize different segments of society under a banner that proclaimed: "We are Aryans, and the Jew is the Semite. The Jew is a foreign substance in the Teutonic body, and in the bodies of all European nations the Jew is a festering splinter." For anything bad that happened, "*der Jude wird verbrennt* [the Jew is burned]."[31]

Jastrow's son, Morris Jastrow Jr., thought otherwise. Trained for the rabbinate, he served one year in a pulpit, but with strong reservations about the future of Judaism in America he left the rabbinate for an appointment as professor of Semitic languages at the University of Pennsylvania in 1892. In the first segment of a lengthy article for the *International Journal of Ethics,* the younger Jastrow denied that racial differences accounted for the new antisemitism. He offered learned arguments on the inaccuracy and unscientific nature of racial categorization; there was no such thing as a pure Jewish or Aryan race. Nor did political or religious factors explain the European persecution. The root cause, he insisted, was *social:* "What we regard as national traits are the result of *tradition,* impressed upon people by virtue of living together under the same influences, sharing their interests with one another, and passing through the same experiences." What was looked on as the Jewish spirit was the product of conditions in the medieval ghetto; race played no part in determining the result, and religion figured only to the extent that it was part of the prevailing conditions.

The second section of the article dealt with the so-called Jewish traits that antisemites were so quick to condemn. Those traits, he insisted, were generated by two factors: the dispersion of the Jews to all corners of the world and the treatment they were accorded by the rulers of the different lands. Restricted to certain limited areas or ghettos and to the sole occupation of money-lending, their isolated life over time made them into a "peculiar" people. Within the ghettos they lived under a single religious influence, that of the Talmud, and their internal life was shaped by a law of countless regulations and ceremonials. Jastrow sympathetically portrayed the pre-modern Jew as the product of his ghetto environment, but he had less patience for those who remained bound to the Talmud and to their own people once the ghetto walls crumbled. That attachment, he predicted, "is certain to preserve peculiarities and to engender new ones." His answer was purposeful assimilation by the Jews and the quicker the better. He praised both the German and Russian Jews in the United States for their rapid assimilation, striking proof, he said, that "the traits peculiar to the Jews have been impressed upon them, not by racial instincts, nor by their religion, but *solely* by the ghetto." It was a far cry from his father's emphasis on the preservation of the Jewish mission and the Jewish heritage. While Jastrow *père* labored to stem the tide of defections from the synagogue, his son looked to the day when Judaism became some vague spiritual and ethical force.[32]

Rabbis suggested a host of additional reasons for the outbreak of the new antisemitism in Germany. Among the most popular were German nationalist and anti-foreign sentiments, Bismarck's political motives, the influence of Jesuitism, and Jewish attachment to Talmudic, or what was perceived as alien, law. Although most shied away from faulting the victims, some did assign a measure of culpability to the German Jews. The *American Israelite* cited Jewish participation in the economic scandals after the Franco-Prussian war, and the *Jewish Messenger* agreed with England's Rothschild that the situation would have been less severe had the German Jews worked to improve the conditions of their poorer brethren. Others like the younger Jastrow encouraged their fellow Jews to avoid the image of clannishness. More common were statements that indifference to religion and the Jewish cultural heritage had brought about the persecution. Since it had appeared for a time as if the upper-class assimilated Jews were the principal target and that the more observant German Jews suffered less, the rabbis who were eager to slow the rate of assimilation among their own congregants doubtless found that message useful for teaching economically mobile American Jews the consequences of religious laxity. Rabbi Leon Straus of Alabama, for example, warned his congregants that God had brought about the European persecutions so that the Jews, who worshiped idols of gold and silver, could return to Him and find safety.[33] The suggestions, however, that Jews remain loyal to the synagogue and resist total assimilation bore little fruit in a materialistic age.

Whatever the cause of the new antisemitism, rabbis also considered the question of an appropriate Jewish response both in Germany and America. Again, a multitude of suggestions surfaced, ranging from sheer passivity to the recommendation that Jews confront antisemitic mobs with physical force. Surprisingly, Rabbi Isaacs's *Jewish Messenger*, usually the most conformist and conservative of the Jewish periodicals, once said: "One determined volley of musketry in the face of the mob would silence the antisemitic agitation *at once.*"[34] While one rabbi suggested that Jews keep the faith and remain silent (Sabato Morais), another said that Jews must act with courage and betray no cowardice (Joseph Krauskopf), and a third urged a vigorous campaign of education from pulpit and press to correct the errors and slanders of the Jew-haters (Joseph Silverman). Of the three the third was most popular. Unfortunately, however, education easily turned into apologetics, and neither Jews nor Christians who repeatedly recounted Jewish contributions to civilization were particularly effective. There were also some, like Rabbi Wise in the *American Israelite*, who insisted that Jews had to be better than non-Jews.[35]

Two weapons usually employed by Jewish defenders of fellow Jews abroad were the plea for government intervention and the mobilization of non-Jewish public opinion. Since the former was rendered useless by the German Jewish insistence that they could handle the situation alone and by Washington's policy of noninvolvement,[36] Jewish laity as well as clergy looked for the support of sympathetic Christians and the religious press. The *Jewish Messenger*, which carefully followed the secular and Christian press, complained that those papers discussed the German situation "as though 500,000 cattle [rather than people] were concerned." When the Congregationalist weekly, the *Independent*, described the persecutions in Western Europe but added that it could not state to what extent they were justified, the *American Hebrew* was outraged. Would the writer of that article have considered the possibility that the Spanish Inquisition had also been justified?[37]

In one episode two rabbis, Marcus Jastrow and Sabato Morais, differed publicly over the desirability of Christian aid. Apparently someone had approached liberal Christian leaders in New York, and on the same Sunday in December 1880 two prominent ministers, Henry Ward Beecher and Robert Collyer, protested German persecution. Jastrow appreciated their comments, adding realistically that the ministers also aimed at shielding their churches from identification with the Stoecker brand of Christianity, but Morais disagreed. Although Jews had for many years sought to enlist non-Jewish allies in campaigns for Jewish causes, he resented what he interpreted as Christian patronage. He therefore urged Jews not to participate in any public rallies on behalf of the victims—"Self-respect suggests that course."[38] Morais, however, was in the small minority, and the defense of Jews by Christians appeared in books and in periodicals around the country.

Of all the antisemitic charges the most worrisome to American Jews was the accusation that Jews, ever the aliens, could not be patriots of the lands in which they lived just because of their Jewishness. It was not a novel indictment; the loyalty of the ancient Israelites was questioned in the biblical books of Exodus and Esther. In the United States at the time of the Revolution and again during the Civil War both sides accused the Jews of disloyalty.[39] The charge persisted, threatening the overriding Jewish desire for equality and acceptance within the body politic. By way of defense,

American Jews censored their own words and actions to guard against any hint of an other-than-American allegiance. They collected statistics on the number and exploits of Jews in the armed forces during America's wars, and they trotted them out regularly in answer to anti-Jewish slanders or when appealing for equal political, civil, or social rights. In 1892 they organized an American Jewish Historical Society, which proceeded to collect documents and publish articles proving how Jews shared in the founding of the country. Little seemed to help. As late as 1896 the *American Hebrew* asked: "Is a Jew always a foreigner and intruder, however many generations back his ancestors may have dwelt in the land?"[40]

At the same time, Jewish religious leaders taught lessons of patriotism in sermons that repeatedly emphasized the glories of America and what the country had done for the Jewish minority. They soon broadened their defense of Jewish loyalties to include all Jews and not merely the Americans. In 1876, for example, with no apparent provocation, the *Jewish Messenger* pointed to Jewish patriotism in France and Germany during the Franco-Prussian War. Should a war break out between Russia and Turkey, the paper predicted, Jews of both Western countries would fight valiantly on behalf of their respective fatherlands.[41]

During the last quarter of the nineteenth century the subject of Jewish patriotism, or the lack thereof, assumed greater significance in the diatribes of the antisemites. The man who awakened the greatest fear and resentment of Jews on both sides of the Atlantic, and the symbol of "respectable" antisemites who were suspicious of Jewish loyalties, was Goldwin Smith. Smith, a wealthy English expatriate who had taught modern history at Oxford, joined Cornell University's faculty in 1868. He retained an honorary professorship and returned to lecture periodically in Ithaca after making his home in Canada. One study that traces various sources of his Jew-hatred shows that his public attacks on Jews drew both from age-old myths like deicide and from events and people of the later Victorian era. Appearing in reputable English and American journals, the attacks were sparked in the 1870s by a bitter critique of Disraeli's policy in the Balkans. Smith charged the prime minister with supporting Turkey at the expense of Bulgaria and Russia in order to further Jewish interests: "Had England been drawn into this conflict, it would have been in some measure a Jewish war, a war waged with British blood to uphold the objects of Jewish sympathy or to avenge Jewish wrongs." Although not germane to his subject, he proceeded to criticize the political objectives of Jews, Jewish racial exclusiveness, and Jewish loyalties.[42] In subsequent well-written but venomous articles dealing with the Jewish situation in both Germany and Russia, he continued to attack Disraeli's "tribe." Tribe and tribalism were among Smith's favorite words for describing Jews. The tribal image echoed even in a textbook he wrote. Referring to Disraeli's father who had converted to Anglicanism, he said that the father "quit the tents of his people," an image that conjured up primitive tribalism.[43]

Smith amplified his anti-Jewish themes of "tribalism": devotion to a biblical and Talmudic law making for exclusiveness and clannishness, identification with a "repellent nationality," lack of patriotism, and Jewish political and economic power dedicated to Jewish racial interests. In a letter to the *Nation* he added that the Jews, who "make race a religion" and act out of "tribal bias," regard "the rest of the community as Gentiles and refuse intermarriage with them." He had supported the enfranchisement of Jews, he said, but "to make them patriots while they remain Jews is beyond the legislator's power." He once predicted to Felix Adler, who trained for the rabbinate but left Judaism to found the Society for Ethical Culture, that in time of crisis Jewish "clan feeling" or inseverable bonds with the Jewish people, would transcend patriotism. Nor did the Englishman see any need for the Jewish Bible. Since civilization rested on the New Testament, he claimed that the Old Testament was but a millstone around Christianity's neck.[44]

Those last remarks called forth criticism from the *New York Times:* "It was bad enough to have been persecuted by Kings and abused by German statesmen, but to have been pronounced unfit to live, and to have their venerable scriptures danced upon by Mr. Smith, must be the last drop in [the Jews'] cup of humiliation." Rabbi Kaufmann Kohler also took issue with Smith's views of the Old Testament. He insisted that the Hebrew Bible and Judaism purveyed a universalist message of a religion of all humanity that rested on faith, love, hope, and peace. Nevertheless, Smith's charges remained part of his general indictment of Judaism as well as of Jews. His attacks persisted through the 1890s. In 1891 at a meeting of the Chautauqua society Rabbi Gustav Gottheil summarized Smith's abuse by calling him "our old enemy, who for the last twenty-five years, has made it his ignoble task to create an anti-Semitic feeling among the English-speaking nations."[45]

Denunciations of Smith resounded in sermons and in the Anglo-Jewish press.[46] As they scrutinized various facets of the Englishman's theories, the rabbis focused mainly on the subject of patriotism. The best-known reply to Smith came in a sermon called "Can Jews Be Patriots?" by the prominent rabbi of England, Hermann Adler. Adler began with the oft-cited verse in Jeremiah (29:7), "And seek the welfare of the city to which I have exiled you and pray to the Lord in its behalf; for in its prosperity you shall prosper," and he developed the thesis that Jews had lived up to the prophet's injunction ever since. As earlier defenders usually had, he pointed to various wars in which Jews throughout the world had participated, the military honors they had won, and their performance as trusted diplomatic envoys in their countries' service. As for England's Jews, there was "no class more deeply concerned for the honor, the highest and truest interests of our beloved country . . . , no class more ready . . . to make every sacrifice of comfort, of substance, nay, of dear life itself." Using biblical and rabbinic sources, Adler also denied Smith's sneers about a Jewish tribal God and a tribal morality. Given all those facts, the conclusion was self-evident: obedience to Jewish law and codes of behavior neither contradicted patriotism nor made Jews morally inferior to Christians.[47]

Shortly after Adler published his reply to Smith, an American pamphlet appeared under the same title. Written by Isaac Schwab, a Reform rabbi in New York, it followed Adler's pattern for the most part. Schwab also claimed most emphatically that patriotism did not contradict Jewish law, and in far greater detail than Adler he traced Jewish loyalty to their countries from ancient times to the nineteenth century. In the periods of the Assyrians and the Persians, the Romans, the dark Middle Ages, and the post-Emancipation era—and with the support of their sages and teachers—Jews fought for and served the nations in whose midst they lived. The love that they bore those countries was a bond as strong as their love for their parents, and their attachment was not diminished even by their religious longing for Palestine. For the benefit of his American readers Schwab also included statements on the American Jewish experience, emphasizing the rights that they enjoyed after the Revolution and their devotion to the Union during the Civil War. Different from Adler in one essential point, Rabbi Schwab conditioned Jewish patriotism on their enjoyment of equality: "The foreigner having settled in [a particular] land permanently, and [having] interwoven his interests with those of the native citizens, will just as heartily be devoted to it as they, provided he have equal rights and liberties, untainted by sectarian prejudices, or the fanaticism of race."[48]

Smith answered Adler in not one but several articles.[49] Courteous in tone, he did not backtrack but instead repeated and elaborated his previous charges. He remained fixed on the point that the Jews constituted a race—one that believed in a tribal god and abided by a tribal morality —and not a very admirable race at that. Now he added a detailed condemnation of the economic and social practices of that alien "jealously separate race." The antisemitic eruptions were not the result of religious fanaticism, he insisted, but rather the consequences of Jewish practices: "The disturbances are essentially not religious, though religion too has played a part, but economical and social. . . . The main cause has always been the unhappy relation of a wandering and parasitic race, retaining its tribal exclusiveness, to the races among which it sojourns, and on the produce of whose labor it feeds." Injecting a new element into the picture of the unsavory Jew, he attacked the Talmud, the base of the Jews' repellent traits and clannishness, and he touted the superiority of Christianity over Judaism. The Hebrew Bible was not so bad, Smith now admitted, but the dry legalistic Talmud, which embodied a message so different from that of Christianity, was something else:

> Talmudism is the matter from which the spirit has soared away, the lees from which the wine has been drawn off. It is a recoil . . . from the Universal Brotherhood of the Gospel into a Tribalism . . . [that] built up ramparts of hatred. . . . It is a recoil from the moral liberty of the Gospel into a legalism which buries conscience under a mountain of formality, ceremony, and casuistry, often portentous in their character. . . . It is a recoil from the spirituality of the Gospel . . . to wealth-worship and plutocracy.

It easily followed from Smith's bill of particulars that patriotism could not be expected from the Jewish race. Rather, the vast wealth amassed by the Jews was used to further only their own interests and aspirations for power. Smith formulated his position in either/or terms—Jew or patriot; a "Jewish patriot" was an oxymoron. Patriotism as defined by the Englishman was more than service to the country in time of war. It meant unqualified exclusive identification with the nation's goals and purposeful assimilation on the part of the Jews. To be sure, many modern Jews were casting Judaism aside and "blending" with their surroundings, but a hard core of "strict" separatists remained. They were the "genuine" Jews, the clannish ones, Smith said, who still practiced the tribal rite of circumcision and who refused to intermarry with the Gentiles.

"Alien," "clannish," and "separatist" were adjectives repeatedly used by Smith about the Jews. A recent biography explains that Smith was a racist in the nineteenth-century meaning of the term. Unlike extremists who defined the Jews as an inferior species like Asiatics, Orientals, or descendants of the Khazars, Smith never preached that Jewishness was a matter of biology or genetics.[50] Nor was it a permanent condition. Jews were trapped by a long history of a fossilized religion, but it was within their power to discard those objectionable traits that were harmful to civilized nations and to themselves. Were they to throw off the dictates of the biblical and Talmudic law, a law that commanded the primitive practices of circumcision and endogamy, and were they to disavow any exclusive Jewish interests, they would be incorporated into society at large. Instead of a Jewish group there would be only individuals who had emancipated themselves from Jewish law and the Jewish collectivity. In short, Jews, sheared of the fundamentals of Judaism, were acceptable.

Smith also considered whether a nation like Germany had a way out if it faced a threat to its political and economic well-being from the sizable Jewish population in its midst. Violence could not be condoned, nor could freedom once granted to the Jews be rescinded, he said, but in self-defense the government had the right to keep the rule of the nation "in German hands." It could, for example, encourage anti-Jewish journals and organizations, and it could limit immigration. Admittedly, some of those actions seemed harsh, but in response to Jewish provocation they were eminently fair. After all, "the land of every nation is its own." Smith never advocated expulsion of the Jews, although he did claim that banishment at the hands of Edward I of England (1290) was intended by the king as a measure of social reform. Nor was a Jewish restoration to Palestine more than a partial remedy. The Turks might be persuaded to relinquish that land, and while a home in Palestine was not desired by the Westernized Jew, it might attract the Eastern Jew whose relations to the native population were particularly bad.

Others like Smith agreed that Jewish clannishness caused Jew-hatred and that conscious or purposeful assimilation was the best antidote. Indeed, the younger Jastrow had given that similar advice to his fellow Jews. Again, when a group of prominent Christian academics and clerics was canvassed by the *American Hebrew* in 1890 to elicit their views on the causes and remedy for antisemitism, many stated openly that Jews themselves were at fault, that their clannishness and their belief that they were the Chosen People accounted for popular ostracism and dislike.[51] Not all those who condemned Jewish separatism advised measures as drastic as Smith had on how much Judaism the Jews should discard. One opinion, like that of the *Nation*, assigned the Jews no specific role in the process of assimilation but merely predicted that within a generation or two the Jews as a separate race would be absorbed by the nations in which they lived.[52]

Rabbis, whether Reformers or Traditionalists, who were out to preserve the synagogue and Judaism, sparred with the assimilationists. Some said that as long as the Jewish mission was unfulfilled, Jews had to retain their separatism.[53] Others had little faith that concessions by Jews, like mixing socially with Gentiles, would guarantee an end to prejudice. Rabbi Marcus Jastrow, still in opposition to his son, put it this way: "I, for my part, was never a believer in a friendship built on bacon and cemented with lard."[54] Indeed, despite Jewish compliance with the demand, for example, that they drop their dietary laws Christians continued to discriminate against Jews in public resorts. American Jewish religious leaders were content neither with discrimination nor with a total abandonment of their practices as Jews. Rather, their aim as always was twofold: they wanted full political and social equality, and they wanted the freedom to choose for themselves how much Judaism to retain.

A series of pogroms that erupted in the spring of 1881 shifted the primary focus of Western Jewry from Germany to Russia. That year enraged mobs of peasants and laborers, abetted by the government's encouragement or inaction, went on a rampage against Jews in cities and villages—killing, maiming and raping, looting, and destroying property. Far different from the relatively nonviolent persecution in Germany, the riots underscored the long and seemingly futile struggle for the emancipation and equal rights of Jews under czarist rule. On several occasions before 1881 the American government had interceded with Russia, either seeking its compliance with a bilateral treaty concerning the rights of American Jews in Russia or requesting more privileges for Russian Jews on humanitarian grounds. In that earlier diplomatic interchange both American and Russian officials had no compunction about referring to the Jews as an alien race. All indications showed that Russia was more than ready for the Western type of racism that prevailed in Germany.[55] Protest meetings organized by Jews and their sympathizers in the United States and England aroused popular opinion, but to no avail. Pogroms in tandem with increased political disabilities continued as long as czarist rule itself.

A widespread racist explanation for the riots of 1881 came from one Mme. Zenaide Ragozin, whose lengthy article in *Century Magazine* (1882) rationalized and exonerated the conduct of Russians and their government. She put the blame squarely on the Jews. Numbering several million within the Romanov Empire, they, despite their outwardly peaceable and timid demeanor, and despite "full" (!) religious and other liberties, were "systematically undermining the well-being of the country they inhabit." A state within a state, their law taught them "to consider the persons and property of their fellow-subjects, if belonging to a different race and religion from theirs, as their natural patrimony." Ragozin added lurid details about a secret organization that governed Jews, material she had gleaned from a book by a Jewish apostate. Most of her animus, however, was reserved for the Talmud, its teachings on how to despoil Gentiles and its responsibility for odious and anti-Gentile social habits. She easily concluded that the Jews were despised not for religious reasons "but because they are a parasitical race who, producing nothing, fasten on the produce of land and labor, and live on it, choking the breath of life out of commerce and industry." Like Goldwin Smith, Ragozin, believed that racial differences could be modified. If Jews were freed of their underhanded communal authorities and their Talmud-sanctioned misconduct, a different climate of opinion would obtain.[56]

American Jews and their periodicals denounced Ragozin's article. The *Jewish Messenger*, for example, called it a "tissue of lies," and Emma Lazarus wrote a stinging detailed critique. Unlike their more timid response to the German situation, they had no hesitation about appealing for government support. Myer Isaacs, son of the late Rabbi Samuel Isaacs, composed a full report of "legalized" Russian atrocities that was based mostly on diplomatic dispatches aired by the press. Meant for presentation to the Committee on Foreign Affairs of the House of Representatives, it requested American intervention with St. Petersburg for the prevention of further outbreaks.[57]

Goldwin Smith also participated in the discussion on the Russian situation. In 1891 he published an article in the prestigious *North American Review* that summarized his interpretation of a decade of persecution. He had first broached the subject of the pogroms in one of his answers to Hermann Adler, and although he called the latest article "New Light on the Jewish Question," he added very little of substance to what he had written since 1878. As Rabbi Isaacs's *Jewish Messenger* suggested, the correct title should have been "Old Spite on the Jewish Question." Again Smith repeated his favorite themes: Jews lusted for wealth and power, Jews lived by a tribal morality and nationality that consumed the nationality of the host country and negated patriotism, and Jewish law promoted clannishness and separatism. He therefore concluded that Russian persecution was not religious but rather an understandable consequence of Russian hatred and envy. Sounding much like Mme. Ragozin, Smith wrote sympathetically about the Russians, and he dismissed Jewish accounts of the atrocities as so much exaggeration. In the "New Light" essay he appeared uncertain whether Jews, the "genuine" Jews of Eastern Europe, or those who clung to Talmudic law, could be "denationalized" as rapidly as they were "derabbinized." The *North American Review* carried several Jewish rejoinders to Smith. One, from Rabbi Adler of England, raised the question that all concerned Jews were asking: Was there a remedy for the Russian Jews?[58]

Incessant persecution and repeated attacks on Talmudic Judaism prompted Kaufmann Kohler to participate actively in Jewish defense. The Reformer raised defense to a higher level. Less concerned with the Ragozins and the Smiths, he determinedly set out to refute the scholars who scoffed at Rabbinic Judaism and maintained that the creed and morality of Christianity, the daughter religion, had far surpassed the mother faith. In 1893–1894 he published a lengthy monograph that was serialized in *American Hebrew* under the title "The Ethics of the Talmud." His central theme was that the ethical doctrines of both the ancient Talmud and the New Testament drew from the same source, the moral teachings of the ascetic Essenes. Jesus, whom he lauded, was the Essene par excellence, and like that sect his religion was Judaism. Drawing on his vast knowledge of classical, rabbinic, and modern scholarship, Kohler argued that the spirit of Talmudic Judaism had always been the "prophetical truth" that embodied the code of humanitarianism. Despite its legalisms, the Talmud's lessons on how to relate to strangers and enemies, including the laws on usury and those on the proper treatment of women, slaves, pagans, and proselytes, proved that Jewish law did not discriminate in essentials against the non-Jew. Kohler pointed out the areas where Judaism and Christianity, after the generation of Jesus, differed, but he claimed that the new directions plotted by the early church reflected the superiority of Judaism. In his opinion the Talmud's love of mankind and its definition of righteousness and holiness set it on a par with, or even above, Christianity: "Has Christian civilization any right to denounce the Talmud when it might yet adopt many of its rules for the improvement of common morality?" In sum, the accusations of the antisemites against the Talmud and the Jews who lived by its laws were invalid.[59]

Years before the new antisemitism blossomed, Kohler had aired his thesis on the Essenes as the model for the rabbis of the Mishnah and the

Talmud and for the New Testament. Now, too, he focused more on earlier European Jew-hatred rather than on the new antisemitism. Several months before his monograph appeared he participated in the World's Parliament of Religions where he expounded the same theories. His own contribution to the international gathering had attempted, albeit in a low key, to show how well Judaism fared in comparison with Christianity. Kohler again defended rabbinic Judaism and its ethical code a short time later in a letter to the *New York Times*.[60] Doubtless he believed that by rebutting the scholars who purveyed a learned rationale for antisemitism, the general problem could be ameliorated.

The question posed by those like Hermann Adler on what was the proper remedy for the Russian Jews underscored important differences between the situations in Germany and the czarist empire. With respect to Germany there were far stronger reasons to view the new antisemitism as a temporary aberration. German Jews had been enfranchised, they had prospered economically and socially, they did not think of fleeing the country, and they did not seek financial relief from abroad. In Russia, where disturbances had become almost an annual rite of the Easter season, many Jews despaired of finding a secure existence. They looked rather to the West and above all to the United States. A mass exodus of hundreds of thousands of Russian Jews, unlike anything that had transpired in Germany, began. From the time of leaving their homes the indigent Russians created serious problems for American Jewish communal leaders. Whether or not they approved of the immigrants, they shouldered the responsibility of overseeing the major steps in the removal process: transportation from Europe, immediate aid for the hungry and sick, settlement and employment, and integration into the American Jewish community and American society at large. American Jews in general were far less than enthusiastic about their new wards, but how they responded to the needs of the immigrants constituted one of the more admirable chapters of their history.[61] Rabbis usually called for sympathy with the new arrivals and defended them against anti-immigrant attacks. Rabbi I. S. Leucht of New Orleans, for example, preached that despite charges by upper-class Jews the immigrants did not arouse anti-Jewish prejudice in America.[62]

Was there any way that Russian Jews could help themselves? Rabbi Abram Isaacs of the *Jewish Messenger* talked of three options available to the Russians. They could convert and submit to the government's policy of Russification, they could emigrate to the West or to Palestine, or they could stay where they were and prove by their deeds that Jews could be patriots. The rabbi preferred the third; conversion, a surrender of Judaism, was unspeakable, and the relocation of one million let alone five million Jews was impossible. Several years earlier Isaacs had denounced Emma Lazarus's defense of a Jewish nationality. At that time he suggested that wealthy Russian Jews underwrite a campaign in Russia for Jewish rights and that they set up "civilizing" schools for teaching proper citizenship to Jewish children.[63]

In 1890 Isaacs canvassed the views of some scholars who were members of the American Historical Association. Including presidents of universities and other well-known intellectuals, the respondents constituted a prestigious group. Isaacs posed one question: What measures should the Jews of Russia adopt to secure civil and religious liberty? The rabbi knew that the subject was new to many, that their sources of information were scanty, and that some could be led astray by personal prejudice. But he called it their duty to defend the victims of religious persecution, and doubtless he hoped that he could enlist their sympathy on behalf of the victims. Of some twenty responses he received and printed in the *Messenger,* opinions varied. A few thought that time would help, and so would opposition from foreign governments, Christian religious leaders, and the public at large. Only one respondent favored emigration while another urged that Russian Jews stand uncompromisingly for equal rights at the same time that they moderated their "peculiarities."

Isaacs's informal symposium brought Goldwin Smith back into the picture. Smith had accepted the invitation to air his opinions, and in a letter in which he admitted that his views were unlikely to gain Jewish approval, he again denied that religious prejudice accounted for the persecution. The solution, he maintained, was simple: "Let the Jews, without compromising any part of their religious belief or worship, only cease to be a separate nationality or tribe, identifying themselves thoroughly with the people among whom they dwell." Were they to mix with their fellow citizens, which included intermarriage, and pursue the same vocations, they would be able to advance to any heights unimpeded by their religion. Denying that social customs which he called *national* traits were integral components of the Jewish faith, he warned: "If you reply that your separate nationality is your religion and cannot be resigned, I can only say that in that case I fear the question which you propounded to me must remain unsolved." Nor did he now agree that a return to Palestine, of which he had once casually approved, was a proper solution.

Isaacs answered Smith privately. Ignoring the religion-versus-nationality question, he argued that identification with the Russians was precisely what the Jews desired. Not only were fifty thousand of them enrolled in the Russian armies, but they also sang Russian hymns in their schools, were proud of their fellow Jews who achieved national prominence in Russian arts and philanthropy, and, as instructed by the prophet Jeremiah, prayed for the welfare of the country. It was the Russian and not the Jew, Isaacs concluded, who insisted on a separate nationality that would make "the Hebrew a foreigner on the soil which is his fatherland." Russian proscriptive laws—disenfranchisement, limits on places of residence, exclusion from trades, professions and schools—were to blame. Neither Smith nor Isaacs convinced the other. A second private letter from Smith to the rabbi followed, but there the correspondence ended.[64]

A few years later, and acting independently, Rabbi Joseph Krauskopf of Philadelphia advanced another scheme. He would travel to Russia, study the condition of the Jews, and petition the czarist government to permit Jewish families to engage in agriculture on land outside the Pale of Settlement. His objective was to relieve the congestion and extreme poverty of Jews within the districts of the Pale that caused so many to emigrate. To validate an *American* interest in internal Russian affairs, he also maintained that reduced emigration would ease the condition of labor in the United States, which was severely hit by the panic of 1893, as well as the burden of relief that fell on the Jewish community. The rabbi explained his plan of colonization to the Russian minister of finance, adding that it would make the settlers "self-supporting tillers of the soil and honorable citizens of your esteemed country." His use of the word "citizens" suggests that he may have thought that the project, to be financed "at our [American Jewish?] expense," would hasten the full emancipation of Russian Jewry. In any case, he was doubtless influenced by the antisemitic charge that the Jews, a nation of petty traders, were a parasitic people shunning agriculture and living off the labor of others. Although Krauskopf's plan was endorsed by Andrew D. White, the American minister to Russia, it went no further.[65]

After the pogroms of 1881, interest in a restoration to Palestine as the solution to antisemitism mounted. Inspired by the writings of people like Leo Pinsker in the East and Emma Lazarus in the West, individuals and small groups in Europe and the United States worked to turn restorationist thought into reality. Before Theodor Herzl organized the political Zionist movement in 1897, those proto-Zionists, who fixed on restoration as the one sure answer to Russian persecution, talked in terms of establishing Jewish colonies in Palestine. They were undeterred by the religious belief that restoration had to wait for the messianic age. As Emma Lazarus had written in her *Epistle to the Hebrews* (1882–1883), the renewal by Jews of Jewish talents in a Jewish land was the answer to racial antisemitism. While prominent Christians also expressed their sympathy with the Palestine solution, most Reform rabbis maintained that proto-Zionism and then Zionism suggested that Jews felt a primary loyalty to Palestine. That assumption in turn vindicated the antisemitic charge that Jews were a separate race and that the allegiance they professed for their country was justifiably suspect.

In 1897, when the first Zionist Congress adopted the Basel program calling for a Jewish homeland, the debate between Zionists and anti-Zionists on the issue of dual allegiance sharpened. American Reform rabbis, who as early as 1869 had disavowed restoration on theological grounds, kept to their initial stand, and their spokesmen repeatedly denounced Herzlian Zionism and Zionists. The hope for restoration, Kaufmann Kohler said, was "a blasphemy and a lie upon the lips of every American Jew." Thus, while Zionism strengthened the case of those, like Emma Lazarus, who believed that racial distinctiveness entitled Jews to a land of their own, it simultaneously strengthened the case of the antisemites.[66]

Supporters of proto-Zionism and then Zionism who worked for Jewish settlement or a state in Palestine vigorously denied that their nationalist sentiments contradicted their patriotism. Some resorted to compromises. For example, both the Traditionalist rabbi H. Pereira Mendes and the Reform rabbi Bernhard Felsenthal argued that Zionism was little more than philanthropy and that its purpose was to provide a refuge for *European* Jewish victims of persecution. In the first decade of its existence the Federation of American Zionists, the first major American Zionist organization, compromised Herzl's demand for statehood and similarly disclaimed any existential commitment on the part of American Zionists to settle in Palestine.[67]

The new antisemitism of the nineteenth century left a legacy for future American Jewish generations. For one thing, it exposed the inadequacies of communal strategy in defense of foreign Jews. How to unite the community and thereby strengthen the voice of American Jews, how to best represent the case of the foreign Jews to Washington, how to arouse public opinion most effectively, how to coordinate defense work with Jewish leaders in Europe—these were only some of the problems that needed to be solved. The weaknesses of defense were answered in turn by the establishment of new national agencies, like the American Jewish Committee, that took command in twentieth-century crises and that then determined the finer points of strategy.[68]

Particularly relevant for our purposes is the influence of the new antisemitism on the discourses of American rabbis. As mentioned earlier, in light of the racist theories that transcended national boundaries, rabbis had to reconsider their remarks on the differences that America made for its Jews. Often the awareness of Jewish vulnerability even in America explained why the optimistic tone that underlay earlier sermons largely evaporated. No longer was it commonplace to insist that civilization was progressing ever forward and with it the Jewish condition. If antisemitism was rife in Germany, and if France, the fount of liberty and equality, could produce a Dreyfus Affair, civilization was obviously retrogressing. Western Jewry had lived off the capital of the Enlightenment for many decades, and their beliefs in reason, liberalism, and ongoing progress were suddenly challenged and even destroyed.

Rabbi Isaac Wise's *American Israelite* reflected the change from optimism to gloom. In 1855 the paper had confidently predicted that all mankind was on its way to embracing the principle of liberty. Thirty-seven years later it wrote in connection with the European situation: "How could the nineteenth century, with all its grand achievements, thus deny and belie its glorious predecessor, the eighteenth century? How could the civilized world so retrograde in moral principle and human sentiment?" Since the Reform movement had incorporated the optimism of the Enlightenment into its very ideology, its rabbis in particular became less sanguine about the future prospects of European Jewry. As Joseph Krauskopf of Philadelphia admitted in a talk on Bismarck and Hermann Ahlwardt, his faith in the progress of mankind had been shaken.[69] True, some held on to their earlier beliefs and none predicted the calamities of the not so far off future, but the words of optimistic sermons often rang hollow. Today, in light of the traumas of the twentieth century, Henry Ward Beecher's statement on the Jewish condition in Germany appears naïve and even childlike. The popular Protestant minister had said in 1880: "No nation can commit with impunity the crime which will be charged to the Germans if they continue to persecute the Jews."[70]

In the end, despite the ongoing talk about remedies for the Jewish condition in Germany and Russia, the new antisemitism—and for that matter, the old—never ceased. The age-old stereotypes of the Jews as well as eruptions of actual discrimination are alive and well over a century later. Neither assimilation, nor "proper" Jewish economic and social behavior, nor memories of the Holocaust, nor even a Jewish state has solved the problem of Jew-hatred.

9

The World's Parliament of Religions

During the last decade of the nineteenth century American Jews heard mixed messages. On the one hand were threats to Jewish security. In Europe czarist persecution of Russian Jews—economic and cultural oppression as well as expulsions and pogroms—intensified, and on the entire Continent the teachings of racism and racial antisemitism increasingly found their way into writings of scholars and sensationalist bigots. In the United States social ostracism of the Jew, now compounded by the influx of thousands of Russian immigrants, grew more rigid, and the Populists, on the way to capturing a major political party, spewed forth their antisemitic venom. While secularism and materialism were driving Jews away from the synagogue, campaigns for national Sunday laws, a Christian amendment to the Constitution, and Protestant practices in the public schools were revived to safeguard the Christian character of the country. All this, plus Justice David Brewer's decision for the Supreme Court in 1892 that America was a Christian nation, alarmed Jews, causing them to wonder whether their quest for full equality had become more elusive.

Scholarship that incorporated the new theories of evolution and biblical criticism contributed to Christian opinions on Jews.[1] Modernists among Protestant ministers like Lyman Abbott and Washington Gladden applied the evolution-inspired concept that the younger was more advanced than the older to uphold the superiority of Christianity, the daughter religion, over Judaism, the mother faith. The modernists said from their pulpits that Christianity embodied higher ideals of morality, love, and universalism and thereby superseded Judaism. Impelled to reply, some rabbis played down the differences between the two religions. For example, they taught that major teachings of the New Testament—the golden rule, the kingdom of heaven, the Lord's Prayer—were Jewish in origin. In those same years Jesus and early Christianity became popular subjects for rabbinical sermons and lectures. Men of the caliber of Bernhard Felsenthal,

David Philipson, and Gotthard Deutsch joined the discussions. Emil G. Hirsch alone published three sermons on Jesus, one on Paul, and one lecture on the crucifixion. Jewish interest in Christianity may have paralleled Protestant interest, but the underlying Jewish motive was the defense of Judaism.

Despite the various forms of anti-Jewish discrimination, condescension, and contempt, there were signs of the liberalization of mainstream Protestantism. Important clerical and lay leaders spoke in more friendly terms of Judaism, and some readily joined Jews on the path to interreligious cooperation.[2] A significant example of the trend to ecumenicism was the World's Parliament of Religions. How well it would serve to counter the anti-Jewish forces was an open question.

The idea of a Parliament of Religions took root in connection with the World's Columbian Exposition of 1893 in Chicago. Mustering widespread enthusiasm, it envisioned an assembly at which representatives of Western and Eastern religions would elucidate the doctrines of their faiths and point up the similarities and differences among the religions. Not all American religious leaders, however, shared these objectives. Some saw the parliament as the opportunity to promote and pay tribute to the superiority of American Christianity; others foresaw a battle for supremacy among the faiths, and still others, like the Jews, hailed the parliament as a welcome boost to religious pluralism and interfaith harmony.[3]

Americans were enchanted by the "brilliant spectacle" of the parliament. One observer commented on the opening procession: The sight was dazzling with

> his Eminence James (Cardinal) Gibbons, magnificent in his robes of red [surrounded by] priests of the Celestial Empire in their long flowing garments of white. . . . [P]atriarchs of the old Greek Church . . . leaning on ivory sticks carved with figures representing ancient rites, [Chinese in robes of mandarin,] Buddhist monks attired in garments of white and yellow. . . . The Greek Archbishop of Zante . . . in purple robe and black cassock, glittering with chains of gold that hung about his neck.

The famous verse from the book of Malachi 2:10 that was chosen as the motto of the Parliament—"Have we not all one father, Hath not one God created us all?"—added to the aura of universalism.[4]

The organizers of the parliament invited American Jews to share in the gala event. Since Reform Jews were the oldest organized Jewish denomination as well as the most familiar to non-Jews, they were tapped to handle Jewish participation. Two branches of the Reform movement, the Central Conference of American Rabbis (CCAR) and the Union of American Hebrew Congregations (UAHC), swung into action. In 1892 the CCAR resolved to cooperate with the parliament, and it drew up an outline of subjects—historical, ethical, statistical, and archeological—for Jewish discussants. It resolved further to act in conjunction with the UAHC. Why laymen were included in what was clearly a rabbinical function was not explained, but the rabbis very likely sought to secure community-wide approval as well as the means to underwrite the expenses of the delegates and the costs of publishing the proceedings. The UAHC appointed a committee of prominent men that included former minister to Constantinople Oscar Straus and philanthropist Jacob Schiff to work with the rabbis. Joined by representatives of the Congress of Jewish Women, still in its formative stage, the enlarged committee planned the Jewish role at the parliament. A list of speakers was drawn up, assignments were parceled out, and some rabbis read the papers of their colleagues in advance. Except for presentations by two Traditionalists, Rabbis H. Pereira Mendes and Alexander Kohut, it was to be a solo performance by Reform.

Preparations for the parliament marked a departure for Jewish women. One story relates that when the women were asked to cooperate in plans for separate religious congresses to be held alongside the parliament, they retorted that they would accept only if they were recognized as "active" participants—that is, if women of their choice would be given spots as speakers. The men finally yielded, and assignments for papers included one to be delivered by Henrietta Szold and one by Josephine Lazarus. Szold spoke on "What Has Judaism Done for Woman?" and on the Jewish Publication Society, and Lazarus on "The Outlook of Judaism." Women's groups exulted in their triumph—one newspaper claimed that it was the first attempt by Jewish women to assemble as a collective entity for a religious gathering. Plans were immediately put into motion to launch a permanent national organization of women, and under the determined leadership of Hannah Solomon, the first sections of the National Council of Jewish Women (NCJW), were founded. Dedicated to religious, educational, and philanthropic works, the NCJW was soon affiliated with other American and foreign associations.[5]

Like the other religions, the Jews were asked to convene a denominational congress, which in their case was held a very short time before the
plenary sessions in September. At that congress, non-Jews had the opportunity to listen to position papers about Judaism by leading rabbis. Other
papers included those by the two women, Szold and Lazarus; the papers
by three non-Jews—D. G. Lyon of Harvard, Archbishop John Ireland, and
the Archbishop of Zante, Greece—rounded out the Jewish panel.[6]

The Christian organizers of the parliament spoke in terms of religious
peace and a "new fraternity . . . to aid in the upbuilding of the kingdom
of God in the hearts of men."[7] They warmly welcomed their Jewish colleagues, but a tone that was patronizing at the very least colored some
statements. John Henry Barrows, a Presbyterian minister and the major
coordinator of the parliament, gave full praise to Jews, "the most won-
derful of all races," but at bottom he still set them apart from Christian
America:

> [These] Jewish friends, some of whom are willing to call themselves Old
> Testament Christians, as I am willing to call myself a New Testament
> Jew, have zealously and powerfully cooperated in this good work. But the
> world calls us, and we call ourselves a Christian people. We believe in
> the gospels and in Him whom they set forth as "the light of the world,"
> and Christian America . . . welcomes to-day the earnest disciples of other
> faiths . . . who . . . have flocked to this jubilee of civilization.

Other religions may have joined the "jubilee" celebration, but Barrows's
words clearly meant that it was celebration of Christianity.

Charles C. Bonney, a jurist whose idea had sparked the organization
of a parliament, also expressed his Christian loyalties in an address of
welcome to the Jewish denominational congress. Calling himself an "ul-
tra and [as] ardent a Christian as the world contains," he explained that
precisely because he and most organizers of the parliament were Christians, "this day deserves to stand gold-bordered in human history as one
of the signs that a new age of brotherhood and peace has truly come."
He told the largely Jewish audience that "we" would prefer that you be
Christians, but that freedom of worship was the right of Jews as well as
Christians. After such words of welcome, Jews might well have wondered
whether their presence was on sufferance alone. To some it might even
have smacked of a Christian attempt at proselytism. Indeed, other speakers affirmed more strongly that "Christianity is the supreme religion" and

that it superseded Judaism. One delegate contended that "the other theistic beliefs have no elements of true theistic conception to give Christianity . . . but Christianity has much to give others." In the words of a contemporary journal, "Christianity is to conquer and supplant all the other religions of the world . . . and this Parliament is one of the steps toward this ultimate triumph."

Rabbis rejoiced in what they preferred to see as the liberal spirit of the parliament, and sentiments of joy and gratitude resounded from their pulpits. Ignoring what might easily be construed as groveling before the religion of the majority, they never voiced any suspicions that they were being used in what some Christian clergymen saw as a tribute to Christian triumphalism. Emil G. Hirsch of Chicago, an enthusiastic participant in the preliminaries leading up to the parliament, confidently foresaw the foundations of a universal religion and the fulfillment of the Jewish mission: "The Messianic kingdom is not yet; but who will doubt that it is to be?" Isaac Mayer Wise, the national leader of Reform Jews, was grateful for the chance—the first and perhaps the last, he mused—to elucidate and defend Judaism to the rest of the religious world. He felt, he said, "like the High Priest on Atonement Day."[8]

At the same time, however, some rabbis advised that the Jewish representatives concentrate at the parliament on defending their people against the rampant antisemitism at home and abroad. Kaufmann Kohler, then rabbi of Temple Beth-El in New York, was particularly concerned about Jew-hatred. At the conference of the CCAR that discussed the parliament, he offered a significant amendment to a committee report endorsing Jewish participation:

> *Whereas,* the anti-Semitic agitation, undeterred by the verdict of the enlightened still continues its own cruel work and forces its way through every land,
>
> *Resolved,* That besides the discussion of topics recommended, the Rabbinical Conference should solicit the co-operation of all American Jews in sympathy with the cause, both private men, societies and congregations to render the participation of the Jews in the Religious Congress of the Columbian World's Exposition, a matter of great international importance, in having the great aim and objects of Judaism clearly and emphatically stated before the entire world *and all the slanderous charges made against it through the successive ages by its declared foes substantially refuted.* (emphasis added)

The amendment went on to suggest that several renowned international scholars be commissioned to write treatises on antisemitic themes, particularly on the ritual murder charge. A joint committee of the CCAR, the UAHC, and the Congress of Jewish Women embraced Kohler's reasoning:

> Although the history of Judaism covers a period of more than three thousand years, no religion has been more thoroughly misunderstood and misinterpreted. Misconceptions of it are so deeply rooted that ours is still the humiliation to see the most enlightened nations of the world not only giving credence to beliefs concerning us that have been invented by fanaticism, and have not the slightest historical foundation, but even persecuting our brethren upon the strength of them.

Therefore, the committee hoped to invite, at their expense, Christian and Jewish scholars to participate in the parliament and to publish "exhaustive" monographs countering the antisemitic charges. They confidently expected that the results would silence the anti-Jewish slander at least within the civilized world.[9]

As it turned out, the words of the Archbishop of Zante, Archbishop John Ireland, and D. G. Lyon fell far short of the mark. The three non-Jewish papers in defense of the Jews barely skimmed over Jew-hatred. Ireland praised Judaism for its gift of monotheism to the world, and he called in general terms for an end to anti-Jewish persecution; the Archbishop of Zante repudiated the ritual murder libel in a few words. Lyon discussed a broader topic, "Jewish Contributions to Civilization." His major themes were the consonance of Jews and Judaism with American ideals and development, and Judaism's legacy to the world. Although highly admiring of the Jewish faith and sounding very much the liberal, he too hoped that Jews would ultimately accept Jesus:

> I do not forget that the Jews have not yet, in large numbers, admitted the greatness of Jesus, but this failure may be largely explained as the effect of certain theological teachings concerning his person, and of the sufferings which Jews have endured at the hands of those who bear his name. But in that name, and that personality rightly conceived, there is such potency to bless and to elevate, that I can see no reason why Jesus should not become to the Jews the greatest and most beloved of all their illustrious teachers.

Even Lyon, a good friend of the Jews, did not hide his belief that their faith was unequal to his.[10]

The Jewish presentations failed to turn out as Kohler had originally hoped. Many rabbis mentioned persecution or oppression of the Jews in history, particularly at the hands of Christianity, but they did so only in an abbreviated fashion. To be sure, on the premise that education, in this case about Judaism, could dispel Gentile ignorance that underlay Judeophobia, they may have thought that by elucidating the tenets of Judaism they could transform bigotry into appreciation. But only one rabbi, Joseph Silverman of New York's Temple Emanu-El, undertook to disprove what he called the "popular errors" about Jews. Silverman began by asserting that historians and other writers had presented a mixed picture of the Jew, portraying him either as totally virtuous or totally evil. He then proceeded to enumerate and refute popular antisemitic charges. Lambasting one so-called "error," he upheld Reform dogma by claiming, first, that Jews were not a separate nation. Contrary to bigots who preached that Jews could not be loyal to the country in which they lived, he argued that most Jews longed for neither a return to Palestine nor the resurrection of their temple. Not a nation, they were only a religious community, like Protestants and Catholics. Second, Jews were not guilty of the charges of clannishness or exclusiveness, and social ostracism for those reasons by fellow citizens were not warranted: "If there is any clannishness in the Jew," he rationalized, "it is due not to any contempt for the outside world, but to an utter abandon to the charm of home and the fascination of confreres in thought and sentiment." As for Jewish aversion to intermarriage, a proof offered by antisemites of Jewish separatism, resistance to mixed marriages was but a "natural barrier" separating denominations. Silverman's words might not have entirely pleased traditional Jews who followed Jewish legal proscriptions against many forms of intercourse with Gentiles, but they accurately expressed Reform sentiments.[11]

Silverman also took up age-old stereotypes and negative images of Jews still circulating in modern America, particularly those of the Jews as Christ-killers and the Jews as ritual murderers. As he said, "If such . . . misrepresentations . . . are taught in this country with the connivance of men who know better it is not difficult to understand how benighted peasants in Europe can be made to believe that Jews use the blood of Christian children at the Passover services, and how such monstrous calumnies could rouse the prejudice and vengeance of the ignorant masses."

Analogous to those extremist slanders and equally false, he added, were the charges that Jews were responsible for natural calamities. It wasn't unusual for some antisemites, for example, to claim that Jews had caused the black death of medieval times by poisoning the wells. The rabbi tackled economic slanders hurled at the Jews in greater detail. The image of the Jew as Shylock had long persisted, and even older were the images of Jews as parasitic nonproducers and deceitful money-lenders. Such stereotypes added up, Silverman summarized, to popular theories of a worldwide Jewish conspiracy: "This whole modern system of anti-Semitic agitation, and of attempts to convert the Jews by any means, reveals to us the erroneous impression entertained by many, it seems, that Jews have entered into a kind of secret competition with the rest of the world for the supremacy of Judaism and its followers." Although the charge of an international conspiracy of Jews, operating principally to destroy Christian civilization through Jewish control of the world's finance and the media, gained credence in the last quarter of the century, Silverman flatly denied it. "Nothing," he said, "could be further removed from the truth."[12]

Unlike some of his colleagues who sketched vague, rosy visions of inevitable improvement in intergroup relations, Silverman used historical examples and a dry, matter-of-fact tone to prove his case. Only when he recounted the virtues of the Jewish group or of selected Jews did he sound apologetic. For the purpose of rectifying the errors about Jews he proposed an extensive publicity campaign utilizing the press and the pulpit to disseminate the truth about Judaism. Calling for the cooperation of religious leaders, he also said that "the Church should . . . in the name of her own principles and teachings rise up in arms" against the antisemitic falsehoods and let the truth be told to the world. He thought that the Parliament of Religions was a good place to start.

Silverman's colleague, Kaufmann Kohler, did not forget about antisemitism, but although he had urged that Jews participate in the parliament in order to combat Jew-hatred, he refrained from addressing the subject directly. Rather, he attempted in a low-keyed fashion to show how favorably Judaism compared with Christianity. Indeed, his words on the superiority of Judaism were no less partisan than the Christian sentiments of Barrows and Bonney. He spoke twice, once on "Synagogue and Church in Their Mutual Relations, Particularly in Reference to the Ethical Teachings" and once on "Human Brotherhood as Taught by the Religions Based on the Bible." Drawing on his lengthy monograph, "The Ethics of the Talmud," he used a scholarly approach to vindicate Judaism against the antisemites.

Careful not to alienate the Christians in his audience, he showed an appreciation of Jesus and his humanitarian teachings at the same time that he depicted the grandeur of Judaism. In but half a sentence he denounced the evils of antisemitism that sharply divided Jews from Christians; historical research taught otherwise, he said. Since some scholars used biblical criticism to degrade Judaism in relation to Christianity, Kohler maintained at the very outset: "Thank Heaven, historical research has begun to bridge the wide gulf and to realize that the Synagogue holds the key to the mysteries of the Church. For after all, Jesus and his Apostles were both in their life and teaching Jews."[13]

As discussed above, Kohler now taught that the religious laws on ethical behavior came from the Old and not the New Testament.[14] In his words, "I learned them from the Talmud." He concentrated on the early period of the church, before Christianity was adopted by the Roman Empire, and the burden of his case was to show how Jesus, "a religious genius," and his followers drew from the teachings of the Essenes—a pietistic Jewish sect dating back to Maccabean times that lived according to the highest standards of purity and holiness. Kohler maintained that Jesus, like the Essene community, affirmed three rules of life: love of God, love of fellow man, and love of virtue. Those principles, found repeatedly in the sayings of the Mishnaic and Talmudic sages, showed conclusively that the early Christians taught nothing not found in Judaism. Even the order of their daily and Sabbath prayers followed the practices of the synagogue. Only when later Christians, having amalgamated pagan elements, changed the man Jesus into a divine being and the son of God did the radical break between Christianity and Judaism occur.

When Christianity proceeded to conquer the Western world, the two faiths went their separate ways. Kohler examined the ethical precepts of the post-Jesus generations and found them wanting:

First, all the salvation preached, the love and charity practiced, were made dependent upon the Creed. The rich treasures of the love of the Father in Heaven were all withheld from those who failed to recognize the sonship of Christ. . . . The world was divided into believers and unbelievers; hence, all the fanaticism and cruelty toward heretics and dissenters. Secondly, to be a true follower of Christ, one had to shape life after the pattern of the Sermon on the Mount—to renounce wife, wealth and comfort, and lead the life of a monk or nun . . . [forgetting] the claims of home and country, of state and society, the demand of justice and manhood, of intellectual progress, and of industrial enterprise. . . . And the third fault of the New Testament ethics is that it turns the human gaze too exclusively to the life beyond the grave, forgetful of the duties of life here on earth.

Not only did Judaism offer a more solid basis for social ethics, but Christians after Jesus, erred again when they defined the Old Testament as legalism and the New Testament as love. Showing that Jesus too demanded the preservation of the Mosaic law, Kohler said that "never was the so-called Sermon on the Mount intended to supplant the Law of Sinai." Moreover, society needed law and the domination of reason for its stability rather than "the mysteries of religion." On all those grounds, Judaism, the older faith which combined love and reason, was superior to Christianity. Having said all that, Kohler concluded on a conciliatory note and in words that smacked of religious pluralism. Truth was multifaceted, he said, and since each religion contributed to the ongoing search for the good and the beautiful, each therefore had an assigned role in God's design.

Kohler neither enumerated nor refuted the age-old antisemitic stereotypes and charges the way Silverman had, but his case against Jew-hatred was skillfully crafted. Praising Christianity as well as Judaism, he often sounded like a neutral adjudicator rather than a defender of the Jews. True, he suggested that the church after Jesus had gone astray, and he also asserted that the church fathers did not show the same good will to the synagogue that Jewish thinkers exhibited to both Christianity and Islam. But he claimed Jesus, a "preacher and saint," for the Jews, and he extolled Jesus' denunciations of hypocritical Jews. More important, albeit indirectly, he charged the post-Jesus church with being the source of Jew-hatred. Avoiding both invective and apologia, he presented the mother faith as a religion that merited neither abuse nor debasement. If not superior to Christianity, it was at least as good.[15] Nevertheless, Kohler sounded far milder than he had when the CCAR discussed participation in the parliament.

A book published in 1894 by the UAHC entitled *Judaism at the World's Parliament of Religions* did not include all of the presentations that bore on Judaism, but its contents reveal that at least twenty-two Reform rabbis spoke—some more than once—at the Jewish denominational congress and the parliament. Most participants expressed genuine enthusiasm over the parliament's ecumenical spirit, but the tone of their papers, whether they discussed theology, or ethics and customs, or the place of the Jew in world history, was unemotional and dignified. Relatively free of apologetics, the papers themselves revealed that some assigned topics often matched the specialties or favorite subject of the speaker. For example, Henry Berkowitz, the social justice activist, emphasized the dignity of labor and the responsibility of society for the disadvantaged; the renowned Talmudic scholar, Moses Mielziner, talked about the ethics of the Talmud; and Gotthard Deutsch, professor of history at Hebrew Union College, discussed the role of the Jews in different historical periods.[16] In addition to the praise of Judaism with respect to Christianity, two other themes were common to most papers—a love and reverence for America, and the merits of Reform over Orthodoxy.

More than half of the rabbis explained aspects of Judaism, and of those the presentations on Jewish theology and Jewish ethics were allotted most time. Isaac Wise introduced both subsections. In a lengthy and heavy paper on theology, he explained that "God-cognition" was the bedrock of all Jewish dogmas: Providence in turn included the covenant between man and God and the election of Israel, atonement, divine worship, human will, duty and accountability of mankind, the future of mankind, and personal immortality. Reason and scripture, he said, were the tools for developing those basic principles.[17] Other rabbis took up separate features of Jewish theology. Joseph Stolz discussed immortality, I. S. Moses the function of prayer, and Isaac Schwab the messianic idea. Bernhard Felsenthal, who developed the theme of the Sabbath presented a paper explaining the lasting importance of the day for the modern Jew. Barely concerned with the ceremonials that marked traditional observance of the day, the rabbi emphasized the moral character of the Sabbath and how it was meant to uplift the character of man in all dealings with his fellows. Jews bequeathed the Sabbath to the Christian world, but for Jews alone it provided a way to preserve their distinctiveness and keep them united. It gave them a day of study, a day of joy, and the strength to bear persecution. He closed with a tribute to the greatness of the United States for permitting the Jews to observe the Sabbath as they saw fit.[18]

One essay included in the section on theology played up the principles and agenda of Reform Judaism more than any other paper at the parliament. Under the lengthy title of "Syllabus of a Treatise on the Development of Religious Ideas in Judaism since Moses Mendelssohn," Rabbi Gustav Gottheil defended the charges leveled against Reform's creation of "a new Judaism." Reform began, he said, with Mendelssohn, a man who sought the harmony of religious practice and modern thought and who urged the acculturation of Jews for the attainment of their emancipation. In essence, "it was not a deflection from the faith on which the synagogue is built; it was life itself that demanded relief." Accordingly, the early Reformers in Germany set out to adjust their faith to the demands of modern life. From studies showing that all layers of the Law went through changes wrought by time, they sifted through the Bible and the Oral Law to discern the meaning of revelation for the modern Jew. They came up with the following precepts: the Unity of God—a commitment to the bond of a common brotherhood with all mankind and an abandonment of all rituals that kept Jews apart from his surroundings; the Chosen People—not a superior people but the people commissioned to execute the divine mission; a return to Palestine—no longer relevant for Jews who identified with the land of their birth or adoption and therefore excised from the Reform prayer book; and the Dispersion of Jews—providentially designed to enable Jews to fulfill their God-given mission worldwide, a mission leading to the peace and harmony of the messianic age. Gottheil did not belabor the essential differences between Reform and Christianity, but Traditionalist or Orthodox Jews were roundly excoriated. They were the illiberal fanatics, those who attempted to crush the inner spiritual freedom of the modern Jew. To be sure, some early Reformers showed excessive zeal regarding the need to advance beyond the age-old traditions, but the future of American Judaism belonged to them, the Reformers, and not to the Orthodox.[19]

Many of Gottheil's colleagues similarly applauded what they saw as the superiority of Reform. Like nineteenth-century Reform sermons in general, their presentations heaped praise on the awe-inspiring character of the Jewish ethical system. Nor did the rabbis, like Silverman, tire of affirming Reform's cardinal axiom: that Jews constituted neither a separate race nor nationality but merely a religious community. Clearly, renunciation of Jewish peoplehood and a search for acceptance by the countries in which Jews lived did more than reflect the beliefs of Reform. First, it countered the popular charge of the Jew as the unassimilable alien; second, it proved how well Judaism fit with Americanism.[20] In sum, the parliament served Reformers more as a platform for equating modern Judaism with their movement than as a way of elucidating the teachings of the Jewish faith to non-Jews.

Wise also delivered the opening paper on the subject of ethics. He outlined a system of ethics that he said flowed from the desire to become

God-like in behavior. He summarized Jewish ethics in three injunctions on individual behavior: the preservation of the human family, the duty of labor, and the duty to develop one's mental powers. Moses Mielziner, Gustav Gottheil, and Maurice Harris continued the discussion. Mielziner's paper on the ethics of the Talmud was a straightforward presentation that upheld the superiority of Judaism over Catholicism. He said, for example, that Judaism avoided extremes like the Catholic Church's rule of clerical celibacy. He also argued against the widespread popular notion that the Talmud was an illiberal source that underlay the unsavory conduct of the Jews. Gottheil spoke on the character and influence of Moses. An example for the church and mosque as well as the synagogue, Moses was forever unequaled as the modest leader, wise legislator, and teacher of morality. A man of God, indeed the prophet of God, but never raised by Judaism to the level of God, he founded a republic based on the idea of the unity of God and God's righteousness.[21]

Harris's paper, "Reverence and Rationalism," argued the inadequacies of philosophic thought for fulfilling the emotional and religious needs of the individual. The rabbi explained that because of a concentration on legalism and ceremonials in medieval times, thinkers of the Enlightenment and French Revolution vehemently attacked organized religion. Their work was continued in the nineteenth century by advances in science, like Darwinian principles, and the emphasis on the scientific method. Harris criticized the modern approach, denying that "the worth of all things in the heaven above and in the earth beneath must be tested in the crucible of logic and be capable of experimental demonstration. This spirit of rationalism has reached religion too. Our beliefs and doctrines must admit of almost mathematical deduction." He insisted rather that skepticism bred in the wake of modern thought failed to fill man's spiritual needs: "Our enthusiasm has carried us too far. In our admiration for mind, we have neglected the claims of emotion. . . . Because religion no longer fears science as an enemy, it need not go to the other extreme and regard it as all-sufficient." Although Harris defended the need of ceremonials along with faith, he deplored excessive legalism and the habit of making fetishes out of religious symbols or customs. His presentation was that of a moderate Reformer; he neither repudiated Traditionalist beliefs and customs out of hand, nor did he parade the accomplishments of Reform. His was also a "safe" paper; avoiding any comparison of Judaism and Christianity, he merely indicated that all religions faced the same challenges.[22]

The two Traditionalist rabbis on the program achieved very little toward dispelling the aura of Reform that emanated from the Jewish presentations. Admittedly, the parliament was hardly the place to air in-house divisions, but the average person in the audience would have been hard put to understand that there were significant numbers of Jews besides the Reform-affiliated. Alexander Kohut, a prominent defender of rabbinic Judaism and a spiritual mentor of the Traditionalists, had publicly debated the teachings and methods of Reform with Kaufmann Kohler in 1885, but at the 1893 parliament, a few years after the Reform movement under Kohler's influence had formally outlined its principles in the Pittsburgh Platform, he refrained from sparring with the Reformers. Doubtless he still found Reform's creed objectionable, but he chose rather to keep strictly to his subject, "What the Hebrew Scriptures Have Wrought for Mankind."

The very topic indicated the obverse of denying antisemitism; instead of answering the charges *against* Jews, it showed why mankind should be *for* Jews. Kohut's dominant theme was that Jews had bequeathed *faith* to the world. Indeed, the Hebrew Bible and its message of religious faith and righteousness had proceeded to infuse and inspire all fields of human enterprise throughout the ages, from architecture to poetry to science. It transcended pagan myths as well as the religions of ancient Egypt, Greece, and Rome. "In religion, Hebrew genius was supreme"; the "inspiration" of morality and righteousness, it was the plant on which both Christianity and Islam were grafted. Nor did Kohut have any qualms about maintaining the superiority of Judaism over Christianity. Although Israel deserved the world's gratitude for their unique gift of faith to all mankind, Jews met with injustice and persecution: "Faith—the Bible creed of Israel—was the first and most vital principle of universal ethics, and it was the Jew, now the Pariah pilgrim of ungrateful humanity, who bequeathed this precious legacy to Semitic and Aryan nations, who sowed the healthy seeds of irradicable [*sic*] belief in often unfertile ground." It was Judaism that "infused *that* inherent vitality of propagation and endurance, which forever marks the progress and triumph of God's chosen, though unaccepted people." The "stone of abuse" borne for countless centuries must be shattered, Kohut insisted, and he called for a new spirit of religion to animate both Islam and Christianity. Why not, he asked, "admit the scions of the mother religion, the Wandering Jew of myth and harsh reality, into the throbbing affections of faith-permeating, equitable peoples?"[23] Although some Reformers at the parliament would doubtless have toned down

Kohut's criticism of Christianity, his emphasis on Israel's legacy of morality sounded very much like their own.

A second address by Kohut, this one on the Talmud, explained in some detail the world of the Talmud, how it contained both *halachah* (law) and *aggadah* (lore) and how each was interpreted. Ignoring Reform's rejection of the authority of the Talmud, he said that the Jews had always been faithful to its teachings. The essay dealt in greater detail with ancient Jewish assessments of the heathen and the Christians. Since antisemites in America and Europe were then reviling the Talmud as the source both of objectionable Jewish characteristics and of nefarious Jewish practices and conspiracies against the Christian world, the subject was most timely.

Kohut, a foremost Talmudic scholar, admitted that the ancient sages had denounced the barbarity of the heathen, but he insisted that despite the fulminations of the church fathers, those passages in the Talmud did not refer to Christians. In Palestine, where early Christianity was known, the rabbis refrained from ridicule: "The worthy founders of the new religion were treated with a large-minded tolerance"—and here Kohut cited chapter and verse in rabbinic discussions— "which the daughter [religion] has never shown to the mother." Again attacking Jew-hatred as he had in his first piece, he hoped that his presentation would help to counter the antisemites: "If we have succeeded in overcoming the innate scruples of the bigots, who, possessed by the erroneous idea (culled chiefly from the calumnies of Jew haters) that the Talmud is a store-house of fetid superstition, where 'corruption is virtue and every aim is vice' . . . then we can triumphantly exclaim, with Darwin's royal judgment, 'The fittest survive.'"[24]

H. Pereira Mendes, rabbi of Shearith Israel of New York City, spoke on "Orthodox or Historical Judaism." A Traditionalist akin to Kohut, and active in the newly established Jewish Theological Seminary, Mendes, like the Reform speakers, devoted a good one-third of his paper to the ethical ideals bequeathed to the world in the Mosaic code and the teachings of the Prophets. He emphasized three ideals in particular: universal peace, universal brotherhood, and universal happiness. But unlike the Reformers he affirmed the belief in the restoration to Palestine and the establishment of a Jewish state. Turning to his major theme, he discussed the function and purpose of Judaism in the history of religion. Filling a twofold role of separation and protest, normative Judaism separated itself from, and denied the veracity of, the many sects, heresies, and ideologies from biblical times to Islam that fell short of Mosaic and Prophetic precepts. One of his examples concerned the divinity of Jesus: "If the Nazarene teacher claimed tacitly or not the title 'Son of God' in any sense save that which Moses meant when he said 'Ye are children of your God,' can we wonder that there was a Hebrew protest?" Mendes found thereby a formula for explaining Jewish separatism, a frequent charge of Jew-haters who blamed antisemitism on Jews who distanced themselves from Christians. Careful not to suggest, however, that Jewish separatism meant separation from the American body politic, he asserted that Traditionalists believed in unity with all Americans on civic, cultural, and humanitarian matters.

The rabbi also explained the opposition of Traditionalists to Reform. Since the former believed that Jewish customs or ideas could be changed only "when effected in accordance with the spirit of God's law and the highest authority attainable," they could not recognize the right of rabbinical conferences whose participants were not empowered by their communities or congregations to represent them. He added several additional requirements: "They [the participants at the conferences] must be sufficiently versed in Hebrew law and lore; they must live lives consistent with Bible teachings and they must be advanced in age so as not to be immature in thought." Given all those stipulations, the decisions of the Reformers at the conferences of Philadelphia (1869) and Pittsburgh (1885) were clearly illegitimate. Furthermore, the rigorous stand of traditional Judaism accounted for its survival even as other faiths perished. Despite all the obstacles, however, he optimistically predicted that the future would bring "an era of reconciliation of all living faiths and systems, the era of all being in "at-one-ment," or atonement, with God."[25]

Aside from the concentration on ethics, theology, and Judaism in history, rabbis also addressed a variety of more mundane topics—help to the Russian immigrant (Radin) and forms of education like the Sabbath schools and the Jewish Chautauqua (Hecht, Felsenthal, Berkowitz).[26] Different too was an essay by Rabbi Max Landsberg on "The Position of Woman among the Jews." Landsberg claimed that Jewish women always ranked higher when compared with other ancient Near Eastern civilizations of biblical times, Greco-Roman culture, or Christianity. He maintained that the Torah and the Talmud built up the role and rights of the woman:"She remained the representative and preserver of idealism and of that genuine prophetic spirit which tends to promote the glorification of Judaism." The feminist movement was still decades away, but Landsberg thought that modern Jewish women had already made great strides; they worked zealously for charitable causes, they were teachers in Jewish religious schools, and they outnumbered the men at religious services.

Calling for "perfect" religious equality, the rabbi asked only that women have a voice in the management of congregations, and he noted with pride that they had served on the school board of his congregation. Henrietta Szold agreed with Landsberg. She called the Jewish woman the guardian of family purity, her husband's upright and respected partner, and the teacher of children.[27] As such, her paper was both a defense of Judaism's views of women and an implied call for equal rights.

Although the atmosphere at the World's Parliament of Religions encouraged talk of interreligious peace and harmony in this world and not merely at the end of time, most Jewish participants shied away from the prospect of one universal or syncretistic religion. Writer Josephine Lazarus, sister of the more famous Emma, was different. She spoke of how Christianity but especially Judaism had drifted from its exalted spiritual moorings. Concerned more about modern Judaism, she called vaguely for a "unity of spirit" between the Jew and non-Jew:

> The Jew must change his attitude before the world, and come into spiritual fellowship with those around him. John, Paul, Jesus himself, we can claim them all for our own. We do not want "missions" to convert us. We cannot become Presbyterians, Episcopalians, members of any dividing sect. . . . Christians as well as Jews need the larger unity that shall embrace them all, the unity of spirit, not of doctrine. *Mankind at large may not be ready for a universal religion, but let the Jews, with their deep prophetic instinct . . . set the example and give the ideal.* (emphasis added)[28]

Lazarus further developed the idea of a nonsectarian ethical monotheism in her book, *The Spirit of Judaism*, which appeared in 1895.

Talk had been heard since 1870 about a merger of Judaism with Unitarianism, but, as historian Benny Kraut has shown, Reform leaders were ambivalent about an actual religious rapprochement. At the parliament or from other platforms most of Josephine Lazarus's colleagues rejected what looked like a Jewish overture to that denomination. Despite its attraction for some Jews and even rabbis, a Jewish flirtation with Unitarianism was strongly condemned by Rabbi Louis Grossman of Detroit: "There is much gossip about the identity of Judaism and Unitarianism. I am sorry that there are Rabbis who are so eager for a premature universalism that they will hurry to engage in any sort of companionship." Even Unitarianism, which he called "the last form of the Christian church" and the "last link" in the evolution of Christianity, could not be anything less than Christian.

As such it differed radically from Judaism: "The difference between Judaism and every phase of Christian theology is clear enough. Judaism is not a chapter in the history of thought, not in the history of zeal; it is the soul of the community, which breaks out into all the moods and movements of the body politic, just as the soul of man breaks through his flesh and bone."[29] The obverse, that a merger could come about if Christians flocked to Judaism, was of course utterly preposterous.

Rabbi Maurice Harris gave a fuller reply in a sermon on "Judaism and Unitarianism." To be sure, both religions were antitrinitarian, both endorsed scientific inquiry and biblical criticism, and both taught the same ethical values. Nevertheless, he saw grave shortcomings in Unitarianism. Since its platform was very broad, its ranks included believers in the transcendent if not divine nature of Jesus, as well as agnostics and pantheists. Having drawn directly from Judaism, Unitarianism had nothing to teach Jews. Furthermore, profound cultural differences in addition to creed separated it from Judaism. Social institutions that involved birth, marriage, and death; holidays and other ceremonials; and even symbols in art and poetry were expressions of two distinct religions. Institutions and separate histories preserved the ties between Unitarians and Christians of all denominations, just as they united both Traditionalists and Reform Jews. For those reasons a merger of Judaism with Unitarianism was highly unnatural.[30]

Rabbi Emil G. Hirsch, an active participant in planning the parliament, went further than most of the rabbis in his presentation, "Elements of Universal Religion." He shrugged off the reality and desirability of national religions, religions coterminous with language or ethnic groups, as well as religions that placed limits on salvation. Rather, he looked forward to a world of righteous men inspired by faith in a loving and just God. According to Hirsch, the elements of that religion rested on the faith of man in God, a universal God who "speaks to all mankind." Knowing God was an ongoing process, but the righteous man with the use of prayer, which was a stirring to love and righteousness, could discover the countless manifestations of God's nature and will. Working with God, man would progress on the path of social justice. Religion would inform all human relationships—man *was* his brother's keeper—and no longer would there be distinctions between sacred and secular. The conduct of men and not formal creed underlay a just society, a society without prejudice and fanaticism, where men freed themselves from hardened, meaningless dogma and base materialism. Hirsch's universal religion, which for want of a better name he called "the Church of God," reflected the approach of a Radical Reformer and the zeal of a crusader for social justice.[31] But his universal religion, which in essence was the humanization of the messianic age, was too extreme a message for most Jews and doubtless for most non-Jews. Despite the negative impact of biblical criticism on religious faith generally, neither Jews, including mainstream Reformers, nor Christians were prepared in 1893 to disavow the distinctive features of their respective creeds and plunge into the sea of humanity.

Hirsch backtracked on the idea of repudiating separate religious identities. His newspaper, the *Reform Advocate*, sneered at the pull of "Jewnitarianism" on some Jews, but he continued to work for interdenominational understanding. In the afterglow of the parliament, he joined a group of liberal clergymen in calling for a Congress of Liberal Religious Societies. The call, which gathered several hundred signatures from American clergymen around the country, outlined the purpose of the projected congress in all-encompassing terms: "Believing in the great law and life of love, and desiring a nearer and more helpful fellowship in the social, educational, industrial, moral and religious thought of the world," we call for a congress of churches and interested organizations "willing to recognize a common duty and to work in the spirit of kinship herein indicated." The meeting of some three thousand participants, including women as well as men, was drawn from ultraliberal religious groups like the Unitarians, Universalists, Free Peoples Churches, and Ethical Culturists. A few Reform rabbis attended the assembly that was hosted in Chicago by Hirsch's temple in May 1894, but mainline Protestants and Catholics absented themselves.

Speakers disavowed intentions of creating a new church and concentrated rather on measures of social and economic reform. Like autonomous units of a federal structure, they suggested that their churches pool resources for publications, free summer schools, ministerial education, and work in isolated churchless communities. When the congress was incorporated later that year, its specific objectives were broadened. It pledged itself to cooperate with all groups in sympathy with the movement toward "undogmatic" religion, to foster the organization of other nonsectarian churches on the basis of absolute mental liberty, and "*to develop the church of humanity, democratic in organization, progressive in spirit aiming at the development of pure and high character, hospitable to all forms of thought, cherishing the spiritual traditions of the past, but keeping itself open to all new light and the higher developments of the future*" (emphasis added). The terms "undogmatic religion," "nonsectarian churches," and "church of humanity" could easily be construed as more threatening to traditional churches than the initial call for a congress. But despite the lofty purposes of the charter, the congress disregarded questions of dogma likely to divide its supporters. Hirsch himself now said that the concern of the congress was primarily sociology, and since Judaism at bottom meant an attachment to humanitarian goals, he repeatedly denied that he had any reason to cut his ties to his religion.

The CCAR endorsed the congress for promoting cooperation between Jew and Christian. Rabbi Joseph Stolz hoped that the new group would fight religious bigotry and religious irreverence in addition to its social program. However, some rabbis, fearing the loss of Jewish identity, argued that the congress should not become a "back door" for "sneaking out" of Judaism. Jews were not ready for one universal church, and Christians, still indulging in antisemitism, were equally unprepared. Some said that only a Jew rooted in Judaism could contribute positively to the congress's work. When the prophetic ideals were achieved, when to be a Jew no longer connoted inferiority—in effect, when Reform's mission was ful- filled at the end of the days—only then could Jews merge with the rest of humanity. In the end, the congress and its plans for interfaith coopera- tion on socioeconomic issues was more an example of the Social Gospel movement than of religious ecumenicism.[32]

The Parliament of Religions was not the first occasion on which rabbis ad- dressed non-Jews. Rabbis had lectured to mixed audiences, and some had exchanged pulpits with their Christian counterparts.[33] But all acknowl- edged that the parliament afforded a singular opportunity to present the case for Judaism before an international assembly. As it turned out, this was their one formal opportunity, for no subsequent parliaments ever fol- lowed. In 1893 the rabbis responded seriously and their papers in different ways included calls for interreligious harmony. Despite the differences in substance and style, their common strategy was to emphasize the ethical legacy bequeathed by Judaism to mankind, to maintain Judaism's equality to Christianity, and to reduce Jew-hatred in America.

During a decade of heightened antisemitism, the Parliament of Re- ligions, a pioneer effort at interfaith dialogue, signaled a ray of hope to those arrayed on the side of religious liberalism. Since acceptance as equals religiously and socially, as well as politically, was always the foremost ob- jective of American Jews, Christian good will had to be cultivated. With that in mind, Reform rabbis showed their eagerness to participate in the parliament and in subsequent attempts at interreligious cooperation. In the end, they failed to achieve true religious pluralism or the acknowledgment of the equal validity of non-Christian faiths in America's religious marketplace. All told, they presented an able defense of Judaism. Very few tackled Jew-hatred head on, but most manifested a deep pride in their faith and a belief that it stood up well in comparisons with Christianity. They had yet to teach their congregations and American Jews at large if and how, in the light of religious harmony, a distinctive Jewish identity merited preservation.

10

Building a Profession

A study of the rabbi and the sermon in the nineteenth century illuminates aspects of American Jewish social history in a period of rapid change. From the data analyzed we can conclude that the average English-speaking rabbi from Central Europe was in many ways a pioneer. Working in a country and in a Jewish community still very much in their youth, he had to master a new language and use a new format, the sermon, for addressing his congregation. Even if he had studied liberal arts as well as Jewish sources, his education in Europe bore little relevance to the demands of an American position. Precedents and usages he had absorbed from his European experiences were often inapplicable to his particular situation, and the Judaism he practiced, whether Traditionalism or Reform, had difficulties in adjusting to a totally free environment. The new rabbi found his tasks and his authority ill defined, the uneducated lay leaders of his synagogue overbearing and often hostile, and the friends he sought usually wanting. What he achieved—as one who carved out a satisfying personal life, or served as the respected spiritual leader of a congregation, or contributed meaningfully to the survival of Judaism in the New World—was in many cases the result of his independent pioneering efforts to break fresh ground.

At the same time that the rabbi was putting his stamp on the style of his synagogue, the forces of Americanization were at work. Scattered throughout communities over the length and the breadth of the land, nineteenth-century Jews were working for rapid acculturation and acceptance as equals. They fulfilled their civic obligations, they joined the mainstream of American economic life, they spoke and dressed like Americans, and they educated their children in American schools. Many also looked to their Protestant neighbors for forms they could adopt in their synagogues. Some changes fell into place almost automatically; the use of Hebrew, for example, yielded more and more ground to English, translations of the prayer books into the vernacular became increasingly common, and a Protestant-like decorum during religious services gradually replaced the customary disorder that had prevailed in traditional European synagogues.[1] Immigrant Jews themselves hastened the process of conformity. The mass immigration of the East Europeans in the last third of the century put a temporary halt to the Americanization of the traditional synagogue, but as the new arrivals rapidly acculturated, they too slowly incorporated American practices into their houses of worship. For example, many synagogues of the Russian newcomers initially featured *magidim* (itinerant preachers) instead of a rabbi, but in a relatively short period of time the *magid* was replaced by the American-like rabbi/preacher.[2]

The Traditionalist Isaac Leeser had purposely borrowed Christian methods and communal practices for his community. An enthusiastic supporter of the Jewish Sunday school, an imitation of the eighteenth-century Protestant model, he prepared catechisms and other materials for its pupils. To counter the Christian missionaries who preyed on the new immigrants, he advocated the distribution of books and pamphlets on the Jewish heritage in the same way that Protestant sects organized Bible and tract societies.[3] Religious leaders besides Leeser also imitated their Gentile neighbors—Rabbi Joseph Krauskopf of Philadelphia even wore a clerical collar![4] An extreme innovation by some Reform congregations was the substitution of Sunday for Sabbath services, a move that both recognized the economic needs of Jewish businessmen and narrowed the gap between them and Christian America. At the end of the century, Reformers also instituted circuit preaching and a Jewish version of the Social Gospel movement. In all those instances, the innovators appropriated *Christian* models to strengthen the *Jewish* community and its public image. As one rabbi noted, "What pleases the *Goy*, the Jew will applaud."[5]

The evolution of a distinctive American Jewish style followed a path that was fraught with obstacles. As mentioned previously, the multiplicity of autonomous congregations over a vast geographic area, whose members stemmed from different European localities, long hindered the emergence of any form of unity. The uncertain tenure of religious leaders also contributed to divisiveness. Since rabbis were in short supply before the Civil War, congregations often competed with each other for an available candidate, and it was not unusual for rabbis to change pulpits frequently in their search for more rewarding employment. It followed that since no two rabbis exactly duplicated each other, synagogues could be exposed to contradictory styles over a period of ten years or less.[6] Nor was any single religious leader the authoritative source to whom the pulpit rabbi turned for counsel on ritual or theological issues. Men in the pulpit, often untrained or otherwise unqualified, might not have recognized or agreed on a reputable authority or model.

Congregations and laity presented other difficulties to the emergence of a single style. Many new immigrants were at first uncomfortable with religious services in English and with a sermon in whatever language. Isaac Leeser, who has been called the father of the Jewish sermon in America, responded to a pressing need by repeatedly encouraging the use of the English sermon and advising the preacher how to construct a proper discourse. He wrote in the *Occident* on the development of new ideas for sermons and the appropriate organization of a sermon, as well as on oratorical proficiency and body language. Although he was cognizant of the lack of model sermons to help guide the rabbi, he cautioned against the imitation of non-Jewish discourses.[7] If followed, Leeser's guidelines would probably have resulted in better sermons and a pattern for an American style.

The equation of a "better" sermon with an effective rabbi, as Leeser's words implied, was soon accepted in most synagogues. In 1876 Rabbi Isaac Mayer Wise printed a lengthy piece in his newspaper, the *American Israelite,* on what made a good rabbi. There he linked the character and abilities of the rabbi to his discourses. Wise wrote:

[The rabbi] must first and foremost be a Jew with heart and soul thoroughly and enthusiastically, a man in whom there is no guile; a teacher who never loses his patience, truthful and reliable as a rock, and benevolent as the palm in the wilderness. The audience must be convinced that whatever this man in the pulpit says is certainly true to the best of his knowledge, and that he does as he teaches. This is a man's moral weight, it is the magnet to attract. . . . A rabbi must be a master of Jewish literature and history or he is a fraud. . . . A rabbi of this age must be a classical and scientific scholar and a pleasant orator, or he is useless to his congregation. . . . The rabbi must speak and preach in the language of the country in which he lives. . . . The rabbi must know and feel the wants of his congregation, he must understand old and young, and they must understand him. The rabbi must stand high, and, if possible, a little higher morally, intellectually, and scholastically than the best of his members. . . . He must not be made by the office he holds; he must make the office respected and honored. He must love his office and his congregation and not the wealth of the individual members.[8]

*

Despite the variety of opinions and resulting disunity that obtained on matters of Jewish beliefs and synagogue style, rabbis of all stripes agreed on at least one major issue, the inadequacies of the American rabbinate. Orthodox rabbis of pre-modern times may not have understood how to lead a congregation in free America, nor did they care about proper pedagogical methods or about inspiring the laity. But their successors in mid-century America were hardly better prepared to fill a rabbinic post. Lack of able leaders compounded in turn the rampant religious indifference and ignorance of American Jews. Leeser, who continually campaigned for proper rabbinic leadership through the pages of his journal, put it this way: "Of spiritual guidance through . . . elected ministers, there has been deplorably little. . . . Where are the preachers who are to be the leaders of the people? Where are the ecclesiastical chiefs who are to instruct?" He explained more fully:

> We in America have scarcely any religious teachers at all; we have readers; a few preachers who occasionally address the public; but we say it with deep humiliation, we have not those whose position enables them to advance the religious sentiment which has so much fallen into decay; the *hazzanim* are too much occupied with their often onerous routine of duty to attend to studies and to prepare weekly sermons even if they had the requisite education; and schools of religion there are scarcely any which deserve the name. We do not therefore wonder that so little religion is seen among us; the wonder is that in spite of all the disadvantages it should not retrograde.

Leeser preferred an American-born, English-speaking rabbi, but first and foremost he demanded an educated one; a higher secular degree was not necessary, but a thorough grounding in Jewish sources, in addition to an extensive knowledge of secular subjects, was. He also faulted congregations who set few standards for the selection of a rabbi. To whom were their members to turn for an appreciation of "the great truths which are entrusted to the safe-keeping of Israel," he asked. He recalled critically that when he was appointed to Mikveh Israel no study was made of his fitness or character. All he was asked to do was to read the services on three successive Sabbaths.[9]

It was one thing to list the requirements of proper rabbis but quite another to find the proper candidates. Understandably, very few rabbis —good, bad, or indifferent—were enticed to leave Europe for the New

World before the Civil War. Whether or not the rabbi was knowledge-able, or whether or not the synagogue of his choice had set appropriate standards of selection, the conditions under which he labored were hardly appealing.[10] His duties were never explicitly defined—as Isaac Wise had said, the early rabbi was a jack-of-all-trades, from teacher to gravedigger —and the tasks that he performed in addition to preaching or reading the service failed to raise his salary or his status. His tenure was uncertain, and he had to work with cantors or sextons in whose choice he had no say. Doubtless most upsetting to a professional was his virtual servitude to the lay leaders of the synagogue. They in turn, the poorly educated and "rich vulgarians," inspired little respect on the part of the rabbi, yet they were the ones who treated him as hired help or, in Rabbi I. L. Leucht's words, a "general utility man."[11] He was denied full freedom of the pul-pit and his sermons in many cases were open for review and criticism; he was excluded from the board's debates on the governance of the syna-gogue and on the discipline of members who disobeyed the board's rul-ings. Under such circumstances many a young man could easily be dis-suaded from electing the rabbinate as his profession.

The private life of the early rabbi was equally difficult. Without books, libraries, religious schools, and colleagues, as Rabbi Abraham Rice had explained on his arrival in the United States, a rabbi's life was extremely lonely. What doubtless rankled the most, however, was the lack of re-spect the average rabbi commanded. Of long duration, that condition provoked bitter comments from some rabbis. At the turn of the century, Reformer David Philipson looked back longingly to the past: "Time was when a Jewish parent considered it the greatest blessing if his son became a rabbi . . . and when the Jewish Croesus regarded it the highest honor to ally himself by the marriage of his daughter with a noted rabbinical fam-ily." Others added that the rabbi, considered inferior to the laity, was not paid adequately for the shabby treatment he received.[12] Individual rabbis gleaned little comfort in the fact that various conditions were replicated in Christian churches.

Over the years, however, some of the rabbis' problems abated. The heavy stream of immigration to America in the 1840s and 1850s and again after 1870 brought new rabbis, trained largely in Central Europe, and strengthened the corps of religious leaders especially in the larger ur-ban areas. By the last quarter of the century, as they and their congregants acculturated, they felt more secure in American surroundings and in their dealings with both their congregants and their non-Jewish neighbors. Democratization within the synagogue and a more equitable distribution of power between the rabbi and the lay officials also improved the rabbi's office and his rights. Many earlier constraints on a free pulpit eased, and salaries too, especially for desirable candidates, edged upward.[13]

Sermons and other public statements of the rabbis, the primary focus of this study, shed but little light on the development of a rabbinical *profession*. To be sure, men like Isaac Leeser, Isaac Mayer Wise, and Sabato Morais commented critically about the conditions under which rabbis labored and whether the rabbis or the congregations were at fault. But not until the establishment of the Central Conference of American Rabbis (CCAR) did rabbis *collectively* address those conditions. The steps first taken by the CCAR in the 1890s began a long process that would lead to a professionalized, and stronger, rabbinate.

Within each major Jewish denomination professionalism rested on several preconditions—intradenominational unity through an organization of congregations, a theological seminary to instill and perpetuate the teachings of the particular denomination, and a rabbinical union to aid rabbis to find, and keep, a satisfactory post. Reform was the first denomination to create a tripartite structure consisting of a rabbinical school and two organizations, one of congregations and one of rabbis, and the other movements followed shortly.[14]

In the preliminaries leading up to the tripartite structures, attention first went to the establishment of a seminary. Since a rabbinical school held out the hope of securing a properly trained and self-respecting ministry, it engaged the attention of leading rabbis as early as the first half of the nineteenth century. Isaac Leeser had supported the creation of a theological school,[15] and because his Reform rivals, Isaac Wise and Max Lilienthal, concurred, an opportunity was created for united action. Wise had thought about a seminary ever since he arrived in Cincinnati, but he realized that the school would need the support of a union of congregations. He joined Leeser in 1848 in a call for a union whose primary goal would be the establishment of a rabbinical school. The conference, which was predicated on the joint action of right-wing and left-wing congregations, never materialized.[16] Six years later, with the backing of a few concerned laymen, Wise founded Zion College in the Queen City. Planned as a Jewish college to train professionals for the rabbinate and for other fields as well, it failed within two years.[17] It was followed by two other unsuccessful attempts shortly after the Civil War: Temple Emanu-El Theological Seminary in New York and Maimonides College in Philadelphia.

Wise had not participated in those projects, and after the Zion College episode he continued to call for a theological school. He warned that without properly trained rabbis independent of European schools, American Judaism would be "reduced to a mere shadow." In 1871 he and Lilienthal organized a conference at which a union of congregations and a rabbinical school were uppermost on the agenda. The conference led shortly thereafter to the founding of the Union of American Hebrew Congregations (UAHC) in 1873 and the Hebrew Union College (HUC) in 1875 under the aegis of the UAHC. Both were milestones in American Jewish history. The UAHC was the first national organization of synagogues, and HUC was the first permanent American theological seminary.[18] For a short while Traditionalists participated in both Reform institutions, but by World War I both the Orthodox and the Conservative denominations had established their own seminaries and congregational unions.[19]

Reformers under Wise's leadership also led in founding an organization of rabbis. They knew that a professional rabbi required the support of his colleagues for meeting his needs and improving his status. The goal was reached when in 1889 the CCAR, which called itself the successor to the German rabbinical conferences of the 1840s, began. It was a daring move. Given business opposition at the time to organized labor and its weapons, the CCAR, a nascent union, could conceivably arouse the suspicions and enmity of those, the lay business leaders of the synagogues, who actually hired the rabbis. Nevertheless, the organization took root, and at almost every annual convention from 1889 to 1900 conditions of the rabbinate were discussed in individual addresses and by the plenum. One resolution summed up the purpose of the deliberations: "The Conference should stand for the dignity of the profession."[20] If achieved, the enhanced dignity of the rabbinate promised to raise the office of the rabbi in the eyes of Jews and non-Jews and to contribute to the rabbi's self-esteem.

The new organization discussed the "dignity of the profession" as it bore on three major areas—the financial problems of the rabbi, the relations between the rabbi and his congregation, and the relations between the rabbi and his colleagues. Deliberations led to a study by a Committee on Rabbinical Ethics that reported on matters like applications for a rabbinical post ("avoid any action that would point to . . . seeking the pulpit of a colleague"), a rabbi's contract with a congregation ("inviolable"), and trial sermons ("embarrassing"). The committee prudently disclaimed any desire to impinge on the autonomy of the congregation:

> The highest confidence, mutual love and reciprocal esteem should be the strong links binding the minister to the congregation and the congregation to the minister. Your committee recognizes that these relations do not always obtain, but regarding the autonomy of the congregation as of the highest import, it does not deem it advisable for this Conference to take these matters into its hands when this mutual relation is broken in upon, but believes in letting the individual and the congregations work out a peaceable solution of their difficulties.

The CCAR was ready to oblige both parties if its assistance in resolving a dispute was requested, but the committee did not elaborate on what methods it was prepared to take. It is interesting that the same resolution did not emphasize the autonomy of the rabbi alongside the "autonomy of the congregation," another hint that the rabbinical organization, still in its infancy, took care not to alienate the powerful laymen.[21]

The first sessions of the CCAR also devoted much thought to the material problems of the pulpit rabbi. Inadequate salaries had long been noted; Rice of Baltimore, for example, had been forced to open a small shop in order to supplement his wages. Others had added that the rabbi, considered inferior to the laity, was not paid adequately for the shabby treatment he received. Prominent rabbis like the renowned Radical Reformer, Samuel Hirsch of Philadelphia, had also suffered. At the celebration of his seventieth birthday, Hirsch's son, Emil, recalled with deep feeling how the rabbi's salary could not compensate for his subordination: "The bread of the Jewish Minister is but seldom buttered. I, who have been privileged from earliest infancy to share the intimacy of such a life . . . know . . . that the bread . . . of the Rabbi is not compensation for the would-be-entailed loss of manhood!"[22]

At least as pressing was the situation of a rabbi, incapacitated by illness or old age and without insurance or pension to relieve his family's basic needs. At the preliminary organizational meeting of the CCAR the rabbis hastened to address the problem. One resolution that was adopted unanimously read: "That in order to prevent any unfortunate colleague or his family from becoming humiliated as objects of charity . . . one half of the annual dues of each member, being $2.50, shall be set aside as a fund designated as the 'Relief Fund of the Conference,' to be used only for the object named." Shortly thereafter, Rabbi Henry Berkowitz of Kansas City provided his colleagues with a graphic picture of the indigent rabbi, and those who were summarily dismissed by their congregations, and he reminded them of their "fraternal" obligations:

> Alas for the Rabbi who happens to get into a difficulty, pecuniary or otherwise. Alas for the Rabbi who has lost the favor of his congregation. What though he has grown old in the service, has given his life's best energies in faithful endeavor, he must be sacrificed to the fashionable whimsies of the "younger elements," or to the factional domination of the elder autocrats. What then? Do the Rabbis, his colleagues in the love of their sacred profession proclaim as one man against the offense which aimed at one smites all? On the contrary (to our shame it must be confessed) we have suffered many a hapless brother to stand alone, struggle alone and fall alone. . . . We have let many a worthy man go about the country as a mendicant and some of us have been gracious enough to rob him of his manhood by supplying him the easy passport of begging letters. We know of those who, spurned by congregations, neglected and shunned by rabbis, their families destitute, all hope forever lost, have gone down broken-hearted to their untimely graves.

After that emotional appeal the CCAR decided to add the proceeds from the sale of its *Union Prayer Book* to the Relief Fund.[23]

Much was said at the conventions about the qualities of a good rabbi. The subject itself was not new; rabbis too had long indulged in self-criticism and in criticism of their colleagues. For the most part the consensus of the members was to follow the essentials which Wise had prescribed in 1876. Often sounding as if they were charging new graduates of HUC rather than addressing their own contemporaries, the rabbis formulated a veritable list of "do's" and "don'ts" for the would-be effective religious leader.[24] After all, as Joseph Krauskopf remarked perhaps with tongue in cheek, the minister and not God was the "polar star" for drawing attendance to the synagogue. Several common conclusions were reached: The focus of the good rabbi was always the spiritual well-being of his congregation, and his primary task was the education of the laity in the meaning and substance of Judaism's ongoing evolution. Rabbi Max Heller offered an alternative. More important than teaching, he said, was the need for the rabbi to transmit to laymen the impulse to study on their own. The CCAR also agreed that the rabbi was linked to the Jewish legacy of the past, but as the representative of Reform Judaism he was enjoined to impart the timely message and meaning of that movement and its mission. Only the "inspired" and honest rabbi could live up to those broad tasks. Highly principled and with the courage of his convictions, the rabbi shared his enthusiastic appreciation of Judaism with his congregation. Nor could he venture beyond his synagogue and offer his services to wider circles within the community until he secured the "love and confidence of his own flock." As guardian of the one true faith, the rabbi taught that fundamental truth belonged neither to science nor Christianity but to his religion. If his approach succeeded, the pulpit rabbi would raise the image of Judaism throughout the world.

Did the pulpit rabbi need to be a scholar? Many answered no. A thorough familiarity with Jewish studies and a broad appreciation of advances in other disciplines was required, but the proper rabbi was neither the dilettante whose sermons touched in cursory fashion on all contemporary topics of fleeting interest nor the student wrapped up in the minutiae of scholarly research. One rabbi added that "the preacher, learned as he may be, has in the pulpit only one legitimate authority, not the authority of the scholar . . . but the force of the morally sublime man." True, the pre-modern traditional rabbi poring over the biblical and Talmudic texts had been ranked according to his scholarship, and his authority had depended on his mastery of Jewish learning. But Reformers had distanced themselves from a Torah- and Talmud-centered world, and, as has been noted, the authority of Reform rabbis and their reverence for rabbinic scholarship were thereby diminished.[25] In short, no longer was the rabbi/ scholar the appropriate model for his modern successors. Some Traditionalists thought otherwise. Alexander Kohut had said in his debate with Kohler that the modern American rabbi preached too much and studied too little. When Reform leader Emil G. Hirsch opposed scholarship as a requisite for the rabbinate, Solomon Schechter, who shortly thereafter succeeded President Sabato Morais at the Jewish Theological Seminary, retorted that "effectiveness in the pulpit never suffered from devotion to learning."[26] A novel idea, but one that was not acted on, was the suggestion that the CCAR sponsor postgraduate refresher courses for its members.[27]

Other rabbis suggested guidelines for the construction of a proper sermon. They admonished the rabbi to avoid polemics, sentimentalism, flattery, and oratorical flourishes. Max Landsberg summed up the message for his colleagues: "Not to give entertainment, or to win applause, is the task of the Rabbi, not to please nor to flatter."[28] If the discourses were better, one speaker said, perhaps attendance at the synagogue would improve. They also talked about the popular lecture and the strong competition it posed to the sermon. By the 1890s the novelty of preaching had worn off, and in place of the sermon many Americans of all faiths were content with the popular lecture.[29] Another victory of secularism over religion, with effects that crossed denominational lines, the lecture could be as "edifying" and moralistic as a sermon, but it spared the audience any religious trappings. Rabbis too hit the lecture circuit, often dividing their thoughts between sermon and lecture or sacrificing one, frequently the sermon, for the other.

In a talk to the CCAR titled "Method in the Pulpit," Rabbi Louis Grossman of Detroit commented cynically that eloquence abounded in this, "the most talkative age of the world," but that neither the sermon nor the lecture was more than mediocre. The former, cut off from the Jewish religious heritage and lacking in fervor, was as "radically un-Jewish" as the latter. As a result, religious services, without a sermon that stirred its listeners to an appreciation of the truths and riches of Judaism, failed to shake the silence and complacency of the congregants. Grossman concluded that "our worship is not intense," that there was a "monotonous sameness" about the rabbi's fifty-two weekly Sabbath sermons, that the synagogue service was arranged "largely to please," and that inspired preaching, like the rabbinate itself, was "on the wane." Emphasizing the shortcomings of the sermons and the rabbi's mechanical delivery, he offered little constructive criticism to remedy the situation.[30]

One analysis that summed up the changes in sermons came from a layman. In 1900 Moritz Ellinger, editor of B'nai B'rith's monthly journal *Menorah*, described how religious discourses had replaced the rabbinic sermons of former years and how the modern rabbi sharply diverged from his prototype, the "ancient rabbi":

> Instead of *Derashoth* [homilies], which were no longer understood or appreciated, sermons had to be delivered, which were freely compared with those of sister creeds, and which run a competitive course. Nor was the theme of the sermons confined any longer to the discussion of dogmatical subjects and the elaboration of theological disquisitions; the sciences and the arts, philosophical questions and social problems, Jewish history and Biblical exercises had to have room and place in it; the progress and

advances made had to be brought in harmony with religion, if the latter was not to be brushed aside. . . . The belief in Divine Providence, in
Revelation, in Immortality, the obligations of ceremonial practices were
questioned, and the weapons with which the doubter be refuted, had to
be taken largely from the armory of reason, history and logic, outside
of Jewish thought and literature. The congregations no longer consisted
exclusively of believers, but were largely sprinkled with skeptics, who did
not keep their doubts to themselves. Altogether, the rabbi, to obtain any
influence among his people, or the world at large, as a representative of
Jewish ideas, had to possess all the varied accomplishments demanded of
the scholar of modern times.[31]

Under the rubric of the rabbinic/lay relationship, the CCAR attempted to
draw the line between the rabbi's rights and his obligations to the laymen on his board. They usually gave the expected answers concerning the
rabbi's independence, but Rabbi Aaron Hahn of Cleveland also included
some words about rabbinic "meddling." He said in part:

A minister must not meddle with party politics, but he would be no man
if he would allow anybody to interfere with his duties as a good citizen.
A minister must not interfere with the rights and duties of the Board of
Trustees . . . but he will command little respect if he would allow every
office-seeker in the congregation to define for him what his rights and
duties are. A minister must not care for what is none of his business, but
it is his duty as a man to intercede when he sees or hears that wrong is
done.[32]

Other addresses at the conventions considered related subjects, like "The
Rabbi and the Charities" by Edward Calisch and "The Rabbi as a Public
Man" by I. L. Leucht. It is impossible to gauge the influence of the various
papers on rabbinical behavior, but the CCAR persisted, and the organization planned future discussions on matters like cooperation between the
synagogues and local fraternal orders and lodges, and an outreach program to the masses of unaffiliated or "unchurched" Jews.[33]

With respect to one rarely mentioned area, the need to alleviate the
loneliness of the congregational rabbi, the CCAR by its very existence
doubtless filled an important function. In an early conference sermon
Rabbi Max Heller of New Orleans reflected in flowery phrases on the

collegial assistance offered by the annual conventions to the rabbi burdened with the manifold responsibilities of a congregation:

> He turns with an expectant joy to the welcome colleague, to seek his counsel, to confide doubts and uncertainties, to exchange thoughts and methods and ideals. He meets the thinker and he meets the man; the former refreshes him with the new lights and interesting reflections of a mind differently made, but it is the latter, the man, who strengthens him; it is the outflow of personalities, here genial and kindly, there fervid and earnest, that cheers to new labors by the imparted electric force and play of a teeming spiritual life.[34]

If the CCAR eased the plight of the rabbi, particularly the one serving in a small town and cut off from professional companionship, it had proved its usefulness.

Matters relating to the rabbi as a professional and the CCAR as a union of professionals overshadowed detailed consideration during the early years of the CCAR about how best to preserve the faith of the Jewish minority within a Christian, and not always friendly, environment. That was a subject on which rabbis differed from the large numbers of American Jews; the latter either denied their Judaism entirely and became Christians, atheists, or freethinkers, or they opted for isolation or ghetto-like seclusion. Indeed, most rabbis followed a third route. They believed that they could successfully ensure Jewish survival by rooting Judaism firmly in American soil. Those who had Americanized as rapidly as or more rapidly than their congregants combined religion with patriotism. The hyperpatriots, or those who equated their theology with American ideals, were most emphatic. Denying any sense of Jewish peoplehood, they never tired of praising America with a religious-like fervor for the freedoms and opportunities it offered Jews. Nor did they set limits, the way some Traditionalists did, on assimilation to American culture. At least for the time being, the CCAR remained content with that consensus. Within those broad parameters, Reform rabbis, closely followed by the moderate Traditionalists, built the framework of a professional rabbinate that would in most respects grow ever stronger in the twentieth century.

An appraisal of the nineteenth-century rabbi must of necessity weave together the highlights of the previous chapters. On that basis we can better judge the contributions of the individual religious leader, the nature of his office, and the legacy he left for his successors.

The picture of the American rabbi etched in the various chapters depicts a man who was born and/or trained abroad, not always officially ordained, and thrust into an alien culture and environment. Separated from family and colleagues, and self-reliant at least until the establishment of rabbinical organizations, he was called to minister to young communities that perhaps more unconsciously than not were buffeted by the forces of religious voluntarism, congregational autonomy, and a dominant Protestantism. Upon the rabbi lay the duty of rapidly accommodating not only himself but also his congregation to American mores and values. At the same time, his primary task was to his flock—to explicate and instill a love of a rich religious faith. Old habits if not completely discarded were forced to meld with new loyalties and patterns of behavior. Acculturation and love of the country proceeded rapidly, but the sensitivity of Jewish religious leaders to the prejudices of Christian America remained.

The nineteenth-century rabbi never enjoyed the authority and respect that the European *Rav* (rabbi) commanded. The learned scholar who studied the sacred tomes and interpreted *halachah* in rabbinical courts for his community was neither replicated nor sought in the United States except by some Orthodox. Instead, the substance of the American rabbi's early sermons was usually moralistic; he dealt not with the nuances of the various commentaries on Talmudic law but for the most part with the attributes of God and the behavioral virtues taught by Judaism to mankind at large. Meantime, lack of respect for the rabbi, or *rabbinerhetze* as Isaac Wise called it, persisted well into the next century.

When, by 1900, restrictions on freedom of the pulpit had largely disappeared, the range of subjects discussed by rabbis increased. Some introduced matters like socioeconomic issues; others spoke on freedom of religion and antisemitism, the condition of world Jewry, and Zionism. Irrespective of content, the format of the edifying sermon remained the same—an introductory verse from the weekly reading of the Torah and Prophets, the lesson to be drawn and applied to contemporary life, and a closing prayer for the welfare of the congregation. The sermon made the rabbi's opinions known to his congregation, and in many cases his lectures and statements to the press disseminated his views to a wider audience.

Of all the subjects that engaged the nineteenth-century rabbis, Jewish education was of primary concern. Laboring to preserve the Jewish heritage, and to arm the Jew against the lures of Christian missionaries, the average rabbi was appalled by the ignorance and, even worse, the indifference on the part of many congregants to things Jewish. Admittedly, the competition he faced, affecting all age groups, was formidable and frequently overwhelming. While parents fell victim to the snares of materialism, they sent their children to the free public school despite its Christian trappings. Older students in high school and college were captivated by the new scientific discoveries and by antireligious ideologies like secularism and socialism. Since sermons and parttime Sabbath or Sunday schools that suffered for want of proper materials and trained teachers were clearly inadequate to the task of instilling the rudiments of Jewish tradition,[35] some rabbis, at times in cooperation with their colleagues, searched for additional means to keep their congregants, particularly the children and young adults, within the fold. Max Lilienthal founded a newspaper for children and Emil G. Hirsch lauded the benefits of university chairs in Jewish studies; their colleague, Henry Berkowitz, supported classes for adults by launching the Jewish Chautauqua Society in 1893.[36] As indicated in the addresses at the first conferences of the CCAR all agreed that the rabbi himself required a rich education in Jewish history and thought.[37] The teacher not only of his own synagogue but often of his non-Jewish neighbors, he had to be well prepared to explain dogma and answer questions.

At the annual conventions of the CCAR, members continually assessed their own performance and the state of their office in general. Numerous sermons and lectures, some followed by resolutions of the plenum, recounted what the rabbis had accomplished and what was still necessary to improve both their situation and their performance. By all those means the CCAR strove to build a dignified and respected profession that would bring satisfaction to its membership.

Ironically, the more the CCAR succeeded, and the more it upgraded and standardized synagogue practices, the more it eclipsed the individual rabbi and the individual congregation. As suggested earlier, it was the denomination, the organizations of congregations and rabbis, that came to represent each of the major movements. Within the larger community the influence of the single rabbi weakened and the less likely were his opinions to be highlighted in the press. But for a few exceptions, the average rabbi now spoke through his denomination on social, political, and constitutional issues as well as on matters of American foreign policy. Often allied with secular defense agencies and even Christian groups, the denomination and not the single rabbi became the defender of Jewish rights and the focus of public attention. And, whereas the denominations participated in community-wide umbrella organizations—most recently the Conference of Presidents of Major American Jewish Organizations— the individual rabbi was rarely heard beyond his particular synagogue.

Assessments of the rabbi, his office, and how they had changed over the years continued in the twentieth century. An examination of two books that appeared in connection with milestone anniversaries in the history of the American rabbinate and published some twenty years apart reveals both old and new trends that shaped the profession. In commemoration of its seventy-fifth anniversary in 1964, and numbering then about nine hundred members, the CCAR marked the occasion with a book of essays on the evolution of Reform's liturgy and ideology and the scope of the rabbis' activities.[38] Of special note were the changed position of the CCAR on Zionism, its increased attention to the problems of European Jewry, and its deep involvement in church-state matters and issues of social justice. Another subject that raised much serious discussion was the idea of a code or guide to Reform practices—something that Leo Levi had desired—but it was rejected. Other pressing matters, like the ongoing tension between religion and science and the need for providing an improved religious education for Jews of all ages, kept alive matters of concern that had antedated 1900.

Contributors to the volume agreed that the duties of the rabbi had expanded dramatically. He was no longer merely the preacher and teacher who inspired his flock in matters of faith and who devoted much of his time to private counseling and pastoral work. He served in addition as the representative of his congregation in community-wide drives for numerous nonreligious causes. Perhaps most important, he had become the CEO of a large plant with an enlarged staff, a post that necessitated guidance and administrative skills. In light of the rabbi's new tasks the president of the CCAR suggested that the curriculum of Hebrew Union College include courses on practical rabbinics, or the duties of the congregational rabbi. Improvement of the rabbi's personal condition also remained a problem. A pension plan and a placement commission, both of benefit to the rabbi, had been put into place by 1964, but rabbinic salaries were not commensurate either with the hours on the job or the salary scale of other professions.[39]

Another book-length assessment of the American rabbinate appeared in 1985 under the sponsorship of the Cincinnati-based American Jewish Archives. Commemorating the one-hundredth anniversary of the first graduation at Hebrew Union College in 1883 and thus the first appearance of American-trained rabbis, the book consisted of lengthy articles by representatives of the three major denominations.[40] Under the theme of continuity and change the writers surveyed and reported on the situation and problems of the rabbi. Much was the same as what had been said in 1964, particularly on the rabbi's ever-increasing duties. Writing about the Conservatives but generally applicable to all groups, Rabbi Abraham Karp listed the expectations of the rabbi on the part of the typical synagogue: "that he [the rabbi] be scholar, pastor, youth worker, preacher, educator, executive, and creative program initiator; and that he have had the wisdom (and good fortune) to have married a woman who would share him with the congregational family and aid him in his work." Karp, more than the other two writers, also emphasized the rabbi's lack of status and how the laity had trivialized his functions. He quoted one colleague who summed up the situation as follows: "We minister to people most of whom fully believe that they are wiser than we, better than we, certainly richer than we."[41]

Education of the laity was still a major problem for all, but advances had been made. For younger children and for college students, new classes, clubs, and summer programs had been created. Efforts by individuals had also borne fruit; Conservative/Reconstructionist Rabbi Mordecai Kaplan inspired and directed the Teachers Institute of the Jewish Theological Seminary for the training of teachers, and Orthodox Rabbi Joseph Lookstein founded Ramaz, which became the model of a modern Jewish day school.[42] Both those institutions served members of other denominations as well as their own. Indeed, unlike conditions in the nineteenth century, instances of interdenominational cooperation had increased.

At the same time, however, the essays in the book showed that diversity within each denomination now prevailed. Some Reformers and their congregations looked very much like Conservatives, and some Conservatives resembled Reformers or the moderate Orthodox. The aim of those nineteenth-century rabbis who sought unity within the denomination had given way to the realities of pluralism. The CCAR went as far as to welcome diversity. In 1976 it issued a "Centenary Perspective" in which it wrote: "Reform Judaism does more than tolerate diversity; it engenders it. In our uncertain historical situation we must expect to have far greater diversity than previous generations knew. . . . We stand open to any position thoughtfully and conscientiously advocated in the spirit of Reform Jewish beliefs." Without diversity, the position paper added, dissent would be stifled and the ability to confront new situations would be paralyzed.[43]

The two twentieth-century assessments of the rabbinate discussed how each denomination labored continuously at the task of adjusting its ideology to the needs of the day. More than dogma was involved. Like their predecessors, the rabbis were well aware of the importance of accommodating to the beliefs and tastes of America and Americans. Always the predominant characteristic of the Jewish minority, accommodationism was so deeply ingrained in the consciousness of the community that it provoked little discussion among the rabbis. Rabbi Herbert Goldstein, a representative of the moderate Orthodox faction, saw fit, however, to invoke accommodationism when he argued for modern, university-trained rabbis. He insisted that only those "reared on American soil, who have breathed the ideal of American democracy, who have been born and bred like other Americans" could minister to Jews desirous of living like their fellow Americans.[44]

Most noteworthy perhaps with respect to ideology was the dramatic shift in Reform's position. In his account of the Reform movement Rabbi David Polish explained how classical Reform's affirmation that Judaism was only a religion had given way to the recognition that the Jewish faith included a national dimension as well. Bonding particularism with universalism in an ongoing process, most rabbis now agreed to increased support of Zionism and permanent ties with the State of Israel.[45]

Nineteenth-century rabbis bequeathed a rich legacy of precedents to their successors. Most of the subjects on which they had commented in sermons and other statements were still relevant after 1900, and so were the principal attributes demanded of the rabbi—a commitment to Jewish tradition and an enthusiasm for the pulpit. To be sure, the questions of unity among the various denominations or freedom of the pulpit was no longer debated publicly, and neither were the distinctions in beliefs and rituals that separated Traditionalists from Reformers. But discussions on other subjects that had begun earlier continued to engage religious leaders, and concern about some matters, like antisemitism, Zionism, and interreligious cooperation, grew stronger. Rabbis, whether priests or prophets as their colleagues variously called them, and particularly their organizations, spoke out on relatively new subjects too. They preached and wrote on relations between pre- and post-1880 immigrants, the position of women in the synagogue, pacifism and American foreign policy, and civil rights issues like equal opportunity for minorities, church/state separation, and social justice. The rabbinical organizations also took stands on "secular" issues, and in time, measures for cooperation with Jewish defense agencies were adopted.

The topics that prompted an airing of rabbinic opinions in the nineteenth century illuminate the major themes that this study identified at the outset—Americanization, denominationalism, and religious identity. Those same themes, albeit with significant modifications that resulted primarily from new demographic and socioeconomic patterns, characterized Jewish religious life in the next century as well. In many instances, they yielded in the attention they claimed to the domestic and foreign crises that engulfed Jews throughout the world. Then, as American Jews built the most powerful Jewish center in history, communal priorities shifted. In those critical days, when American Jews were forced to look beyond their community, a strong rabbinate, a rabbinate that first took shape in the nineteenth century, became one of their principal resources.

Notes

NOTES TO THE INTRODUCTION

1. Throughout this book I use the word "Traditionalism" to connote what will become modern Orthodoxy and Conservatism.

2. Two studies consulted for this book are Robert V. Friedenberg, *"Hear O Israel": The History of American Jewish Preaching* (Tuscaloosa, AL, 1980), and Nathan M. Kaganoff, "The Traditional Jewish Sermon in the United States from Its Beginnings to the First World War" (Ph.D. diss., American University, 1961). A recent book edited by Elliot B. Gertel, *Jewish Belief and Practice in Nineteenth Century America* (Jefferson, NC, 2006), is a collection of eighteen essays by prominent rabbis.

3. See, for example, Friedenberg, *"Hear O Israel,"* ch. 1; Kaganoff, "Traditional Jewish Sermon," chs. 1–2, p. 207. For an in-depth study of the colonial New England sermon, including the "occasional" sermons that commented on various events, see Harry S. Stout, *The New England Soul* (New York, 1986), ch. 1.

4. Abraham J. Karp, "An East European Congregation on American Soil," in Bertram W. Korn, ed., *A Bicentennial Festschrift for Jacob Rader Marcus* (Waltham, MA, 1976).

5. Kaganoff, "Traditional Jewish Sermon," pp. 152–59; Moshe Davis, *The Emergence of Conservative Judaism* (Philadelphia, 1963), p. 122; Charles Reznikoff, *The Jews of Charleston* (Philadelphia, 1950), pp. 125–34.

6. Central Conference of American Rabbis (CCAR), *Sermons by American Rabbis* (Chicago, 1896), pp. x–xiv; Bertram W. Korn, *Eventful Years and Experiences* (Cincinnati, 1954), pp. 157, 208; Samuel E. Karff, ed., *Hebrew Union College–Jewish Institute of Religion at One Hundred Years* (Cincinnati, 1976), pp. 20–21, 31.

7. James Parton, "Our Israelitish Brethren," *Atlantic Monthly* 26 (Oct. 1870): 395. A recent study of East European immigrant rabbis and their sermons is Kimmy Caplan, *Orthodoxy in the New World* ([in Hebrew] Jerusalem, 2002). Moshe D. Sherman, "Struggle for Legitimacy," *Jewish History* 10 (Spring 1996): 63–70, discusses a few Orthodox rabbis who arrived before 1880. Comments on the rabbis and congregations in Orthodox communities of new immigrants in New York, Philadelphia, and Chicago at the turn of the century are found in studies compiled by Charles S. Bernheimer, *The Russian Jew in the United States*

(Philadelphia, 1905), pp. 149–50, 164–65, 179–80. For ways in which the new immigrants accommodated their synagogues to established Jewish or Americanized patterns, see Jonathan D. Sarna, *American Judaism* (New Haven, 2004), pp. 176–79.

8. Friedenberg, *"Hear O Israel,"* p. 42; Kaganoff, "Traditional Jewish Sermon," pp. 109–10. For estimates of rabbis who preached regularly in English before the arrival of waves of East Europeans, see Jacob R. Marcus, *United States Jewry, 1776–1985* (Detroit, 1993), vol. 3, p. 74, and Caplan, *Orthodoxy in the New World,* p. 36. Caplan adds (p. 278) that with the influx of the East Europeans more opposition to the English sermon was heard from immigrant Orthodox rabbis and preachers,

9. Unlike the established American Traditionalists and Reformers, the newer immigrant rabbis often expressed negative opinions of America, and many despaired of a future for Judaism in their new land. Caplan, *Orthodoxy in the New World,* pp. 222–53.

10. On European models, see, for example, Alexander Altmann, "The New Style of Preaching in Nineteenth-Century German Jewry," in Altmann, ed., *Studies in Nineteenth-Century Jewish Intellectual History* (Cambridge, 1964), and Michael A. Meyer, "Christian Influence on Early German Reform Judaism," in Charles Berlin, ed., *Studies in Jewish Bibliography, History and Literature in Honor of I. Edward Kiev* (New York, 1971). A study of nineteenth-century sermons in Germany in addition to American sermons in German is Adolf Kober, "Jewish Preaching and Preachers," *Historia Judaica* 7 (Oct. 1945): 103–34.

11. On the synthesis of Americanism and Judaism by laymen and rabbis in the nineteenth and twentieth centuries, see Jonathan D. Sarna, "The Cult of Synthesis in American Jewish Culture," *Jewish Social Studies* 5 n.s. (Fall 1998/Winter 1999): 52–75.

12. Hyman B. Grinstein, *The Rise of the Jewish Community of New York* (Philadelphia, 1945), ch. 5; Jacob R. Marcus, *United States Jewry, 1776–1985* (Detroit, 1989), vol. 1, p. 280.

13. Allan Tarshish, "Jew and Christian in a New Society," in Korn, *Bicentennial Festschrift,* pp. 579–80; Benny Kraut, "The Ambivalent Relations of American Reform Judaism with Unitarianism in the Last Third of the Nineteenth Century," *Journal of Ecumenical Studies* 23 (Winter 1986): 60–61.

14. Jacob R. Marcus, *American Jewry: Documents* (Cincinnati, 1959), p. 53.

15. Grinstein, *Jewish Community of New York,* p. 340.

16. Maurice H. Harris, "The Dangers of Emancipation," *Central Conference of American Rabbis Yearbook (CCARY)* 4 (1893): 55–63.

17. I. J. Benjamin, a Romanian self-styled Orthodox Jew, toured the United States on the eve of the Civil War. He reported on the empty synagogues, but he spoke more positively about the Reform congregations. I. J. Benjamin, *Three*

Years in America, translated from the German by Charles Reznikoff (Philadelphia, 1956), vol. 1, pp. 82–83.

18. Hasia Diner, *A Time for Gathering* (Baltimore, 1992), p. 119. For a brief summary of Orthodox reactions to Reformers and their sermons at the turn of the century, see Caplan, *Orthodoxy in the New World*, pp. 260–65.

19. Leeser was acquainted with most of his rabbinical colleagues and their congregations. His periodical, the *Occident*, enjoyed a nationwide readership. Lance J. Sussman, *Isaac Leeser and the Making of American Judaism* (Detroit, 1995).

20. For example, see Marcus, *United States Jewry*, vol. 1, p. 645; Alan Silverstein, *Alternatives to Assimilation* (Hanover, NH, 1994), p. 35; Joseph L. Blau and Salo W. Baron, *The Jews of the United States, 1790–1840* (New York, 1963), vol. 2, pp. 588–90; Sherman, "Struggle for Legitimacy," pp. 64–70. For Schwab, see chapter 8 in this volume.

21. Cf. Marc Saperstein, *Jewish Preaching, 1200–1800* (New Haven, 1989), introduction. Some of the same difficulties are mentioned by Saperstein in his introduction to a book on his father's sermons. Harold I. Saperstein, *Witness from the Pulpit*, ed. Marc Saperstein (Lanham, MD, 2000).

22. CCAR, *Sermons by American Rabbis*, p. xiv.

NOTES TO CHAPTER 1

1. Isaac M. Fein, *The Making of an American Jewish Community* (Philadelphia, 1971), pp. 56–57. See also Jacob R. Marcus, *United States Jewry, 1776–1985* (Detroit, 1991), vol. 2, ch. 9. This chapter has been reworked from my essay, "Sermons and the Contemporary World," in Geoffrey Wigoder, ed., *Contemporary Jewry: Studies in Honor of Moshe Davis* (Jerusalem, 1984). I obtained permission to reproduce the material from the late Dr. Wigoder.

2. Saul I. Teplitz, "Synagogue Life and Thought in Nineteenth Century America as Reflected in the English Sermon" (D.H.L. diss., Jewish Theological Seminary of America, New York, n.d.), pp. 3–5, 7.

3. Bertram W. Korn, *American Jewry and the Civil War* (Philadelphia, 1951), pp. 206–12, 221–22.

4. The sermons of New England before the Revolution, the occasions on which they were delivered, and their function as a means of social control are discussed in Harry S. Stout, *The New England Soul* (New York, 1986); see esp. ch. 1.

5. Jacob R. Marcus, *United States Jewry, 1776–1985* (Detroit, 1989), vol. 1, p. 281; David and Tamar De Sola Pool, *An Old Faith in the New World* (New York, 1955), p. 499.

6. *Occident (OCC)* 3 (Mar. 1846): 578.

7. Sabato Morais Letters, American Jew Archives, microfilm reel 203: M. Ellinger to M. Sulzberger, 5 Apr. 1877.

8. Jacob R. Marcus, *United States Jewry, 1776–1985* (Detroit, 1993), vol. 3, p. 699.

9. Harold I. Saperstein, "The Origin and Authority of the Rabbi," in Elliot L. Stevens, ed., *Papers Presented before the Ninety-First Annual Convention of the Central Conference of American Rabbis, Central Conference of American Rabbis Yearbook (CCARY)* 90, part 2 (1982): 22–23; *CCARY* 2 (1891): 84–128, 3 (1892): 35.

10. Isaac M. Wise, *Reminiscences*, translated from the German and edited by David Philipson (Cincinnati, 1901), p. 45; *Israelite*, 3 Aug. 1855.

11. *American Israelite (AI)*, 3 May 1878, and partially quoted in Paul A. Carter, *The Spiritual Crisis of the Gilded Age* (De Kalb, IL, 1971), p. 12.

12. James G. Heller, *Isaac M. Wise* (New York, 1965), ch. 12.

13. Lance J. Sussman, *Isaac Leeser and the Making of American Judaism* (Detroit, 1995), ch. 3; Maxwell Whiteman, "Isaac Leeser and the Jews of Philadelphia," in Abraham J. Karp, ed., *The Jewish Experience in America* (Waltham, MA, 1969) vol. 3, p. 33; Nathan M. Kaganoff, "The Traditional Jewish Sermon in the United States from Its Beginnings to the First World War" (Ph.D. diss., American University, 1961), p. 152. On Leeser's method of constructing a sermon, see Robert V. Friedenberg, *"Hear O Israel": The History of American Jewish Preaching, 1654–1970* (Tuscaloosa, AL, 1989), ch. 2; *OCC* 11 (Jan. 1854): 510.

14. For a fuller discussion of this and the following two paragraphs, see Naomi W. Cohen, *Encounter with Emancipation* (Philadelphia, 1984), pp. 129–41. For Leeser's opinion on the separation between Jews and politics, albeit laden with contradictions, see Cohen, "Pioneers of American Jewish Defense," *American Jewish Archives* 29 (Nov. 1977): 126–27.

15. The code may have rested in part on British precedent as well. In 1817 the lay leaders of England's foremost synagogue, Bevis Marks in London, forbade any sermon critical of British institutions. Friedenberg, *"Hear O Israel,"* pp. 23–24.

16. Ibid., p. 28.

17. Cohen, *Encounter with Emancipation*, pp. 131, 134–35; Korn, *American Jewry and the Civil War*, pp. 22, 41–42.

18. *American Hebrew (AH)*, 20 Apr. 1894; Melvin I. Urofsky, *A Voice That Spoke for Justice* (Albany, NY, 1982), ch. 4.

19. Particularly advantageous were periodicals edited by rabbis themselves, like the *Jewish Messenger* and the *American Israelite*.

20. I. L. Leucht, "The Rabbi as a Public Man," *CCARY* 8 (1897): 14.

21. Kaganoff, "Traditional Jewish Sermon," pp. 113–16.

22. *AI*, 21 Nov. 1889; Naomi W. Cohen, "The Challenges of Darwinism and Biblical Criticism to American Judaism," *Modern Judaism* 4 (May 1984): 136–37.

23. Although Morais was usually a severe critic of Reformers, he sounded very much like them when he called for discarding significant portions of the ritual. *The American Jewish Pulpit* (Cincinnati, 1881), pp. 14–15.

24. Jacob R. Marcus, *To Count a People* (Lanham, MD, 1990), pp, 65, 87, 90.

25. *American Jewish Pulpit*, pp. 79–80; *New York Times*, 3–6 May 1879.

26. For example, *American Jewish Pulpit*, pp. 6, 130–33, 149, 157–61, 240–41.

27. Ibid., pp. 88–89.

28. Ibid., pp. 54, 57, 72–73, 149–51, 193.

29. Ibid., pp. 13, 57, 72–73, 89–91, 149–51, 193; Sidney Mead, "American Protestantism since the Civil War," *Journal of Religion* 36 (Apr. 1956): 77–78.

30. *American Jewish Pulpit*, pp. 72–73, 149–51.

31. Ibid., pp. 6, 90, 157, 160–64, 241. Some years earlier Isaac Wise had called Darwinism "Homo-Brutalism," a theory that "is nugatory to morals, robs man of the consciousness of his dignity and pre-eminence, and brutalizes him." Cohen, "Challenges of Darwinism and Biblical Criticism," pp. 123–24.

32. Emil G. Hirsch, *My Religion* (New York, 1925), p. 83.

33. *American Jewish Pulpit*, pp. 72, 160.

34. Translated from the German and quoted in Gershon Greenberg, "The Significance of America in David Einhorn's Conception of History," *American Jewish Historical Quarterly* 63 (Dec. 1973): 163.

35. *American Jewish Pulpit*, pp. 100, 129–32, 161–63.

36. Ibid., pp. 8, 14, 68–69, 72–73, 195, 197.

37. The Seligman-Hilton affair refers to the exclusion of the prominent banker Joseph Seligman from a hotel in Saratoga just because he was Jewish. On European antisemitism there was only a brief mention of two virulent German Jew-baiters. Ibid., p. 196.

38. *American Jewish Pulpit*, pp. 8–9.

39. *CCARY* 5 (1894): 25, 43; CCAR, *Sermons by American Rabbis* (Chicago, 1896).

40. CCAR, *Sermons by American Rabbis*, pp. 14, 29, 36, 49, 105, 107–8, 226, 289–90, 309. The text of the Pittsburgh Platform is included by Nathan Glazer in *American Judaism* (Chicago, 1957), pp. 151–52. Rabbi Joseph Krauskopf of Philadelphia, who claimed that he had studied the subject thoroughly, defended evolution in 1887 in a talk reconciling the new science with religion. Krauskopf, "Evolution and Judaism," in Elliot B. Gertel, *Jewish Belief and Practice in Nineteenth Century America* (Jefferson, NC, 2006), pp. 132–41.

41. CCAR, *Sermons by American Rabbis*, pp. 49, 99, 117, 223–32, 289. See also the discourse by Rabbi Henry Berkowitz on the "Great Infidel," Robert Ingersoll. Berkowitz, *Judaism and Ingersollism* (Philadelphia, 1894).

42. CCAR, *Sermons by American Rabbis*, pp. 13, 34, 91–92, 152, 221.

43. Berkowitz in CCAR, *Sermons by American Rabbis*, pp. 197–99; Hirsch, "The Harvest Festival," in ibid., pp. 94–113; see also Cohen, *Encounter with Emancipation*, pp. 197–202.

44. For example, see Kaufmann Kohler in *CCARY* 5 (1894): 132–36, 141–43.

45. Glazer, *American Judaism*, p. 53; CCAR, *Sermons by American Rabbis*, p. 92; Benny Kraut, "The Ambivalent Relations of American Reform Judaism with Unitarianism in the Last Third of the Nineteenth Century," *Journal of Ecumenical Studies* 23 (Winter 1986): 58–68. Rabbi Gustav Gottheil was another outspoken opponent of merger with the Unitarianism. See his printed letter, "The Great Refusal," in Gertel, *Jewish Belief and Practice*, pp. 122–31.

46. CCAR, *Sermons by American Rabbis*, pp. 176–79; Jonathan D. Sarna, "Passover Raisin Wine, the American Temperance Movement, and Mordecai Noah," *Hebrew Union College Annual* 59 (1988): 281, 287–88.

47. CCAR, *Sermons by American Rabbis*, pp. 105–6, 119, 261, 268.

48. Ibid., pp. 316–28.

49. Joseph Stolz, "Judaism and the Congress of Liberal Religious Societies," CCAR, *Sermons by American Rabbis*, pp. 244–49; Moses J. Gries, "Reform Judaism and Liberal Christianity," in ibid., pp. 250–58; Maurice H. Harris, "Judaism and Unitarianism," in ibid., pp. 270–84.

50. CCAR, *Sermons by American Rabbis*, pp. 53, 121, 141–44, 151, 235.

51. Ibid., pp. 92, 97–98, 102, 113, 132–34, 161–62, 191, 214, 235.

52. Ibid., pp. 233, 241.

53. Ibid., pp. 122–46. For a full discussion of the Hanukkah sermon, see chapter 8 in this volume.

NOTES TO CHAPTER 2

1. The most recent full biography of Leeser is Lance J. Sussman, *Isaac Leeser and the Making of American Judaism* (Detroit, 1995).

2. Moshe Davis Papers (MDP), courtesy of Mrs. Lottie K. Davis: sermon by Morais, "Anniversary of My 45 Years with the Congregation Mikveh Israel [1896]." Morais's background and education are discussed in Arthur Kiron, "Dust and Ashes," *American Jewish History* 84 (Sept. 1996): 158–63, 187–88.

3. Arthur Kiron, "Golden Ages, Promised Lands" (Ph.D. diss., Columbia University, 1999). Since the dissertation was inaccessible to me, I used the twenty-one-page abstract available on the internet, http://proquest.umi.com/pqdweb?dis =733502571&sid=1&fmt=28=clientd=11916&rqt=309&vname=pqd.

4. Bertram W. Korn, *American Jewry and the Civil War* (Philadelphia, 1951), p. 38.

5. Morais once wrote that in his later years he preferred the *Jewish Record* of Philadelphia to the *Jewish Messenger*. *Jewish Messenger (JM)*, 6 Jan. 1882. The Morais Ledger is in the Schoenberg Center for Electronic Text and Image, University of Pennsylvania.

6. Unsorted Morais Papers (UMP), Hebrew Union College (HUC): microfilm reel 199, sermon by Morais, "A Few Words about the Necessity of Continuing to

Deliver Lectures [undated]." For a fuller discussion of lay control of the pulpit, see chapter 1 in this volume.

7. Moshe Davis, *The Emergence of Conservative Judaism* (Philadelphia, 1963), pp. 99–100; Morris U. Schappes, ed., *A Documentary History of the Jews in the United States* (New York, 1971), p. 674; MDP: sermon by Morais, "On the Anti-Jewish League in Germany [1881]."

8. *American Hebrew (AH)*, 28 Jan. 1881, 4 Feb. 1881.

9. Korn, *American Jewry and the Civil War*, pp. 38–39; a slight variation appears in Davis, *Emergence of Conservative Judaism*, pp. 110–12; UMP microfilm reel 206: undated sermon by Morais on the Pharisees; Morais to L. Liberman, 14 Dec. 1864. In a letter to the president of the congregation Morais said that since the constitution of Mikveh Israel made no mention of sermons, he wanted precise instructions from the board on the contents of acceptable sermons. UMP microfilm reel 206: Morais to A. Hart, 11 Jan. [1865]. In neither of the two letters found in UMP does Morais discuss the issue of a free pulpit.

10. *Philadelphia Inquirer*, 28 Nov. 1884; *Public Ledger*, 9 May, 29 Nov. 1892. References to Philadelphia newspapers are from clippings in the Morais Ledger.

11. *JM*, 15 May 1863; MDP: sermon by Morais, "For the Day of Thanksgiving Proclaimed by President Lincoln [undated]." For a list of his Civil War sermons, see Korn, *American Jewry and the Civil War*, p. 222; Kiron, "Dust and Ashes," p. 164. One source reports that Morais was the most quoted rabbi in the daily press during the war. Nathan M. Kaganoff, "The Traditional Jewish Sermon in the United States from Its Beginnings to the First World War" (Ph.D. diss., American University, 1961), p. 82.

12. Naomi W. Cohen, *Encounter with Emancipation* (Philadelphia, 1984), pp. 72–75; *JM*, 11 Dec. 1868.

13. MDP: statement by Morais on Thanksgiving, 5 Nov. 1868; *JM*, 13, 27 Nov., 11 Dec. 1868; Davis, *Emergence of Conservative Judaism*, pp. 95–96.

14. *Jewish Record (JR)*, 12 Nov. 1880.

15. *JM*, 11 Dec. 1880.

16. *Sunday Dispatch*, 28 Oct. 1877; *JR*, 2 Nov. 1877; UMP microfilm reel 207: undated and untitled sermon by Morais. For the background of Sunday laws in America in the nineteenth century, see Naomi W. Cohen, *Jews in Christian America* (New York, 1992), pp. 55–64. In 1876, when America celebrated its centennial and suggestions were made on bringing Christianity into the celebrations, Morais also protested. For example, see *JR*, 3 Mar. 1876.

17. *Sunday Dispatch*, 27 Feb. 1870, 28 Oct. 1877; *JM*, 4 Mar. 1870; *Jewish Exponent (JE)*, 12 Apr. 1889; UMP microfilm reel 206: undated and untitled sermon by Morais. In connection with the rights of labor, Morais mediated a strike by garment workers in 1890. Kiron, "Dust and Ashes," p. 165.

18. UMP microfilm reel 207: undated and untitled sermon by Morais; *Sunday Dispatch*, 20 June 1869.

19. MDP: Sermon by Morais, "On the Attempt to Christianize the Constitution, 1894."

20. *JM*, 10 Mar. 1871, 11 Apr. 1873; *The Press*, 28 Jan. 1871; Davis, *Emergence of Conservative Judaism*, pp. 189–90; Cohen, *Jews in Christian America*, pp. 65–72, 91–92; MDP: sermon by Morais, "On the Attempt to Christianize the Constitution, 1894."

21. *The Press*, 29 Apr. 1867, 10 May 1867; *The Age*, 28 Jan. 1871; *JR*, 13 Apr. 1877, 18 Nov. 1882; to editor of *North American*, 13 Aug. 1878; unnamed and undated source in Morais Ledger, p. 453.

22. UMP microfilm reel 206: sermon by Morais, "A Few Words on the Hilton Affair [undated]"; undated and untitled sermon by Morais on the Union League club incident.

23. *JM*, 21 Jan. 1876; Martin E. Marty, *Righteous Empire* (New York, 1970), pp. 162–64, 180–81.

24. Kiron, "Golden Ages," abstract, p. 18; MDP: sermon by Morais, "Anniversary of My 45 Years . . . [1896]"; MDP: Morais to A. Isaacs, 12 Nov. 1878.

25. Although not yet a movement in the nineteenth century, a "middle way" between Orthodoxy and Reform had been recognized since the 1860s. In 1866 Julius Bondi, a rabbi and editor, called it a golden mean that was termed "Orthodox" by Reformers and "Reform" by the Orthodox. Noting its rapid progress, he added that it was "hated on both sides." Abraham J. Karp, "The Conservative Rabbi," in Jacob R. Marcus and Abraham J. Peck, eds., *The American Rabbinate* (Hoboken, NJ, 1985), pp. 105–7.

26. Sermon by Morais in *The American Jewish Pulpit* (Cincinnati, 1881), pp. 14–15.

27. Many early sermons in the Morais Ledger criticized Reform and Reformers; for example, clippings in the Ledger from the *Asmonean* for 1854 and 1859.

28. For this and the next paragraph, see MDP: sermon by Morais, "A Scolding Lecture on the 30th Anniversary of My Ministry 5641 [1881]"; MDP: M. Montefiore to Morais, 20 July 1881; MDP: Morais to B. Felsenthal, 30 Apr. 1889; to editor *AH*, 24 June 1865; *JM*, 18 Mar. 1859, 4 June 1869, 13 Dec. 1872; UMP microfilm reel 206: sermons by Morais on the Pharisees and "On Religion and Reason [undated]."

29. *JR*, 1 Oct. 1875 (Morais to I. Wise), 8 Sept. 1876; Moshe Davis, "Sabato Morais: A Selected and Annotated Bibliography of His Writings," *Publications of the American Jewish Historical Society* 37 (1947): 56; MDP: Morais to B. Felsenthal, 20 Apr. 1889; UMP microfilm reel 199: untitled and undated sermon by Morais on the Hebrew Union College.

30. *JM*, 1 Feb., 8 Mar. 1867, 3 Nov. 1871; see also *JR*, 1 Oct. 1875, 15 Aug. 1879.

31. The proceedings of the conferences in Germany and in Philadelphia were published by the CCAR in its *Yearbook (CCARY)* 1 (1890); MDP: statement by

Morais dated 8 Nov. 1869 prepared for the *JM*; MDP: sermon by Morais, "On the Pittsburgh Convention in 1885," also contains material on the Philadelphia conference. Morais's statement along with correspondence and editorials on the subject appeared in the *JM*, 12, 19 Nov. 1869. For an analysis of the leading figures at the Philadelphia conference, the divisions within Reform ranks, and the aftermath of the conference, see Sefton D. Temkin, *The New World of Reform* (Bridgeport, CT, 1974), pp. 1–29.

32. *JM*, 12–26 Nov., 10–24 Dec. 1875; Davis, *Emergence of Conservative Judaism*, pp. 162–65. Morais saw no need to placate the right-wing Orthodox. They too were troubled by the assimilatory forces that undercut the membership and vibrancy of their synagogues, and they therefore might not be totally averse to Morais's suggestions.

33. UMP microfilm reel 199: undated sermon by Morais for Parashat Bamidbar; cf. Hasia Diner, "Like the Antelope and the Badger," in Jack Wertheimer, ed., *Tradition Renewed* (New York, 1997) vol. 1, 11–13; *CCARY* 1 (1890): 15. An abbreviated overview of the differences between the Reformers and the Traditionalists in the 1880s, based mainly on the *American Hebrew*, is Charles Wyszkowski, *A Community in Conflict* (Lanham, MD, 1991), ch. 5.

34. Series of open letters to Kaufmann Kohler, *AH*, 26 June, 3, 10, 17 1885; MDP: sermon by Morais, "On the Pittsburgh Convention in 1885"; Michael A. Meyer, *Response to Modernity* (New York, 1988), pp. 265–70; Jonathan D. Sarna, *American Judaism* (New Haven, CT, 2004), pp. 144–50.

35. Kiron, "Golden Ages," abstract, p. 20; *JE*, 11 Oct. 1889, 8 July 1892; *AH*, 2 Sept. 1887; *JR*, 14 Mar. 1884, 3–17 July 1885.

36. *JR*, 11 Dec. 1889; *AH*, 2 Sept. 1887; Davis, *Emergence of Conservative Judaism*, pp 59–63, 231–35; MDP: a call for a seminary by Morais, Oct. 1871. Before the founding of HUC in 1875, Morais's desire for an educated ministry explained his interest in the short-lived Maimonides College in Philadelphia.

37. MDP: sermon by Morais, "On the Pittsburgh Convention in1885"; MDP: sermon by Morais, "About the Education of the Young [undated]"; MDP: sermon by Morais, "On the Jewish Theological Seminary, 1894"; MDP: printed leaflet by Morais, 26 Nov. 1885; Davis, *Emergence of Conservative Judaism*, pp. 231–35; Kiron, "Golden Ages," abstract, p. 11. For a short resume of the debate among historians, see Kiron, "Dust and Ashes," p. 163 n.26, and Diner, "Like the Antelope and the Badger," pp. 12–13.

38. MDP: Morais' call for a seminary [Oct. 1871]; MDP: sermon by Morais, "On the Jewish Theological Seminary, 1894"; UMP microfilm reel 207: several sermons by Morais on the need for a Jewish Theological Seminary; Diner, "Like the Antelope and the Badger," p. 17; Sarna, *American Judaism*, pp. 184–85; *AH*, 7 May 1897.

39. Joseph H. Hertz, "Sabato Morais: A Pupil's Tribute," in Cyrus Adler, ed., *The Jewish Theological Seminary of America* (New York, 1939), pp. 46–49.

NOTES TO CHAPTER 3

1. Nathan M. Kaganoff, "The Traditional Jewish Sermon in the United States from Its Beginnings to the First World War" (Ph.D. diss., American University, 1961), p. 50; Hyman B. Grinstein, *The Rise of the Jewish Community of New York* (Philadelphia, 1945), p. 88; Lance J. Sussman, *Isaac Leeser and the Making of American Judaism* (Detroit, 1995), p.102. Although the two sons, Myer and Abram, moved away from their father's strict Traditionalism, I use the words "Isaacs," meaning Samuel and/or his sons, and *"Jewish Messenger"* interchangeably in the following discussion.

2. Allan Tarshish, "The Board of Delegates of American Israelites (1859–1878)," in Abraham J. Karp, ed., *The Jewish Experience in America* (Waltham, MA, 1969), vol. 3, p. 128.

3. George L. Berlin, *Defending the Faith* (Albany, 1989), pp. 87–92.

4. Naomi W. Cohen, "Pioneers of American Jewish Defense," *American Jewish Archives* 29 (Nov. 1977): 116–50.

5. H. L. Ginsberg, ed., *The Five Megilloth and Jonah* (Philadelphia, 1969), pp. 82, 88.

6. For this and the next three paragraphs, see *Jewish Messenger (JM)*, 27 Feb. 1857, 22 Mar. 1867.

7. Ibid., 22 Feb. 1861, 3 May 1867.

8. Ibid., 22 Mar. 1861, 23 Feb. 1877.

9. Ibid., 22 Mar., 3 May 1867. Other calls for representative men and Mordecais appeared in the *JM* in 1858, 1871, 1873, 1875, and 1876. The paper may also have been encouraged in its use of the name Mordecai by George Eliot's novel *Daniel Deronda* (1876) in which Daniel's idealistic mentor is called Mordecai.

10. *JM*, 3 May 1867. On one Purim a Jewish children's magazine, *Sabbath Visitor*, picked up the same theme and talked of men like Riesser and Crémieux, "Our Modern Mordecais," who fought for Jewish rights. *Sabbath Visitor* 3 (Mar. 1876): 76.

11. *JM*, 22 Mar. 1867.

12. Cohen, "Pioneers of American Jewish Defense," pp. 120–33. A recent biography of Leeser discusses the many fronts on which Leeser fought. Sussman, *Leeser*.

13. Heller, "Silence Means Ruin," in Central Conference of American Rabbis (CCAR), *Sermons by American Rabbis* (Chicago, 1896), pp. 151–57.

14. *Jewish Encyclopedia*, vol. 1, p. 483; *Encyclopedia Judaica*, vol. 2, p. 791.

15. A recent interpretation of the Book of Esther removes the embarrassment by cogently explaining the *megillah* in terms of basic moral precepts and political realities. Yoram Hazony, *The Dawn*, rev. ed. (Jerusalem, 2003). For interpretations of Amalek by several writers of ancient times, see Louis H. Feldman, *Remember Amalek* (Cincinnati, 2004).

16. *JM,* 17 Aug. 1888; CCAR, *Sermons by American Rabbis,* p. xiv.

17. Bertram W. Korn, *American Jewry and the Civil War* (Philadelphia, 1951), pp. 7–9, 20–22.

18. Ibid., pp. 17–19.

19. For this and the next two paragraphs, see David Einhorn, *War with Amalek!* (Philadelphia, 1864).

20. Naomi W. Cohen, *Encounter with Emancipation* (Philadelphia, 1984), pp. 253–54.

21. For this and the next two paragraphs, see *Jewish Times,* 1 Mar. 1870.

22. For the material on Schwab, see *American Israelite (AI),* 17 Mar. 1876.

23. For this and the next two paragraphs, see Henry Vidaver in *American Jewish Pulpit* (Cincinnati, 1881), pp. 25–30.

24. Hermann Baar, *Addresses on Homely and Religious Subjects Delivered before the Children of the Hebrew Orphan Asylum* (New York, 1885), vol. 2, pp. 85–88; *American Hebrew (AH),* 16 Sept. 1904.

25. On the Washington synagogue, see Marc L. Raphael, "Our Treasury Is Empty . . . ," *American Jewish History* 84 (June 1996): 81–98.

26. *AH,* 15 Mar. 1895.

27. For example, Naomi W. Cohen, "Antisemitism in the Gilded Age," *Jewish Social Studies* 41 (Summer–Fall 1979): 200–201. See also Louise A. Mayo, *The Ambivalent Image* (Rutherford, NJ, 1988), pp. 54–70.

28. Abraham J. Feldman, "Does the Jew Remember Too Well?" in *Beth Israel Pulpit,* Series 4, no. 7 (Hartford, Conn., 1930).

29. In 1912 a Jewish children's magazine, the *Ark,* retold the Purim story and added: "In every Jewish lad there is a possible Mordecai." *Ark* 2 (Feb. 1912): 108.

30. Feldman, "Does the Jew Remember Too Well?"; Israel H. Levinthal, *Judaism Speaks to the Modern World* (New York, 1963), pp. 77–84; Samuel Rosenblatt, *Hear, Oh Israel* (New York, 1958), pp. 261–66. The quotation is from Rosenblatt.

NOTES TO CHAPTER 4

Notes to the *Sabbath Visitor (SV)* are for direct quotations and for ideas mentioned only once. Only those issues of the *SV* that appeared monthly are paginated.

1. R. Gordon Kelly, *Mother Was a Lady* (Westport, CT, 1974); John M. Blum, *Yesterday's Children* (Cambridge, 1959), introduction; *SV* 5 (14 Jan. 1878); Naomi M. Patz, "Jewish Religious Children's Literature in America," *Phaedrus* 7 (1980): 28 n.4. Although the *Visitor* claimed on occasion that it was the first American journal for Jewish children, it had been preceded by the *Young Israel* of New York, founded in 1871 and lasting about five years, and by the *Hebrew Sabbath School Companion,* also of New York, that appeared only in 1872–1873. Julia Richman, "The Jewish Sunday School Movement in the United States," *Jewish Quarterly Review* 12 (July 1900): 574.

2. Unless otherwise noted the material for this and the next paragraph comes from Bruce L. Ruben, "Max Lilienthal: Rabbi, Educator, and Reformer in Nineteenth-Century America" (Ph.D. diss., City University of New York, 1997), pp. 228–42.

3. Morton J. Merowitz, "Max Lilienthal (1814–1882)," *YIVO Annual of Jewish Social Studies* 15 (1974): 48–49.

4. *SV* 1 (Jan. 1874): 1–8.

5. Merowitz, "Lilienthal," pp. 57–58; Alan Silverstein, *Alternatives to Assimilation* (Hanover, NH, 1994), pp. 31–34. At a meeting in 1871 that led to the establishment of a short-lived American Jewish Publication Society, Lilienthal spoke of the need to provide Jewish children with books in English. Jonathan D. Sarna, *JPS: The Americanization of Jewish Culture, 1888–1988* (Philadelphia, 1989), p. 9.

6. *SV* 1 (Jan., Feb. 1874): 6, 7, 24. Nellie lasted for two years, the Visitor and his group even longer.

7. *SV* 1 (Jan. 1874): 2, 7.

8. *SV* 2 (Aug. 1875): 120; 3 (Jan. 1876): 76.

9. *SV* 1 (Jan. 1874): 24; 2 (May 1875): 64; 3 (July 1876): 223; 6 (12 Dec. 1879).

10. *SV* 3 (Jan. 1876): 12; 6 (10 Jan. 1879).

11. *SV* 1 (Mar. 1874): 34.

12. Lilienthal served on Cincinnati's Board of Education where he worked for the removal of Bible-reading from the classroom. Naomi W. Cohen, *Jews in Christian America* (New York, 1992), pp. 83–84; David Philipson, *Max Lilienthal* (New York, 1915), pp. 474–87.

13. *SV* 1 (Jan. 1874): 5; 3 (Dec. 1876): 404. An opponent of large standing armies, Lilienthal also counseled an American policy of noninterference in European affairs. *SV* 1 (June 1874): 92. For the West Point story, see *SV* 2 (May 1875): 36.

14. *SV* 6 (1 Aug. 1879); 2 (7 Apr. 1875); 1 (July 1874): 98.

15. *SV* 5 (4 Apr. 1878).

16. *SV* 7 (4 June, 13 Aug., 8 Oct. 1880). The Seligman-Hilton affair refers to the exclusion of banker Joseph Seligman from a hotel in Saratoga in 1877 because he was a Jew. The affair highlighted public awareness of increasing social discrimination against Jews.

17. *SV* 7 (8 Oct. 1880).

18. *SV* 21 (1 May 1891).

19. *SV* 21 (29 May 1891).

20. *SV* 7 (2 July 1880); 16 (May 1886): 1; 21 (1 May 1891).

21. Hyman Bogen, *The Luckiest Orphans* (Urbana, IL, 1992), chs. 1–5; Hyman B. Grinstein, *The Rise of the Jewish Community of New York* (Philadelphia, 1945), pp. 145–48; *SV* 13 (7 Nov. 1884). A detailed study of the HOA and other Jewish orphanages in the United States is Reena S. Friedman, *These Are Our Children* (Hanover, NH, 1994), esp. chs. 5–6 on the norms and values of the HOA.

22. Isaac Markens, *The Hebrews in America* (New York, 1888), p. 197; Bogen, *Luckiest Orphans*, ch. 6.

23. *SV* 13 (21 Nov., 26 Dec. 1884); 17 (Apr. 1888): 739; [22] (2 Dec. 1892). Volume 22 of the *SV* is numbered incorrectly in the copy I used, and I have therefore put the correct number in brackets.

24. *SV* 18 (July 1888): 133–35.

25. *SV* 18 (Mar. 1889): 663–65.

26. Friedman, *These Are Our Children*, pp. 135–36; *SV* 14 (Oct. 1885): 497.

27. *SV* 14 (31 July 1885).

28. *SV* 17 (Dec. 1887): 451–53; 16 (June 1886): 72–73.

29. *SV* 13 (14–21 Nov.1884); Friedman, *These Are Our Children*, p. 134.

30. *SV* 19 (15 Dec. 1889; 16 (Apr. 1887): 719; Friedman, *These Are Our Children*, p. 129.

31. *SV* 14 (27 Nov. 1885); 16 (Sept. 1886): 267–69.

32. Bogen, *Luckiest Orphans*, pp. 94–96.

33. *SV* [22] (6 May 1892).

34. *SV* 18 (Sept. 1888): 271–72.

35. *SV* 16 (Sept. 1886): 267, 269.

36. Bogen, *Luckiest Orphans*, p. 86; *SV* 16 (Aug. 1886): 219–21.

37. *SV* 19 (1 Oct. 1889); [22] (28 Oct. 1892).

38. *SV* 17 (Feb. 1888): 587–88.

39. *SV* 21 (17 July, 9 Oct., 25 Dec. 1891); [22] (9 Sept. 1892); Friedman, *These Are Our Children*, pp. 26, 44.

40. *SV* 19 (15 May 1889).

41. Bogen, *Luckiest Orphans*, p.106; *SV* 14 (19 June 1885). For a different comment by Baar on his use of corporal punishment, see Friedman, *These Are Our Children*, p. 44.

42. *SV* 18 (June 1888): 78–80; [22] (24 Mar. 1893).

43. Bogen, *Luckiest Orphans*, ch. 7.

44. Ibid., p. 93.

45. *SV* 20 (15 Apr. 1891).

46. *SV* 19 (1 May 1889).

47. *SV* 16 (Sept. 1886): 267–69.

48. Bogen, *Luckiest Orphans*, chs. 7–9.

49. Ibid., p. 94.

50. Kelly, *Mother Was a Lady*, introduction.

NOTES TO CHAPTER 5

1. Naomi W. Cohen, *Jews in Christian America* (New York, 1992), pp. 11–33.

2. Maurice H. Harris, "The Dangers of Emancipation," *Central Conference of American Rabbis Yearbook (CCARY)* 4 (1893): 55–63.

3. *Occident (OCC)* 2 (June, Sept. 1844): 122, 291.

4. Moshe Davis, *The Emergence of Conservative Judaism* (Philadelphia, 1963), pp. 127–28; Michael A. Meyer, *Response to Modernity* (New York, 1988), ch. 6.

5. *OCC* 2 (May 1844): 67–78.

6. The references to the *Occident* for this and the following paragraph, except for a few quotations, are too numerous to cite. See especially vols. 2 (1844–1845), 8 (1850–1851), 12–14 (1854–1857).

7. *OCC* 12 (Oct. 1854): 329–38.

8. Ibid., 8 (Oct. 1850): 325–33.

9. Ibid., 12 (Nov. 1854): 386.

10. For example, ibid., 3 (Jan., Feb. 1846): 520, 536.

11. Davis, *Emergence of Conservative Judaism*, pp. 125–30; Bruce L. Ruben, "Max Lilienthal: Rabbi, Educator, and Reformer in Nineteenth-Century America" (Ph.D. diss., City University of New York, 1997), pp. 141–44; Lance J. Sussman, *Isaac Leeser and the Making of American Judaism* (Detroit, 1995), pp. 169–70.

12. *OCC* 1 (July 1843): 253–61. Similar criticism came from Rabbi Samuel Isaacs, ibid., 2 (June 1844): 150–53. See also Allan Tarshish, "The Charleston Organ Case," in Abraham J. Karp, ed., *The Jewish Experience in America* (Waltham, MA, 1969), vol. 2, pp. 281–315.

13. *OCC* 12 (June 1854–Mar. 1855); Sussman, *Leeser*, pp. 145–46, 194–95.

14. Ruben, "Lilienthal," pp. 181–97; Davis, *Emergence of Conservative Judaism*, pp. 130–34; Sussman, *Leeser*, pp. 196–200; Meyer, *Response to Modernity*, pp. 238–43; *OCC* 14 (Feb. 1857): 505–9.

15. Lilienthal's European background, his Russian experience, and his educational work in New York are discussed in Ruben, "Lilienthal," chs. 1–3.

16. Numerous articles are in *OCC* 13 (1855–1856) and 14 (1856–1857) by Leeser and other Traditionalists on the arguments of the two disputants; see especially in *OCC* 14 (July, Nov. 1856): 180–87, 378–87.

17. Max Lilienthal, "The Spirit of the Age," *Israelite* (Dec. 1856), reprinted with slight variations in David Philipson, *Max Lilienthal* (New York, 1915), pp. 367–97. The fifth installment by Lilienthal, which repudiated the claim that the *Shulchan Aruch* was the final authority, is also included in Elliot B. Gertel, *Jewish Belief and Practice in Nineteenth Century America* (Jefferson, NC, 2006), pp. 45–50.

18. *OCC* 14 (Jan. 1857): 475–80.

19. Philipson, *Lilienthal*, pp. 387–91.

20. *OCC* 14 (Jan. 1857): 534–38.

21. Ibid., 15 (June 1857): 109–20; *Israelite*, 20 Feb. 1857.

22. Kaufmann Kohler, *Studies, Addresses and Personal Papers* (New York, 1931), pp. 539–42.

23. Moshe Davis mentions earlier public disputes between Reformers and Traditionalists, *Emergence of Conservative Judaism* (pp. 219–22), over the retention of Hebrew in the services and over the observance of Shabbat and dietary laws.

24. Alexander Kohut, *The Ethics of the Fathers*, edited and revised by Barnett N. Elzas (New York, 1920), pp. xxxiv–xxxvi.

25. Ibid., pp. xxxii–xxxvi; Davis, *Emergence of Conservative Judaism*, pp. 222–25.

26. For this and the next two paragraphs, see a summary of the debate in Naomi W. Cohen, *Encounter with Emancipation* (Philadelphia, 1984), pp. 181–84.

27. H. G. Enelow, "Kaufmann Kohler," *American Jewish Year Book* 28 (1926–1927): 235–50; Kohler, *Studies*, p. 211.

28. Kohler, *Studies*, pp. 201–35.

29. Ibid., pp. 201–8.

30. Ibid., p. 211.

31. In 1887, when the Statue of Liberty was dedicated, Kohut was one of the speakers, and his theme was "Liberty Enlightening the World." Kohut, *Ethics*, pp. xcii–xciii. Kohler's fifth discourse discussed his choice of American Judaism above what he called Palestinian Judaism. Kohler, *Studies*, pp. 229–35.

32. Kohut, *Ethics*, pp. c–ciii.

33. Jonathan D. Sarna, "New Light on the Pittsburgh Platform of 1885," *American Jewish History* 76 (Mar. 1987): 358–68; Meyer, *Response to Modernity*, pp. 268–70; Beryl H. Levy, *Reform Judaism in America* (New York, 1933), pp. 60–63; Davis, *Emergence of Conservative Judaism*, pp. 225–28.

34. Two interesting exceptions to that general pattern and featuring an individual rabbi sparring publicly with another occurred in connection with the Jewish response to the New Christian Right. One, in 1980, concerned the remarks of a Fundamentalist leader, Bailey Smith, which elicited accusations of antisemitism from Reform Rabbi Alexander Schindler and a defense of Smith by Orthodox Rabbi Marvin Antelman. A second instance arose when Arthur Hertzberg and Marc Tanenbaum, both Conservative rabbis, clashed over the desirability of cooperating with the Evangelicals in return for their support of Israel. Naomi W. Cohen, *Natural Adversaries or Possible Allies?* (New York, 1993), pp. 8–10, 16–17.

35. Marc Lee Raphael, *Profiles in American Judaism* (New York, 1984). For developments in the Reform movement, see Alan Silverstein, *Alternatives to Assimilation* (Hanover, NH, 1994), ch. 4.

36. For two overviews of the rabbi's functions, one in 1890 and one seventy years later, see Aaron Hahn, "The Relation of the Rabbi to the Congregation," *CCARY* 1 (1890): 67–79, and Jacob K. Shankman, "The Changing Role of the Rabbi," in Bertram W. Korn, ed., *Retrospect and Prospect* (New York, 1964), pp. 230–51.

NOTES TO CHAPTER 6

1. Rudolf Glanz, *Studies in Judaica Americana* (New York, 1970), pp. 367, 380; *American Israelite (AI)*, 15 Sept. 1876, 24 Jan. 1879; Milton Plesur, "The American

Press and Jewish Restoration," in Isidore S. Meyer, ed., *Early History of Zionism in America* (New York, 1958); Robert T. Handy, *The Holy Land in American Protestant Life* (New York, 1981). Quotation from Luther in Salo W. Baron, "Changing Patterns of Antisemitism," *Jewish Social Studies* 38 (Winter 1976): 15.

2. Salo W. and Jeannette M. Baron, *Palestinian Messengers in America, 1849–79* (reprinted from *Jewish Social Studies* [New York, 1943]).

3. *Central Conference of American Rabbis Yearbook (CCARY)* 1 (1890): esp. 81–88, 117–18.

4. Jonathan D. Sarna, *American Judaism* (New Haven, CT, 2004), pp. 148–50.

5. Charles Reznikoff, *The Jews of Charleston* (Philadelphia, 1950), pp. 140, 269 n.182.

6. The story of Reform's opposition to Zionism and its fear of the charge of dual allegiance has often been told. For a recent account, see Naomi W. Cohen, *The Americanization of Zionism* (Hanover, NH, 2003), ch. 2. On the minority who supported some form of restoration to Palestine, see Michael A. Meyer, "American Reform Judaism and Zionism," *Studies in Zionism* 7 (Spring 1983), and Jonathan D. Sarna, "Converts to Zionism in the American Reform Movement," in S. Almog, ed., *Zionism and Religion* (Hanover, NH, 1998).

7. *Jewish Times*, 28 Apr. 1871; *AI*, 16 Dec. 1870, 3 Oct. 1879; David Philipson, *Max Lilienthal* (New York, 1915), pp. 62–64. As mentioned in chapter 5, Lilienthal also rejected Israel's nationhood when he abolished the day of mourning commemorating the destruction of the first and second temples. Bruce L. Ruben, "Max Lilienthal: Rabbi, Educator, and Reformer in Nineteenth-Century America" (Ph.D. diss., City University of New York, 1997), pp. 208–9.

8. Abraham J. Karp, "The Zionism of Warder Cresson," in Isidore S. Meyer, ed., *Early History of Zionism in America* (New York, 1958), p. 13; Selig Adler, "Backgrounds of American Policy toward Zion," in Moshe Davis, ed., *Israel: Its Role in Civilization* (New York, 1956), p. 259.

9. Isaac Leeser, "The Future of Palestine," *Occident (OCC)* 22 (Apr. 1864): 5–15; Maxine S. Seller, "Isaac Leeser's Views on the Restoration of a Jewish Palestine," *American Jewish Historical Quarterly* 58 (Sept. 1968): 118–35. See also George L. Berlin, *Defending the Faith* (Albany, NY, 1989), p. 27; Marnin Feinstein, *American Zionism, 1884–1904* (New York, 1965), p. 12; Hyman B. Grinstein, "Orthodox Judaism and Early Zionism," in Isidore S. Meyer, ed., *Early History of Zionism in America* (New York, 1958), pp, 219–24.

10. *Jewish Messenger (JM)*, 20 Aug., 3 Sept. 1869.

11. Federation of American Zionists, *George Eliot as a Zionist*, reprinted in Aaron S. and Adrian L. Klieman, eds., *American Zionism: A Documentary History* (New York, 1990–1991), vol. 1; *JM*, 9 June, 8, 15 Sept.1876.

12. Reprinted in *AI*, 15 Sept. 1876; see also James Parton, "Our Israelitish Brethren," *Atlantic Monthly* 26 (Oct. 1870): 387–88.

13. *AI*, 15 Sept. 1876, 19 Jan., 9, 16 Feb., 23 Mar. 1877, 24 Jan. 1879.

14. Sermon by Morais in *AI*, 9 Feb. 1877; *Jewish Record (JR)*, 7 May 1880, 29 July 1881, 21 July 1882, 16 Feb. 1883; *Hebrew Standard*, 26 Nov. 1886.

15. Feinstein, *American Zionism*, chs. 1–2. For a discussion of Orthodox rabbis on Zionism, see Kimmy Caplan, *Orthodoxy in the New World* ([in Hebrew] Jerusalem, 2002), pp. 285–302.

16. *JM*, letter to the editor, 9, 23 Feb. 1883; Arthur Zeiger, "Emma Lazarus and Pre-Herzlian Zionism," in Isidore S. Meyer, ed., *Early History of Zionism in America* (New York, 1958), p. 96; Bette Roth Young, "Emma Lazarus and Her Jewish Problem," *American Jewish History* 84 (Dec. 1996): 291–313; cf. a recent biography of Lazarus by Esther Schor, *Emma Lazarus* (New York, 2006), especially part 3.

17. *JM*, 26 Jan., 9 Feb. 1883.

18. Emma Lazarus, "The Jewish Problem," *Century Magazine* 25 (Feb. 1883): 602–11; Abram S. Isaacs, letter to the editor, *Century Magazine* 26 (May 1883): 156–57.

19. For the Kohut-Kohler debate, see chapter 5 in this volume; Kaufmann Kohler, *Studies, Addresses, and Personal Papers* (New York, 1931), pp. 229–35.

20. Anna Laurens Dawes, *The Modern Jew: His Present and Future* (Boston, 1884; reprinted 1889).

21. Anita L. Lebeson, "Zionism Comes to Chicago," in Isidore S. Meyer, ed., *Early History of Zionism in America* (New York, 1958), pp. 165–72, 179–81; Handy, *Holy Land in American Protestant Life*, pp. 194–97; Feinstein, *American Zionism*, ch. 3; *JM*, 27 Mar. 1891.

22. Naomi W. Cohen, *Encounter with Emancipation* (Philadelphia, 1984), pp. 247–49. Two Germans who preached antisemitism to American audiences were Adolf Stoecker, ex-court chaplain of Berlin who was known as the "leader of the Jew-baiters," and Hermann Ahlwardt, pamphleteer and lecturer. *New York Times*, 2 Sept., 4, 5, Oct. 1893, 22, 30 Nov., 4–15 Dec. 1895. At the same time the respected British historian, Goldwin Smith, was writing articles charging that Jewish racial exclusiveness prevented Jews from becoming patriots of the lands in which they lived. See chapter 8 in this volume.

23. Sarna, "Converts to Zionism in the American Reform Movement," pp. 194–96; Gottheil, "Syllabus of a Treatise on the Development of Religious Ideas in Judaism since Moses Mendelssohn," *Judaism at the World's Parliament of Religions* (Cincinnati, 1894), p. 31; Melvin I. Urofsky, *American Zionism from Herzl to the Holocaust* (Garden City, NY, 1975), p. 92.

24. David Philipson, *Centenary Papers* (Cincinnati, 1919), p. 178; *CCARY* 8 (1897): xli.

25. For a similar statement made after the Zionist Congress, see Bernhard Felsenthal, "Some Remarks Concerning Zionism," *H.U.C. Journal* 4 (Dec. 1899).

26. Among the first officers of the Federation of American Zionists were

Rabbis Gustav Gottheil and Stephen Wise; seven of the ten vice-presidents were also rabbis. Herbert Parzen, "The Federation of American Zionists (1897–1914)," in Isidore S. Meyer, ed., *Early History of Zionism in America* (New York, 1958), p. 247.

NOTES TO CHAPTER 7

1. Michael A. Meyer, *Response to Modernity* (New York, 1988), ch. 7.

2. Kimmy Caplan, *Orthodoxy in the New World* ([in Hebrew] Jerusalem, 2002), pp. 227–28, 243–53.

3. Naomi W. Cohen, "The Challenges of Darwinism and Biblical Criticism to American Judaism," *Modern Judaism* 4 (May 1984): 121–57.

4. Barnett Elzas, *A Memoir of Alexander Kohut,* quoted in Rebekah Kohut, *My Portion* (New York, 1927), p. 80.

5. Nathan Glazer, *American Judaism* (Chicago, 1957), ch. 4.

6. For example, Moses A. Dropsie, *On Deform in Judaism and the Study of Hebrew* (Philadelphia, 1895).

7. *Leo N. Levi Memorial Volume* (Chicago, 1905), pp. 5–15.

8. *American Israelite (AI),* 29 Mar.–7 Aug. 1885.

9. *Levi Memorial Volume,* pp. 177–313.

10. For this and the preceding paragraph, see Leo N. Levi, "Tell Us What Is Judaism," *Menorah* 3 (July 1887): 51–57. Answers to Levi appeared in *Menorah* 3 (Sept.–Nov. 1887), and Levi referred to the replies he received in his address to the UAHC.

11. *Levi Memorial Volume,* pp. 12–15; Annie Nathan and Harry I. Cohen, *The Man Who Stayed in Texas* (New York, 1941), esp. pp. 73, 84–85, 121–22; A. Stanley Dreyfus, comp., *Henry Cohen* (New York, 1963), pp. 13, 37–38; *American Jewish Year Book* 5 (1903–1904): 48.

12. The address appeared in the *Proceedings* of the UAHC for 1894 and was reprinted in installments in the *American Hebrew (AH),* Dec. 1894 and Jan. 1895 and with minor changes in the *Levi Memorial Volume.* Text and quotes in this and the following three paragraphs are from this address.

13. Meyer, *Response to Modernity,* pp. 265–70; Moshe Davis, *The Emergence of Conservative Judaism* (Philadelphia, 1963), pp. 223–28.

14. Jerold S. Auerbach, *Rabbis and Lawyers* (Bloomington, 1990), pp. 85–88.

15. Unless otherwise noted, this and the next two paragraphs are based on material in *AH,* 7, 14 Dec. 1894.

16. *New York Times,* 6 Dec. 1894; *AI,* 20 Dec. 1894; UAHC, *Proceedings* 1894, pp. 3394–3416; David Philipson, *My Life as an American Jew* (Cincinnati, 1941), pp. 97–98.

17. *AH,* 21 Dec. 1894; *AI,* 13 Dec. 1894; *Central Conference of American Rabbis Yearbook (CCARY)* 2 (1891): 41–47.

18. *AH*, 7 Dec. 1894; A. Moses in *AI*, 27 Dec. 1894; Meyer, *Response to Modernity*, p. 282.

19. *AI*, 20 Dec. 1894, 10 Jan. 1895; Philipson, *My Life*, pp. 96–97.

20. These conclusions are based on a reading of the *AH*, *AI*, *Jewish Comment*, *Jewish Exponent*, *Menorah*, and *Reform Advocate*.

21. *AH*, 28 Dec. 1894, 21 Feb. 1895; *Reform Advocate*, 25 May 1895.

22. L. Grossman in *AI*, 17 Jan. 1895; H. P. Mendes in *AH*, 11 Jan. 1895; *Jewish Comment*, 27 Dec. 1894; *Reform Advocate*, 2 Mar. 1895.

23. Josephine Lazarus, *The Spirit of Judaism* (New York, 1895); *AH*, 8, 15 June 1894; Charlotte Baum et al., *The Jewish Woman in America* (New York, 1975), p. 48. Kaufmann Kohler devoted an entire article to a critique of Lazarus in "The Spirit of Judaism," *Menorah* 39 (Dec. 1895): 321–33.

24. *Jewish Messenger*, 14 Dec. 1894.

25. *AH*, 7 Dec. 1894; *Reform Advocate*, 12 Jan. 1895; editorial, *Menorah* 18 (Jan. 1895): 60. At the convention of the CCAR in 1895 Rabbi Samuel Sale doubtless meant Levi when he said that a lay critic who wanted a definition of Judaism lacked the proper knowledge to raise the question. *CCARY* 6 (1895): 137–38.

26. *Reform Advocate*, 22 Dec. 1894, 12 Jan. 1895.

27. *AH*, 28 Dec. 1894.

28. *AI*, 3,10 Jan. 1895.

29. See especially *Reform Advocate*, 22 Dec. 1894, 2 Mar. 1895 ("Ben Tanhum"); *AI*, 27 Dec. 1894 (A. Moses), 17, 24 Jan., 21 Feb. 1895; *AH*, 4 Jan. 1895 (Kohler); Emil G. Hirsch, "The Philosophy of the Reform Movement in American Judaism," *CCARY* 6 (1895): 96; Hirsch, "The Harvest Festival," in CCAR, *Sermons by American Rabbis* (Chicago, 1896), p. 105.

30. Kaufmann Kohler, "The Spiritual Forces of Judaism," *CCARY* 5 (1894): 131–45.

31. For Kohler's views, see ibid; see also Kohler, "Judaism and Reform," *Menorah* 18 (Jan. 1895): 36–48; Kohler, "The Relation between Jew and Non-Jew," *Menorah* 26 (June 1899): 351–53. For Hirsch's views, see his "Philosophy of the Reform Movement," pp. 90–122; *Reform Advocate*, 3 Mar. 1895, 7, 21 Mar. 1896, 21 Aug. 1897, 28 May 1898; Cohen, "Challenges of Darwinism and Biblical Criticism," pp. 125–30. For the rabbis' talk of race at the end of the century, see Eric L. Goldstein, *The Price of Whiteness* (Princeton, NJ, 2006), pp. 27–29.

32. Kohler in *AH*, 4 Jan. 1895.

33. Mendes in *AH*, 11 Jan., 8 Feb. 1895, Kohler in *AH*, 18 Jan. 1895.

34. *Jewish Spectator* (in *Reform Advocate*), 29 Dec. 1894; Kohler in *AH*, 4 Jan. 1895; I. S. Moses, "A Definition of Judaism," CCAR, *Sermons by American Rabbis*, pp. 74–75.

35. Frankel in *Jewish Exponent*, 7 June 1895.

36. *AI*, 20 Dec. 1894; *Reform Advocate*, 15 Dec. 1894, 6 Jan. 1895.

37. *Reform Advocate*, 12 Jan. 1895. It was not the first occasion on which Hirsch

defended the Radicals. At the celebration of the seventieth birthday of his father, Rabbi Samuel Hirsch of Philadelphia, who was one of the first Radical Reformers in America, the son exchanged harsh words with his opponents. *AI*, 10 July 1885.

38. C. H. Levy in *Jewish Messenger*, 8 Dec. 1894. On the subject of countering lay indifference to religion, Levy also blamed synagogues that were governed by a "plutocratic oligarchy" and that limited membership to the wealthy. *AH*, 8 Feb. 1895.

39. *Levi Memorial Volume*, pp. 13–15.

40. *CCARY* 5 (1894): 25, 43; CCAR, *Sermons by American Rabbis.*

NOTES TO CHAPTER 8

1. *Nation*, 24 June 1880, p. 469.

2. Two important accounts are Leonard Dinnerstein, *Anti-Semitism in America* (New York, 1994), and David A. Gerber, ed., *Anti-Semitism in American History* (Urbana, IL, 1986).

3. Jewish leaders were especially opposed to racial classification by the government. Naomi W. Cohen, *Encounter with Emancipation* (Philadelphia, 1984), p. 273.

4. *American Hebrew (AH)*, 13 Mar. 1884.

5. Moshe Davis Papers, courtesy of Mrs. Lottie K. Davis: sermon by Sabato Morais, "On the Anti-Jewish League in Germany [1881]"; *AH*, 21 Jan. 1881,

6. *AH*, 25 Nov. 1898.

7. Israel Cohen, *Anti-Semitism in Germany* (London, 1918), pp. 1–20. Putting greater weight on the influence of nationalism, Salo W. Baron once wrote: "The National State, feeling strongly the strangeness of the Jew in its otherwise homogeneous body . . . has always tried to eliminate it by full assimilation, which often took the shape of enforced conversion, or by full exclusion, which generally meant expulsion." Salo W. Baron, "Changing Patterns of Antisemitism," *Jewish Social Studies* 38 (Winter 1976): 15, 18–22.

8. Henry Vidaver, *Ancient and Modern Anti-Semitism* (Baltimore, 1882), p. 7; Marcus Jastrow, *The Causes of the Revived Disaffection against the Jews* (New York, 1890), pp. 9–10; Louis Grossman in *AH*, 5 Apr. 1895.

9. *Jewish Messenger (JM)*, 18 July 1879.

10. *JM*, 20 May 1878; *AH*, 5 Dec. 1879.

11. For example, *AH*, 14 June 1895, 23 Mar. 1896.

12. John Higham, *Send These to Me* (New York, 1975), pp. 129–30, 148–51; Dinnerstein, *Anti-Semitism in America*, ch. 3; Edward N. Saveth, *American Historians and European Immigrants* (New York, 1965), pp. 20, 23–24, 47–48; Richard Hofstadter, *Social Darwinism in American Thought* (Philadelphia, 1945), pp. 148–50.

13. *Judas Iscariot* (New York, 1888); see also Telemachus T. Timayenis, *The Original Mr. Jacobs* (New York, 1888); *New York Times,* 2 Sept., 4, 5, Oct. 1893; *AH,* 15, 29 Sept., 13 Oct. 1893; Dinnerstein, *Anti-Semitism in America,* p. 272 n.45; Louise A. Mayo, *The Ambivalent Image* (Rutherford, NJ, 1988), pp. 132–36.

14. The three major American Jewish periodicals, *American Israelite (AI), AH,* and *JM,* contain countless analyses and comments on the new antisemitism that reveal the inconsistencies and contradictions that abounded. The *JM,* for example, generally shied away from the concept of racism, but it praised George Eliot and Benjamin Disraeli as racists. *JM,* 6 Mar. 1868, 8 Sept. 1876, 23 Mar. 1877, 22 Mar. 1878, 13 June 1879, 21 Jan. 1881, 15 Aug. 1884.

15. In 1858 Edgar Mortara, a little Jewish boy of Bologna, Italy, whose nurse-maid had secretly arranged for his baptism, was forcibly abducted from his parents' home by papal guards.

16. Union of American Hebrew Congregations, *Proceedings* 2 (1881): 1079.

17. Eric L. Goldstein, *The Price of Whiteness* (Princeton, NJ, 2006), esp. introduction and ch. 1. With respect to lay as well as rabbinic opinion, the material I used for this chapter emphasizes the confusion and inconsistency over the terms "race" and "people" that do not always fit Goldstein's categories.

18. See below for the views of Morris Jastrow; Joseph Silverman, "Popular Errors about the Jews," *Judaism at the World's Parliament of Religions* (Cincinnati, 1894), p. 287; *JM,* 21 Jan. 1881; *Nation,* 24 June 1880, p. 469.

19. Mayer Sulzberger, letter to the editor, *Penn Monthly* 12 (Feb. 1881): 102.

20. *AI,* 4 May 1893.

21. *AI,* 20 Apr. 1893.

22. *JM,* 26 Mar. 1880.

23. Silverman, "Popular Errors," pp. 285, 294.

24. Ibid., p. 291. See *AH,* 3 Dec. 1880 (de Sola Mendes); *AI,* 21 Jan. 1881, 8 Dec. 1892.

25. The *AI* retorted that if indeed the Jews enjoyed such power, they should have been able to prevent persecution. *AI,* 14 Nov. 1879, 16 June 1882, 22 Feb. 1884, 22 May 1895, 3 Sept. 1886.

26. Silverman, "Popular Errors," p. 286; cf. *JM,* 9 Jan. 1880; *AI,* 21 Nov. 1879, 16 Jan. 1880.

27. *AI,* 30 Jan., 6 Feb., 5 Nov. 1880, 23 Feb., 1883, 10 Dec. 1896.

28. Hirsch in CCAR, *Sermons by American Rabbis* (Chicago, 1896), pp. 122–46. Hirsch doubtless knew that bigots in Germany argued that Jewish adherence to classical liberalism worked against the interests of nationalism and monarchism in the country. Uriel Tal, *Christians and Jews in Germany,* translated by Noah Jacobs (Ithaca, NY, 1975), p. 43.

29. John Higham, "Social Discrimination against Jews in America, 1830–1930," *Publications of the American Jewish Historical Society* 47 (1957): 1–33, and Higham,

"Anti-Semitism in the Gilded Age: A Reinterpretation," *Mississippi Valley Historical Review* 43 (1957): 559–78. Both articles were revised and reprinted in Higham's *Send These to Me.*

30. Naomi W. Cohen, "Antisemitism in the Gilded Age," *Jewish Social Studies* 41 (Summer–Fall 1979): 187–210.

31. *JM*, 21 Jan. 1881; Jastrow, *Causes of the Revived Disaffection.*

32. Morris Jastrow Jr., "The Jewish Question in Its Recent Aspects," *International Journal of Ethics* 6 (July 1896): 457–79. On Jastrow's assessment of the state of American Judaism, an assessment that contributed to his choice of the academy above the rabbinate, see Harold S. Wechsler, "Pulpit or Professoriate," *American Jewish History* 74 (June 1985): 338–55.

33. *AI*, 27 Aug. 1880, 17 Aug. 1883; *JM*, 27 June 1879, 28 Jan. 1881, 30 Nov. 1883; *AH*, 22 Aug. 1884.

34. *AI*, 19 Dec. 1879; *JM*, 6 Oct. 1882.

35. Morais in *AH*, 21 Jan. 1881; Krauskopf in *AI*, 20 Apr. 1893; Silverman in "Popular Errors"; *AI*, 9 Dec. 1881, 11 Feb. 1897.

36. The newspaper *American Correspondence* reported that Minister Andrew White in Berlin was instructed to do what he could for the German Jews on an informal basis. *American Correspondence*, 11 Dec. 1880; Cyrus Adler and Aaron M. Margalith, *With Firmness in the Right* (New York, 1946), pp. 354–62.

37. *JM*, 12 Mar., 12 July 1880; *AH*, 31 Aug. 1888.

38. *New York Times*, 27 Dec. 1880; *JM*, 21 Jan. 1881; *AH*, 28 Jan. 1881.

39. For example, Edwin Wolf II and Maxwell Whiteman, *The History of the Jews of Philadelphia from Colonial Times to the Age of Jackson* (Philadelphia, 1975), chs. 5–6; Bertram W. Korn, *American Jewry and the Civil War* (Philadelphia, 1951), ch. 7.

40. *AH*, 2 Oct. 1896.

41. *JM*, 20 Oct., 3 Nov. 1876.

42. Colin Holmes, "Goldwin Smith: A 'Liberal' Antisemite," *Patterns of Prejudice* 6 (1972): 25–30; Gerald Tulchinsky, *Taking Root* (Hanover, NH, 1992), pp. 231–38.

43. Goldwin Smith, *A History of England*, 2nd ed. (New York, 1957), p. 630.

44. Holmes, "Goldwin Smith," p. 29; *Nation*, 3 Mar. 1881, p. 148.

45. Felix Adler, *The Revival of Anti-Semitism* (New York, 1921), p. 9; Goldwin Smith, "The Jewish Question," *Nineteenth Century* 5 (Oct. 1881): 514–15; *New York Times*, 20 Oct. 1881; *JM*, 3 Jan. 1896; *AI*, 10 Sept. 1891.

46. In the three major Anglo-Jewish periodicals—the *JM*, *AI*, *AH*—hardly a month went by without some comment about Smith. See also *JM*, 27 Feb. 1880, *AH*, 2 Feb. 1880, 6 May 1885.

47. Hermann Adler, *Can Jews Be Patriots?* (London, 1878); *JM*, 15 Mar., 17 Apr. 1878. The sermon was reprinted by the *JM* and sold for ten cents a copy.

48. Isaac Schwab, *Can Jews Be Patriots?* (New York, 1878).

49. Goldwin Smith, "Can Jews Be Patriots?" *Nineteenth Century* 1 (May 1878): 875–87; Smith, "The Jewish Question," in ibid. 5 (Oct 1881): 494–515; Smith, "The Jews: A Deferred Referender," in ibid. 11 (Nov. 1882), 687–709. The material in this and the next three paragraphs is drawn from those articles.

50. Paul T. Phillips, *The Controversialist* (Westport, CT, 2002), ch. 6; Robert Singerman, "The Jew as Racial Alien," in Gerber, *Anti-Semitism in American History*, pp. 103–28.

51. Reprinted as Philip Cowen, *Prejudice against the Jew* (New York, 1928).

52. *Nation*, 24 June 1880, p. 469.

53. For example, Gustav Gottheil in *JM*, 26 Mar. 1880.

54. Jastrow, *Causes of the Revived Disaffection*, p. 10.

55. Adler and Margalith, *With Firmness in the Right*, pp. 171–207.

56. Zenaide Ragozin, "Russian Jews and Gentiles," *Century Magazine* 23 (Apr. 1882): 905–20.

57. *JM*, 24 Mar. 1882; Emma Lazarus, "Russian Christianity versus Modern Judaism," *Century Magazine* 24 (May 1882): 48–56; Myer S. Isaacs, *The Persecution of the Jews in Russia* (New York, 1882).

58. Smith in *Nineteenth Century*, Nov. 1882; Smith, "New Light on the Jewish Question," *North American Review* 153 (Aug. 1891): 129–42; *JM*, 24 July 1891; Hermann Adler, "Russian Barbarities and Their Apologist," *North American Review* 153 (Nov. 1891): 513–23. Smith amplified his views on how the Jews were to blame for the new antisemitism in his book *Questions of the Day* (New York, 1893), pp. 221–60.

59. *AH*, 24 Nov., 1, 29 Dec. 1893, 12 Jan., 16, 23 Feb., 2, 9, 23, 30 Mar., 20 Apr. 1894. See also *American Jewish Year Book* 28 (1926–1927): 258–59.

60. See chapter 9 in this volume and *AH*, 22 Sept., 3 Nov. 1893.

61. I have discussed how the Americans tried to share the burden of emigration with their European counterparts in Naomi W. Cohen, *Relief and Relocation*, Occasional Papers, Hunter College Jewish Studies Program (New York, 2000).

62. *AI*, 8 July 1887.

63. *JM*, 14 Jan. 1890; Abram S. Isaacs, letter to the editor, *Century Magazine* 26 (May 1882): 156–57.

64. *JM*, 14, 21 Nov. 1890; American Jewish Archives microfilm no. 148: A. Isaacs to Smith, 17 Oct. 1890.

65. Union of American Hebrew Congregations, *Proceedings* 4 (1894): 3359–61.

66. The material used in the paragraphs on Zionism is discussed more fully in chapter 6 in this volume. The quote from Kohler is from his *Studies, Addresses, and Personal Papers* (New York, 1931), pp. 229–35.

67. Naomi W. Cohen, *The Americanization of Zionism, 1897–1948* (Hanover, NH, 2003), ch. 1.

68. Strategy, for example, involved, decisions on the value of publicizing anti-semitic outbreaks. For comments on publicity, see *JM*, 7 Sept. 1888, 16 Dec. 1892; *AI*, 31 July 1890.

69. *AI*, 13 July 1855, 22 Sept. 1892, 20 Apr. 1893; *Central Conference of American Rabbis Yearbook (CCARY)*, 1 (1890): 7–9.

70. *New York Times*, 27 Dec. 1880.

NOTES TO CHAPTER 9

1. For this and the next paragraph, see text and notes in Naomi W. Cohen, "The Challenges of Darwinism and Biblical Criticism to American Judaism," *Modern Judaism* 4 (May 1984): 138–42.

2. For relevant background, see Egal Feldman, *Dual Destinies* (Urbana, IL, 1990), esp. chs. 10–11; Leonard Dinnerstein, *Anti-Semitism in America* (New York, 1994), ch. 3; Naomi W. Cohen, *Encounter with Emancipation* (Philadelphia, 1984), chs. 5–6. On Jewish-Christian relations before 1880, see Allan Tarshish, "Jew and Christian in a New Society," in Bertram W. Korn, ed., *A Bicentennial Festschrift for Jacob Rader Marcus* (Waltham, MA, 1976), pp. 565–88.

3. On the idea of a parliament and its organization, see UAHC, *Judaism at the World's Parliament of Religions,* hereinafter noted as *JWP* (Cincinnati, 1894); Feldman, *Dual Destinies*, pp. 127–29; Richard H. Seager, *The World's Parliament of Religions* (Bloomington, IL, 1995), pp. ix–xxix.

4. For the scene at the parliament, see Egal Feldman, "American Ecumenicism: Chicago's World's Parliament of Religions of 1893," *Journal of Church and State* 9 (Spring 1967): 180–99.

5. Hannah G. Solomon, *Fabric of My Life* (New York, 1946), chs. 10–12; Deborah G. Golomb, "The 1893 Congress of Jewish Women," *American Jewish History* 70 (Sept. 1980): 52–67.

6. *JWP*, introduction.

7. For this and the next paragraph, see John H. Barrows, ed., *The World's Parliament of Religions* (Chicago, 1893), pp. 74, 1462; Donald J. Bishop, "Religious Confrontation: A Case Study," *Numen* 16 (Apr. 1969): 64–67.

8. *Reform Advocate,* 29 Apr. 1893; Hirsch also published sermons on the need to universalize Judaism (for example, ibid., 8 Mar. 1893); James G. Heller, *Isaac M. Wise* (Cincinnati, 1965), pp. 487–88.

9. *JWP*, pp. v, xi, 391–407, 410–13; *Central Conference of American Rabbis Yearbook* 5 (1894): 39.

10. D. G. Lyon, "Jewish Contributions to Civilization"; "Archbishop of Zante on the Blood Accusation"; John Ireland, "Remarks on Anti-Semitism," all in *JWP*, pp. 391–407, 410–13.

11. Joseph Silverman, "Popular Errors about the Jews," *JWP*, pp. 285–94; Silverman's paper is also discussed in chapter 8 in this volume.

12. Ibid. For examples of conspiracy theories that antedated the notorious *Protocols of the Elders of Zion* in the first decade of the 1900s, see Cohen, *Encounter with Emancipation,* pp. 266–71.

13. For this and the next three paragraphs, see *JWP,* pp. 116–26, 164–71.

14. See chapter 8 in this volume.

15. H. G. Enelow, "Kaufmann Kohler," *American Jewish Year Book* 28 (1926–1927): 258. Kohler had discussed the Essene roots of Christianity for a popular English-speaking audience in "The Cradle of Christianity," *Menorah* 3 (July 1892): 17–29.

16. Moses Mielziner, "Ethics of the Talmud," Gotthard Deutsch, "The Share of the Jewish People in the Culture of the Various Nations and Ages," and Henry Berkowitz, "The Voice of the Mother of Religions on the Social Question," all in *JWP,* pp. 107–13, 175–92, 367–72.

17. Isaac M. Wise, "An Introduction to the Theology of Judaism," *JWP,* pp. 1–25.

18. Bernhard Felsenthal. "The Sabbath in Judaism," Joseph Stolz, "The Doctrine of Immortality in Judaism," I. S. Moses, "The Function of Prayer According to Jewish Doctrine," and Isaac Schwab, "A Review of the Messianic Idea from the Earliest Times to the Rise of Christianity," all in *JWP,* pp. 35–41, 49–55, 72–78, 79–95.

19. Gustav Gottheil, "Syllabus of a Treatise on the Development of Religious Ideas in Judaism since Moses Mendelssohn," *JWP,* pp. 26–34.

20. See especially David Philipson, "Judaism and the Modern State," *JWP,* pp. 257–67. Defining Jews as a religious community exclusively also helped Rabbi Adolph Moses refute the doctrines of racism and a Jewish race. "Judaism a Religion, and Not a Race," *JWP,* pp. 268–84.

21. Isaac M. Wise, "The Ethics of Judaism," Moses Mielziner, "Ethics of the Talmud," and Gustav Gottheil, "The Greatness and Influence of Moses," all in *JWP,* pp. 99–106, 107–13, 159–63.

22. Maurice H. Harris, "Reverence and Rationalism," *JWP,* pp. 147–58.

23. Alexander Kohut, "What the Hebrew Scriptures Have Wrought for Mankind," *JWP,* pp. 42–48.

24. Alexander Kohut, "The Genius of the Talmud," *JWP,* pp. 373–85.

25. H. Pereira Mendes, "Orthodox or Historical Judaism," *JWP,* pp. 230–40.

26. S. Hecht, "A Sabbath-School Union," A. M. Radin, "Popular Lectures," Henry Berkowitz, "What Organized Forces Can Do for Judaism," all in *JWP,* pp. 313–18, 342–47, 353–57.

27. Max Landsberg, "The Position of Woman among the Jews," *JWP,* pp. 241–54; Henrietta Szold, "What Has Judaism Done for Woman?" *JWP,* pp. 305–10.

28. Josephine Lazarus, "The Outlook of Judaism," *JWP,* pp. 295–303.

29. Louis Grossman, "Judaism and the Science of Comparative Religions," *JWP,* pp. 56–71. For a thoughtful analysis of the relations between Reformers and Unitarians, see Benny Kraut, "The Ambivalent Relations of American Reform

Judaism with Unitarianism in the Last Third of the Nineteenth Century," *Journal of Ecumenical Studies* 23 (Winter 1986): 58–68.

30. CCAR, *Sermons by American Rabbis* (Chicago, 1896), pp. 270–84; letter by Gustav Gottheil, "The Great Refusal," in Elliot B. Gertel, *Jewish Belief and Practice in Nineteenth Century America* (Jefferson, NC, 2006), pp. 122–31.

31. Emil G. Hirsch, "Elements of Universal Religion," *JWP*, pp. 386–90; Bishop, "Religious Confrontation," pp. 68–69.

32. Cohen, "Challenges of Darwinism and Biblical Criticism," pp. 145–48; Kraut, "Ambivalent Relations," pp. 62–68.

33. Feldman, *Dual Destinies*, pp. 125–26.

NOTES TO CHAPTER 10

1. Jacob R. Marcus, *United States Jewry, 1776–1985* (Detroit, 1993), vol. 3, pp. 141–42.

2. Nathan M. Kaganoff, "The Traditional Jewish Sermon in the United States from Its Beginnings to the First World War" (Ph.D. diss., American University, 1961), pp. 106, 118–23.

3. For Leeser's activities, see the recent biography by Lance J. Sussman, *Isaac Leeser and the Making of American Judaism* (Detroit, 1995).

4. Marcus, *United States Jewry*, vol. 3, p. 657.

5. Naomi W. Cohen, *Encounter with Emancipation* (Philadelphia, 1984), pp. 185–201; I. L. Leucht, "The Rabbi as a Public Man," *Central Conference of American Rabbis Yearbook (CCARY)* 8 (1897): 13.

6. Jonathan D. Sarna, *American Judaism* (New Haven, CT, 2004), p. 100.

7. Kaganoff, "Traditional Jewish Sermon," pp. 152–59; Robert V. Friedenberg, *"Hear O Israel": The History of American Jewish Preaching* (Tuscaloosa, AL, 1980), ch. 2.

8. Henry B. May, *Isaac Mayer Wise* (New York, 1916), pp. 190–92.

9. *Occident (OCC)* 2 (Sept., Oct. 1844, Mar. 1845): 265–72, 315–16, 569.

10. Some of the material in this and the following paragraph is discussed in chapter 1 of this volume. See also Cohen, *Encounter with Emancipation*, pp. 192–93, 367 n.55; Jacob R. Marcus, *United States Jewry, 1776–1985* (Detroit, 1991), vol. 2, p. 231; Emil G. Hirsch, *Reform Judaism* (n.p., 1885), pp. 11–13.

11. Leucht, "Rabbi as a Public Man," pp. 11–18.

12. David Philipson, *Centenary Papers and Others* (Cincinnati, 1919), pp. 229–46; Myer S. Isaacs, *The Old Guard and Other Addresses* (New York, 1906), pp. 150–53.

13. The *American Israelite* commented in 1888: "A quarter of a century ago and even now in many places [the rabbi] was the ill-paid servant of a congregation which was ruled over by a few dominant spirits to whom he was forced to bow.

. . . Today the rabbi of even mediocre ability can command a position of from 2 to $3000 a year and upward." Quoted in Alan Silverstein, *Alternatives to Assimilation* (Hanover, NH, 1994), p. 28. Silverstein notes that at the same time skilled workers and doctors, lawyers, and other professionals usually earned no more than $1,000 annually. The salaries compared very favorably with those received by rabbis some forty years earlier. Sefton D. Temkin, *Isaac Mayer Wise* (Oxford, 1992), p. 45. For an intensive study of rabbis' salaries, Orthodox as well as Reform, between 1881 and 1924, see Kimmy Caplan, "In God We Trust," *American Jewish History* 86 (Mar. 1998): 77–106.

14. Reform established the Union of American Hebrew Congregations, Hebrew Union College, and the Central Conference of American Rabbis; the Conservative tripartite structure included the Jewish Theological Seminary of America, the United Synagogue of America, and the Rabbinical Assembly; the Orthodox establishment consisted of Yeshiva University, the Union of American Orthodox Congregations, the Union of Orthodox Rabbis, and after 1935 the Rabbinical Council of America. On the emergence of the three structures, see Marc L. Raphael, *Profiles in American Judaism* (New York, 1984), chs. 6–7.

15. The *Occident,* in almost every single issue in vol. 2 (1844–1845) and vol. 3 (1845–1846), spoke of the need for proper rabbinical training. See esp. 2 (Sept., Oct. 1844, Mar. 1845): 265ff., 314–21, 569. At one point Leeser also suggested that the Board of Delegates of American Israelites establish a school for training rabbis. Leon A. Jick, *The Americanization of the Synagogue* (Hanover, NH, 1976), p. 171.

16. James G. Heller, *Isaac M. Wise* (New York, 1965), pp. 151–53.

17. Ibid., pp. 224, 273–82; Samuel E. Karff, ed., *Hebrew Union College–Jewish Institute of Religion at One Hundred Years* (Cincinnati, 1976), pp. 15–17.

18. Bertram W. Korn, "The Temple Emanu-El Theological Seminary," *Essays in American Jewish History* (Cincinnati, 1958), pp. 359–71; Heller, *Wise,* pp. 224, 405–20; Bruce L. Ruben, "Max Lilienthal: Rabbi, Educator, Reformer in Nineteenth-Century America" (Ph.D. diss., City University of New York, 1997), pp. 292–94.

19. Raphael, *Profiles in American Judaism,* chs. 6–7.

20. *CCARY* 11 (1900): 63.

21. Ibid., pp. 57–58.

22. Isaac M. Fein, *The Making of an American Jewish Community* (Philadelphia, 1971), pp. 56–57; Hirsch, *Reform Judaism,* p. 5.

23. *CCARY* 3 (1892): 120; 8 (1897): 15–16.

24. Unless otherwise noted, material for this and the next three paragraphs comes from the following rabbinic addresses and sermons in the *Yearbooks* of the CCAR. (I found several errors in the numbering of the volumes that I used at the Hebrew Union College in Jerusalem; the corrected numbering follows.) Aaron Hahn, "The Relation of the Rabbi to the Congregation," 1 (1890): 62–79; Max Heller, "Conference Sermon," 2 (1891): 41–47; Henry Berkowitz, "The Opportunity of

the American Jewish Ministry," 3 (1892): 115–23; Max Landsberg, "The Duties of the Rabbi in the Present Time," 5 (1894): 121–30; Samuel Sale, "Conference Sermon," 6 (1895): 134–43; Louis Grossman, "Method in the Pulpit," 7 (1896): 114–28; I. L. Leucht, "The Rabbi as a Public Man," 8 (1897): 11–18; Edward N. Calisch, "The Rabbi and the Charities," Special Convention (1899): 133–46; Joseph Krauskopf, "How We Can Enlist Our Young Men in the Service of the Congregation," Special Convention (1899): 147–60; Rudolph Grossman, "The Rabbi as a Scholar," 11 (1900): 133–47. See also Isaac Wise's annual addresses to the conventions until his death in 1900.

25. Jerold S. Auerbach, *Rabbis and Lawyers* (Bloomington, IN, 1990), pp. 85–86; Jacob K. Shankman, "The Changing Role of the Rabbi," in Bertram W. Korn, ed., *Retrospect and Prospect* (New York, 1965), pp. 233–34.

26. On Kohut, see chapter 5 in this volume; Shankman, "Changing Role of the Rabbi," p. 235.

27. R. Grossman, "Rabbi as a Scholar," pp. 133–47.

28. Landsberg, "Duties of the Rabbi," pp. 121–20.

29. Kaganoff, "Traditional Jewish Sermon," pp. 110–11.

30. L. Grossman, "Method in the Pulpit," pp. 114–28.

31. Moritz Ellinger, "From the Old to the New," *Menorah* 29 (Nov. 1900): 253–69.

32. Hahn, "Relation of the Rabbi to the Congregation," pp. 62–79.

33. *CCARY* 11 (1900): 25.

34. Heller, "Conference Sermon," pp. 41–47.

35. Julia Richman, "The Jewish Sunday School Movement in the United States," *Jewish Quarterly Review* 12 (July 1900): 577–80, 584–88. The CCAR in 1895 considered plans for improving the Sabbath school by the adoption of a uniform five-year curriculum plus postconfirmation classes. *CCARY* 6 (1895): 26–30.

36. For a full study of the Jewish Chautauqua Society, see Peggy K. Pearlstein, "Understanding through Education" (Ph.D. diss., George Washington University, 1993).

37. See talks listed in n. 24, especially those by Samuel Sale, Louis Grossman, I. L. Leucht, Rudolph Grossman, and Max Landsberg.

38. Korn, *Retrospect and Prospect*.

39. Sidney L. Regner, "The History of the Conference," and Leon I. Feuer, "Summary and Prospect," both in Korn, *Retrospect and Prospect*, pp. 13–14, 257–58.

40. Jacob R. Marcus and Abraham J. Peck, eds., *The American Rabbinate* (Hoboken, NJ, 1985); includes Jeffrey S. Gurock, "Resistors and Accommodators," Abraham J. Karp, "The Conservative Rabbi: 'Dissatisfied but Not Unhappy,'" and David Polish, "The Changing and the Constant in the Reform Rabbinate."

41. Karp, "Conservative Rabbi," pp. 104, 139, 156.

42. Gurock, "Resistors and Accommodators," p. 49; on Kaplan's interest in the education of the children of immigrants, see pp. 28, 31.

43. Michael A. Meyer, *Response to Modernity* (New York, 1988), p. 392.

44. Gurock, "Resistors and Accommodators," p. 34.

45. Polish, "The Changing and the Constant," pp. 186–96, 200–5, 231–33, 243–46.

Index

Abbott, Lyman, 177

accommodationism, 215

acculturation: of American Jewry, 5–6, 17–18, 19, 72, 198–199; Emancipation, 188; Jewish religion combined with, 93; Morais and, 34, 40, 46

Addresses on Homely and Religious Subjects (Baar), 69, 85

Adler, Felix, 29, 164

Adler, Hermann: "Can Jews Be Patriots?" (Adler), 164–165; Schwab and, 10; Smith and, Goldwin, 164–166, 169, 170

Adler, Samuel, 106

aggadah (Jewish lore), 191

Ahlwardt, Hermann, 154, 175, 233n22

Alliance Israélite Universelle, 79

Amalek, 63–73; Baar on, 69–71; discomfort with, 61–62; Einhorn on, 62–66; as impersonal, timeless force, 72; Jewish blame for, 67, 70, 72; Mendes on, 71–72; Moses and, 61, 68; rabbinic stress on self-improvement, 72; Schwab on, 67–68; slavery as, 63–64; as symbol of evil, 53, 61–62, 63–73; in twentieth century, 73; Vidaver on, 68–69

Amalekites, 60–61

American Council for Judaism, 129

American Hebrew (newspaper): Christian view of antisemitism, 167; "The Ethics of the Talmud" (Kohler), 170; *Independent*'s response to antisemitism, 162; Jewish loyalty to America, 163; Jewish racial superiority, 151; Levi's criticism of Reform rabbis, 140, 141, 142; "Sermons for the Young" in, 69

American Historical Association, 172

American Israelite (newspaper): attributes of good rabbis, 200; bad sermons, 16; editor, 134; German antisemitism, 161;

"The Jews of Today: Their Status and Duties" (Levi), 134; Levi and, 139; Levi's criticism of Reform rabbis, 146–147; Lilienthal in, 76; non-kosher food at Hebrew Union College, 50; rabbinic salaries, 242n13; racial antisemitism, analysis of, 158; retrogression in nineteenth century, 175; Wise and, Isaac Mayer, 119–120, 134, 146–147, 162, 200

American Jewish Archives, 214

American Jewish Committee, 73, 175

American Jewish Congress, 73

American Jewish Historical Society, 163

American Jewish Publication Society, 228n5

The American Jewish Pulpit (Bloch and Company), 22–24, 25

American Jewry: accommodationism, 215; acculturation, 5–6, 17–18, 19, 72; affluent Jews, 57–58; alliances with non-Jewish groups, 112; Anglo-Jewish periodicals of, 55; assimilation, 13; Christian opinion of, 177; colonial period, 94; common liturgy/ platform, 112; congregationalism, 8–9, 55, 96, 149; contributions to United States, 42; denominationalism, 8–9, 199–200, 214; enlistment of Christians to speak for Jewish causes, 36, 55; gap between Jewish and non-Jewish Americans, 99; influence of nineteenth-century Jewry on, 1; intermarriage by, 13; Jeffersonianism, 15; Jewish nationalism, 113; lay control of synagogues, 14, 202, 203, 205, 209; managerial revolution among, post-World War I, 73; materialism, 25, 64–65, 212; middle-class Jews, 24; national leadership, 10, 54–55, 70–71, 73; political abstinence/ invisibility, 16–19, 21, 27, 35, 72–73; quasi-"Marranoism" of, 18; rabbis as representatives of, 4–5, 6, 10; religious apathy and

American Jewry (*continued*)
indifference, 7, 13, 25, 34, 65, 75, 100, 142, 201, 212; representative men among, 53, 54; secularization, 13, 34, 72, 212; separation of church and state, 18, 43; split into two wings, 52; Thanksgiving Day celebrations, participation in, 38–40; tripartite structure, 203; unification of, 112

American rabbis, 131–149; 1840s, 13; acculturation of American Jews, 5–6; Americanization of, 5–6, 19; Americanization of traditional synagogues, 198–199; assessments of, 213–215; authority of, 15, 130, 199–200, 207, 211; borrowings from Protestants, 198–200; central problem facing, 32; Christian leaders, 6; as communal activists, 74; congregational restraints on, 13–20, 32; criticism of non-Jewish spokesmen, 66; criticism of Reform rabbis, Heller's, 139; criticism of Reform rabbis, Levi's, 131, 133–142, 144–149; criticism of Reform rabbis, women's, 140–141; desired characteristics of, 15; duties, 213; education of, 202, 203–204, 207, 212, 213; equation of proper Jewish deportment with virtuous American behavior, 93; European rabbis, 10–11; faith in progress of mankind, 175; functions of, 5–6; good rabbis defined, 200, 201, 206–207; immigrant rabbis, 218n9; inadequacies of, 201; independence of, 16, 19; influence of individual rabbis, 112, 212–213; Jewish survivalists among, 95; job hopping, 199; job security, 15, 18; Kohut on, Alexander, 108; lay control of synagogues, 14, 202, 203, 205, 209; Leeser on, 201; legacy of nineteenth-century rabbis, 215–216; loneliness, 209–210; moral aspects of public issues, 19–20; need for questioned, 2; nineteenth-century rabbis, 1; Orthodox rabbis, 201, 211; pensions, 205–206, 213; private life, 202, 209–210; professionalization, 203–210; profile of, 211; public discourse of (*see* rabbinic sermons); rabbinic scholarship, 207; religious disputations between rabbis, 111–112, 231n34; as representatives of American Jewry, 4–5, 6, 10; respect for, 146, 202, 211; salary, 15, 18, 202, 205, 213, 242n13; seminaries for, 203–204; sermons

by (*see* rabbinic sermons); social reform, 19–20; status of, 15, 27; twentieth-century rabbis, 112; Union of American Hebrew Congregations (UAHC), 14; Wise on, Isaac Mayer, 200, 202; working conditions, 202–203; Zionism, 129–130

Americanism, 4–6, 81, 105

Americanization: of immigrant children, 87; *Jewish Messenger* on, 57; of rabbis, 5–6, 19; of traditional synagogues, 198–199

"Ancient and Modern Amalek" (Baar), 69

"The Ancient Anti-Semite and His Modern Successors" (Hirsch), 32

Anglo-Jewish periodicals, 55

Antelman, Marvin, 231n34

Anti-Defamation League, 73

anti-Zionism, 115–118, 126–130. *See also* Palestine, restoration to

antisemitism, 150–176; after 1860, 113; after 1870, 150–151; appeals for government support against, 169; assimilation, 160, 161, 167–168; Baar on, 70, 72; Christians on, 167; coverage in *Visitor*, 82; Darwinism, 150; Eastern European immigrants, 106–107, 153, 171; economic jealousy, 157–159, 166; in Europe, 114, 127, 155; faith in progress of mankind, 175; in Germany, 36, 151–153, 155, 157, 158, 159, 161, 162, 167, 171, 175; Gottheil on, 156–157; Harris on, 151–152; Hirsch on, Emil G., 158–159; Jastrow on, Marcus, 152, 159, 162, 168; Jastrow on, Morris, Jr., 160; Jewish clannishness, 166–167; Jewish emphasis on business, 92; Jewish international conspiracy, 184; Jewish loyalty to America, 162–163; Jewish response to, 161–162, 168; Jewish traits, 160; Jewish tribalism, 164; Kohler on, 170–171, 186; Krauskopf on, 161; legacy of nineteenth-century antisemitism, 174–176; materialism, 158; modernity, 158; Morais on, 36, 43–45, 151, 161, 162; Mortara affair (1858), 35–36, 237n15; Moses on, Adolph, 155–156; nationalism, 150, 236n7; nouveaux riches, behavior of, 158–159; racial antisemitism, 150, 154–155, 158, 160, 166–167; racial superiority and inferiority, 151, 177; religious antisemitism, 150, 155–157, 159; in Russia, 158, 171–174; Russian pogroms, 168–170, 173–174; secularization, 158;

Seligman-Hilton affair (1877), 26, 82, 221n37, 228n16; Shylock image, 158, 184; Silverman on, 157, 161, 183–184; Smith's, Goldwin, 163–167, 171–173; social discrimination, 158; as subject of rabbinic sermons, 26, 31–32; as subject of World's Parliament of Religions (1893), 181–182, 183–184, 186; Talmud, 166, 169, 170, 191; in United States, 43–45, 132, 152, 153–154, 158–159, 175; Wise on, Isaac Mayer, 162; the word coined, 152; Zionism, 126

assimilation: American Jewry, 13; antisemitism, 160, 161, 167–168; conversion, 236n7; nationalism, 236n7; racism, 151

Atlantic Monthly (magazine), 119

Autoemancipation (Pinsker), 122

Baar, Hermann, 84–93; advice to boys, 91–92; on Amalek, 69–71; on antisemitism, 70, 72; behavior taught by, 93; biblical models chosen by, 86–87; character building, importance of, 85–86; on family life, 88–89; genteel tradition, 92–93; Hebrew Orphan Asylum (HOA), 84–85; Kohler on, 85, 91; labor unrest, condemnation of, 92; national leadership of American Jews, 70–71; orphaned, 88; Reform Judaism, 87; in *Sabbath Visitor*, 85; sensitivity, lack of, 88–89; sermons of, 74, 87–88; on truthfulness, 89–90; *Visitor* (magazine), 87

"Backward or Forward" (Kohler), 109

Balfour Declaration (1917), 129

Baltimore, Maryland, 13, 21

Baron, Salo W., 236n7

Barrows, John Henry, 180

Basel Congress (1897), 113, 127, 129

Beecher, Henry Ward, 18, 162, 175

Benjamin, I. J., 218n17

Berkowitz, Henry: on authority of American rabbis, 15; classes for adults, 212; on indigent rabbis, 206; Jewish social action to ameliorate abuses of capitalism, 9; social justice, 20, 28; World's Parliament of Religions (1893), 187, 192

Beth Elohim (Charleston), 2, 98

bilu movement, 121

Bismarck, Otto von, 43, 151, 161, 175

Blackstone, William, 126–127

Blackstone Memorial (1891), 126

B'nai B'rith, 133, 148

B'nai Israel (Galveston), 133, 135

B'nai Jeshurun (New York), 54

Board of Delegates of American Israelites, 55, 154

Bogen, Hyman, 91, 92

Bondi, Julius, 224n25

Bonney, Charles C., 180

Breslau Theological Seminary, 106

Brewer, David, 177

Briggs, Charles, 30

Buchanan, James, 35–36

Calisch, Edward, 209

Calvin, John, 39

"Can Jews Be Patriots?" (Adler), 164–165

"Can Jews Be Patriots?" (Schwab), 165

Central Conference of American Rabbis (CCAR), 203–210; 1892 meeting, 15; 1896 collection of sermons, 26–32, 148; 1897 convention, 19; annual conventions, 212; Calisch and, 209; "Centenary Perspective" (1976), 214–215; circumcision for proselytes, 15; Committee on Rabbinical Ethics, 204; Congress of Liberal Religious Societies, 196; diversity, 214–215; first sessions, 205; focus of, 204–205; founding, 204; on good rabbis, 206–207; Grossman and, 208; Heller and, 139; Hirsch and, Emil G., 147; Kohler and, 144, 181–182, 186; Leucht and, 209; Levi's criticism of Reform rabbis, 138–139, 140; national leadership of American Jews, 10; officers, 142; placement commission, 213; professionalization of American rabbis, 203–210; rabbinic authority, 207; rabbinic education, 207, 212, 213; rabbinic/lay relationship, 205, 209; rabbinic loneliness, 209–210; rabbinic pensions, 205–206, 213; rabbinic salary, 205, 213; rabbinic scholarship, 207; rabbinic status, 27; Reform Judaism, 243n14; Relief Fund of the Conference, 205–206; restoration to Palestine, 115–116; Sabbath schools, 244n35; seventy-fifth anniversary commemoration, 213; *Union Prayer Book*, 206; Wise and, Isaac Mayer, 15, 142; World's Parliament of Religions (1893), 179

Century Magazine, 123, 124, 168

Channing, William Ellery, 78

Christianization of the Constitution, 41–43, 58, 64
Church Universal, 141
Cincinnati, Ohio, 76, 101
circumcision for proselytes, 15
Cleveland Conference (1855), 100, 101
Cohen, Henry, 135
Collyer, Robert, 162
Conference of Presidents of Major American Jewish Organizations, 213
Congregation Ahavath Chesed (New York), 106–107, 108
congregationalism, 8–9, 55, 96, 149
Congress of Jewish Women, 140, 179, 182
Congress of Liberal Religious Societies, 195–196
"Conservative" (the term), 46
Conservative Judaism: hatred of, 224n25; Jewish Theological Seminary, 52, 111, 243n14; as "middle way" between Orthodoxy and Reform, 224n25; Morais and, 34; Rabbinical Assembly, 243n14; tripartite structure, 204, 243n14; United Synagogue of America, 243n14
Constitution, Christianization of, 41–43, 58, 64
Crémieux, Adolphe, 58, 78, 226n10
Cresson, Warder, 116–117

Daily Gazette (Cincinnati newspaper), 119
Daniel Deronda (Eliot), 118, 123–124
Darwin, Charles, 22, 132
Darwinism, 22–24, 150, 221n31. See also evolutionary theory
Dawes, Anna Laurens, 125
De Sola, Abraham, 23, 24
Democratic Party, 18
denominationalism, 8–9, 199–200, 214
Derashoth (homilies), 208
The Descent of Man (Darwin), 22
Detroit, Michigan, 108
Deutsch, Gotthard, 178, 187
din (a basic law), 98
Diner, Hasia, 8
Disraeli, Benjamin, 163
Dreyfus Affair, 127, 175

Eastern European Jews: antisemitism, 106–107, 153, 171; Orthodox Judaism, 106, 132; rabbinic sermons, 3; Society for the

Improvement and Emigration of East European Jews, 122; Traditional Judaism, 3
ecumenicism, 178
Edward I, King of England, 167
Einhorn, David, 62–67; on Amalek, 62–66; on Catholic Church, 66; on Christianization of the Constitution, 64; Darwinism, 24; on enslavement of the spirit, 64–65; German antisemitism, 153; in Germany, 62; Har Sinai Temple (Baltimore), 62, 63; influence of, 66–67; Keneseth Israel (Philadelphia), 63; Kohler and, 24, 109; on materialism of American Jews, 25, 64–65; Mendes on, H. Pereira, 145; in New York, 65; Orthodox Judaism, 63, 65; polemics in sermons, 62; on Protestantism, 66; on religiously indifferent Jews, 65; Shabbat Zakhor sermon (1864), 63; slavery, opposition to, 63; son-in-law, 24; on Syllabus of Errors, 66; university training of, 14
"Elements of Universal Religion" (Hirsch), 194–195
Eliot, George, 118, 122
Ellinger, Moritz, 208–209
Emancipation: acculturation, 188; allegiance of Jews to their country of residence, 115; Harris on, 94; Jewish identity, 17; Lilienthal on, 103; options for reconciling Judaism with modern world, 95; quasi-"Marranoism" of American Jewry, 18; religious apathy and indifference, 7, 94
Emerson, Ralph Waldo, 121
Enlightenment, 67, 75
Epistle to the Hebrews (Lazarus), 121, 123, 174
Essenes, 170–171, 185
Esther, 60, 73
Esther, Book of, 56, 226n15
Ethical Culture movement, 29, 133. See also Society for Ethical Culture
Ethics of the Fathers, 107
"The Ethics of the Talmud" (Kohler), 170, 184
evil: Amalek as symbol of, 53, 61–62, 63–73; Haman as symbol of, 53, 59, 60–61, 62, 70, 73
evolutionary theory, 22–24, 132, 177, 221n40. See also Darwinism

Federation of American Zionists, 128, 233n26
Felsenthal, Bernhard: on authority of American rabbis, 15; Blackstone and, 126; on Christianity and Islam, 26; on early Christianity, 177–178; on Judaism and science, 23–24; Morais and, 47; refuge for foreign victims of persecution, 129; sermons of, 177–178; World's Parliament of Religions (1893), 187, 192; Zionism, 174
Frankel, Lee K., 146, 149
Frankel, Zachariah, 145
French Revolution, 94
Friedman, Reena, 87
Fuller, Margaret, 79

Galveston, Texas, 133, 135
Geary, John, 38–39, 40
Geiger, Abraham, 145
German Jewish immigrants, 2, 99
Germany: antisemitism in, 36, 151–153, 155, 157, 158, 159, 161, 162, 167, 171, 175; nationalism in, 161; racism in, 152
Gibbons, James, 178
Gladden, Washington, 177
Glazer, Nathan, 29
Goldman, Solomon, 130
Goldsmid, Francis, 58–59
Goldstein, Herbert, 215
good, Mordecai as symbol of, 53, 56–60, 73
Gottheil, Gustav: on antisemitism, 156–157; Federation of American Zionists, 127–128, 233n26; "Judaism and Temperance," 29–30; on Moses, 189; on prohibition, 29–30; on Reform Judaism, 187–188; restoration to Palestine, 128; Silverman and, 157; Smith and, Goldwin, 164; Temple Emanu-El (New York), 29; World's Parliament of Religions (1893), 128, 187–188, 189; Zionism, 127–128
Grand Union Hotel (Saratoga), 44
Gries, Moses, 31
Grinstein, Hyman, 5–6
Grossman, Louis, 30, 140, 193–194, 208

Hahn, Aaron, 209
halachah (Jewish law), 4, 5, 50, 98, 191
Haman: affluent American Jews, 57–58; destruction of, 60; European antisemitism,

155; Mordecai and, 56, 60; as symbol of evil, 53, 59, 60–61, 62, 70, 73
Har Sinai Temple (Baltimore), 62, 63
Harris, Maurice: on antisemitism, 151–152; on differences between Christianity and Judaism, 31; on Emancipation, 94; on Judaism, 142–143; "Judaism and Utilitarianism," 194; on laxity in observance among American Jews, 7; as moderate Reformer, 189; at World's Parliament of Religions (1893), 189, 194
Harrison, Benjamin, 126
Harrison, Leon, 28
hazzan, usage of, 11
Hebrew Benevolent and Orphan Asylum Society, 84
Hebrew Benevolent Society, 84
Hebrew Free Schools, 79
Hebrew Orphan Asylum (HOA), 84–92; Americanization of children, 87; Baar and, 84–85; behavior expected of orphans, 89; Bogen on, 91; discipline, 90, 92; "half orphans," 84; Kohler and, 84; marching band, 87; meals, 91; monitors, 90–91; parental visits, 91; play time, 91; punishments for infractions of rules, 91; regimentation, 91, 92; religious services, 87; supporters, 92; Temple Emanu-El (New York), 87; training provided by, 89; uniforms, 91; wards, number of, 88
Hebrew Sabbath School Companion (magazine), 227n1
Hebrew Sabbath School Visitor. See Visitor (magazine)
Hebrew Technical Institutes, 91
Hebrew Union College (HUC): courses on practical rabbinics, 213; coverage in *Visitor*, 80; Deutsch and, 187; founding, 204; Heller and, 60; homiletics, study of, 3; hundredth anniversary commemoration, 214; Levi on, 135–136; Morais and, 48, 51; non-kosher food at, 49–50; Reform Judaism, 106, 243n14; restoration to Palestine, 116; status of American rabbis, 27
Hecht, Sigmund, 192
Heller, Max, 60, 139, 206, 209–210
Hertz, Joseph H., 52
Hertzberg, Arthur, 231n34
Herzl, Theodor, 113, 127, 128, 173
Higham, John, 153, 158–159

Hirsch, Emil G., 141–144; on antisemitism, 158–159; on authority of American rabbis, 15; Blackstone Memorial (1891), 126; Central Conference of American Rabbis (CCAR), 147; Congress of Liberal Religious Societies, 195–196; Darwinism, 24; on early Christianity, 178; "Elements of Universal Religion," 194–195; on freedom of thought within Judaism, 30; French Enlightenment, 143; independence of, 19; influence of, 3–4; on Jesus, 178; on Judaism and science, 23–24; Lazarus and, Moritz, 143; Levi's criticism of Reform rabbis, 141, 147; Mendelssohn and, 143; on "rabbi haters," 147; rabbinic salaries, 205; on rabbinic scholarship, 207; on Radical Reformers, 147, 235n37; *Reform Advocate*, 141; on Reform Judaism, 142; Reform Judaism's reliance on reason, 143–144; sermons of, 178; social justice, 28–29; Temple Sinai (Chicago), 141, 147; "The Ancient Anti-Semite and His Modern Successors," 32; uniform liturgy to unite congregations, 9; university chairs in Jewish studies, 212; University of Chicago, 159; World's Parliament of Religions (1893), 181, 194–195
Hirsch, Samuel, 14, 106, 205, 235n37
House of Rothschild, 114
hovevei Zion (Lovers of Zion), 121, 129
Hoyt, Henry, 39, 40
"Human Brotherhood as Taught by the Religions Based on the Bible" (Kohler), 184
Huxley, Thomas Henry, 24

"The Ideal Rabbi" (Levi), 133, 138, 140
Independent (newspaper), 162
International Journal of Ethics, 160
Ireland, John, 180, 182
Isaacs, Abram, 123, 124, 127, 171–173
Isaacs, Myer, 169
Isaacs, Samuel M.: B'nai Jeshurun (New York), 54; idealism, 58; influence of, 3–4; *Jewish Messenger*, 34, 53–54, 55, 118, 123, 226n1; on laxity in observance among American Jews, 7; Leeser and, 59–60; Mordecai as symbol of resistance to tyranny, 56; Noah and, Mordecai Manuel, 59; ordination of, 11; "Palestine Restored," 118; Shaaray Tefila (New York), 54

Israel, Vidaver on, 68–69
"Israel a Missionary People" (Vidaver), 68
Israelite (newspaper), 15, 55, 101, 102
"The Israelites and Their Detractors" (Morais), 45

Jastrow, Marcus: on antisemitism, 152, 159, 162, 168; on legitimate province of the pulpit, 20; Morais and, 36; son, 160
Jastrow, Morris, Jr., 160, 167
Jefferson, Thomas, 56
Jeffersonianism, 15
Jesus: Hirsch on, Emil G., 178; Jewish acceptance of, 182; Kohler on, 170, 185, 186; Mendes on, H. Pereira, 191–192; Moses and, 191–192; in rabbinic sermons, 177–178
Jewish Chautauqua Society, 212
Jewish/Christian relations, 30–31, 80
Jewish Chronicle (newspaper), 140
"Jewish Contributions to Civilization" (Lyon), 182–183
Jewish denominational congress (1893), 30–31
Jewish identity: Americanism, 4–6; Emancipation, 17; evolutionary theory, 22–23; rabbinic sermons, 6–7; racism, 151; religious apathy and indifference, 6–7; requirements for molding, 74; retention of, 32
Jewish Messenger (newspaper), 55–60; "A Problematic Champion" (editorial), 123; on affluent American Jews, 57–58; on Americanization, 57; attachment to Judaism, emphasis on, 57; call for representative men, 53, 54, 58–59, 73, 226n9; ceased publication, 54; Christian press coverage of German antisemitism, 162; on Christianization of the Constitution, 58; *Daniel Deronda* review, 118; founder/publisher, 34, 123; founding, 53–54; Isaacs and, Abram, 123; Isaacs and, Samuel M., 34, 53–54, 55, 118, 123, 226n1; Jewish patriotism, 163; Jewish response to antisemitism, 161; Levi's criticism of Reform rabbis, 141, 147–148; Levy in, 147–148; Morais in, 48; Mordecai as symbol of good, 56–60; "Palestine Restored" (editorial), 118; on racial antisemitism, 155; on Ragozin, 169; readership, 54; restoration

to Palestine, 127; Smith in, Goldwin, 172–173
Jewish Ministers' Association, 152
Jewish nationalism, 113. *See also* Zionism
Jewish Publication Society, 179
Jewish Question, 151. *See also* antisemitism
Jewish Spectator (newspaper), 146
The Jewish State (Herzl), 127
Jewish survivalists, 95
Jewish Theological Seminary: Conservative Judaism, 52, 111, 243n14; founding, 34, 52, 145; Mendes and, H. Pereira, 145, 191; Morais and, 34, 52, 207; Reform Judaism, 132; Schechter and, 207; Shearith Israel (New York), 52; Teachers Institute, 214
Jewish women, 179, 192–193
The Jews of America (Levi), 134
"The Jews of Today: Their Status and Duties" (Levi), 134
Judaism: in America (*see* American Jewry); in England, 55; faith in, 116; faith in America, 116; in France, 55; freedom of thought within, 30; Harris on, 142–143; "legalism" of, 30; meaning of, 135, 137; merger with Unitarianism, 29, 193–194; options for reconciling with modern world, 95; science, 23–24
"Judaism and Temperance" (Gottheil), 29–30
"Judaism and Utilitarianism" (Harris), 194
Judaism at the World's Parliament of Religions (UAHC), 186–187
Judas Iscariot (1888 book), 153
juvenile periodicals, 74–75, 83, 92. See also *Visitor* (magazine)

Kahn, Zadoc, 140
Kaplan, Mordecai, 214
Karp, Abraham, 214
kehillah (community), 9–10
Kelly, R. Gordon, 92
Keneseth Israel (Philadelphia), 51, 63
Kiron, Arthur, 33, 46, 51
Kohler, Kaufmann, 108–111; on antisemitism, 170–171, 186; on Baar, 85, 91; "Backward or Forward," 109; birth, 108; Central Conference of American Rabbis (CCAR), 144, 181–182, 186; Congress of Jewish Women, 182; Darwinism, 24; in Detroit, 108; on early Christianity, 185;

education, 108; Einhorn and, 24, 109; Essenes as model for rabbis, 170, 185; "The Ethics of the Talmud," 170, 184; Hebrew Orphan Asylum (HOA), 84; individualism in Reform Judaism, 144; influence of, 3–4; on Jesus, 170, 185, 186; on Jewish situation in America, 26; Kohut and, Alexander, 105–106, 109–111, 124–125, 137, 207; on laity, 146, 149; Lazarus and, Moritz, 143; Mendes and, 145–146; minutiae of traditional laws/customs, 109; Morais and, 51; Pittsburgh Platform (1885), 111; prophetism, emphasis on, 110; on Rabbinism, 110; on Reform Judaism, 109–111; Reform Judaism's reliance on reason, 143–144; restoration to Palestine, 124–125, 174; Smith and, Goldwin, 164; spirituality through rituals, 144; on superiority of Judaism, 184–186; Temple Emanu-El (New York), 107; Union of American Hebrew Congregations (UAHC), 182; university training of, 14; World's Parliament of Religions (1893), 171, 181, 184–186
Kohut, Alexander, 106–111; on American rabbis, 108; birth, 106; Congregation Ahavath Chesed (New York), 106–107, 108; death, 105, 145; dictionary of the Talmud, 106; education, 106; failure to unify American Jewry, 112; Kohler and, 105–106, 109–111, 124–125, 137, 207; on Reform Judaism, 107–108; sermons of, 107; Statue of Liberty dedication, 231n31; superiority of Judaism, 190–191; Traditional Judaism, 111; World's Parliament of Religions (1893), 179, 190–191
Kohut, George Alexander, 52
Korn, Bertram, 36
Krauskopf, Joseph: clerical collar worn by, 199; evolutionary theory, 221n40; faith in progress of mankind, 175; on good rabbis, 206; Jewish response to antisemitism, 161; Keneseth Israel (Philadelphia), 51; Morais and, 51; National Farm School (Doylestown), 9; settlement of Russian Jews outside the Pale of Settlement, 173
Kraut, Benny, 29, 193

The Land of Gilead (Oliphant), 122
Landsberg, Max, 21, 192–193, 207–208

Lasker, Eduard, 78
Lazarus, Emma, 121–124; in *Century Maga-zine*, 123; Emerson and, 121; *Epistle to the Hebrews*, 121; influences on, 122; Isaacs on, Abram, 123, 124, 172; *Jewish Mes-senger* on, 123; Mendes and, H. Pereira, 122; on Ragozin, 169; restoration to Palestine, 122, 123–124, 173–174; Society for the Improvement and Emigration of East European Jews, 122; Wise and, Isaac Mayer, 122
Lazarus, Josephine, 140–141, 179–180, 193
Lazarus, Moritz, 143
Leeser, Isaac, 101–105; borrowings of Chris-tian methods, 199; Cleveland Conference (1855), 100; congregational approval for sermonizing, 16; congregational restraints on, 14; contributions to Jewish com-munity, 59–60; on *din* (a basic law), 98; failure to unify American Jewry, 112; first sermon, 16; on *halachah* (Jewish law), 98; influence of, 3–4; Isaacs and, Samuel M., 59–60; Jewish separatism, 95, 97; Jewish Sunday schools, 199; Lilienthal, debate with, 99, 101–105, 111, 137; Mayer and, 99; Mikveh Israel (Philadelphia), 2, 14, 33, 201; Morais and, 33; national leader-ship of American Jews, 10; *Occident*, 55, 97, 101–102, 117, 200; ordination of, 11; Poznanski and, 98–99; rabbinic seminar-ies, need for, 203; rabbinic sermons, 2, 3; on rabbis, 201; readiness to compromise with Reformers, 98, 102; Reform Juda-ism, critique of, 46, 97–99, 102–105; as representative man, 59–60; restoration to Palestine, 117–118; sermons of, 98, 200; synagogue schools/classes by, 74; transla-tions into English, 98; Wise and, Isaac Mayer, 101, 203; writing style, 101
legalism, 30
Leo N. Levi Memorial Volume, 135
Leucht, I. L., 19, 171, 202, 209
Levi, Leo N., 133–142, 144–149; *American Israelite*, 139; B'nai B'rith (Galveston), 133; B'nai B'rith presidency, 148; B'nai Israel (Galveston), 133, 135; Cohen and, 135; criticism of Reform rabbis, 131, 133–142, 144–149; death, 135; education, 133; guidelines for Reform practices, 213; on Hebrew Union College (HUC), 135 –136;

Hirsch and, Emil G., 141, 147; "The Ideal Rabbi," 133, 138, 140; *The Jews of America*, 134; "The Jews of Today: Their Status and Duties," 134; Kohler-Kohut debate, 137; *Leo N. Levi Memorial Volume*, 135; Levy on, 147–148; lobbying for Romanian, Russian Jews, 148; meaning of Judaism, 135, 137; in *Menorah*, 134–135, 140, 141; Pittsburgh Platform (1885), 137; religious rituals, 137; Roosevelt and, 148; Union of American Hebrew Congregations (UAHC), 133–134, 135; Wise and, Isaac Mayer, 139–140
Levy, C. H., 147
Lilienthal, Max, 74–76, 100–105; in *Ameri-can Israelite*, 76; Americanism of, 81, 105; behavior taught by, 93; birth, 75; children's books in English, need for, 228n5; in Cincinnati, 76, 101; Cleveland Conference (1855), 100, 101; death, 75; on Emancipation, 103; emigration to Amer-ica, 76; genteel tradition, 92–93; *haskalah* (Enlightenment), 75; as headmaster, 101; historical development, deterministic scheme of, 103; influence of, 3–4; Israel's nationhood, rejection of, 232n7; Jewish schools in Russia, 75–76; juvenile maga-zines, 74–75, 83 (see also *Visitor*); Leeser, debate with, 96, 101–105, 111; loyalty to America, 129; as moderate Reformer, 101, 106; in Munich, 75; newspaper for children, 212; on Passover, 81; rabbinic seminaries, need for, 203–204; relation-ship between Jews and the United States, 116; restoration to Palestine, 116; in Riga, 75; on scientific theories, 23; sermons of, 101; "The Spirit of the Age," 102–103, 104; synagogue schools/classes by, 74; Uni-versity of Cincinnati, 76; West Pointer recommended by, 81; Wise and, Isaac Mayer, 76, 98, 101, 204; writing style, 101
Lincoln, Abraham, 36, 38
Lookstein, Joseph, 214
Lovers of Zion (*hovevei Zion*), 121, 129
Luther, Martin, 43, 114
Lyon, D. G., 180, 182–183

Madison, James, 17
mah yomru ha-goyyim (what will the Gentiles say?), 127

Maimonides College (Philadelphia), 3, 204

Marr, Wilhelm, 152

Marshall, Louis, 10

materialism: American Jewry, 25, 64–65, 212; antisemitism, 158; Harrison on, Leon, 28

Mayer, Maurice, 99

Mead, Sidney, 23

megillah (scroll, of Esther), 56, 226n15

Mendelssohn, Moses, 102, 143, 187–188

Mendes, Frederick de Sola, 71–72

Mendes, H. Pereira: on Einhorn, 145; on Jesus, 191–192; Jewish Theological Seminary, 145; Kohler and, 145–146; Lazarus and, Emma, 122; as moderate Traditionalist, 122, 145; on opposition of Traditionalists to Reform Judaism, 191; refuge for foreign victims of persecution, 129; restoration to Palestine, 191; Shearith Israel (New York), 122, 145; World's Parliament of Religions (1893), 179, 191–192; Zionism, 174

Menorah (journal), 134–135, 140, 141, 208

"Method in the Pulpit" (Grossman), 208

Mielziner, Moses, 187, 189

Mikveh Israel (Philadelphia): constitution of, 223n9; hard times at, 47; Leeser and, 2, 14, 33, 201; Morais and, 33, 36–37, 45, 223n9; Sephardic *minhag*, 48

"Minhag America," 112

minhag (mode), 48

Mizrachi, 128–129

The Modern Jew (Dawes), 125

modernity, 158

Montefiore, Moses, 33, 47, 58, 78

Moody, Dwight, 44–45, 70

Morais, Sabato: acculturation, belief in need for, 34, 40, 46; agitation for Traditionalist seminary, 48, 51–52; America, praise for, 37–38; American exceptionalism, belief in, 34; American Jewish equality, defense of, 37–45; *The American Jewish Pulpit*, 21; on antisemitism, 36, 43–45, 151, 161, 162; Buchanan and, 35–36; on Christian support for Jews, 36; on Christianization of the Constitution, 41–43; Conservative Judaism, 34; death, 33; death penalty, Judaism and, 41; in England, 33, 43; Felsenthal and, 47;

Geary and, 38–39, 40; as Hebrew teacher, 33; Hebrew Union College (HUC), 48, 51; Hoyt and, 39, 40; influence of, 3–4, 223n11; "The Israelites and Their Detractors," 45; Jastrow and, Marcus, 36; on Jewish contributions to United States, 42; Jewish education, 47–48; Jewish Theological Seminary, 34, 52, 207; Jewish unity, 47; on Judaism and science, 23; Kohler and, 51; Kohut on, George Alexander, 52; Krauskopf and, 51; labor unrest, sermon on, 41; Leeser and, 33; Lincoln, support for, 36, 38; on Luther, 43; Mikveh Israel (Philadelphia), 33, 36–37, 45, 223n9; as moderate Traditionalist, 34, 47; Montefiore and, 33, 47; on Moody, 44–45; Mortara affair (1858), 35–36; Orthodox Judaism, 225n32; patriotism of, 38; on Pittsburgh Platform (1885), 50–51; plan for uniform synagogue ritual, 9, 48–49; preaching by, 35; prohibition, Judaism and, 41; publications by, 34; quotation in daily press, 223n11; Reform Judaism, critique of, 46–51, 220n23; restoration to Palestine, 120–121, 122; right to free pulpit, 35–37; secular enlightenment, 33–34; on the Seligmans (Joseph and Theodore), 44; separation of church and state, 43; Shearith Israel (New York), 51; slavery, opposition to, 36; Sunday laws, constitutionality of, 40; synagogue schools/classes by, 74; Thanksgiving Day messages, 38–40; Traditionalism, defense of, 34, 46–51; Union, support for, 36, 38; Union of American Hebrew Congregations (UAHC), 47, 51; visibility where constitutional rights were concerned, 37; Wise and, Isaac Mayer, 51

Mordecai: Haman and, 56, 60; as representative man, 56–58; as symbol of good, 53, 56–60, 73; as symbol of resistance to tyranny, 56

Mortara affair (1858), 35–36, 237n15

Moses: Amalek and, 61, 68; to Baar, 86; Bezalel and, 91; curses proclaimed by, 66; Gottheil on, 189; as hero, 53; influence of, 189; Jesus and, 191–192; Kohut on, Alexander, 107

Moses, Adolph, 155–156

Moses, I. S, 187

Napoleon, 94

Nation (magazine), 150, 163, 167

National Council of Jewish Women (NCJW), 140, 179

National Farm School (Doylestown), 9

National Reform Association (NRA), 41–42

nationalism: antisemitism, 150, 236n7; assimilation, 236n7; German, 161; Jewish, 113

"New Light on the Jewish Question" (Smith), 169–170

New York Times (newspaper), 138, 164, 171

Noah, Mordecai Manuel, 59

North American Review (journal), 169, 170

"nothingarian" attitudes, 7, 133

Occident (journal): Leeser and, 55, 97, 101–102, 117, 200; letters in, 98

"The Offering of Isaac" (Landsberg), 21

Oliphant, Laurence, 122, 123

The Origin of Species (Darwin), 22

Orthodox Judaism: divisiveness within, 8; Eastern European Jews, 106, 132; Einhorn and, 63, 65; Morais and, 225n32; rabbinic sermons, 3, 8; Rabbinical Council of America, 243n14; rabbis, 201, 211; restoration to Palestine, 116; tripartite structure, 204, 243n14; Union of American Hebrew Congregations (UAHC), 243n14; Union of Orthodox Rabbis, 243n14; Yeshiva University (New York), 243n14

"Orthodox or Historical Judaism" (Mendes), 191–192

Paine, Thomas, 56

Palestine: American Jews' interest in, 114; Christian interest in, 113–114; Jewish efforts to buy Jerusalem, 114; Lazarus and, Emma, 122; relief for needy Jews in, 114; restoration to (*see* Palestine, restoration to)

Palestine, restoration to, 114–129; *bilu* movement, 121; Blackstone on, 126; Central Conference of American Rabbis (CCAR), 115–116; Dawes on, 125; God's role in, 116–117, 120–121; Gottheil on, 128; Hebrew Union College (HUC), 116; *hovevei Zion* (Lovers of Zion), 121; international diplomacy, 119; Isaacs on, Abram, 124; Isaacs on, Samuel M., 118;

Jewish Messenger on, 127; Kohler on, 124–125, 174; Lazarus on, Emma, 122, 123–124, 173–174; Leeser on, 117–118; Lilienthal on, 116; loyalty to America, 115–116, 126–127; Luther on, 114; *mah yomru ha-goyyim* (what will the Gentiles say?), 127; Mendes on, H. Pereira, 191; Morais on, 120–121, 122; Orthodox Judaism, 116; Pittsburgh Platform (1885), 115; Reform Judaism, 114–116, 126–127, 129, 174; revival of agriculture, commerce in Palestine, 119; Russian pogroms, 121, 173–174; Smith on, Goldwin, 167, 172; Traditional Judaism, 116–118; Union of American Hebrew Congregations (UAHC), 115–116; Wise on, Isaac Mayer, 119–120; World War II, 128

"Palestine Restored" (Isaacs), 118

parnas (lay leader of the synagogue), 14

Penn, William, 79

Philipson, David, 20, 142, 178, 202

Phillips, Paul, 166

Phillips, Wendell, 18

Pinsker, Leo, 122, 173

Pittsburgh Platform (1885): changes to, 111; *halachah* (Jewish law), 50; Kohler and, 111; Levi and, 137; Mendes on, H. Pereira, 192; Morais on, 50–51; Mosaic-rabbinic law, repudiation of, 137; Reform Judaism, 115, 148; restoration to Palestine, 115; on science and Judaism, 28

Polish, David, 215

"The Position of Woman among the Jews" (Landsberg), 192–193

Poznanski, Gustav, 98–99, 115

prohibition, 29–30, 41

proselytes, circumcision for, 15

Protestant Reformation, 102

Protestantism, 66, 178, 198–200

Puritanism, 66, 113–114

"The Rabbi and the Charities" (Calisch), 209

"The Rabbi as a Public Man" (Leucht), 209

Rabbinerhetze (rabbi-baiting), 140, 146–147, 211

rabbinic sermons, 1–12; Amalek in (*see* Amalek); American colonial period, 2; Americanism, 4–6; among European Jews, 2; analyses of, 1, 11–12; antisemitism as a subject, 26, 31–32; avoidance of sociopolitical themes, 24; bad sermons defined, 16; congregational restraints on, 16; contemporary events, discussion of, 13–15, 18, 32; on early Christianity, 177–178; early nineteenth century, 2–3, 4–5; East European Jews, 3; as educational lessons, 9–10, 27; English language, use of, 3, 6, 198–199, 200; European rabbis, influences of, 10–11; faith in progress of mankind, 175; format of edifying sermons, 211; German Jewish immigrants of 1830s and 1840s, 2; Haman in (*see* Haman); heroes cited often, 53; on Jesus, 177–178; Jewish education as subject, 211–212; Jewish identity, 6–7; as lectures, 208–209; Leeser and, 2, 3; as lessons in morality, 53; love of the United States, 32; Mordecai in (*see* Mordecai); on need of Jews to accommodate the United States, 95; noteworthiness of, 112; opposition to including them in religious services, 16; optimism in, 175; Orthodox Judaism, 3, 8; polemics in, 62; political abstinence/invisibility of American Jews, 17, 21, 27, 35, 72–73; Purim sermons, 73 (see also *Shabbat Zakhor*); reasons for, 2; Reform Judaism, 2; on religious apathy and indifference, 7; styles of, 4; subjects discussed, 211; substance of, 211; synagogue members' desires for, 4; Traditional Judaism, 3; usual bases of, 53; villains cited often, 53; Wise on, Isaac Mayer, 12; Yiddish language, use of, 3; youth and, 74

Rabbinical Assembly, 243n14
Rabbinical Council of America, 243n14
rabbis. *See* American rabbis
racism: antisemitism, 150, 154–155, 158, 160, 166–167; assimilation, 151; in Germany, 152; Jewish identity, 151
Radin, A. M., 192
Ragozin, Zenaide, 168–169
Ramaz, 214
Raphall, Morris, 11, 63
Readers' Guide to Periodical Literature, 127
Reform Advocate (newspaper), 141, 147, 195
Reform Judaism: 1869 Philadelphia conference resolutions, 48–49; affluence, 96; appeal of, 45; to average layman, 29; Baar and, 87; cardinal axiom, 188;

Central Conference of American Rabbis (CCAR), 243n14; criticism of Reform rabbis, Heller's, 139; criticism of Reform rabbis, Levi's, 131, 133–142, 144–149; criticism of Reform rabbis, women's, 140–141; Dispersion of Jews, 188; diversity, 214–215; in Europe, 8, 45; evolutionary theory, 22–23, 23–24; Gottheil on, 187–188; growth, 96; guidelines for, authoritative, 137, 213; Hebrew Union College (HUC), 106, 243n14; hegemony of, challenges to, 131–133; Hirsch on, Emil G., 142; individualism in, 144; integration and equality of Jews in America, 154; Jewish Theological Seminary, 132; Judaism as a religious faith free of national dimension, 154, 188, 215; Kohler on, 109–111; Kohut on, Alexander, 107–108; lack of unity among American counter-Reformers, 47; Leeser's critique of, 46, 97–99, 102–105; mantra of, 98; moderate Reformers, 96, 101, 189; Morais's critique of, 46–51, 220n23; morality, reliance on, 20; official creed, 115, 148; opposition of Traditionalists to, 191; organization, 96; Philadelphia conference (1869), 192; Pittsburgh Platform (1885), 115, 148; problems facing, 96; rabbinic sermons, 2, 3; racial antisemitism and, 154–155; Radical reformers, 147; rationalism, 133, 143–144; relief for needy Jews in Palestine, 114; restoration to Palestine, 114–116, 126–127, 129, 174; Social Gospel movement, 199; social justice, 132; spiritual crisis facing, 29; spirituality, 143, 144; status within American society, 3; teachings/principles, cardinal, 65, 68; Traditional Judaism, rift with, 8, 99, 100, 101, 112, 146; tripartite structure, 131, 203, 243n14; Union of American Hebrew Congregations (UAHC), 106, 243n14; Unity of God, 188; universalism, 133, 154; *Visitor* (magazine) and, 79–80; World's Parliament of Religions (1893), 179, 186, 197; Zionism, 120, 132, 174, 215
Reform's Declaration of Independence. *See* Pittsburgh Platform (1885)
religion: science and, 22–23, 28, 221n40; social justice as surrogate for, 32
representative men, 53, 54, 58–60
"Reverence and Rationalism" (Harris), 189

Rice, Abraham, 13, 202, 205
Riesser, Gabriel, 58, 226n10
Rochester, New York, 2, 21
Roman Catholic Church, 66
Roosevelt, Theodore, 148
Rothschild family, 43, 120
Ruskay, Esther, 140–141
Russian Jewry: Blackstone Memorial (1891), 126; Isaacs on, Abram, 124; Levi's lobbying for, 148; remedies for Russian antisemitism, 171–174; restrictions on immigration of, 127; Russian pogroms, 121, 168–170, 173–174

Sabbath Visitor. See *Visitor* (magazine)
Salomon family, 43
Salomons, David, 58
Schechter, Solomon, 207
Schiff, Jacob, 10, 179
Schindler, Alexander, 231n34
Schindler, Solomon, 126
Schwab, Isaac: Adler and, 10; on Amalek, 67–68; "Can Jews Be Patriots?" 165; on the Enlightenment, 67; in Evansville, Indiana, 67; on Smith, Goldwin, 165; Smith and, Goldwin, 10; World's Parliament of Religions (1893), 187
science: Darwinism, 22–24, 150, 221n31; evolutionary theory, 22–24, 132, 177, 221n40; Judaism, 23–24, 28; religion and, 22–23, 28, 221n40
secularization: of American Jews, 13, 34, 72, 212; antisemitism, 158; Reform Judaism, 132
Seixas, Gershom Mendes, 5–6
Seligman, Joseph, 44, 221n37, 228n16
Seligman, Theodore, 44
Seligman-Hilton affair (1877), 26, 82, 221n37, 228n16
separation of church and state, 18
sermons. See rabbinic sermons
"Sermons for the Young" (Baar), 69
Shaaray Tefila (New York), 54
Shabbat Zakhor (the Sabbath of Remembrance): Baar sermon (1880s), 69–70; Deuteronomy 25:17–19, 61; Einhorn sermon (1864), 63; Mendes sermon (1895), 71; Vidaver sermon (1881), 68
Shearith Israel (New York): among Sephardic congregations, 145; authority

of the *parnas*, 14; Jewish Theological Seminary, 52; Mendes and, H. Pereira, 122, 145; Morais and, 51; Seixas and, 5
Shylock, 79, 158, 184
Silver, Abba Hillel, 112, 130
Silverman, Joseph: on antisemitism, 157, 183–184; Gottheil and, 157; Jewish clannishness, 183; Jewish response to antisemitism, 161; Temple Emanu-El (New York), 20; World's Parliament of Religions (1893), 182–183
slavery, 36, 63–64
Smith, Bailey, 231n34
Smith, Goldwin, 163–170; Adler and, Hermann, 164–166, 169, 170; antisemitism of, 163–167, 172–173; assimilation of Jews, 167–168; denunciations of, 164–165; Disraeli and, 163; Gottheil and, 164; Jewish clannishness, 166–167; in *Jewish Messenger*, 172–173; Jewish tribalism, 164; Kohler and, 164; in the *Nation*, 164; "New Light on the Jewish Question," 169–170; on Old Testament, 164; restoration to Palestine, 167, 172; Schwab and, 10, 165; Talmud, 166, 170
Social Gospel movement, 132, 196, 199
social justice: Berkowitz and, 20, 28; Hirsch and, Emil G., 28–29; Reform rabbis, 132; as surrogate for religion, 32
social reform, 19–20
Society for Ethical Culture, 164
Society for the Improvement and Emigration of East European Jews, 122
Solomon, Hannah, 179
Spencer, Herbert, 132
The Spirit of Judaism (Lazarus), 193
"The Spirit of the Age" (Lilienthal), 102–103, 104
Stoecker, Adolf, 85, 153–154, 162, 233n22
Stolz, Joseph, 31, 187, 196
Straus, Leon, 161
Straus, Oscar, 179
Sunday laws, constitutionality of, 40
"Syllabus of a Treatise on the Development of Religious Ideas in Judaism since Moses Mendelssohn" (Gottheil), 187–188
Syllabus of Errors, 66
"Synagogue and Church in Their Mutual Relations" (Kohler), 184

Szold, Benjamin, 23
Szold, Henrietta, 179–180, 193

Tanenbaum, Marc, 231n34
Temple Beth-El (New York), 109
Temple Emanu-El (New York): Board of
Delegates of American Israelites, 55;
Gottheil and, 29; Hebrew Orphan Asylum (HOA), 87; Kohler and, 107; Silverman and, 20; Wise and, Isaac Mayer, 19
Temple Emanu-El Theological Seminary
(New York), 204
Temple Sinai (Chicago), 141, 147
Thanksgiving Day celebrations, 38–40
Traditional Judaism: divisiveness within, 8,
45, 96; East European Jews, 3; in Europe,
8; evolutionary theory, 23–24; Kohut
and, Alexander, 111; moderate Traditionalists, 34, 47, 96, 101, 116–117, 122, 141, 145,
210; Morais and, 34; Morais's defense of,
34, 46–51; problems facing, 96; rabbinic
sermons, 3; Reform Judaism, rift with, 8,
99, 100, 101, 112, 146; relief for needy Jews
in Palestine, 114; restoration to Palestine,
116–118; retention of the loyalty of the
faithful, 46; Zionism, 118
"Traditionalism" (the term), 217n1
transcendentalism, 23
Treitschke, Heinrich von, 152
Tyndall, John, 24, 132

Union League club, 44
Union of American Hebrew Congregations
(UAHC): American rabbis, 14; Board
of Delegates of American Israelites, 154;
founding, 204; Kohler and, 182; Levi and,
133–134, 135; Morais and, 47, 51; Ortho-
dox Judaism, 243n14; Reform Judaism,
106, 243n14; support for/coverage of in
Visitor, 79, 80; support for in *Visitor,* 79;
World's Parliament of Religions (1893),
179
Union of American Orthodox Congrega-
tions, 243n14
Union of Orthodox Rabbis, 243n14
Union Prayer Book (CCAR), 206
Unitarianism, merger with Judaism, 29,
193–194
United Synagogue of America, 243n14
University of Chicago, 159

University of Cincinnati, 76
University of Leipzig, 106
University of Pennsylvania, 160

Vatican Council (1869-1870), 66
Vidaver, Henry, 21, 26, 68–69
Visitor (magazine), 76–84; aim, 77, 83;
antisemitism, coverage of, 82; audience,
74–75, 79, 81; avoidance of controversial
subjects, 83; Baar and, 87; Baar in, 85; call
for representative men, 226n10; changes
after Lilienthal's death, 82–83; charity,
emphasis on, 79; "Cousin Sadie" department, 78; current events, coverage of, 82,
83; editorial board, 87; editors, 75, 82–83;
first issue, 76–77; flaws, 83; genteel tradition, 92; glory of America, 80–81; heroes
in, 78; "I love my religion" (editorial), 80;
Jewish/Christian relations in, 80; on Jewish patriotism, 81; lesson plans in, 83;
Lilienthal and, 75, 83; moralistic character, 75, 77; non-Jewish sources, 81;
outlook, 78, 81–82; popularity of, 78;
predecessor, 227n1; purposes, 75; Reform
Judaism, 79–80; respect for readers, 78–
79; on Seligman-Hilton affair (1877), 82;
sponsors of, 88; story about Abraham's
sacrifice of Isaac, 80; typical issue, 78–79

Wagner, Richard, 70
Washington, George, 79
Wesley, John, 39
West End Synagogue (New York), 71
Western Christian Advocate (newspaper), 15
"What Has Judaism Done for Woman"
(Szold), 179
"What the Hebrew Scriptures Have
Wrought for Mankind" (Kohut), 190–191
White, Andrew D., 173
Wise, Isaac Mayer, 100–104; *American
Israelite,* 119–120, 134, 146–147, 162; *The
American Jewish Pulpit,* 21; antisemitism,
Jewish response to, 162; on author-
ity of American rabbis, 15; brawl with
congregants, 16; Central Conference of
American Rabbis (CCAR), 15, 142; in
Cincinnati, 76; Cleveland Conference
(1855), 100; on Darwinism, 221n31; Dem-
ocratic Party, 18; on good rabbis, 200,
206; influence of, 3–4; *Israelite,*

Wise, Isaac Mayer (*continued*)
15, 55; Lazarus and, Emma, 122; Leeser and, 101, 203; Levi and, 139–140; Levi's criticism of Reform rabbis, 146–147; Lilienthal and, 76, 98, 101, 204; on materialism of post-Civil War America, 25; "Minhag America," 112; as moderate Reformer, 106; Moody and, 45; Morais and, 51; political activism of, 18–19; rabbinic seminaries, need for, 203–204; on rabbinic sermons, 12; on rabbis, 202; on religious antisemitism, 156; restoration to Palestine, 119–120; synagogue schools/classes by, 74; Temple Emanu-El (New York), 19; World's Parliament of Religions (1893), 181, 187, 188–189; Zion College (Cincinnati), 203

Wise, Stephen, 19, 130, 233n26

women, Jewish, 179, 192–193

Women's Christian Temperance Union, 72

Women's Columbian Exposition (1893), 178

World Zionist Organization, 127

World's Parliament of Religions (1893), 178–197; 1896 CCAR collection of sermons, 30; antisemitism as a subject, 181–182, 183–184, 186; Barrows and, 180; Berkowitz at, 187, 192; Bonney and, 180; Central Conference of American Rabbis (CCAR), 179; Christian organizers, 180; Congress of Jewish Women, 140; denominational congresses, 180; Deutsch at, 187; Felsenthal at, 187, 192; Gottheil at, 128, 187–188, 189; Harris at, 189, 194; Hecht at, 192; Hirsch at, Emil G., 181, 194–195; Ireland and, John, 180; Jewish presentations at, 183–197; Jewish women, participation

by, 179; *Judaism at the World's Parliament of Religions* (UAHC), 186–187; Kohler and, 171, 181, 184–186; Kohut at, Alexander, 179, 190–191; Landsberg at, 192–193; Lazarus and, Josephine, 179; Lyon and, 180, 182–183; Mendes at, H. Pereira, 179, 191–192; Mielziner at, 189; Moses at, I. S., 187; motto, 178; opening procession, 178; Radin at, 192; Reform Judaism, 179, 186, 197; Schiff and, 179; Schwab at, 187; Silverman at, 182–183; Stolz at, 187; Straus and, 179; superiority of Christianity as ⸗subject, 178, 180–181; superiority of Judaism as subject, 184–186, 189, 190–191; syncretistic religion as subject, 193–196; Szold and, Henrietta, 179; Traditionalist rabbis on the program, 190–192; Union of American Hebrew Congregations (UAHC), 179; univeralism, 178; Wise at, Isaac Mayer, 181, 187, 188–189; Zante, Greece, Archbishop of, 180, 182

Yeshiva University (New York), 243n14

Young Israel (magazine), 227n1

Zante, Greece, Archbishop of, 180, 182

Zion College (Cincinnati), 3, 203–204

Zionism: "agrarian myth," 119; American rabbis, 129–130; antisemitism, 126; Basel Congress (1897), 113; Felsenthal and, 174; Gottheil and, 127–128; loyalty to America, 129, 174; Mendes and, H. Pereira, 174; Reform Judaism, 120, 132, 174, 215; refugeeism, 129; Traditional Judaism, 118. *See also* anti-Zionism; Palestine, restoration to

Zionist Organization of America, 128

About the Author

Naomi W. Cohen, a retired professor of history now residing in Jerusalem, has written extensively on American Jewry. The recipient of various prizes for her scholarship, she has twice been awarded the National Jewish Book Award for history. Her most recent books are *Jacob H. Schiff: A Study in American Jewish Leadership* (1999) and *The Americanization of Zionism* (2003).